SERMONS THAT
SHAPED AMERICA

SERMONS THAT SHAPED AMERICA

REFORMED PREACHING FROM 1630 TO 2001

EDITED BY

WILLIAM S. BARKER AND

SAMUEL T. LOGAN JR.

PUBLISHING

P.O. BOX 817 • PHILLIPSBURG • NEW JERSEY 08865-0817

Italics within Scripture quotations indicate emphasis added.

Page design and typesetting by Lakeside Design Plus

Printed in the United States of America

Library of Congress Cataloging-in-Publication Data

Sermons that shaped America : Reformed preaching from 1630 to 2001 / edited by William S. Barker and Samuel T. Logan, Jr.
    p. cm.
    Includes bibliographical references.
    ISBN 0-87552-003-0 (pbk.)
    1. Reformed Church—Sermons. 2. Sermons, American. I. Barker, William S. II. Logan, Samuel T., 1943–

BX9495.S47 2003
252'.057—dc22

2003062628

To the memory of Theodore Roosevelt Barker (1908–1982) and Nancy Edwards Barker (1909–1998), loving and faithful parents who made sure that I heard and listened to biblical sermons.

To the memory of Samuel Talbot Logan (1910–1985) and Annie Mary Yerger Logan (1910–1998), whose lives were gospel sermons that shaped me.

Contents

Preface

"How shall they hear without a preacher?" the apostle Paul asks in Romans 10, as part of his argument for the critical importance of the "foolishness" of preaching.

Without a doubt, the church stands or falls, grows or dies according to the quality of the weekly diet that it is fed. From the prophetic orations of the Old Testament to and beyond the missionary sermons of the New, what the people of God are *told* matters. The use of words (and use of the symbolism of God's Word) has always been and will always be a uniquely formative activity in the life of the church.

And not just in the church.

To the degree that the church affects the world in which God has placed it, to the degree that the worldview of the church shapes the society in which the church functions, to that very degree what is said in the pulpit on Sunday morning produces direct consequences, some intended and some not, in the entire community on Monday, Tuesday, and the rest of the week.

Harry Stout has probably stated it best in his study of "The New England Soul." And while his comments apply most directly and most clearly to an earlier American culture, they unquestionably apply as well to a modern culture in which thousands listened to a sermon just days after and blocks from the site of the terrorist attacks on September 11, 2001. These are Stout's words:

> The sermon stood alone in local New England contexts as the only regular (or at least weekly) medium of public communication. As a channel of information, it combined religious, educational, and journalistic functions, and supplied all the key terms necessary to understand existence in this world or the next.[1]

---

1. Harry Stout, *The New England Soul: Preaching and Religious Culture in Colonial New England* (New York: Oxford University, 1986), 3.

How *do* we understand existence in a world where terrorism is as real as an airline boarding pass? Or in a world where human beings are bought and sold as slaves? Or in a world where another nation, the nation from which we came, seems bent on destroying us? Or in a world where we are given the opportunity to start a Holy Commonwealth from scratch?

And when all the cultural and ethical and technological changes of the past 380 years are amassed, how *do* we understand existence in the next world? To what degree do the societal changes we are experiencing affect our understanding of the next world? *Are* there any unchanging words to be spoken in or to this changing world?

Sermons preached in American pulpits from 1630 to 2001 still provide answers to these seven questions. And some of those answers singularly shaped the United States as a nation.

One of the values of this collection of sermons, therefore, is historical. Each of them played a unique and critical role in what America has become. Lengthy volumes such as Ola Winslow's *Meetinghouse Hill* and Alan Heimert's *Religion and the American Mind* and Bernard Bailyn's *The Ideological Origins of the American Revolution* and Colleen Carroll's *The New Orthodoxy* trace the historical impact of religious ideas on American society. We have tried to briefly suggest the specific historical impact of each sermon included here and have frequently suggested other sources that can be used to pursue in more depth the themes introduced by individual sermons.

But there is even more here than matters of historical interest.

Precisely because the preachers of these sermons believed that there is an unchanging Word from God and precisely because they sought to faithfully speak that Word into the changing world they faced, what they said matters greatly to those who, today, continue to believe in the power and sufficiency and authority of that Word.

No, of course these sermons are not inspired. Some of them will even seem foolish to modern readers (as they did to some who heard them when they were first preached). But God's Word, when faithfully preached, never returns to Him void (Isa. 55:11). Sometimes, in fact, the preaching of that Word produces thirtyfold, or sixtyfold, or hundredfold results (Matt. 13:23). When sermons produced results like that in earlier generations (as these appear to have done), they may do the same in ours.

And that is precisely our prayer!

—Samuel T. Logan

Acknowledgments

We are deeply indebted to the exceptional research work for this volume done by Dr. Jan Van Vliet. Jan worked through countless volumes in innumerable libraries to make sure that the texts of the sermons we printed were the most accurate possible. He then, probably at great cost to his future eyesight, transferred the material he found from dusty manuscripts to computer disks. The project would not have happened without you, Jan. Thank you!

We also want to thank the Board of Trustees of Westminster Theological Seminary (Pennsylvania) for the support that made this project possible. We believe that the Lord continues to use this institution to shape his creation to the end that "the earth will be covered with the knowledge of the glory of God in Christ as the waters cover the sea"!

Introduction

Four centuries of Reformed and Presbyterian preaching in North America provide windows on significant periods of American history. From colonial foundations through the Great Awakening, the American Revolution, nineteenth-century revivals, the Civil War, the Modernist–Fundamentalist controversy, the emergence of biblically faithful denominations in the twentieth century, down to the shock of the terrorist attacks on September 11, 2001, one can see the sermons reflecting the providence of the sovereign and gracious Lord God. The Holy Spirit is faithfully guiding his people through these events.

As one reads these historic sermons, one can sense their impact on their hearers. The vision of a theocentric community, as enunciated by John Cotton and John Winthrop, helped to shape the Puritan society of New England. The distinction between genuine Christianity and a counterfeit faith is set forth by Jonathan Edwards in the eighteenth century and also by Clarence Macartney and J. Gresham Machen in a more modern context. The sermons of Gilbert Tennent and Archibald Alexander deal with the qualifications for ministry, and that of Francis Schaeffer with the nature of leadership in the church. Asahel Nettleton and James W. Alexander provide examples of Reformed revivalism in a context of awe before a holy and sovereign God. The comfort of a sovereign God is shown in the sermons of Cotton Mather and John L. Girardeau in the face of suffering and death. Geerhardus Vos brings home the impact of the resurrection, as does Timothy Keller in response to personal and corporate tragedy. Reformed doctrine is expounded and applied by Benjamin M. Palmer and James M. Boice. The hearers of the Word from such preachers must have been inspired to become doers of the Word as well in the varying circumstances of life.

The preachers themselves show us God's servants as instruments of his grace. From English, Scottish, French, and Dutch backgrounds, from the South and from the North, from various social and educational upbringings, they manifest in their lives the flaws of fallen, sinful human nature and yet the penetrating insight and eloquence of men who have experienced the grace of God and have confidence in the truth of his Word.

Altogether, the sermons contained in this book manifest God's use of the preaching of his Word as the main means of advancing his kingdom in this world.

What of the future prospects for preaching in the twenty-first century and beyond? The events of September 11, 2001 suggest an ongoing conflict between Christianity and radical Islam, perhaps a climactic worldwide conflict. What will still be needed—whatever the future brings—is the faithful preaching of the Word of God: "speaking the truth in love" or "the foolishness of preaching," as the apostle Paul put it in Ephesians 4:15 and 1 Corinthians 1:21. The Scriptures of the Old and New Testaments are indeed the only infallible rule of faith and practice, and they must be applied by faithful servants of the Lord to every area of thought and life, both at the individual level and at the corporate level. Both the purity and the unity of the church must be maintained as we contend for the truth while also ultimately manifesting esteem for Jesus our Lord.

Faith comes by hearing, and hearing by the Word of God. But how shall they hear without a preacher? (Rom. 10:17, 14). The Great Commission of our Lord to make disciples of all the nations will be fulfilled as the coming generations continue the faithful preaching of the gospel of our Lord Jesus Christ.

—William S. Barker

1

God's Promise to His Plantation

2 Samuel 7:10

JOHN COTTON

From his pulpit at St. Botolph's Parish Church in Boston, England, John Cotton (1584–1652) set forth, in this 1630 sermon, an encouragement for members of his congregation to consider "building a house" in the New World. Many of those who heard the sermon did, in fact, take up Cotton's challenge, and the house they built reflects the encouragement they were given.

But there is a great deal of history behind Cotton's sermon, and without at least a glance at that history, we cannot fully appreciate what Cotton said in Boston, England, or what his people did in Boston, New England.

Innumerable factors helped to produce English Christianity in the first third of the seventeenth century, but one that shaped most of the others was the publication, in 1563, of John Foxe's most famous work, popularly known as the *Book of Martyrs*. Foxe was born in 1517, right in Boston, less than a quarter mile from the spot on which Cotton preached his sermon in 1630. (The site of Foxe's birthplace is now occupied by a pub called Martha's Vineyard.)

In 1554, Foxe invited the wrath of Queen Mary by joining others in protesting her planned reintroduction into the English church of the largely

1

Roman Catholic Six Articles of Religion that had been originally forced on the church by Mary's father, Henry VIII. Because of his opposition to the Crown, Foxe, with many of his compatriots, was forced to flee England, and his personal journey took him first to Strasbourg and then to Frankfurt, where he met Edmund Grindal, who seems to have been the one who gave Foxe the idea for the *Book of Martyrs*.

Foxe, with many others, returned to England from exile after Elizabeth's accession to the throne in 1558, and in 1563, he published his work under the decidedly Puritanesque title *Actes and Monuments of these Latter and Perillous Dayes, Touching Matters of the Church, Wherin Ar Comprehended and Described the Great Persecutions and Horrible Troubles, That Have Been Wrought and Practised by the Romish Prelates, Speciallye in this Realme of England and Scotlande, From the Yeare of our Lorde a Thousand, Unto the Tyme Now Present. Gathered and Collected According to the True Copies & Wrytings Certificatorie as wel of the Parties Them Selves that Suffered, As also out of the Bishop's Registers, Which wer the Doers Thereof.*

The *Book of Martyrs* functioned almost like a second Bible to the Christians of Foxe's generation and was later regarded by no less than John Bunyan as being, next to the Bible, the reason for the Puritan movement in England. Why? William Haller suggests one reason: "The book expressed the exultancy of the returned exiles at the intervention of providence in their behalf, but also their increasing concern lest divine justice be given occasion to withdraw the favour divine grace had bestowed."[1]

True to their name, the Puritans sought to purify both church and state according to the Word of God. They believed that God expects obedience from his people in all spheres of their lives, in the state no less than in the church. To use more modern terminology, there is no neutral area of human experience and no source other than the Bible to which men and women can look for absolutely certain knowledge of what duties God requires of man.

Foxe's *Book of Martyrs* added a sense of urgency to this covenantal view of the Christian's relation to both church and state. The martyrs spilled their blood and gave their lives for a cause, which the church now had the opportunity to honor under a Protestant monarch. That cause was to build a church and a state that fully conformed to God's Word and therefore fully

---

1. William Haller, *The Elect Nation: The Meaning and Relevance of Foxe's Book of Martyrs* (New York: Harper and Row, 1963), 119.

brought honor to God. If the Christians of Foxe's and later generations in England failed to seize this opportunity, they should expect that "divine justice" would "withdraw the favour divine grace had bestowed."

The next six decades of English church history were characterized by the Puritan attempt to do just that, to seize the opportunity to reform England—both church and state—according to the Scriptures, the Word of God. From Thomas Cartwright's lectures on the book of Acts in 1570 at Cambridge to the Puritan "showdown" with King James I at the Hampton Court Conference in 1604 to John Cotton's move from Emmanuel College, Cambridge, to the St. Botolph's pulpit in 1612, there was constant agitation toward the goal implied by Foxe. And when mainstream Puritan efforts seemed to fail, some of Foxe's heirs sought "reformation without tarrying for any," and the Separatist movement was formed.[2]

But the Separatists were considered radicals by Puritan leaders such as William Perkins and William Ames and John Cotton himself. They knew further changes were needed in the church (and the state); they believed that Foxe's vision was essentially correct; but they were also firmly committed to the unity of the church. One did not split the church with impunity. How to move toward appropriate reform without doing unbiblical violence to the Body of Christ—this was the challenge they faced, one not unknown even in today's ecclesiastical environment. If anything, those mainstream Puritan giants would find twentieth-century Reformed churchmen (in the U.S., in Scotland, in South Korea, and in most other places) far too quick to split the church. They certainly rejected the efforts of those whom we call Pilgrims and who, after being briefly imprisoned less than a mile from St. Botolph's, sailed to the New World in 1620 to found Plimoth Plantation in Massachusetts.

But by the mid-1620s, even the mainstream Puritans were wondering what could and should be done. After James I died in 1625, his son came to the throne as Charles I and, two months later, married Henrietta Maria, sister of the French king, Louis XIII. Having entered into an agreement, supposedly secret, to support English Catholics, Charles embarked on a vigorous persecution of Puritans in England and Presbyterians in Scotland, and this led to the first very open and very public quarrel between Charles

---

2. Robert Browne, the first of the "Separatists," published his treatise in 1582. The title says it all: "A Treatise of Reformation Without Tarrying for Anie and of the Wickedness of Those Preachers Which Will Not Reforme Till the Magistrate Commande or Compell Them."

and the English Parliament, a quarrel that eventually produced civil war and, in 1649, Charles's own execution as an enemy of the state.

In the late 1620s, civil war was a barely discernible possibility and the execution of the king totally unimaginable. But John Cotton, John Winthrop, and many other Puritan leaders had come to realize the complete failure of the strategy for church reform that they had been following. And thus they came to the strategy that produced both Cotton's "God's Promise to His Plantation" and Winthrop's sermon "A Model of Christian Charity" (the second sermon printed in this collection).

For the reasons outlined above, these two sermons stand first among those that shaped the American church and, more specifically, the American Reformed church.

Cotton's sermon addresses the fundamental strategy that was being adopted and Winthrop's the particular model that the newly Reformed church should set. Together, they give an excellent picture of precisely why those who left Boston (England) to come to Boston (New England) did so. And together, they offer one biblical perspective to those who, in the twenty-first century, find themselves living in a state or in a church that, they are convinced, is not all that Scripture requires.

Cotton preached his sermon in Boston, England, to a congregation in which many were considering the possibility of dealing with the perceived rottenness in England and the Church of England by emigrating to the New World. Cotton himself had not yet decided to leave England—perhaps he was preaching to himself as well. But in both Cotton's sermon and Winthrop's sermon, one finds rationale for emigration that differs markedly from that in a Separatist work such as William Bradford's "Of Plimoth Plantation."

Most significantly, Cotton and Winthrop wanted such emigration to occur with the full knowledge and approval of the Crown. They were not Separatists; they remained members of the Church of England and English citizens. Their strategy was to seek official governmental approval for a new colony and, at the same time, official governmental permission to structure that colony according to their own theological commitments and understandings. Without either of these, there would have been no emigration.[3]

---

3. These conditions were clearly set forth in "The Cambridge Agreement," signed by Winthrop and numerous other Puritan leaders on August 26, 1629.

In God's providence both conditions were met, and it was in this context that Cotton described "God's Promise to His Plantation." This sermon was remarkable for many reasons—not least for its setting of a vision before the people, a vision of God's expectations and of God's promise to his people, a vision intended to define the New World to which the emigrants were going. Read carefully, this sermon makes clear both the link between Bostonians John Foxe and John Cotton and the fundamental ideological gulf between the Pilgrims at Plymouth and the Puritans at Boston.

From Foxe to Cotton and Winthrop and beyond, the emphasis is on *what God deserves* far more than it is on what men might want or even need. Especially in his use of Acts 17:26–27, Cotton emphasizes what "the landlord," i.e., God, is due and he urges his people to "defraud him not of his rent." Cotton's vision is of a theocentric community, one with its very reason for being in the One who does the planting, does the growing, does the protecting.

And for those who are correctly "centered," Cotton does indeed have a promise: "Neglect not walls, and bulwarks, and fortifications for your own defense; but ever let the name of the Lord be your strong tower, and the Word of his promise the rock of your refuge. His Word that made heaven and earth will not fail, till heaven and earth be no more."

God's Promise to His Plantation

John Cotton

Moreover I will appoint a place for my people Israel, and I will plant them, that they may dwell in a place of their own, and move no more. (2 Sam. 7:10)

I n the beginning of this chapter, we read of David's purpose to build God a house, who thereupon consulted with Nathan about it, one prophet standing in need of another's help in such weighty matters. Nathan encourages the king unto this work (2 Sam. 7:3). God the same night meets Nathan and tells him a contrary purpose of his. But God refuses David's offer, with some kind of earnest and vehement dislike (vv. 4–5). Secondly, he refuses the reason of David's offer, from his long silence. For four hundred years together he spoke of no such thing unto any of the tribes of Israel, saying, "Why build you not me a house?" (vv. 6–7).

Now lest David should be discouraged with this answer, the Lord bids Nathan to shut up his speech with words of encouragement, and so he removes his discouragement two ways.

First, by recounting his former favors dispensed unto David. Secondly, by promising the continuance of the like or greater: and the rather, because of this purpose of his. And five blessings God promises unto David, and his, for his sake.

The first is in verse 10: "I will appoint a place for my people Israel."

Secondly, seeing it was in his heart to build him a house, God would therefore "build him a house renowned forever" (v. 11).

Thirdly, that he would accept a house from Solomon (v. 12).

Fourthly, he will be a father to his son (vv. 14–15).

Fifthly, that he will "establish the throne of his house forever" (v. 13).

In this verse 10 a double blessing is promised:

First, the designment of a place for his people.

Secondly, a plantation of them in that place, from whence is promised a threefold blessing.

First, they shall dwell there like freeholders in a place of their own.

Secondly, he promises them firm and durable possession; they shall move no more.

Thirdly, they shall have peaceable and quiet resting there; the sons of wickedness shall afflict them no more, which is amplified by their former troubles, as before time.

From the appointment of a place for them, which is the first blessing, you may observe this note:

The placing of a people in this or that country is from the appointment of the Lord.

This is evident in the text, and the apostle speaks of it as grounded in nature in Acts 17:26: "God has determined the times before appointed, and the bounds of our habitation." In Deuteronomy 2:5, 9, God would not have the Israelites meddle with the Edomites or the Moabites, because he had given them their land for a possession. God assigned out such a land for such a posterity, and for such a time.

Question: Wherein does this work of God stand in appointing a place for a people?

Answer: First, when God espies or discovers a land for a people, as in Ezekiel 20:6, he brought them into a land that he had espied for them; and that is, when either he gives them to discover it themselves or hear of it discovered by others, and fitting them.

Secondly, after he espies it, when he carries them along to it, so that they plainly see a providence of God leading them from one country to another, as in Exodus 19:4: "You have seen how I have borne you as on eagles' wings, and brought you unto myself." So that though they met with many difficulties, yet he carried them high above them all, like an eagle, flying over seas and rocks, and all hindrances.

Thirdly, when he makes room for a people to dwell there, as in Psalm 80:9: "You prepared room for them." When Isaac sojourned among the Philistines, he dug one well, and the Philistines strove for it, and he called it Esek; and he dug another well, and for that they strove also; therefore, he called it Sitnah; and he removed thence, and dug another well, and for that they strove not, and he called it Rehoboth, and said, "For now the Lord has made room for us, and we shall be fruitful in the land" (Gen. 26:22). Now no Esek, no Sitnah, no quarrel or contention, but now he sits down in Rehoboth, in a peaceable room.

Now God makes room for a people three ways:

First, when he casts out the enemies of a people before them by lawful war with the inhabitants, which God calls them unto: as in Psalm 44:2: "You did drive out the heathen before them." But this course of warring against others, and driving them out without provocation, depends upon special commission from God, or else it is not imitable.

Secondly, when he gives a foreign people favor in the eyes of any native people to come and sit down with them either by way of purchase, as Abraham did obtain the field of Machpela; or else when they give it in courtesy, as Pharaoh did the land of Goshen unto the sons of Jacob.

Thirdly, when he makes a country though not altogether void of inhabitants, yet void in that place where they reside. Where there is a vacant place, there is liberty for the sons of Adam or Noah to come and inhabit, though they neither buy it nor ask their leave. Abraham and Isaac, when they[4] sojourned among the Philistines, did not buy that land to feed their cattle, because they said, There is room enough. And so did Jacob pitch his tent by Shechem. There was room enough; as Hamor said, "Let them sit down among us" (Gen. 34:21). And in this case if the people who were former inhabitants did disturb them in their possessions, they complained to the kings, as of wrong done unto them, as Abraham did because they took away his well (Gen. 21:25). For his right whereto he pleads not his immediate calling from God (for that would have seemed frivolous among the heathen), but his own industry and culture in digging the well (v. 30). Nor does the king reject his plea (with what had he to do to dig wells in their soil?), but admits it as a principle in nature, that in a vacant soil, he that takes possession of it and bestows culture and husbandry upon it, his right it is. And the ground of this is from the grand charter given to Adam and his posterity in Paradise in Genesis 1:28: "Multiply, and replenish the earth, and subdue it." If therefore any son of Adam comes and finds a place empty, he has liberty to come, and fill, and subdue the earth there. This charter was renewed to Noah in Genesis 9:1—"Fulfill the earth and multiply"—so that it is free from that common grant for any to take possession of vacant countries. Indeed, no nation is to drive out another without special commission from heaven, such as the Israelites had, unless the natives do unjustly wrong them, and will not recompense the wrongs done in peaceable sort, and then they may right themselves by lawful war, and subdue the country unto themselves.

This placing of people in this or that country is from God's sovereignty over all the earth and the inhabitants thereof, as in Psalm 24:1: "The earth is the Lord's, and the fullness thereof." And in Jeremiah 10:7 God is there

---

4. This sojourning was a constant residence there, as in a possession of their own; although it was called sojourning or dwelling as strangers, because they neither had the sovereign government of the whole country in their own hand, nor yet did incorporate themselves into the commonwealth of the natives, to submit themselves unto their government.

called The King of Nations, an idea supported by Deuteronomy 10:14. Therefore it is meet he should provide a place for all nations to inhabit, and have all the earth replenished. Only in the text here is meant some more special appointment, because God tells it to them by his own mouth; he does not so with other people; he does not tell the children of Seir that he has appointed a place for them. That is, he gives them the land by promise; others take the land by his providence, but God's people take the land of promise. And therefore the land of Canaan is called a land of promise, which they discern, first, by discerning themselves to be in Christ, in whom all the promises are, yea and amen.

Secondly, by finding his holy presence with them, that is, when he plants them in the holy mountain of his inheritance (Ex. 15:17). And that is when he gives them the liberty and purity of his ordinances. It is a land of promise, where they have provision for soul as well as for body. Ruth dwelt well for outward respects while she dwelt in Moab, but when she comes to dwell in Israel, she is said to come under the wings of God (Ruth 2:12). When God wraps us in with his ordinances, and warms us with the life and power of them as with wings, there is a land of promise.

This may teach us all where we do now dwell, or where after we may dwell: be sure you look at every place appointed to you, from the hand of God. We may not rush into any place, and never say to God, By your leave; but we must discern how God appoints us this place. There is poor comfort in sitting down in any place if you cannot say, This place is appointed me of God. Can you say that God spied out this place for you, and there has settled you above all hindrances? Did you find that God made room for you either by lawful descent, or purchase, or gift, or other warrantable right? Why then this is the place God has appointed you; here he has made room for you; he has placed you in Rehoboth, in a peaceable place. This we must discern, or else we are but intruders upon God. And when we do discern that God gives us these outward blessings from his love in Christ, and makes comfortable provision as well for our soul as for our bodies, by the means of grace, then we enjoy our present possession as well by gracious promise, as by the common, and just, and bountiful providence of the Lord. Or if a man does remove, he must see that God has espied out such a country for him.

Secondly, though there are many difficulties, yet he has given us hearts to overlook them all, as if we were carried upon eagles' wings.

And thirdly, see God making room for us by some lawful means.

Question: But how shall I know whether God has appointed me such a place; if I am well where I am, what may warrant my removal?

Answer: There are four or five good things, for procurement of any of which I may remove. Secondly, there are some evil things, for avoiding of any of which we may transplant ourselves. Thirdly, if we find some special providence of God concurring in either of both concerning ourselves, and applying general grounds of removal to our personal estate.

First, we may remove for the gaining of knowledge. Our Savior commends it in the Queen of the South, that she came from the uttermost parts of the earth to hear the wisdom of Solomon (Matt. 12:42). And surely with him she might have continued for the same end, if her personal calling had not recalled her home.

Secondly, some remove and travail for merchandise and gain's sake: "Daily bread may be sought from far" (Prov. 31:14). In Matthew 13:45–46, our Savior approves travail for merchants when he compares a Christian to a merchant-man seeking pearls; for he never fetches a comparison from any unlawful thing to illustrate a thing lawful. The comparison from the unjust steward, and from the thief in the night, is not taken from the injustice of the one, or the theft of the other, but from the wisdom of the one, and the suddenness of the other, which in themselves are not unlawful.

Thirdly, to plant a colony, that is, a company that agree together to remove out of their own country, and settle a city or commonwealth elsewhere. Of such a colony we read in Acts 16:12, which God blessed and prospered exceedingly, and made it a glorious church. Nature teaches bees to do so: as when the hive is too full they seek abroad for new dwellings, so when the hive of the commonwealth is so full that tradesmen cannot live one by another, but eat up one another, in this case it is lawful to remove.

Fourthly, God allows a man to remove when he may employ his talents and gifts better elsewhere, especially when where he is, he is not bound by any special engagement. Thus God sent Joseph before to preserve the church: Joseph's wisdom and spirit were not fit for a shepherd, but for a counselor of state, and therefore God sent him into Egypt. "To whom much is given, of him God will require the more" (Luke 12:48).

Fifthly, for the liberty of the ordinances. In 2 Chronicles 11:13–15, when Jeroboam made a desertion from Judah, and set up golden calves to worship, all that were well affected, both priests and people, sold their possessions, and came to Jerusalem for the ordinances' sake. This case was of seasonable use to our fathers in the days of Queen Mary, who removed to France and Germany in the beginning of her reign, upon proclamation of alteration of religion, before any persecution began.

Secondly, there are evils to be avoided that may warrant removal. First, some grievous sins that overspread a country may threaten desolation. Micah 2:6–11 informs us that when the people say to them that prophesy, "Prophesy not," then God responds: "Arise then, this is not your rest" (v. 10). These words are a threatening, not a commandment; yet as in a threatening a wise man foresees the plague, so in the threatening he sees a commandment, to hide himself from it. This case might have been of seasonable use unto them of the Palatinate, when they saw their orthodox ministers banished, although they themselves might for a while enjoy liberty of conscience.

Secondly, if men are overburdened with debts and miseries, as David's followers were; they may then retire out of the way (as they retired to David for safety), not to defraud their creditors, for "God is an avenger of such things" (1 Thess. 4:6), but to gain further opportunity to discharge their debts, and to satisfy their creditors (1 Sam. 22:1–2).

Thirdly, in case of persecution, so did the apostles in Acts 13:46–47.

Thirdly, as these general cases, where any of them do fall out, do warrant removal in general, so there are some special providences or particular cases which may give warrant unto such or such a person to transplant himself, and which apply the former general grounds to particular persons.

First, if sovereign authority commands and encourages such plantations by giving way to subjects to transplant themselves, and set up a new commonwealth, this is a lawful and expedient case for such particular persons as are designed and sent (Matt. 8:9) and for such as they who are sent have power to command.

Secondly, when some special providence of God leads a man unto such a course, this may also single out particulars. Psalm 32:8 tells us: "I will instruct, and guide you with my eye." As the child knows the pleasure of his father in his eye, so does the child of God see God's pleasure in the eye of his heavenly Father's providence. And this is done three ways.

First, if God gives a man an inclination to this or that course, for that is the spirit of man; and "God is the Father of spirits" (Heb. 12:9; Rom. 1:12; 1 Cor. 16:12). Paul discerned his calling to go to Rome by his to prothymon, his ready inclination to that voyage; and Paul accepted Apollos' loathness to go to Corinth as a just reason of his refusal of a calling to go thither. And this holds: when in a man's inclination to travail, his heart is set on no by-respects, as to see fashions, to deceive his creditors, to fight duels, or to live idly, there are vain inclinations; but if his heart is inclined upon right judgment to advance the gospel, to maintain his family, to use his talents fruitfully, or the like good end, this inclination is from God. As the beams of the moon darting into the sea lead it to and fro, so does a secret inclination darted by God into our hearts lead and bow (as a bias) our whole course.

Secondly, when God gives other men hearts to call us, as the men of Macedonia did Paul, "Come to us into Macedonia, and help us" (Acts 16:9). When we are invited by others who have a good calling to reside there, we may go with them unless we are detained by weightier occasions. One member has interest in another, to call to it for help, when it is not diverted by greater employment.

Thirdly, there is another providence of God concurring in both these: that is, when a man's calling and person is free, and not tied by parents, or magistrates, or other people that have interest in him, or when abroad he may do himself and others more good than he can do at home. Here is then an eye of God that opens a door there, and sets him loose here, inclines his heart that way, and outlooks all difficulties. When God makes room for us, no binding here, and an open way there, in such a case God tells them, he will appoint a place for them.

Use 2.

Secondly, this may teach us in every place where God appoints us to sit down to acknowledge him as our Landlord. The earth is the Lord's, and the fullness thereof; his are our countries, our towns, our houses; and therefore let us acknowledge him in them all. The apostle makes this use of it among the Athenians in Acts 17:26–27: "He has appointed the times and places of our habitation, that we might seek, and grope after the Lord." There is a threefold use that we are to make of it, as it appears there: Let us seek after the Lord—why? Because if you come into a house, you will ask for the owner of it; and so if you come into a foreign land, and there find a house and land provided for you, will you not enquire, where is the Landlord?—where is that God that gave me this house and land? He is missing—and therefore seek after him.

Secondly, you must feel after him, grope after him by such sensible things, strive to attain the favor of your Landlord, and labor to be obedient to him that has given you such a place.

Thirdly, you must labor to find him in his ordinances, in prayer, and in Christian communion. These things I owe him as my Landlord, and by these I find and enjoy him. This use the very pagans were to make of their several plantations; and if you knew him before, seek him yet more and feel after him till you find him in his ordinances, and in your consciences.

Use 3.

Thirdly, when you have found God making way and room for you, and carrying you by his providence unto any place, learn to walk thankfully before him, defraud him not of his rent, but offer yourselves unto his service: Serve that God, and teach your children to serve him, who has appointed you and them the place of your habitation.

2. Observation: *A people of God's plantation shall enjoy their own place with safety and peace.*

This is manifest in the text: I will plant them; and what follows from thence? They shall dwell in their own place. But how? Peaceably, they shall not be moved any more. Then they shall dwell safely, then they shall live in peace. The like promise you read of in Psalm 89:21–22: "The enemy shall not exact upon them any more." And in Psalm 92:13: "Those that are planted in the house of the Lord shall flourish in the courts of our God." And in Amos 9:15: "God's plantation is a flourishing plantation."

Question: What is it for God to plant a people?

Answer: It is a metaphor taken from young Impes: I will plant them; that is, I will make them to take root there—and that is where they and their soil agree well together, when they are well and sufficiently provided for, as a plant sucks nourishment from the soil that fits it.

Secondly, when he causes them to grow as plants do, in Psalm 80:8–11. When a man grows like a tree in tallness and strength to more firmness and eminency, then he may be said to be planted.

Thirdly, when God causes them to fructify (Ps. 1:3).

Fourthly, when he establishes them there, then he plants and roots not up.

But there is something more especial in this planting; for they were planted before in this land, and yet he promises here again that he will plant them in their own land, which implies, first, that whatever former good estate they had already, he would prosper it and increase it.

Secondly, God is said to plant a people more especially when they become "trees of righteousness" (Isa. 61:3). That they may be called trees of righteousness, the planting of the Lord. So that there is implied not only a continuance of their former good estate, but that he would make them a good people, a choice generation: which he did, first, by planting the ordinances of God among them in a more glorious manner, as he did in Solomon's time.

2. He would give his people a nail, and a place in his Tabernacle (Isa. 56:5). And that is to give us part in Christ, for so the Temple typified. So then he plants us when he gives us root in Christ.

Thirdly, when he gives us to "grow up in him as calves in the stall" (Mal. 4:2–3).

Fourthly, to "bring forth much fruit" (John 15:1–2).

Fifthly, to continue and abide in the state of grace. This is to plant us in his holy sanctuary; he is not rooting us up.

Reason.

This is taken from the kind acceptance of David's purpose to build God a house: because he saw it was done in the honesty of his heart, therefore he promises to give his people a place wherein they should abide forever as in a house of rest.

Secondly, it is taken from the office God takes upon him: when he is our planter, he becomes our husbandman; and if he plants us, who shall pluck us up? (Isa. 27:1–2). When he gives quiet, who can make trouble? (Job 34:29). If God is the gardener, who shall pluck up what he sets down? Every plantation that he has not planted shall be plucked up, and what he has planted shall surely be established.

Thirdly, from the nature of the blessing he confers upon us: when he promises to plant a people, their days shall be as the days of a tree (Isa. 65:22), as the oak is said to be a hundred years in growing, and a hundred years in full strength, and a hundred years in decaying.

Question: But, it may be demanded, how was this promise fulfilled by the people, seeing after this time they met with many persecutions, at home and abroad; many sons of wickedness afflicted them: Jeroboam was a son of wickedness, and so was Ahab, and Ahaz, and various others.

Answer: Because after David's time they had more settledness than before. Secondly, to the godly these promises were fulfilled in Christ.

Thirdly, though this promise was made that others should not wrong them, yet it follows not but that they might wrong themselves by trespassing against God, and so expose themselves to affliction. While they continued God's plantation, they were a noble vine, a right seed; but if Israel will destroy themselves, the fault is in themselves. And yet even in their captivity the good among them God graciously provided for: the basket of good figs God sent into the land of Chaldea for their good (Jer. 24:5). But if you rebel against God, the same God that planted you will also root you out again, for all the evil which you shall do against yourselves (Jer. 11:17). When the Israelites liked not the soil, grew weary of the ordinances, and forsook the worship of God, and said, "What part have we in David?"— after this they never got so good a king, nor any settled rest in the good land wherein God had planted them. As they waxed weary of God, so he waxed weary of them, and cast them out of his sight.

Use 1.

To exhort all that are planted at home, or intend to plant abroad, to look well to your plantation, as you desire that the sons of wickedness may not afflict you at home, nor enemies abroad, look that you be right planted, and then you need not fear; you are safe enough. God has spoken it: I will plant them, and they shall not be moved; neither shall the sons of wickedness afflict them any more.

Question: What course would you have us take?

Answer: Have special care that you always have the ordinances planted among you, or else never look for security. As soon as God's ordinances cease, your security ceases likewise; but if God plants his ordinances among you, fear not—he will maintain them. Isaiah 4:5–6 says: "Upon all their glory, there shall be a defense"; that is, upon all God's ordinances, for so was the ark called "the Glory of Israel" (1 Sam. 4:22).

Secondly, have a care to be implanted into the ordinances, that the Word may be ingrafted into you, and you into it. If you take root in the ordinances, grow up thereby, bring forth much fruit, continue and abide therein, then you are a vineyard of red wine, and the Lord will keep you (Isa. 27:2–3), that no sons of violence shall destroy you. Look into all the stories, whether divine or human, and you shall never find that God rooted out a people that had the ordinances planted among them, and themselves planted into the ordinances. Never did God suffer such plants to be plucked up; on all their glory shall be a defense.

Thirdly, be not unmindful of our Jerusalem at home, whether you leave us or stay at home with us. "Oh pray for the peace of Jerusalem; they shall prosper that love her" (Ps. 122:6). "They shall all be confounded and turned back that hate Zion" (Ps. 129:5). As God continues his presence with us (blessed be his name), so you are present in spirit with us, though absent in body. Forget not the womb that bore you, and the breasts that gave you suck. Even ducklings hatched under a hen, though they take water, yet will still have recourse to the wing that hatched them; how much more should chickens of the same feather and yolk? In the amity and unity of brethren, the Lord has not only promised, but commanded a blessing: life forevermore (Ps. 133:1–2).

Fourthly, go forth, every man that goes, with a public spirit, looking not on your own things only, but also on the things of others (Phil. 2:4). This care of universal helpfulness was the prosperity of the first plantation of the primitive church (Acts 4:32).

Fifthly, have a tender care that you look well to the plants that spring from you (that is, to your children), that they do not degenerate as the Israelites did, after which they were vexed with afflictions on every hand. How came this to pass? As Jeremiah 2:21 asks: "I planted them a noble vine, holy [wholly], a right seed; how then have you degenerated into a strange vine before me?" Your ancestors were of a noble divine spirit, but if they suffer their children to degenerate, to take loose courses, then God will surely pluck you up. Otherwise, if men have a care to propagate the ordinances and religion to their children after them, God will plant them, and not root them up. For want of this, the seed of the repenting Ninevites was rooted out.

Sixthly, and lastly, offend not the poor natives, but as you partake in their land, so make them partakers of your precious faith; as you reap their temporals, so feed them with your spirituals; win them to the love of Christ, for whom Christ died. They never yet refused the gospel, and there is therefore more hope they will now receive it. Who knows whether God has reared this whole plantation for such an end?

Use 2.

Secondly, for consolation to them that are planted by God in any place, that find rooting and establishing from God, this is a cause of much encouragement unto you, that what he has planted he will maintain. Every plantation his right hand has not planted shall be rooted up, but his own plantation shall prosper and flourish. When he promises peace and safety, what enemy shall be able to make the promise of God of no effect? Neglect not walls, and bulwarks, and fortifications for your own defense; but ever let the name of the Lord be your strong tower, and the Word of his promise the rock of your refuge. His Word that made heaven and earth will not fail, till heaven and earth be no more.

Amen.

2

A Model of Christian Charity

JOHN WINTHROP

This sermon was preached in 1630 by John Winthrop (1588–1649) aboard
the ship *Arbella* as Winthrop led a group of Puritans from England to New
England in fulfillment of the sort of challenge laid down by John Cotton
in "God's Promise to His Plantation." In many ways, this sermon builds directly on that earlier one. But Winthrop puts his own spin on the Puritan
vision, and given the role he was to play in the Massachusetts Bay Colony,
it is important to take note of both aspects ("building" and "spinning") of
this sermon.

First, of course, we must note that Winthrop was a layman, not an ordained clergyman, and that this sermon was not delivered in a church or
meetinghouse, but in a more secular setting. A number of conclusions can
be drawn from these initial observations.

Obviously, the Puritan vision was not restricted to the clergy. In fact, it
might not be too much to affirm that the impetus to implement this vision
came at least as much from the laity as it did from the clergy. It was, after
all, Winthrop, not Cotton, who actually led the first group of Puritans who
acted on Cotton's admonition to "build a house" in the New World. This is
not to suggest any kind of tension between the clergy and the laity; it is, in

fact, to suggest exactly the opposite. The Puritan movement was a joint effort of clergy and laity, very much in keeping with that fundamental Reformational conviction of "the priesthood of all believers." Those who claim that the Massachusetts Bay Colony very quickly became a "clerocracy," more on a Roman Catholic model than on a Protestant model, simply fail to recognize the significance of the leadership provided, from the very beginning of the New England experiment, by Winthrop and other lay leaders.

Another tentative conclusion is closely related to the first. The Reformed church in early Massachusetts did not seem to restrict theological insight or ecclesiastical leadership to the ordained clergy. There is no question that ministers provided the bulk of this leadership, but New England Puritans obviously saw no biblical reasons why members of the laity should not preach and teach as well. Some, on both sides of the Antinomian Controversy (which arose in the mid-1630s), have argued that those problems were rooted in the fact that the protagonist, Anne Hutchinson, represented a challenge to the authority of the clergy. Such an interpretation simply does not square with the fact of Winthrop's obviously accepted lay leadership—both in his preaching on board the *Arbella* and later in the Antinomian Controversy when he clashed with none other than John Cotton.

Winthrop's sermon builds on Cotton's in that Winthrop assumes the truth of the fundamental vision that informs Cotton's. Both men are heirs of John Foxe. Both men believed that God expects absolute obedience to his Word by both church and state. Neither man encouraged settlement of the New World for the sake of "freedom." Admittedly, this interpretation of the Puritan vision runs counter to the views of many secular critics and historians. Those who take issue with the actions of the Massachusetts Bay Colony often argue that the Puritans who led it were among the most inconsistent and hypocritical of men—they came to the New World for religious freedom, but as soon as they arrived here, they began denying that very freedom to others (such as Anne Hutchinson and Roger Williams).

But this distressingly common interpretation simply misses the primary reason for the emigration to the New World. Like Cotton, Winthrop was far more concerned about what God deserved than he was about what man needed or desired. To the degree that issues of political and religious freedom were addressed at all, they were addressed by Winthrop, both here in this sermon and later in his political leadership of the Massachusetts Bay

Colony, as a means to an end—a "Holy Commonwealth" that brought honor to God. When, therefore, values of freedom or liberty came into conflict with values of holiness and righteousness before God, the latter values always took precedence. One might argue that the Puritans' value priorities were wrong (certainly not an argument I would make), but one cannot accuse them of acting inconsistently with respect to their value priorities.

For reasons outlined in detail elsewhere, these value priorities did not necessarily make the Puritans "theonomists."[1] It did not lead them all—and it certainly did not lead Winthrop—to the conclusion that all the laws laid down in the Bible, both in the Old Testament and in the New Testament, should be enacted in civil societies today. It did lead them to the conclusion that the aim of any corporate grouping of human beings had to be, first and foremost, to bring honor to God. No matter what the specific limited purpose of any such group, its first priority had to be to perform its tasks in a way that brought honor to the Lord. Even if that first priority put further limits on the specific limited purpose for which the group was formed, the responsibility to "do all to the glory of God" was absolute and could never be compromised.

One of the most fascinating studies of the long-term impact of this way of thinking is E. Digby Baltzell, *Puritan Boston and Quaker Philadelphia: Two Protestant Ethics and the Spirit of Class Authority and Leadership* (New York: The Free Press, 1979). With a clearly secular methodology, Baltzell analyzes the difference that the fundamental mind-sets of the Boston Puritans and the Philadelphia Quakers made in the societies they created—the former essentially focused on the whole and the latter essentially focused on the individual.[2] Or, if we must use the language of "freedom," the former was focused on the freedom of an entire community to determine what would be the community's purposes and modes of action and the latter was focused on the freedom of the individual to do anything he or she wanted to do.

Regardless of how we, in the twenty-first century, might state our preference for one mind-set or the other, Baltzell is correct in his analysis of

---

1. Samuel T. Logan Jr., *"New England Puritans and the State,"* in *Theonomy: A Reformed Critique* (Grand Rapids: Zondervan, 1990) William S. Barker and W. Robert Godfrey, eds., 353–84.

2. E. Digby Baltzell, *Puritan Boston and Quaker Philadelphia: Two Protestant Ethics and the Spirit of Class Authority and Leadership* (New York: The Free Press, 1979), 76, 119.

what drove the Puritan community in Massachusetts Bay. In fact, I would argue that this was *the* defining characteristic of Puritanism.

In most ways, the Puritans (of Old and New England) were simply heirs of the Reformation and specifically of the theology of John Calvin. They saw themselves that way, and we should as well. Added to their Reformed theology was the conviction that the church (initially the Church of England) needed purification. But desire to purify a church on the basis of Reformed or Calvinistic theology does not, in our use of terms today, lead us to identify an individual as a Puritan. There must have been something more, and Baltzell identifies that something more.

The Puritans were committed corporate thinkers—not in a business sense but in a "body" sense, or even in a "covenant" sense. They certainly believed that the *individual's* relationship with God was foundational; individuals had to exercise personal trust in Jesus Christ, and individuals would go to heaven. But corporate entities were real as well, and while the blessings or judgments given to corporate entities were temporal rather than eternal, those blessings and judgments were real.

This is not necessarily a point that would be denied by other Calvinists who wanted to purify their churches, but it was a major aspect of Puritan theology. They thought and wrote and preached with corporate realities very much in view, much more so than has been the case with many other Reformed leaders, and this, more than anything else, gives us a way of understanding the full significance of the term "Puritan."

John Winthrop was a Puritan, and "A Model of Christian Charity" is a Puritan sermon. It could be argued that while they are all Reformed, none of the rest of the sermons in this volume are Puritan. (It might also be argued that there should be a return to genuinely Puritan preaching, but that argument must wait for another day.)

Winthrop does, therefore, assume the validity of the basic vision that informed John Cotton's sermon. He is preaching to a group of Christians who are about to embark on house-building in the New World. He emphasizes, toward the end of his sermon, the spiritual responsibilities that define their work. Those to whom he is preaching are not to do their building simply as individuals who owe personal obedience to God. It is the entire community that owes obedience to God (note how often that word "community" is used).

And Winthrop calls the entire community to obedience for reasons that far transcend the blessings they might enjoy as a result of obedience—though those blessings are real. Fundamentally, the danger of disobedience is what it will mean in relation to God himself. If we disobey the Lord, Winthrop argues, "we shall be made a story and a by-word through the world; we shall open the mouths of enemies to speak evil of the ways of God." It is precisely in this context that Winthrop makes his famous "city upon a hill" comment. The greatest concern of the Massachusetts Bay colonists must be whether their behavior, whether the house they build, when seen by the rest of the world, will produce appropriate praise to the Lord. It is a *theo*centric political vision if ever there was one.

In all of this, therefore, Winthrop is carrying forward the vision communicated earlier in Boston, England, by John Cotton. But Winthrop does put his individual spin on this vision.

In reading just the title of the sermon (even more, of course, in reading the entire sermon), one is impressed with Winthrop's description of the exact nature of the obedience that God expects of his people. Contrary to most stereotypes of the Puritans, the sermon's emphasis is not on narrowly defined personal ethical issues. The focus is on what the title announces: "Christian charity." And while the introductory statement might lead one to believe that Winthrop's emphasis will be on the rights of the wealthy, exactly the opposite proves to be the case.

In reading the sermon, note the distinctions Winthrop makes between the laws of nature and the laws of grace. Note the incredible obligations placed on those to whom the Lord has given great gifts. And note how Winthrop urges his hearers to see that it is in fulfilling these laws of grace that they will build a city on a hill that will bring praise and honor and glory to God.

After considering all these things, consider one more thing: is it possible that, in the twenty-first century, some African-American preachers who proclaim the necessity of corporate as well as individual obedience to God and who define that corporate obedience in terms of "Christian charity" are more in the tradition of Cotton and Winthrop than are those of us whose sermons never make such proclamations?

We must remember that we who name the name of Jesus "shall be as a city upon a hill; the eyes of all people are upon us." Are we sure that what they see tends to lead them to praise and worship the Lord?

A MODEL OF CHRISTIAN CHARITY

JOHN WINTHROP

G od Almighty in his most holy and wise providence has so disposed of the condition of mankind as in all times some must be rich, some poor, some high and eminent in power and dignity, others mean and in subjection.

THE REASON HEREOF

1. Reason: First, to hold conformity with the rest of his works, being delighted to show forth the glory of his wisdom in the variety and difference of the creatures and the glory of his power, in ordering all these differences for the preservation and good of the whole, and the glory of his greatness that as it is the glory of princes to have many officers, so this great King will have many stewards counting himself more honored in dispensing his gifts to man by man than if he did it by his own immediate hand.

2. Reason: Secondly, that he might have the more occasion to manifest the work of his Spirit: first, upon the wicked in moderating and restraining them so that the rich and mighty should not eat up the poor, nor the poor and despised rise up against their superiors, and shake off their yoke; secondly, in the regenerate in exercising his graces in them, the great ones in their love, mercy, gentleness, temperance, etc.; and in the poor and inferior sort, their faith, patience, obedience, etc.

3. Reason: Thirdly, that every man might have need of each other, and from hence they might be all knit more nearly together in the bond of brotherly affection. From hence it appears plainly that no man is made more honorable than another or more wealthy, etc., out of any particular and singular respect to himself but for the glory of his Creator and the common good of the creature, man. Therefore, God still reserves the property of these gifts to himself; in Ezekiel 16:17 he there calls wealth his gold and his silver, etc., and in Proverbs 3:9 he claims their service as his due: honor the Lord with your riches, etc. All men are thus (by divine providence) ranked into two sorts, rich and poor. Under the first are comprehended all such as are able to live comfortably by their own means duly improved; and all others are poor according to the former distribution. There are two rules whereby we are to walk one towards another: *justice* and *mercy*. These are always distinguished in their act and in their object, yet may they both concur in the same subject in each respect; sometimes there may be an occasion of showing mercy to a rich man in some sudden danger of distress, and also doing of mere justice to a poor man in regard of some particular contract, etc. There is likewise a double law by which we are regulated in our conversation one towards another: in both the former respects, the law of nature and the law of grace, or the moral law or the law of the gospel, to omit the rule of justice as not properly belonging to this purpose otherwise than it may fall into consideration in some particular cases. By the first of these laws man as he was enabled so is commanded to love his neighbor as himself; upon this ground stands all the precepts of the moral law, which concerns our dealings with men. To apply this to the works of mercy this law requires two things: first, that every man afford his help to another in every want or distress; secondly, that he perform this out of the same affection that makes him careful of his own good. According to our Savior, "Whatever you would that men should do to you" (Matt. 7:12). This was practiced by Abraham and Lot in entertaining the angels and the old man of Gibeah.

The law of grace or the gospel has some difference from the former in these respects: first, the law of nature was given to man in the estate of innocency, the law of the gospel in the estate of regeneracy. Secondly, the former propounds one man to another, as the same flesh and image of God—this as a brother in Christ also and in the communion of the same spirit, and so teaches us to put a difference between Christians and others. Do good to all, especially to the household of faith; upon this ground the Israelites were to put a difference between the brethren of such as were strangers, though not of the Canaanites. Thirdly, the law of nature could give no rules for dealing with enemies, for all are to be considered as friends in the estate of innocency, but the gospel commands love to an enemy: "If your enemy hungers, feed him; love your enemies and do good to them that hate you" (Matt: 5:44).

This law of the gospel propounds likewise a difference of seasons and occasions. There is a time when a Christian must sell all and give to the poor, as they did in the apostles' times. There is a time also when a Christian (though they give not all yet) must give beyond their ability, as they of Macedonia (2 Cor. 8:2–6). Likewise, community of perils calls for extraordinary liberality, and so does community in some special service for the church. Lastly, when there is no other means whereby our Christian brother may be relieved in his distress, we must help him beyond our ability, rather than tempt God in putting him upon help by miraculous or extraordinary means.

This duty of mercy is exercised in giving, lending, and forgiving.

Question: What rule shall a man observe in giving in respect of the measure?

Answer: If the time and occasion are ordinary, he is to give out of his abundance—let him lay aside, as God has blessed him. If the time and occasion are extraordinary, he must be ruled by them; also taking this, that then a man cannot likely do too much especially, if he may leave himself and his family under probable means of comfortable subsistence.

Objection: A man must lay up for posterity, the fathers lay up for posterity and children, and he is worse than an infidel that provides not for his own.

Answer: For the first, it is plain that it being spoken by way of comparison it must be meant of the ordinary and usual course of fathers and cannot extend to times and occasions extraordinary; for the other place, the apostle speaks against such as walked inordinately, and it is without question that he is worse than an infidel who through his own sloth and voluptuousness shall neglect to provide for his family.

Objection: The wise man's eyes are in his head (Solomon says) and foresees the plague; therefore, we must forecast and lay up against evil times when he or his may stand in need of all he can gather.

Answer: This very argument Solomon uses to persuade to liberality: "cast your bread upon the waters . . . for you know not what evil may come upon the land" (Eccl. 11:1). And in Luke 16: make you friends of the riches of iniquity. You will ask how this shall be? Very well. For first he that gives to the poor lends to the Lord, and he will repay him even in this life a hundredfold to him or his. The righteous is ever merciful and lends, and his seed enjoys the blessing; and besides, we know what advantage it will be to us in the day of account, when many such witnesses shall stand forth for us to witness the improvement of our talent. And I would know of those who plead so much for laying up for time to come, whether they hold that to be gospel. As Christ says in Matthew 16:19: "Lay not up for yourselves treasures upon earth. . . ." If they acknowledge it, what extent will they allow it? If only to those primitive times, let them consider the reason whereupon our Savior grounds it. The first is that they are subject to the moth, the rust, the thief. Secondly, they will steal away the heart: where the treasure is, there will the heart be also. The reasons are of like force at all times; therefore, the exhortation must be general and perpetual which applies always in respect of the love and affection to riches and in regard of the things themselves when any special service for the church or particular distress of our brother do call for the use of them; otherwise, it is not only lawful but necessary to lay up as Joseph did to have ready upon such occasions as the Lord (whose stewards we are of them) shall call for them from us. Christ gives us an instance of the first, when he sent his disciples for the ass, and bids them answer the owner thus: "The Lord has need of him." When the Tabernacle was to be built, his servant sends to his people to call for their silver and gold, etc., and yields them no other reason but that it was for his work. When Elisha comes to the widow of Sareptah and finds her preparing to make ready her pittance for herself and family, he bids her first provide for him; he challenges first God's part, which she must first give before she must serve her own family. All these teach us that the Lord looks that when he is pleased to call for his right in anything we have, our own interest we have must stand aside till his turn be served. For the other, we need look no further than to that of 1 John 3:17: "He who has this world's goods and sees his brother in need, and shuts up his compassion from him, how dwells the love of God in him?" This comes punctually to this conclusion: if your brother is in want and you can help him, you need not doubt what you should do: if you love God, you must help him.

Question: What rule must we observe in lending?

Answer: You must observe whether your brother has present, probable, or possible means of repaying you. If there are none of these, you must give him according to his necessity, rather than lend him as he requires; if he has present means of repaying you, you are to look at him, not as an act of mercy, but by way of commerce, wherein you are to walk by the rule of justice; but if his means of repaying you are only probable or possible, then he is an object of your mercy, and you must lend him, though there is danger of losing it. Deuteronomy 15:7 tells us that if any of your brethren are poor, etc., you shall lend him sufficient that men might not shift off this duty by the apparent hazard. He tells them that though the Year of Jubilee were at hand (when he must remit it, if he were not able to repay it before), yet he must lend him cheerfully. It may not grieve you to give him (he says), and because some might object that I should soon impoverish myself and my family, he adds with all your work, etc., for our Savior, "From him that would borrow of you turn not away" (Matt. 5:42).

Question: What rule must we observe in forgiving?

Answer: Whether you did lend by way of commerce or in mercy, if he has nothing to pay you, you must forgive him (except in cause where you have a surety or a lawful pledge) (Deut. 15:2). Every seventh year the creditor was to quit that which he lent to his brother if he were poor, "save when there shall be no poor with you" (v. 4). In all these and like cases, Christ gave a general rule: "Whatever you would that men should do to you, do the same to them also" (Matt. 7:12).

Question: What rule must we observe and walk by in cause of community of peril?

Answer: The same as before, but with more enlargement towards others and less respect towards ourselves and our own right. Thus it was that in the primitive church they sold all and had all things in common, neither did any man say that that which he possessed was his own; likewise in their return out of the captivity, because the work was great for the restoring of the church, and the danger of enemies was common to all. Nehemiah exhorts the Jews to liberality and readiness in remitting their debts to their brethren, and disposes liberally of his own to such as wanted and stands not upon his own due, which he might have demanded of them. Thus did some of our forefathers in times of persecution here in England, and so did many of the faithful in other churches; therefore, we keep an honorable remembrance of them. And it is to be observed that both in Scriptures and latter stories of the churches, such as have been most bountiful to the poor saints, especially in these extraordinary times and occasions, God has left them highly commended to posterity, such as Zacchaeus, Cornelius, Dorcas, Bishop Hooper, the Cuttler of Brussells, and various others. Observe again that the Scripture gives no cause to restrain any from being overliberal this way, but all men to the liberal and cheerful practice hereof by the sweetest promises. For instance, one of many is in Isaiah 58:6–7: "Is not this the fast that I have chosen to loose the bonds of wickedness, to take off the heavy burdens to let the oppressed go free and to break every yoke, to deal your bread to the hungry and to bring the poor that wander into your house, when you see the naked to cover them, etc. Then shall your light break forth as the morning, and your health shall grow speedily, your righteousness shall go before you, and the glory of the Lord shall embrace you, then you shall call and the Lord shall answer you . . ." (vv. 8–9). "If you pour out your soul to the hungry, then shall your light spring out in darkness and the Lord shall guide you continually, and satisfy your soul in drought, and make fat your bones, you shall be like a watered garden, and they shall be of you that shall build the old waste places . . ." (vv. 10–12). On the contrary, most heavy curses are laid upon such as are straightened towards the Lord and his people. "Curse Meroshe because they came not to help the Lord . . ." (Judg. 5:23). "He who shuts his ears from hearing the cry of the poor, he shall cry and shall not be heard" (Prov. 21:13). "Go, you cursed, into everlasting fire . . ." (Matt. 25:41). "I was hungry and you fed me not" (v. 42). "He that sows sparingly shall reap sparingly" (2 Cor. 9:6).

Having already set forth the practice of mercy according to the rule of God's law, it will be useful to lay open the grounds of it also being the other part of the commandment, and that is the affection from which this exercise of mercy must arise. The apostle tells us that this love is the fulfilling of the law, not that it is enough to love our brother and go no further, but in regard of the excellency of his parts giving any motion to the other, as the soul to the body and the power it has to set all the faculties to work in the outward exercise of this duty. For example, when we bid one make the clock strike, he does not lay hand on the hammer, which is the immediate instrument of the sound, but sets to work on the first mover or main wheel, knowing that will certainly produce the sound which he intends. Thus, the way to draw men to the works of mercy is not by force of argument from the goodness or necessity of the work, for though this course may enforce a rational mind to some present act of mercy as is frequent in experience, yet it cannot work such a habit in a soul as shall prompt it upon all occasions to produce the same effect except by framing these affections of love in the heart, which will as natively bring forth the other as any cause produces the effect.

The definition which the Scripture gives us of love is this: Love is the bond of perfection. First, it is a bond, or ligament. Secondly, it makes the work perfect. Each body consists of parts, and that which knits these parts together gives the body its perfection, because it makes each part so contiguous to the other as thereby they do mutually participate with each other, both in strength and infirmity, in pleasure and pain. For instance, in the most perfect of all bodies, Christ and his church make one body: the several parts of this body considered apart before they were united were as disproportionate and as much disordering as so many contrary qualities or elements, but when Christ comes and by his Spirit and love knits all these parts to himself and each to the other, it becomes the most perfect and best-proportioned body in the world. "Christ by whom all the body being knit together by every joint for the furniture thereof" (Eph. 4:16) according to the effectual power which is in the measure of every perfection of parts a glorious body without spot or wrinkle, the ligaments hereof being Christ or his love, for Christ is love (1 John 4:8). So this definition is right: Love is the bond of perfection.

From hence we may frame these conclusions.

First, all true Christians are of one body in Christ (1 Cor. 12:12–13, 27). You are the body of Christ and members of [your?] part.

Secondly, the ligaments of this body which knit together are love.

Thirdly, no body can be perfect which wants its proper ligaments.

Fourthly, all the parts of this body being thus united are made so contiguous in a special relation as they must needs partake of each other's strength and infirmity, joy and sorrow, weal and woe. "If one member suffers, all suffer with it; if one be in honor, all rejoice with it" (1 Cor. 12:26).

Fifthly, this sensibleness and sympathy of each other's conditions will necessarily infuse into each part a native desire and endeavor to strengthen, defend, preserve, and comfort the other.

To insist a little on this conclusion being the product of all the former, the truth hereof will appear both by precept and pattern. "You ought to lay down your lives for the brethren" (1 John 3:16). "Bear one another's burdens and so fulfill the law of Christ" (Gal. 6:2).

For patterns we have that first of our Savior, who out of his good will in obedience to his Father, becoming a part of this body, and being knit with it in the bond of love, found such a native sensibleness of our infirmities and sorrows as he willingly yielded himself to death to ease the infirmities of the rest of his body and so heal their sorrows. From the like sympathy of parts did the apostles and many thousands of the saints lay down their lives for Christ again, the like we may see in the members of this body among themselves. In Romans 9:3, Paul could have been contented to have been separated from Christ so that the Jews might not be cut off from the body. It is very observable which he professes of his affectionate partaking with every member: "Who is weak, he says, and I am not weak? Who is offended and I burn not"? (2 Cor. 11:29). And again in 2 Corinthians 7:13: "Therefore, we are comforted because you were comforted." Of Epaphroditus he speaks in Philippians 2:30 that he regarded not his own life to do him service; Phoebe and others are called the servants of the church. It is apparent that they served not for wages or by constraint but out of love, the like we shall find in the history of the church in all ages: the sweet sympathy of affections which was in the members of this body one towards another, their cheerfulness in serving and suffering together, how liberal they were without repining, harborers without grudging, and helpful without reproaching, and all from hence they had fervent love among them, which only makes the practice of mercy constant and easy.

The next consideration is how this love comes to be wrought. Adam in his first estate was a perfect model of mankind in all their generations, and in him this love was perfected in regard of the habit. But Adam rent himself from his Creator, rent all his posterity also one from another, whence it comes that every man is born with this principle in him, to love and seek himself only, and thus a man continues till Christ comes and takes possession of the soul and infuses another principle: love to God and our brother. And this latter has continual supply from Christ, as the head and root by which he is united get the predominancy in the soul, so little by little expels the former. "Love comes of God, and everyone that loves is born of God" (1 John 4:7). Thus, this love is the fruit of the new birth, and none can have it but the new creature; now when this quality is thus formed in the souls of men, it works like the Spirit upon the dry bones (Ezek. 37:7). Bone comes to bone; it gathers together the scattered bones of perfect old man Adam and knits them into one body again in Christ, whereby a man is become again a living soul.

The third consideration is concerning the exercise of this love, which is twofold: inward or outward. The outward has been handled in the former preface of this discourse. For unfolding the other we must take in our way that maxim of philosophy, *Simile simili gaudet*, or like will to like; for as it is things which are carved with disaffection to each other, the ground of it is from a dissimilitude . . . arising from the contrary or different nature of the things themselves, so the ground of love is an apprehension of some resemblance in the things loved to that which affects it. This is the cause why the Lord loves the creature, so far as it has any of his image in it: he loves his elect because they are like himself, and he beholds them in his beloved son. So a mother loves her child, because she thoroughly conceives a resemblance of herself in it. Thus it is between the members of Christ: each discerns by the work of the Spirit his own image and resemblance in another, and therefore cannot but love him as he loves himself. Now when the soul which is of a sociable nature finds anything like to itself, it is like Adam when Eve was brought to him. She must have it one with herself. "This is flesh of my flesh, she says, and bone of my bone." She conceives a great delight in it; therefore, she desires nearness and familiarity with it. She has a great propensity to do it good and receives such content in it, as fearing the miscarriage of her beloved she bestows it in the inmost closet of her heart. She will not endure that it shall want any good which she can give it. If by occasion she is withdrawn from the company of it, she is still looking towards the place where she left her beloved. If she hears it groan, she is with it presently; if she finds it sad and disconsolate, she sighs and mourns with it. She has no such joy as when she sees her beloved merry and thriving. If she sees it wronged, she cannot bear it without passion. She sets no bounds of her affections, nor has any thought of reward; she finds recompense enough in the exercise of her love towards it. We may see this acted to life in Jonathan and David. Jonathan, a valiant man endued with the spirit of Christ, so soon as he discovers the same spirit in David, had presently his heart knit to him by this ligament of love, so that it is said he loved him as his own soul. He takes so great pleasure in him that he strips himself to adorn his beloved; his father's kingdom was not so precious to him as his beloved David. David shall have it with all his heart; he himself desires no more but that he may be near to him to rejoice in his good. He chooses to converse with him in the wilderness even to the hazard of his own life, rather than with the great courtiers in his father's palace; when he sees danger towards him, he spares neither care, pains, nor peril to divert it; when injury was offered his beloved David, he could not bear it, though from his own father; and when they must part for a season only, they thought their hearts would break for sorrow, had not their affections found vent by abundance of tears. Other instances might be brought to show the nature of this affection, as of Ruth and Naomi and many others, but this truth is made clear enough. If any shall object that it is not possible that love should be bred or upheld without hope of requital, it is granted but that is not our cause, for this love is always under reward. It never gives, but it always receives with advantage: first, in regard that among the members of the same body, love and affection are reciprocal in a most equal and sweet kind of commerce. Secondly, in regard of the pleasure and content that the exercise of love carries with it, we may see in the natural body that the mouth is at all the pains to receive and mince the food which serves for the nourishment of all the other parts of the body; yet it has no cause to complain, for first, the other parts send back by secret passages a due proportion of the same nourishment in a better form for the strengthening and comforting of the mouth. Secondly, the labor of the mouth is accompanied with such pleasure and content as far exceeds the pains it takes. So it is in all the labor of love among Christians. The party loving reaps love again as was showed before, which the soul covets more than all the wealth in the world. Thirdly, nothing yields more pleasure and content to the soul than when it finds that which it may love fervently, for to love and live beloved is the soul's paradise, both here and in heaven. In the state of wedlock there are many comforts to bear out the troubles of that condition; but let such as have tried the most say if there be any sweetness in that condition comparable to the exercise of mutual love.

From the former considerations arise these conclusions.

First, this love among Christians is a real thing, not imaginary.

Secondly, this love is as absolutely necessary to the being of the body of Christ as the sinews and other ligaments of a natural body are to the being of that body.

Thirdly, this love is a divine, spiritual nature, free, active, strong, courageous, permanent, undervaluing all things beneath its proper object, and of all the graces this makes us nearer to resembling the virtues of our heavenly Father.

Fourthly, it rests in the love and welfare of its beloved, for the full and certain knowledge of these truths concerning the nature, use, and excellency of this grace, that which the Holy Ghost has left recorded in 1 Corinthians 13. This may give full satisfaction which is needful for every true member of this lovely body of the Lord Jesus, to work upon their hearts by prayer, meditation, continual exercise at least of the special power of this grace till Christ is formed in them and they in him, all in each other knit together by this bond of love.

It rests now to make some application of this discourse by the present design which gave the occasion of writing of it. Herein are four things to be propounded: first, the persons; secondly, the work; thirdly, the end; fourthly, the means.

First, for the persons, we are a company professing ourselves fellow members of Christ, in which respect only though we were absent from each other many miles, and had our employments as far distant, yet we ought to account ourselves knit together by this bond of love, and live in the exercise of it, if we would have comfort of our being in Christ. This was notorious in the practice of the Christians in former times, as is testified of the Waldenses from the mouth of one of the adversaries, Aeneas Sylvius: *mutuo [solent amare] penè antequam norint*, they use to love any of their own religion even before they were acquainted with them.

Secondly, for the work we have in hand, it is by a mutual consent through a special overruling providence, and a more than ordinary approbation of the churches of Christ to seek out a place of cohabitation and consortship under a due form of government both civil and ecclesiastical. In such cases as this the care of the public must oversway all private respects, by which not only conscience but mere civil policy binds us; for it is a true rule that particular estates cannot subsist in the ruin of the public.

Thirdly, the end is to improve our lives to do more service to the Lord to comfort and increase the body of Christ whereof we are members, that we ourselves and posterity may be the better preserved from the common corruptions of this evil world to serve the Lord and work out our salvation under the power and purity of his holy ordinances.

Fourthly, for the means whereby this must be effected, they are twofold: a conformity with the work and end we aim at. These we see are extraordinary; therefore, we must not content ourselves with usual ordinary means whatsoever we did or ought to have done when we lived in England. The same must we do and more also where we go. That which the most in their churches maintain as a truth in profession only we must bring into familiar and constant practice; as in this duty of love we must love brotherly without dissimulation, we must love one another with a pure heart fervently, we must bear one another's burdens, we must not look only on our own things, but also on the things of our brethren, neither must we think that the Lord will bear with such failings at our hands as he does from those among whom we have lived, and that for three reasons.

1. In regard of the more near bond of marriage between him and us, wherein he has taken us to be his after a most strict and peculiar manner which will make him the more jealous of our love and obedience, so he tells the people of Israel, "You only have I known of all the families of the earth; therefore, I will punish you for your transgressions."

Secondly, because the Lord will be sanctified in them that come near him. We know that there were many that corrupted the service of the Lord, some setting up altars before his own, others offering both strange fire and strange sacrifices also; yet there came no fire from heaven or other sudden judgment upon them as did upon Nadab and Abihu, who yet we may think did not sin presumptuously.

Thirdly, when God gives a special commission he looks to have it strictly observed in every article. When he gave Saul a commission to destroy Amalek, he indented with him upon certain articles, and because he failed in one of the least, and that upon a fair pretense, it lost him the kingdom, which should have been his reward, if he had observed his commission. Thus stands the cause between God and us: we are entered into covenant with him for this work, we have taken out a commission, the Lord has given us leave to draw our own articles, we have professed to enterprise these actions upon these and these ends, and we have hereupon besought him of favor and blessing. Now if the Lord shall please to hear us, and bring us in peace to the place we desire, then he has ratified this covenant and sealed our commission, and will expect a strict performance of the articles contained in it, but if we shall neglect the observation of these articles which are the ends we have propounded, and dissembling with our God, shall fall to embrace this present world and prosecute our carnal intentions, seeking great things for ourselves and our posterity, the Lord will surely break out in wrath against us, be revenged of such a perjured people, and make us know the price of the breach of such a covenant.

Now the only way to avoid this shipwreck and to provide for our posterity is to follow the counsel of Micah, to do justly, to love mercy, to walk humbly with our God, for this end: we must be knit together in this work as one man; we must entertain each other in brotherly affection; we must be willing to abridge ourselves of our superfluities for the supply of others' necessities; we must uphold a familiar commerce together in all meekness, gentleness, patience, and liberality; we must delight in each other, make others' conditions our own, rejoice together, mourn together, labor and suffer together, always having before our eyes our commission and community in the work, our community as members of the same body. When we shall keep the unity of the Spirit in the bond of peace, the Lord will be our God and delight to dwell among us as his own people and will command a blessing upon us in all our ways, so that we shall see much more of his wisdom, power, goodness, and truth than formerly we have been acquainted with. We shall find that the God of Israel is among us when ten of us shall be able to resist a thousand of our enemies, when he shall make us a praise and glory, that men shall say of succeeding plantations: the Lord make it like that of New England. For we must consider that we shall be as a city upon a hill; the eyes of all people are upon us, so that if we shall deal falsely with our God in this work we have undertaken and so cause him to withdraw his present help from us, we shall be made a story and a by-word through the world; we shall open the mouths of enemies to speak evil of the ways of God and all professors for God's sake; we shall shame the faces of many of God's worthy servants, and cause their prayers to be turned into curses upon us till we are consumed out of the good land whither we are going. And to shut up this discourse, we give that exhortation of Moses, that faithful servant of the Lord, in his last farewell to Israel in Deuteronomy 30:

> Beloved, there is now set before us life and good, death and evil, in that we are commanded this day to love the Lord our God and to love one another, to walk in his ways and to keep his commandments, his ordinances, and his laws, and the articles of our covenant with him, that we may live and be multiplied, and that the Lord our God may bless us in the land whither we go to possess it. But if our hearts shall turn away so that we will not obey, but shall be seduced and worship other gods, our pleasures, and profits, and serve them, it is propounded unto us this day, we shall surely perish out of the good land whither we pass over this vast sea to possess it.

> Therefore, let us choose life,
> that we and our seed
> may live by obeying his
> voice and cleaving to him,
> for he is our life and
> our prosperity.

3

The Loss of a
Desirable Relative,
Lamented and Improved

Ezekiel 24:16

COTTON MATHER

The Mather family was unquestionably the most dominant family in seventeenth-century New England Puritanism. Richard (grandfather), Increase (father), and Cotton (son) (1663–1728) led the church and the academy and influenced the state in ways too numerous to mention. Robert Middlekauff, in his excellent work *The Mathers: Three Generations of Puritan Intellectuals*, details the case for the dominance of the Mather family over the first century of New England life.

Michael Hall has produced the definitive work on Increase Mather, and the title of his work is most significant for our purposes. Hall called his study *The Last American Puritan: The Life of Increase Mather, 1639–1723*. Why would Hall call Increase Mather the last American Puritan, and how is this insight relevant to Cotton Mather's sermon on Ezekiel 24:16? Answering these questions not only will serve as an introduction to this sermon but also will provide a framework within which to understand all the remaining sermons in this volume.

New England Puritanism might be said to have ended with Increase Mather for reasons that arise directly out of the earlier introductions to John Cotton and John Winthrop. If the point made there about the corporate nature of the Puritan visions of Cotton and Winthrop is valid, then we might expect to see the loss of that vision as integrally involved in the disappearance of that vision in American ecclesiastical life. And so we do.

The political situation that made possible Cotton's and Winthrop's intentions for the Holy Commonwealth of Massachusetts Bay was the peculiar arrangements that had been negotiated for the charter, which provided legal warrant for the colony. All British colonies in the seventeenth century needed a legal charter from the king to be legitimate, and the kings, in order to maintain their control over these colonies, always stipulated that at least once a year the individuals to whom the charter was granted (the "company") would meet in London, where they would be directly accessible to him. Well, not always! For some reason that scholars have never been able to precisely identify, the charter of the Massachusetts Bay Colony contained no such clause. This meant that the company that controlled Massachusetts Bay (which included John Winthrop) was, for all practical purposes, out of the reach of the sovereign and could therefore construct the colony as they saw fit. This is why Massachusetts Bay could institute such dramatic innovations as the requirement that the franchise (the vote) be based on membership in a Puritan church in the colony.

Obviously, therefore, the preservation of the charter was foundationally important to the corporate vision of the early-seventeenth-century Puritans. If they lost the charter, they could be forced to revert to the English franchise basis, which was wealth (a forty-shilling freehold) rather than spiritual identity. While this change would not increase the *number* of those who could vote, it would surely change the character of the community and could easily cause the community to seek to become a "model of capitalism" rather than a "model of Christian charity." [This is not to say that these two are necessarily mutually exclusive; it *is* to say that when financial return becomes the most important societal priority, the results can be quite different than they might be if Christian charity were the most important societal priority. And it *is* to say that, as heirs of John Foxe, the

New England Puritans thought that the economic base for the English fran-chise was one of the reasons why that state was not primarily concerned with giving God the honor and worship that he deserves.]

So the preservation of their original charter was exceedingly important to the first generation of Puritan leaders in New England. Equally, those who wished to undermine and replace the Puritan vision for the colony knew that all they had to do to accomplish this goal was to get the charter revoked. Accordingly, in the mid-1640s, when he was denied membership in a local Puritan congregation, Dr. Robert Child, a wealthy physician who would certainly have been able to vote in England, returned to London and petitioned the king to void the original Massachusetts Bay charter. There is every indication that, all other things being equal, Child's peti-tion would have been successful and the Puritan experiment would have ended then and there. But of course, all other things were not equal for the English king in the late 1640s—he was facing a war with Parliament, and in 1649 he faced his own execution by Parliament.

Thus, the goals of a Holy Commonwealth, based on the corporate theol-ogy of Foxe and Cotton and Winthrop, continued, and sermons such as the first two in this volume continued as well.

But after the restoration of the Stuart line to the monarchy in 1660, it was just a matter of time. In October 1684, a letter arrived in Boston from King Charles II revoking the Massachusetts Bay charter and installing a royal governor, Sir Edmund Andros, as the supreme authority in Massa-chusetts.

Nothing has ever changed the nature of American preaching so dra-matically as these events in 1684. In the immediate aftermath of the ar-rival of Andros, sermons of even the most orthodox of Puritan ministers came to ring with such phrases as "natural rights of Englishmen," "liberty," and "freedom." It is actually to this period rather than to the founding pe-riod of the colony that the cultural values announced in the Declaration of Independence and the Constitution should be traced.

Because of their dominance in Massachusetts, the Mathers took on the role as the primary colonial spokesmen in the attempt to get the 1684 de-cision reversed. Indeed, Increase Mather was in London more than he was in Boston from 1686 to 1691, and the story of his negotiations with the Crown is told thoroughly and fairly by Hall in his biography of Mather.

The original goal with which Mather went to London—the restoration of the original charter—was gradually forgotten as it became clear that neither Parliament nor the king would consider such an option. Slowly but surely, Mather adapted his requests, and finally, a couple of years after the Glorious Revolution when William and Mary replaced James II/VII on the throne, he was "successful."

The word "successful" must be placed in quotation marks because what Mather got was very different from what he had said he wanted when he originally went to London. He did not get the original Massachusetts Bay charter restored. He did get a new charter, which guaranteed self-government to New England on the condition that New England enact laws that were in no way "inimical" to the laws of England.

Cotton and Winthrop would have said that Mather betrayed the entire Puritan enterprise. Mather, in his own defense, said this: "God has been so gracious to me as to make me instrumental in obtaining for my country a Magna Charta, whereby religion and English liberties, with some peculiar privileges, liberties, and all men's properties, are confirmed and secured (allowance being given for the instability of all human affairs) to them and their posterity forevermore."[1]

Hall has several superb summaries of the impact of Mather's accomplishment. I quote them at length in order to set the context for Cotton Mather's sermon on Ezekiel 24:

> The new charter of 1691 was far different. The new charter brought about fundamental changes in Massachusetts society, and what it did not cause, it symbolized. The royal charter of 1691 was the turning point in the history of Puritan New England. . . . Prominent among the new legislation was a "Bill for the General Rights and Liberties." This legislation was in effect a bill of rights, and while it established the general design of political rights and liberties as they would develop in America down to the War for Independence, it just as clearly replaced the "Body of Liberties" which had served Massachusetts in a similar way from 1641. The contrast is as night with day. Whereas the "Body of Liberties" was infused with the concern to create a religious state, the "Bill for the General Rights and Liberties" dropped all reference to church

---

1. Increase Mather, quoted by Michael Hall in *The Last American Puritan: The Life of Increase Mather, 1639–1723* (Middletown, Conn.: Wesleyan University Press, 1988), 251.

and religion. Perhaps even more dramatic than the thoroughgoing secularism of the new statute was its acceptance by the clergy. . . . Life, liberty, and property, not religion, were the concerns of the government in Massachusetts now. . . . The old Puritan state was gone for good.[2]

With the disappearance of the Puritan state came a significant change in orthodox Reformed preaching. The kind of theological framework assumed in sermons such as those of Cotton and Winthrop was replaced by a new framework. Whereas Cotton's and Winthrop's sermons had had strong corporate elements, sermons now took on a much more individualistic character. Of course, this point can be exaggerated. Orthodox Reformed sermons before 1691 certainly did contain elements directed primarily to individuals. And sermons after 1691 did (and do) contain some elements related to corporate entities. But the fundamental character of preaching in the Reformed tradition in America did shift, and it is therefore appropriate in some ways to consider Increase Mather to be the last American Puritan preacher.

It is also appropriate in some ways to consider Cotton Mather to be the first orthodox Reformed non-Puritan American preacher, an appellation confirmed by the sermon that follows and, at least to some degree, by all of the other sermons that follow his in this volume.

Cotton Mather's life and ministry were even more extraordinary than those of his father and his grandfather. As an ecclesiastical leader in New England during the charter controversy and during the Salem witchcraft trials, a participant in the founding of Yale, a pastor during the horrific smallpox epidemic of 1721, an elected member of the Royal Society of London (only the eighth colonial to be elected to this most prestigious of scientific societies), and the author of 388 publications (and as many more manuscripts, which were yet unpublished at the time of his death), no one—not even John Winthrop two generations earlier—had a higher profile in New England in his lifetime than did Cotton Mather.[3]

Mather's sermon on Ezekiel 24 is seldom (if ever) anthologized. And one may rightly ask, in what way is this a Reformed sermon that shaped America? It must be granted that any one of a number of Mather's sermons could

---

2. Ibid., 264–65.

3. See Kenneth Silverman, *The Life and Times of Cotton Mather* (New York: Harper and Row, 1984).

have been chosen for this volume. No single Mather sermon had the impact of Cotton's sermon or Winthrop's sermon (or, for that matter, Edwards's sermon to follow). But the kind of preaching done by Mather is absolutely crucial in the development of Reformed preaching in America. It would perhaps not be too much to say that Mather's preaching, as represented by this sermon, is the key homiletical transition that leads to the type of preaching exemplified by Tim Keller in the last sermon in this volume.

Cotton Mather's personal life was as turbulent as the life of his culture. His personal finances were often in chaos (largely because of his charitable nature), and the response to his public positions was often violently negative (for example, because he supported inoculation against smallpox, he was ridiculed by the newspapermen James Franklin and his younger brother Benjamin, who so inflamed public opinion against Mather that someone threw a bomb into his living room). But the severest trials Mather faced were family-related. Put simply, during his lifetime, Mather endured the deaths of two wives and of thirteen of his fifteen children. It is impossible even to imagine this kind of grief!

How does a Christian, and particularly a Reformed Christian who believes in the sovereignty of God, handle such suffering? What indeed can we say to others who face such things? How does the preacher speak of these things to his people?

That is the context of Mather's sermon on Ezekiel 24:16, the passage in which God announces to his prophet that he is about to take Ezekiel's wife, "the delight of your eyes," from him. As the preface to the sermon points out, Mather had already lost five children, including his firstborn son. Now their mother, Mather's beloved wife Abigail, is dead. What does the preacher say to his congregation when this has happened?

One might surmise that John Cotton or John Winthrop would have approached the subject with theology identical to Mather's but that they would have provided a theological framework leading them to draw corporate conclusions from the personal disaster. Not so Mather. His sermon describes a personal, private, individual response to God's action. Whether one is inclined to applaud or lament this new direction in Reformed preaching, one cannot avoid being caught up in the resilient faith of one who has lost all that Mather has and who can yet say, in words reminiscent of the conclusion of Habakkuk's prophecy, "Heaven, heaven, will make amends for all"!

THE LOSS OF A DESIRABLE RELATIVE, LAMENTED AND IMPROVED

COTTON MATHER

Son of Man, behold, I take away the desire of your eyes with a stroke. (Ezek. 24:16)

I am this day myself a sad commentary upon my text. The Holy God has, in my deadly calamity, given you its lively commentary. Your eyes do behold what it is for the God of heaven to take away from a Son of Man the desire of his eyes with a stroke.

That one of so little use or worth as I am, and one who has so much deserved the displeasure of heaven, should feel such a stroke from God, nobody may wonder at it. But why must such an eminent man of God as the prophet Ezekiel be thus dealt with? The blessed God would not only try the virtue of his holy servant, but also make the trial of the prophet a thing prophetical of what was to come upon all the people. It is often so that the things befalling of one considerable person, who has been much concerned for the welfare of a people, are ominous of what is to befall all the people for whom he has been concerned. The case of David in the Fifty-first Psalm, the fate of Miriam in her leprosy and exclusion, and many more such things were types of what was to befall the Israelitish nation. The angels of the seven churches had in their condition that of their churches. Though this minister of God, our Ezekiel, was a most unspotted liver and a most excellent preacher, and his hearers would also confess him so to be, yet he had enemies among them. Heaven took notice of it, with much offense at it.

Son of Man, the children your people are still talking against you. It may be that some of these would be so malignant as to rejoice in the affliction that now befell him. Rejoice not against me, O my enemies (might our prophet now say); for the affliction upon my family is but a sign of a greater confusion to come upon the public. When God was going to cast off a people whom he had once espoused and married unto himself, he does by death cut off the happy marriage which there had been between his prophet and a daughter of Israel. When God was going to deprive the people of the dear enjoyments which their hearts were most of all set upon, he takes away from his prophet the dearest thing he had in the world. And because the judgments coming upon that people would be such that they should not have liberty to mourn with due compassion and solemnity for one another, therefore the Lord forbids now unto his prophet the solemn rites of mourning, which else on this mournful occasion would have been proper for him. Thus Ezekiel is unto you a sign, says the Lord.

We have in the words before us the preparation for this grievous matter. There is first a commination to the prophet. The thing threatened unto him is a death, and as distressing a death as could have come upon him; his own death would not have been more uneasy.

The subject of the death here threatened is the desire of his eyes—that is to say, his wife, who, it seems, was a very lovely person, whom he loved very much to look upon. His eyes, he thought, could not be charmed with a more desirable creature.

The manner of the death here threatened is with a stroke, that is to say, very suddenly. She did not lie languishing for many months; he had not opportunity by long languishments upon her to fortify his mind against the loss that was now to befall him. Some quick disaster snatched away from him the brightest jewel he had in his house. He had but short warning of the sore trouble that was now coming upon him. She died that very night. A stroke indeed! But unto him, rather than her.

But then, there is a compellation of the prophet: Son of Man. A title near one hundred times over addressed unto him. For a Son of Man to have the amiable companion of his life torn from him—oh! 'Tis a sorrowful thing! He must be more than a man (or worse than a brute!) who feels not more than ordinary sorrows upon it. He and his rare contemporary Daniel were admitted unto an astonishing familiarity with the angels of God: The angels of heaven flew down to them in their studies, and ravished them with sensible and most heavenly communications. Now, lest they should forget themselves to be feeble men, and that they might not forget to be humble men, the angels that favored them with their visits would still use that style, Son of Man! Son of Man! Accordingly, we find them at the very mention of that word sometimes falling down into the dust before the glorious angels of the Lord. The angels of God would have this brave man feel that he was but a Son of Man. And surely there would soon arrive mortifications enough in that one point—"I take away the desire of your eyes with a stroke"—to convince him of his being so.

But heaven does now call me to treat upon this uneasy

DOCTRINE.

When the desire of our eyes, or a relative that was very desirable in our eyes, is taken away from us, 'tis God that has taken it, and stricken us by taking it.

These things are now to be observed.

I. The children of men are sometimes blessed with such desirable relatives as may be very justly called the desire of their eyes. The blessed God makes a various distribution of his blessings among the children of men. But not the least of those blessings are enwrapped in the relations which the children of men bear to one another. Inasmuch as we are the children of men, we are in various respects related unto one another; and the all-wise Maker and Ruler of the world has made a manifold provision for our mutual comfort in those relations.

Now, 'tis a special favor of God granted unto some among the children of men that relatives can take much delight in one another. Indeed, sometimes 'tis otherwise; and it is a fearful curse upon the children of men when 'tis otherwise. Relatives there are who have no desire, but rather a distaste of one another; so little do they desire, that they can't endure one another. Their persons, their tempers, their manners make them so disagreeable to one another that they do not love, but loathe each other. It is not altogether unusual in this woeful world that relatives are not only weary of each other, but also make each other weary of the world. Thus the lady of old made that complaint about her daughters-in-law in Genesis 27:46: "I am weary of my life because of them." Nevertheless, there are many instances of that compassion in our good God upon the unworthy children of men: that relatives are made highly desirable and agreeable to one another.

And it is especially thus in the conjugal relation. The God of love sometimes disposes those whom he has made consorts in the conjugal relation greatly to love and prize one another. The consorts are to each other the desire of their eyes; and they so love each other that they love to be as much as may be in the sight of each other. About one of these relatives, 'tis said in Proverbs 18:22: "He that finds it finds a good thing, and obtains favor of the Lord." And that is the opinion which both of them have of each other: This is a good and a great gift of God unto me! Highly favored of God was I, in his giving of it. It may be, before they were first acquainted, they humbly cried unto God, that he would choose for them what consorts they should live with; and God so answers those prayers and cries that every day afterwards, as long as they live together, they give thanks unto God for giving them to live together. They live together like Abraham and Sarah, like Isaac and Rebekah, like Jacob and Rachel. They live together in such harmony and happiness that they could freely die for one another; and when either of them does die, it gives a thousand deaths to the survivor. They set a mighty value upon one another. The satisfaction which they take in one another is inexpressible. The husband is of great esteem in the eyes of his wife. She loves to see him and, much more, loves to please him. Such a covering of the eyes he is unto her that all the men upon earth are nothing in her eyes, in comparison of him. And she will no more look upon another than the wife of Tigranes, who after the wedding of Cyrus, whom everyone did commend as the rarest person in the company, being asked by her husband what she thought of him, answered, "In truth, I looked at nobody there but you, my husband." But her esteem for him is like that in the wife of Phocion, who, when a lady had shown her treasures and jewels unto her, by way of requital only showed her Phocion, saying, "All my treasures and jewels are in him!" The wife is of as great esteem in the eyes of her husband. He loves her and her love, and rejoices in his loving hind and his pleasant roe. He would rather lose all his possessions than suffer the loss of one whom God had thus enriched him with. He can scarce relish anything if his eyes have not her also before him. If by death she leaves him, he can, it may be, say, as one once of his Lady Crescentia, "She never grieved me but once, and that was by her death!" And he is ready to write upon all his other entertainments the motto written upon one of his by a worthy man among ourselves, when he became a widower: *In Lugenda Compare, vitae spacium compleat Orbus.*

And the affection which these relatives have to each other sometimes is raised unto the more of rapture, upon the most religious and honorable principles. When 'tis thus, I may use the exclamation which Tertullian of old, writing to his consort, used about a Christian marriage: *Undo Sufficiam ad Enorrandam fœlicitatem Ejus Matrimonij!* (Who can declare the happiness of such a marriage!). Our Ezekiel was a prophet as well as a priest, and a man full of God and Christ and heaven, a man of a most holy and heavenly character. He had the glory of the Lord, and the presence of his angels, in his eyes. And yet his consort was the desire of his eyes. *And yet!* said I? Nay, rather let me say, Therefore she was so. Breeding will do very much to endear consorts unto one another, but virtue will do more. The filthy papists decry the married state, as if it were a very polluted state and inconsistent with the most consummate sanctity. But the Bible calls them dogs for it, and it is well known that infandous abominations at the same time are continually perpetrated by those impious dogs. The Nazirites that were purer than snow, whiter than milk, and brighter than pearl by their vow of holiness did not become defiled by being married. The married society was well called by Paphnutius of old, An Holy Chastity. The holy martyr Bradford, whom they have sometimes well styled An Angel of God, when there was talk of hope that he might be delivered out of prison, on being asked what he would do upon his deliverance, answered, He would marry. What a heavenly man was Enoch the seventh from Adam? A man so full of heaven that God would never let him die, but would fetch him away to heaven both body and spirit. And yet this walker of God was a married man, and had both sons and daughters. It may be that there never were two men more full of grace and heaven than Moses and Isaiah. They both of them were taken into heaven before they died and saw the Son of God with his angels about him in his glory there. And yet these were married men. The solace of the married state is mightily advanced by the Christian religion. The more of Christianity there is in any man, the more of honor and value he is ready to put upon the desire of his eyes, and the more will he desire to render himself on all accounts a blessing unto her. So far is the married state from hurting of a heavenly mind that the more heavenly mind there is in any man, the more tenderness he has for her that is the desire of his eyes. The thoughts of such a man are, *My Lord Jesus Christ has bidden me to love this dear creature with all possible tenderness; and the more I love her, the more shall I exhibit the kindness which the Lord Jesus Christ has for his church. By well treating her, who is to be the desire of my eyes, I shall adorn the doctrine of God my Savior, and make his religion appear the more lovely in the eyes of my neighbors.* Such thoughts do ennoble the married conversation of them that would eminently approve themselves the children of God as well as the children of men. And the beastly satyrs against marriage which affront the sober part of mankind in many printed pamphlets have a most noble confutation in that conversation.

But I am now called off to a more melancholy proposition.

II. Very desirable relatives may be—yea, shall be—taken away from one another; and the more they have been the desire of our eyes, perhaps the sooner they must be taken from us. What are earthly comforts? Truly, very short-lived comforts. We read in 1 Chronicles 29:15: "Our days on the earth are as a shadow, and there is none abiding." Relatives that would gladly live together, and unto whom it is a death to think of parting, must in a little while be parted by death. Let relatives be never so strongly engaged unto one another, it won't be long before death brings a terrible dissolution upon all their engagements. Their love may be strong as death, yet strong death will dissolve all the ties of it. Are there any relatives which are unto us the desire of our eyes? It won't be long before they take that long farewell of us: "The eye of him that has seen me shall see me no more" (Job 7:8). A time will come when one shall say with her in 2 Kings 4:1, "My husband is dead." A time will come when another shall say with him in Genesis 23:4, "I must bury my dead out of my sight."

Our Ezekiel was doubtless very much a favorite of God; and no doubt he made the most fervent intercessions to God for the sparing of the dearly beloved of his soul. But it might not be granted. That servant of God had his heart exceedingly set upon the glorifying of the Lord. He had already glorified God, first in a single state, and then in a married state; and now the Lord must be glorified by him in a holy widowhood.

Sometimes when a sentence of death is passed upon our desirable relatives, we may by prayer and faith obtain a short reprieve. The relatives may by prayer and faith be rescued from the jaws of death one time after another, until the Lord shall say unto us: *Now be content; I have granted as long as I see convenient. Say no more; be willing to take up with spiritual and eternal blessings, and with what I shall order for you. What I do you know not now, but you shall know hereafter.* And when our hearts are perhaps thus fitted for it, *Son of Man, behold, the Lord now takes away the desire of your eyes with a stroke.* Though we bring the desire of our eyes unto the Lord, with never such a fountain of tears in our eyes, and spread the desire of our souls with never such importunity before Him for the continuance of it, yet it must, when God sees meet, be taken away. Death will first or last accomplish that lamentable thing; according to Lamentations 2:4, "He slew all the desirable of the eye in the tabernacle of the daughter of Zion."

Yea, sometimes desirable relatives must be taken from us, for this very reason: because we too much make them the desire of our eyes. When our hearts are inordinately set upon anything, we pay for our inordinateness by our having that thing taken from us. It is many ways necessary and profitable for the disciples of him who died upon the cross to be often under the cross. And a man may make a shrewd guess what cross he is most likely to meet from this token: What is the point which is most of all desirable in the eyes of the man, and which he is most loath to be crossed in? There, most probably, must the man be most severely afflicted. Thus, when a man loses the desire of his eyes, or any very desirable relative, he may often say with Job: "The thing which I greatly feared is come upon me, and that which I was afraid of is come unto me" (Job 3:25).

But whence comes it? Let a third proposition answer that.

III. When desirable relatives are taken away from us, 'tis God that has taken them. We must have the providence of God in our eyes when the desire of our eyes is taken away from us. Our eyes must not be so put out by our having the desire of our eyes taken away that we shall not see the hand of God in all that befalls us. There is the providence of God, ordering and inflicting all the afflictions that befall the children of men. As it was said in Amos 3:6: "Shall there be evil in a city and the Lord has not done it?" So we may say, Shall there be evil in a family, and it not be the Lord's doing? To have desirable relatives taken away is an affliction of so much consequence that we need think seriously, *What hand is it that lays this affliction upon us?* Oh, let us awfully think with ourselves, *I have to do with God in this dispensation.* There is nothing to be ascribed unto happenstance and fortune; 'tis blind paganism to see no further than such a blind original for the loss of desirable relatives. Nor must we consider diseases or accidents as being in any higher form than that of second causes. God, the great God, is to be considered as the first cause of all. When any of our desirable relatives are taken away, we must say with Job, "The Lord gave, and the Lord has taken away" (Job 1:21). It is a vile stupidity and profanity to be insensible of a divine hand ordering, disposing, directing our loss of desirable relatives when it comes upon us. When our families are wounded by having desirable relatives taken out of them, if we regard not the works of the Lord, nor the operation of his hands, we may fear that he will go on in wounding of us; yea, that he will destroy us, and not build us up.

IV. And now, a fourth proposition comes to challenge a share in my discourse, which would have been that when desirable relatives are taken away, there is a dreadful stroke of God upon us in the taking of them. But my best way of speaking to this proposition will be only to say that I am not at present well able to speak to it; I do not yet know all the evil that is to be spoken to it. [Only I know what dread in the twelfth of Job and the fourteenth!] We will proceed therefore unto the

APPLICATION.

I. Are the children of men sometimes blessed with desirable relatives? 'Tis then a lamentable thing when relatives do not study to render themselves desirable. When relatives have no desire, no respect, no honor for one another, they are very unhappy in one another. The yoking of such relatives is almost as great an unhappiness as the torment invented by the Turian, who fastened a dead body to a living one. Relatives there are who are not the desire of the eyes to those unto whom they stand related, but the terror of their eyes, or the contempt of their eyes, a very smoke in their eyes, and an abominable eyesore; or, as 'tis expressed in 1 Samuel 2:33, "To consume their eyes, and grieve their hearts." A most lamentable thing when relatives are so little desired that they are taken away from each other without being much lamented. We read of such a one in 2 Chronicles 21:20: "He departed without being desired."

It is a lamentable thing when parents are so fierce and harsh or foolish that the children can have no desire to appear in their presence. And it is a lamentable thing when children are so graceless and wicked that the parents have no desire to have them appear before them.

It is a lamentable thing when brethren and sisters are of such ill qualities that they don't care to see one another.

It is a lamentable thing when rulers are not such as people can desire, but such roaring lions and ranging bears that they would rejoice to be rid of them. And it is a lamentable thing when people are so unreasonably hard to please that the rulers, or any man of sense, would say, They had rather have the government of wild creatures committed unto them.

We read concerning a renowned minister of God in Daniel 9:23. He was a man of desires, a very desirable man. It is a lamentable thing when ministers are so ignorant or so negligent or so criminal that their hearers have no cause to desire their ministry, but wish they would lay it down. And it is a lamentable thing when hearers are so captious or so ungrateful that the ministers have no cause to desire to have anything to do with them.

It is most of all to be lamented when consorts cannot make a consort, but cease to be desirable unto one another. Let all such relatives, the most nearly related of any under heaven, beware of everything that may render them unacceptable unto one another and beware of all tendencies or temptations to weariness of one another. It is required: "Let every one of you in particular so love his wife even as himself, and the wife see that she reverence her husband" (Eph. 5:33). Let the fear of God cause you to oblige one another with all suitable expressions of goodness and kindness, and let the fear of God fill you with love to one another. Oh, let there be nothing in your conduct but what shall be an emblem of the goodness and kindness that passes between the Lord Jesus Christ and his church.

II. Must very desirable relatives be taken from one another? It becomes relatives, then, to live together as not being always to live together. When we have any desire of our eyes before us, let us hear that admonition from heaven given to us in Proverbs 23:5: "Will you set your eyes upon that which is not? For these things certainly make themselves wings; they fly away as an eagle towards heaven." Concerning the desirable relatives whose conversation with us is the very salt of our lives, and without whom life itself is hardly to be desired, let us remember that ere long, either we shall be taken from them or they be taken from us. In the midst of all our entertainments with our desirable relatives, oh, remember the days of darkness, and think, *Shortly we must part*. It would not have been the ancient custom to introduce a death's head at a wedding feast if such thoughts were at all impertinent or unprofitable. Oh, let us take heed of too violent affections towards each other, lest we hasten the parting time upon us, and lest when the parting time comes, we make it a bitter one. Christians, fortify yourselves with a spirit of self-denial and resignation. Mortify your passions, that you may be ready for that which mortality has to do upon you. Wholesome is that advice of 1 Corinthians 7:29–30: "This I say, brethren, the time is short; it remains that both they that have wives be as though they had none; and they that weep (supposedly at the death of their wives) as though they wept not."

And O my hearers, let this meditation awaken you so faithfully to discharge your duty to each other that at the parting time you may with joy reflect upon your faithfulness. Parents and children, masters and servants, and all others, howsoever you be related, call to mind, I beseech you, 'tis but a little time that you have to be together. Oh, improve this little time to the best advantage for eternity. It is urged in Ecclesiastes 9:10: "Whatever your hand finds to do, do it with your might, for there is no work . . . in the grave, where you go." Have you nothing to do for the souls of each other? Oh, do it as well as you can and as fast as you can, so that, a little while hence, when you can do no more, you may make this joyful reflection: I have left nothing undone that was to be done for the good of the friend that is now taken away.

But most of all, may all consorts attend this lesson of wisdom. Take heed of grieving one another. A sad parting time is at hand; but, I do assure you, it will very much abate the sadness of it if you may then say, I have lovingly, honestly, and unfaintingly done all the service that I could for the relative that is now taken away. In a peculiar manner, we owe very much of service to the souls of each other. It was said in 1 Corinthians 7:16: "How do you know, O wife, whether you shall save your husband? Or how do you know, O man, whether you shall save your wife?" Thus, O wife, have you nothing to do for the salvation of your husband? Or, O man, for the salvation of your wife? Oh, do it out of hand. Pray with one another, as well as for one another. Propound unto each other the articles of the covenant of grace, and assist each other in a consent unto those articles. Forward each other in the exercises of piety, and assist each other in your endeavors at those exercises. As it is in general a true and a good observation that they that would have the comfort of relations must be careful to do the duty of them, so, more particularly, I will freely say this unto my hearers: It will be an unspeakable consolation unto a man who has the desire of his eyes going from him to hear his desirable relatives saying unto him: *I bless God that ever he gave me to you; 'tis my acquaintance with you, and with your prayerful and watchful and holy example, that has been the salvation of my soul.* Oh! Live together here as the heirs of everlasting life and resolving, if you can, to help each other unto that inheritance. Live together as those that would meet each other shortly in heaven, and there be able to say unto each other, It was you that helped me hither.

III. Is it God who takes away from us our desirable relatives? O realize and reverence the hand of God in such bereavement.

'Tis a season wherein desirable relatives are taken away from very many of our neighbors. Many eyes are weeping because the desire of those eyes is taken away. But he that is tasting of the cup given to the prophet Ezekiel has peculiar cause and call to attend unto the admonitions of God. First, it is the hand of God which takes away our desirable relatives. Oh, patiently resign them into that hand. When the prophet had the desire of his eyes extinguished, he received this order to signalize his patience: "You shall neither mourn nor weep, neither shall your tears run down." And that holy and patient servant of God could say, "My wife died, and I did as I was commanded." Whatever evil we sustain in losing the desire of our eyes, yet considering what hand it is that sends that evil upon us, it becomes us to say, as did Job in Job 2:10, "Shall we receive good at the hand of God (such a good as we had in the desire of our eyes), and shall we not receive evil?" (such an evil as the loss of that good). Those that were the desire of our eyes, and as the very apple of our eyes—'tis God that has taken them. Say then with the psalmist in Psalm 39:9: "I was dumb, I opened not my mouth, because you did it." We never do more honor to the blessed God than by a patient and profound submission unto his will in our adversity. Behold, when in a stroke of adversity we are submissive unto the will of God, it may honor him more than all our active obedience! When a servant of God sees the desire of his eyes taking wing, he may then kneel down by her and take into his hands that hand which has been dearer to him than all the world beside, and there with all possible solemnity resign unto the Lord the friend for whose life he would freely have given all he had in the world as a ransom, and hear her thereupon saying to him, whom she preferred above the whole world, Sir, I sign and seal your act of resignation! Methinks I see my Ezekiel doing so in the black day when the great God said unto him, "Son of Man, behold, I take away the desire of your eyes with a stroke." Certainly, it is no dishonorable testimony to the glories of Christianity.

Remember, O Christians, our God is a sovereign God. Were the desire of our eyes never so bright a thing, 'twas but a bright piece of clay, and absolutely at the disposal of the eternal Potter. Our God is a righteous God. When the desire of our eyes is ravished from us, rivers of tears may run down our eyes for the sins by which we forfeited it. Our God is an all-sufficient God. Our Creator, our Savior, our Comforter is infinite and immortal; we may enjoy him when the finest creature dies. Though a lovely creature is snatched from us, have we not a lovely Jesus left us for our consolation? When the desire of our eyes is gone, we may still converse with him, who should be the Desire of all Nations. Why say we not now with David in Psalm 73:25: "Lord, there is none upon earth that I desire besides you"? When David had lost the desire of his eyes, we read, "He encouraged himself in the Lord his God." Oh, let this encouragement make us very patient; we still have the Lord for our God! In the Marian persecution, there was a woman brought before the bloody Bishop of London on the score of the gospel. He threatened to take away her husband from her; said she, "Christ is my husband." He threatened to take away her child from her; said she, "Christ is better to me than ten sons." He said he would strip her of all her outward comforts; her answer was, "But Christ is mine, and you cannot strip me of him." Admirably spoken! Let my sex, too, learn of that admirable woman how to encourage ourselves under the worst of our bereavements.

Secondly, it is the hand of God which takes away our desirable relatives. But let us hear the voice of God in that work of his hand. Oh, hear the rod, for there is a voice in it.

The voice of God unto us, in taking away the desire of our eyes, is: Humble yourself under the mighty hand of God. It is now, if ever, a season for that practice: "Let us search and try our ways, and turn again unto the Lord" (Lam. 3:40). Let us now search and try whether the just God have no controversy with us. Now search and try what may be the sins by which the desire of our eyes has been confiscated. Search and try whether we did carry towards the desire of our eyes as we ought to do. Let this our self-examination issue in a deep abhorrence of ourselves, and a true repentance of our sins. That, that is the right mourning, which is a sorrowing to repentance, and a being sorry after a godly manner. But now, by fresh applications with faith to the blood of the Lord Jesus Christ, the Son of God, which cleanses from all sin, obtain the pardon of all the sins whereof we do thus repent. And, oh, be very cautious of again falling into the sins, or being like that man of whom it is said, "In the time of his distress, he trespassed yet more against the Lord."

Another voice of God unto us is: Be strongly convinced of human weakness and frailty. We read it in the divine oracle of Psalm 103:15–16: "As for man, his days are as grass; as a flower in the field, so he flourishes: for the wind passes over it, and it is gone, and the place thereof shall know it no more." Do we not now read it in our own experience? When we see beauty turned into ashes, loveliness become loathesomeness, the greatest charms become a prey to worms, and the desire of our eyes become the horror of our eyes, how can we forbear crying out, "Lord, what fading flowers are those that we most of all dote upon! Lord, when you correct us with your rebukes, you make our beauty consume away like a moth; surely we are vanity."

A third voice of God unto us is: Prepare to follow. When the desire of our eyes is taken away, the language of it is this: "Be also ready" (Matt. 24:44). They that are gone from us were a part of ourselves and, it may be, not so old as ourselves. How inexcusable are we if we do not say with ourselves, "I shall not be long after them"? 'Twas the manner of old for them to lay and leave their friends in their graves with these words: *Vale, Vale, nos te sequemur* (Farewell, farewell, we shall quickly follow)! What? Is one half of us already in a coffin? Surely it becomes us to expect that the rest of us will soon be there. They that are gone from us are gone but a very little before us.

Oh! That we might now today hear the voice of God, and not burden our hearts.

Thirdly, it is the hand of God which takes away our desirable relatives. Well, then, watch very much against all the temptations of Satan, which may be likely to assault us under this hand of God. Is the desire of our eyes taken away? It may now be said unto us: "Behold, Satan has desired to have you, that he may sift you as wheat" (Luke 22:31). All new conditions have some new temptations. When any irksome thing befalls us, and especially when we are deprived of the desire of our eyes, than which what can be more irksome? We may be sure Satan will take advantage from it. For to have the desire of our eyes taken away brings a dark time upon us. The powers of darkness may, ere we are aware, hurry us on to unaccountable inconveniences. Now more than ever is that counsel seasonable: "Watch and pray that you enter not into temptation" (Matt. 26:41). If God by taking away the desire of our eyes brings us particularly into a state of widowhood, oh! How solicitous ought we to be of a holy widowhood! But that it may be so, it should be a very prayerful one. The very first thing we are to do, as soon as we can look about us, methinks, should be to pray, and fast, and weep in secret places before the Lord, and beg of God that he would pardon all our miscarriages in our former condition, and preserve us from all further miscarriages in the new and sad condition that is now come upon us. Alas, what wrong steps, what foolish ones, and what fatal ones are commonly taken in that state by those who, being desolate, continue not in supplications and prayers night and day! And they are never more unhappily taken than in precipitated proceedings unto second marriages. For though it was an indefensible severity in many of the ancients absolutely to forbid them, nevertheless, 'tis a dishonorable levity to make too much haste unto them, and especially for those aged men, to whom a Jerom would say, *Cogitate quotidie moriturum et de secundis nuptiis numquam cogitabis* (It were fitter for you to think of dying than of wedding). The Duchess of Millain, being made a widow, stamped that motto on her coin: *Sola facta, solum deum sequor* (Being left alone, I converse with God alone). It becomes both sexes, when the state of widowhood is come upon them, to converse with God more than ever they did in their lives before.

Lastly, it is the hand of God which takes away our desirable relatives. But let it be a very rich anodyne and cordial unto us to think unto whom and what he has taken them. Were the relatives rendered principally by the fear and grace of God, the desire of our eyes? The God who has taken them away has then taken them to himself. Were they in Christ? They are now with Christ, where to be is by far the best of all. And as well as they loved us, they would be loath to return from him unto us. They were the desire of our eyes, but will it have no pacifying influence upon us to think they are gone where all tears are wiped from their eyes? The relation between them and us is lost, but the remembrance of the relatives may continue more with them than with us. And when we meet them again in the heavenly world, there will doubtless be some rapturous expressions of gladness agreeable to the heavenly state upon the meeting of such as have been instrumental to bring each other unto it.

In conclusion: We encounter many grievances in this present evil world. Our desirable relatives have got the start of us to the blessedness of a better world! We shall shortly see the period of all our grievances, as well as they, and in the society of them, that are got before us. And give me leave to conclude my sermon with the words wherewith the desire of my eyes has newly concluded her life—words which, I pray God, help me to make the solace of mine: Heaven, heaven, will make amends for all.

4

The Distinguishing Marks of a Work of the Spirit of God

1 John 4:1

JONATHAN EDWARDS

First things first—Jonathan Edwards (1703–58) was the greatest pastor/theologian that America has yet seen. Jonathan Edwards possessed the greatest intellect of any American thinker, Christian or otherwise. Jonathan Edwards was a powerful revival preacher and was one of those whose preaching the Lord used to bring about the Great Awakening.

But Jonathan Edwards was not a Puritan. He operated in a culture and in a church where the original "Holy Commonwealth" dreams of men such as John Cotton and John Winthrop no longer structured the thinking of Reformed ecclesiastical leaders. The church within which Edwards preached was increasingly confronted with challenges to the fundamentals of the Christian faith (the Trinity, the imputation of Adam's sin, the sovereignty of God), and therefore, Edwards's preaching often involved what later Reformed theologians would call "the defense of the faith."

At the same time, Edwards was profoundly involved in the greatest re-vival in American history.

For these reasons and many more besides, Edwards's preaching may be more instructive than the preaching of any other single individual both for those who wish to understand the history of the American church and for those who wish to shape, in a biblical fashion, both the present and the fu-ture of the American church.

Still in the category of "first things," it should be said that the 2003 biography of Edwards written by George Marsden and published by Yale University Press is far and away the best book ever written about Edwards. Those who would understand the man, the Christian, the pastor, and the theologian must start their secondary reading here. Though that work be-came available only after most of the materials for this volume had been prepared, it is an incredibly valuable resource for understanding not only Edwards's sermon that follows, but also many of the other sermons here as well.

Several themes recurred throughout Edwards's ministry, and that pre-sented in "Distinguishing Marks" is one of the most prominent. It is also one of the themes with the greatest direct relevance to the church of Christ (Re-formed and otherwise) in America today. That theme might be stated briefly as follows: "How can we discern what is *genuinely* Christian and distinguish between that and what might be considered 'counterfeit' Christianity?"

This is a concern that Edwards encountered in his reading of Scripture, in specific situations faced by his congregation, and, indeed, in his own life. Perhaps the most obvious of the forms in which it was manifested had to do with the Great Awakening. From at least 1734, Edwards experienced revival blessings upon his preaching in Northampton, and several of his earlier treatises focused on those blessings.

"A Narrative of Surprising Conversions" was Edwards's first formal at-tempt to describe what he had seen the Lord do among his people in the 1734 revival, and the name of that work accurately describes its content. It is basically an uncritical description of what Edwards saw as genuine con-versions in his own parish and in surrounding ones. But that revival was relatively short-lived and largely confined to western Massachusetts. It was the trauma of the Great Awakening that produced Edwards's most profound preaching and writing on the subject.

By the late 1740s, all of New England was caught up in what we now know to have been the most dramatic religious event (in terms of the proportion of the population involved) that America has ever experienced. And as with any such event, there were extremes—some opposing everything that was happening and some engaging in the most bizarre forms of behavior imaginable. At Yale, during the first half of 1741, the cumulative effects of recent campus visits by revival preachers George Whitefield and Gilbert Tennent left the campus in a state of extraordinary spiritual fervor and the conservative rector, Thomas Clap, in a state of angry antagonism. Then came September, the time for Yale's commencement, and James Davenport, perhaps the wildest of the revival preachers. Arriving uninvited in New Haven, Davenport held a series of revival meetings on the New Haven common during which, among other things, he denounced New Haven clergy and urged students to abandon their churches. Clap immediately clamped down on the students and banned them from attending religious services held by itinerant preachers.

It was in this context that Edwards preached "Distinguishing Marks" as the commencement address at Yale on September 10, 1741. In this sermon, Edwards lays out the following purpose:

> My design therefore at this time is to show what are the true, certain, and distinguishing evidences of a work of the Spirit of God, by which we may safely proceed in judging of any operation we find in ourselves, or see in others.

But this is not a matter of merely historical or cultural interest for Edwards; it gets at the very heart of "what makes a person a Christian," and therefore it gets at the heart of his ministry as a Christian preacher and pastor.

The sermon itself is clear and relatively easy to read and understand. Just a couple of points might be made to highlight its themes and historical significance.

First, it is crucial to note the sentence immediately following Edwards's statement of purpose quoted above. Edwards's purpose, as he spoke to the Yale community, was to provide guidance in discerning the work of the Spirit of God. "And here I would observe that we are to take the *Scriptures* as our guide in such cases." A subtle point, perhaps, but neither Cotton nor Winthrop nor Mather had found it necessary to make this point in exactly this way.

By the 1740s, however, the exclusive role of God's revealed Word was being slowly but surely undermined by arguments built on "common sense" or "the natural light of reason." Read carefully, Charles Chauncey's *Seasonable Thoughts on the State of Religion in New England*, the most influential attack on the Great Awakening, is nothing short of an "ode to reason." Edwards was affirming that, in this matter as in all others, God has given us his special revelation to be our infallible guide. No one used his mind better than Edwards, but Edwards knew and was affirming that the mind truly knows only on the basis of the Scriptures.

At the same time, Edwards was responding to the James Davenports who were, in 1741, increasingly hijacking the Awakening, moving it in the direction of mindless "enthusiasm," and building justification for outlandish behavior on the foundation of the extraordinary effects seen in their ministries. Later, in his treatise on *Qualifications for Communion*, Edwards would make this powerful statement: "God has not given us his *providence*, but his *word*, to be our governing *rule*."[1] Over and over again, Edwards would return to his argument that only the Scriptures provide adequate guidance in spiritual matters. Edwards may not have been a Puritan, but he surely was an heir of the Reformation and of the Reformers' commitment to "sola scriptura."

But there is more. The seed that was to grow into the massive oak of Edwards's most significant theological contribution to the church is found at the very beginning of Section 2 of the sermon. Edwards asks, "What are distinguishing Scripture evidences of a work of the Spirit of God?" And he answers, "When the operation is such as to raise their esteem of that Jesus who was born of the Virgin . . . is a sure sign that it is from the Spirit of God."

Esteem for Jesus—here is a key to Edwards's thinking and preaching throughout his life. Here is a key to the matter of discerning "counterfeit" religion. Do the actions or activities in question promote esteem for Jesus? Not simply whether they evoke fear and guilt and even repentance. Not simply whether they evoke a vague sense of gratitude. But do they promote esteem? Do they prompt us to worship and adore and delight in the Savior? If they do, they are genuinely Christian. If they do not, they may not be Christian.

---

1. Jonathan Edwards, *An Humble Inquiry into the Rules of the Word of God Concerning the Qualifications Requisite to a Complete Standing and Full Communion in the Visible Church*, in *The Works of Jonathan Edwards*, vol. 1 (Edinburgh: Banner of Truth Trust, 1974), 477.

The radical way in which Edwards described God's sheer worthiness and called himself and his people to make it the ground of all their Christian words and deeds was at the very heart of his ministry. And that radical call is right here in seminal form in his 1741 sermon. Later that call gets even clearer, and in *The Treatise on Religious Affections* it becomes definitive, such that that treatise is probably the most important book ever written by an American.

Having argued that Edwards was not a Puritan, I would now like to suggest that, in fact, he developed more completely than anyone else one of the fundamental elements of Puritan thinking. In the introduction to John Cotton's "God's Promise to His Plantation," I made this comment: "From Foxe to Cotton and Winthrop and beyond, the emphasis is on *what God deserves* far more than it is on what men might want or even need." In terms of the application of this insight to individual spirituality and to the life of the church in a pluralistic environment, no one accomplished more than Edwards. And since most of us now live as individual Christians in a pluralistic environment, no human being can be more helpful to us than Jonathan Edwards.

THE DISTINGUISHING MARKS
OF A WORK OF THE SPIRIT
OF GOD

JONATHAN EDWARDS

Beloved, believe not every spirit, but try the spirits whether they are of God; because many false prophets are gone out into the world.
(1 John 4:1)

I n the apostolic age, there was the greatest outpouring of the Spirit of God that ever was, both as to his extraordinary influences and gifts and as to his ordinary operations in convincing, converting, enlightening, and sanctifying the souls of men. But as the influences of the true Spirit abounded, so counterfeits did also abound: the devil was abundant in mimicking both the ordinary and extraordinary influences of the Spirit of God, as is manifest by innumerable passages of the apostles' writings. This made it very necessary that the church of Christ should be furnished with some certain rules, distinguishing and clear marks by which she might proceed safely in judging of the true from the false without danger of being imposed upon. The giving of such rules is the plain design of this chapter, where we have this matter more expressly and fully treated than anywhere else in the Bible. The apostle, of set purpose, undertakes to supply the church of God with such marks of the true Spirit as may be plain and safe, and well accommodated to use and practice; and that the subject might be clearly and sufficiently handled, he insists upon it throughout the chapter, which makes it wonderful that what is here said is no more taken notice of in this extraordinary day, when there is such an uncommon and extensive operation on the minds of people, such a variety of opinions concerning it, and so much talk about the work of the Spirit.

The apostle's discourse on this subject is introduced by an occasional mention of the indwelling of the Spirit as the sure evidence of an interest in Christ. "And he that keeps his commandments dwells in him, and he in him; and hereby we know that he abides in us, by the Spirit which he has given us." From this we may infer that the design of the apostle is not only to give marks whereby to distinguish the true Spirit from the false, in his extraordinary gifts of prophecy and miracles, but also in his ordinary influences on the minds of his people, in order to their union to Christ and being built up in him, which is also manifest from the marks themselves that are given, which we shall hereafter notice.

The words of the text are an introduction to this discourse of the distinguishing signs of the true and false spirit. Before the apostle proceeds to lay down these signs, he exhorts Christians, first, against an overcredulousness and a forwardness to admit every specious appearance as the work of a true spirit. "Beloved, believe not every spirit, but try the spirits whether they are of God." And second, he shows that there were many counterfeits, "because many false prophets were gone out into the world." These did not only pretend to have the Spirit of God in his extraordinary gifts of inspiration, but also to be the great friends and favorites of heaven, to be eminently holy persons, and to have much of the ordinary saving, sanctifying influences of the Spirit of God on their hearts. Hence we are to look upon these words as a direction to examine and try their pretenses to the Spirit of God in both these respects.

My design therefore at this time is to show what are the true, certain, and distinguishing evidences of a work of the Spirit of God by which we may safely proceed in judging any operation we find in ourselves or see in others. And here I would observe that we are to take the Scriptures as our guide in such cases. This is the great and standing rule which God has given to his church in order to guide them in things relating to the great concerns of their souls, and it is an infallible and sufficient rule. There are undoubtedly sufficient marks given to guide the church of God in this great affair of judging of spirits, without which it would lie open to woeful delusion and would be remedilessly exposed to be imposed on and devoured by its enemies. And we need not be afraid to trust these rules. Doubtless that Spirit who indited the Scriptures knew how to give us good rules by which to distinguish his operations from all that is falsely pretended to be from him. And this, as I observed before, the Spirit of God has here done of set purpose, and done it more particularly and fully than anywhere else, so that in my present discourse I shall go nowhere else for rules or marks for the trial of spirits, but shall confine myself to those that I find in this chapter. But before I proceed particularly to speak to these, I would prepare my way by, first, observing negatively, in some instances, what are not signs or evidences of a work of the Spirit of God.

SECTION 1

Negative Signs: What are no signs by which we are to judge of a work— and especially: What are no evidences that a work is not from the Spirit of God?

I. Nothing can be certainly concluded from this: that a work is carried on in a way very unusual and extraordinary, provided the variety or difference is such as may still be comprehended within the limits of Scripture rules. What the church has been used to is not a rule by which we are to judge, because there may be new and extraordinary works of God, and he has heretofore evidently wrought in an extraordinary manner. He has brought to pass new things, strange works, and has wrought in such a manner as to surprise both men and angels. And as God has done thus in times past, so we have no reason to think but that he will do so still. The prophecies of Scripture give us reason to think that God has things to accomplish which have never yet been seen. No deviation from what has hitherto been usual, let it be never so great, is an argument that a work is not from the Spirit of God if it is no deviation from his prescribed rule. The Holy Spirit is sovereign in his operation, and we know that he uses a great variety; and we cannot tell how great a variety he may use within the compass of the rules he himself has fixed. We ought not to limit God where he has not limited himself.

Therefore, it is not reasonable to determine that a work is not from God's Holy Spirit because of the extraordinary degree in which the minds of persons are influenced. If they seem to have an extraordinary conviction of the dreadful nature of sin and a very uncommon sense of the misery of a Christless condition—or extraordinary views of the certainty and glory of divine things—and are proportionably moved with very extraordinary affections of fear and sorrow, desire, love, or joy; or if the apparent change is very sudden, and the work is carried on with very unusual swiftness—and the persons affected are very numerous, and many of them are very young, with other unusual circumstances—not infringing upon Scripture marks a work of the Spirit. These things are no argument that the work is not of the Spirit of God. The extraordinary and unusual degree of influence and power of operation, if in its nature it is agreeable to the rules and marks given in Scripture, is rather an argument in its favor; for by how much higher the degree which in its nature is agreeable to the rule, so much the more is there of conformity to the rule, and so much the more evident that conformity. When things are in small degrees, though they are really agreeable to the rule, it is not so easily seen whether their nature agrees with the rule.

There is a great aptness in persons to doubt things that are strange, especially elderly persons to think that to be right which they have never been used to in their day, have not heard of in the days of their day, and have not heard of in the days of their fathers. But if it is a good argument that a work is not from the Spirit of God, that it is very unusual, then it was so in the apostles' days. The work of the Spirit then was carried on in a manner that, in very many respects, was altogether new, such as never had been seen or heard since the world stood. The work was then carried on with more visible and remarkable power than ever, nor had there been seen before such mighty and wonderful effects of the Spirit of God in sudden changes and such great engagedness and zeal in great multitudes—such a sudden alteration in towns, cities, and countries; such a swift progress and vast extent of the work—and many other extraordinary circumstances might be mentioned. The great unusualness of the work surprised the Jews; they knew not what to make of it, but could not believe it to be the work of God. Many looked upon the persons that were the subjects of it as bereft of reason, as you may see in Acts 2:13, 26:24, and 1 Corinthians 4:10.

And we have reason from Scripture prophecy to suppose that at the commencement of that last and greatest outpouring of the Spirit of God that is to be in the latter ages of the world, the manner of the work will be very extraordinary, and such as never has yet been seen, so that there shall be occasion then to say, as in Isaiah 66:8: "Who has heard such a thing? Who has seen such things? Shall the earth be made to bring forth in one day? Shall a nation be born at once? For as soon as Zion travailed, she brought forth her children." It may be reasonably expected that the extraordinary manner of the work then will bear some proportion to the very extraordinary events and that glorious change in the state of the world which God will bring to pass by it.

II. A work is not to be judged by any effects on the bodies of men, such as tears, trembling, groans, loud outcries, agonies of body, or the failing of bodily strength. The influence persons are under is not to be judged one way or other by such effects on the body, and the reason is because the Scripture nowhere gives us any such rule. We cannot conclude that persons are under the influence of the true Spirit because we see such effects upon their bodies, because this is not given as a mark of the true Spirit; nor, on the other hand, have we any reason to conclude, from any such outward appearances, that persons are not under the influence of the Spirit of God, because there is no rule of Scripture given us to judge spirits by that does either expressly or indirectly exclude such effects on the body, nor does reason exclude them. It is easily accounted for from the consideration of the nature of divine and eternal things, the nature of man, and the laws of the union between soul and body how a right influence, a true and proper sense of things, should have such effects on the body, even those that are of the most extraordinary kind, such as taking away the bodily strength or throwing the body into great agonies and extorting loud outcries. There are none of us but do suppose, and would have been ready at any time to say it, that the misery of hell is doubtless so dreadful, and eternity so vast, that if a person should have a clear apprehension of that misery as it is, it would be more than his feeble frame could bear, and especially if at the same time he saw himself in great danger of it, and to be utterly uncertain whether he should be delivered from it, yea, and to have no security from it one day or hour. If we consider human nature, we must not wonder that when persons have a great sense of that which is so amazingly dreadful, and also have a great view of their own wickedness and God's anger, that things seem to them to forebode speedy and immediate destruction. We see the nature of man to be such that when he is in danger of some terrible calamity to which he is greatly exposed, he is ready upon every occasion to think that *now* it is coming. When persons' hearts are full of fear, in time of war, they are ready to tremble at the shaking of a leaf, to expect the enemy every minute, and to say within themselves, *now* I shall be slain. If we should suppose that a person saw himself hanging over a great pit, full of fierce and glowing flames, by a thread that he knew to be very weak and not sufficient to bear his weight, and knew that multitudes had been in such circumstances before and that most of them had fallen and perished, and saw nothing within reach that he could take hold of to save him, what distress would he be in! How ready to think that *now* the thread was breaking, that now, *this minute*, he should be swallowed up in those dreadful flames! And would not he be ready to cry out in such circumstances? How much more those that see themselves in this manner hanging over an infinitely more dreadful pit, or held over it in the hand of God, who at the same time they see to be exceedingly provoked! No wonder that the wrath of God, when manifested but a little to the soul, overbears human strength.

So it may easily be accounted for that a true sense of the glorious excellency of the Lord Jesus Christ and of his wonderful dying love, and the ex-

ercise of a truly spiritual love and joy, should be such as very much to overcome the bodily strength. We are all ready to own that no man can see God
and live and that it is but a very small part of that apprehension of the glory
and love of Christ, which the saints enjoy in heaven, that our present frame
can bear; therefore, it is not at all strange that God should sometimes give
his saints such foretastes of heaven as to diminish their bodily strength. If
it was not unaccountable that the queen of Sheba fainted and had her bodily strength taken away when she came to see the glory of Solomon, much
less is it unaccountable that she who is the antitype of the queen of Sheba,
that is, the church, that is brought, as it were, from the utmost ends of the
earth from being an alien and stranger, far off in a state of sin and misery,
should faint when she comes to see the glory of Christ, who is the antitype
of Solomon—and especially will be so in that prosperous, peaceful, glorious kingdom which he will set up in the world in its latter age.

Some object against such extraordinary appearances that we have no instances of them recorded in the New Testament under the extraordinary
effusions of the Spirit. Were this allowed, I can see no force in the objection, if neither reason nor any rule of Scripture excludes such things, especially considering what was observed under the foregoing particular. I do
not know that we have any express mention in the New Testament of any
person's weeping, groaning, or sighing through fear of hell, or a sense of
God's anger; but is there anybody so foolish as from hence to argue that in
whomsoever these things appear, their convictions are not from the Spirit
of God? And the reason why we do not argue thus is because these are easily accounted for, from what we know of the nature of man and from what
the Scripture informs us in general, concerning the nature of eternal things
and the nature of the convictions of God's Spirit; so that there is no need
that anything should be said in particular concerning these external, circumstantial effects. Nobody supposes that there is any need of express Scripture for every external, accidental manifestation of the inward motion of
the mind; and though such circumstances are not particularly recorded in
sacred history, yet there is a great deal of reason to think, from the general
accounts we have, that it could not be otherwise than that such things must
be in those days. And there is also reason to think that such great outpouring of the Spirit was not wholly without those more extraordinary effects on persons' bodies. The jailer in particular seems to have been an in-

stance of that nature when he, in the utmost distress and amazement, came trembling and fell down before Paul and Silas. His falling down at that time does not seem to be a designed putting himself into a posture of supplication or humble address to Paul and Silas, for he seems not to have said anything to them then; but he first brought them out, and then he says to them, "Sirs, what must I do to be saved?" (Acts 16:29–30). But his falling down seems to be from the same cause as his trembling. The psalmist gives an account of his crying out aloud, a great weakening of his body under convictions of conscience, and a sense of the guilt of sin: "When I kept silence my bones waxed old, through my roaring all the day long; for day and night your hand was heavy upon me: my moisture is turned into the drought of summer" (Ps. 32:3–4). We may at least argue this much from it: that such an effect of conviction of sin may well in some cases be supposed; for if we should suppose anything of an auxesis in the expressions, yet the psalmist would not represent his case by what would be absurd and to which no degree of that exercise of mind he spoke of would have any tendency. We read of the disciples in Matthew 14:26 that when they saw Christ coming to them in the storm, and took him for some terrible enemy threatening their destruction in that storm, *they cried out for fear*. Why then should it be thought strange that persons should cry out for fear when God appears to them, as a terrible enemy, and they see themselves in great danger of being swallowed up in the bottomless gulf of eternal misery? The spouse, once and again, speaks of herself as overpowered with the love of Christ, so as to weaken her body and make her faint: "Stay me with flagons, comfort me with apples; for I am sick of love" (Song 2:5). And in 5:8: "I charge you, O you daughters of Jerusalem, if you find my Beloved, that you tell him that I am sick of love." From this we may at least argue that such an effect may well be supposed to arise from such a cause in the saints in some cases, and that such an effect will sometimes be seen in the church of Christ.

It is a weak objection that the impressions of enthusiasts have a great effect on their bodies. That the Quakers used to tremble is no argument that Saul (afterwards Paul) and the jailer did not tremble from real convictions of conscience. Indeed, all such objections from effects on the body, let them be greater or less, seem to be exceedingly frivolous. They who argue thence proceed in the dark; they know not what ground they go upon, nor by what rule they judge. The root and course of things is to be looked at and the nature of the operations and affections are to be inquired into and examined by the rule of God's Word, and not the motions of the blood and animal spirits.

III. It is no argument that an operation on the minds of people is not the work of the Spirit of God if it occasions a great deal of noise about religion. For though true religion is of a contrary nature to that of the Pharisees—which was ostentatious, and delighted to set itself forth to the view of men for their applause—yet such is human nature that it is morally impossible that there should be a great concern, strong affection, and a general engagedness of mind among a people without causing a notable, visible, and open commotion and alteration among that people. Surely it is no argument that the minds of persons are not under the influence of God's Spirit if they are very much moved; for indeed spiritual and eternal things are so great and of such infinite concern that there is a great absurdity in men's being but moderately moved and affected by them. And surely it is no argument that they are not moved by the Spirit of God if they are affected with these things in some measure as they deserve, or in some proportion to their importance. And when was there ever any such thing since the world stood as a people in general being greatly affected in any affair whatsoever without noise or stir? The nature of man will not allow it.

Indeed, Christ says in Luke 17:20: "The kingdom of God comes not with observation." That is, it will not consist in what is outward and visible; it shall not be like earthly kingdoms, set up with outward pomp in some particular place, which shall be especially the royal city and seat of the kingdom, as Christ explains himself in the words next following: "Neither shall they say, Lo here, or lo there; for behold, the kingdom of God is within you." Not that the kingdom of God shall be set up in the world, on the ruin of Satan's kingdom, without a very observable, great effect: a mighty change in the state of things, to the observation and astonishment of the whole world—for such an effect as this is even held forth in the prophecies of Scripture, and is so by Christ himself in this very place, and even in his own explanation of these aforementioned words in verse 24: "For as the lightning that lightens out of one part under heaven shines unto another part under heaven, so shall also the Son of man be in his day." This is to distinguish Christ's coming to set up his kingdom from the coming of false christs, which he tells us will be in a private manner in the deserts and in the secret chambers; whereas this event of setting up the kingdom of God should be open and public, in the sight of the whole world with clear manifestation, like lightning that cannot be hid but glares in everyone's eyes and shines from one side of heaven to the other. And we find that when Christ's kingdom came by that remarkable pouring out of the Spirit in the apostles' days, it occasioned a great stir everywhere. What a mighty opposition was there in Jerusalem on occasion of that great effusion of the Spirit! And so in Samaria, Antioch, Ephesus, Corinth, and other places! The affair filled the world with noise and gave occasion to some to say of the apostles that they had turned the world upside down (Acts 17:6).

IV. It is no argument that an operation on the minds of a people is not the work of the Spirit of God if many who are the subjects of it have great impressions made on their imaginations. That persons have many impressions on their imaginations does not prove that they have nothing else. It is easy to be accounted for that there should be much of this nature among a people where a great multitude of all kinds of constitutions have their minds engaged with intense thought and strong affections about invisible things; yea, it would be strange if there should not. Such is our nature that we cannot think of things invisible without a degree of imagination. I dare appeal to any man of the greatest powers of mind whether he is able to fix his thoughts on God, Christ, or the things of another world without imaginary ideas attending his meditations. And the more engaged the mind is and the more intense the contemplation and affection, still the more lively and strong the imaginary idea will ordinarily be, especially when attended with surprise. And this is the case when the mental prospect is very new and takes strong hold of the passions, as fear or joy; and when the change of the state and views of the mind is sudden, from a contrary extreme, as from that which was extremely dreadful to that which is extremely ravishing and delightful. And it is no wonder that many persons do not well distinguish between that which is imaginary and that which is intellectual and spiritual and that they are apt to lay too much weight on the imaginary part and are most ready to speak of that in the account they give of their experiences, especially persons of less understanding and of distinguishing capacity.

As God has given us such a faculty as the imagination, and so made us that we cannot think of things spiritual and invisible without some exercise of this faculty, so, it appears to me, that such is our state and nature that this faculty is really subservient and helpful to the other faculties of the mind when a proper use is made of it—though oftentimes, when the imagination is too strong and the other faculties weak, it overbears and disturbs them in their exercise. It appears to me manifest, in many instances with which I have been acquainted, that God has really made use of this faculty to truly divine purposes, especially in some that are more ignorant. God seems to condescend to their circumstances and deal with them as babes, as of old he instructed his church, while in a state of ignorance and minority, by types and outward representations. I can see nothing unreasonable in such a position. Let others who have much occasion to deal with souls in spiritual concerns judge whether experience does not confirm it.

It is no argument that a work is not of the Spirit of God if some who are the subjects of it have been in a kind of ecstasy wherein they have been carried beyond themselves and have had their minds transported into a train of strong and pleasing imaginations and a kind of visions, as though they were rapt up even to heaven, and there saw glorious sights. I have been acquainted with some such instances, and I see no need of bringing in the help of the devil into the account that we give of these things, nor yet of supposing them to be of the same nature with the visions of the prophets or St. Paul's rapture into paradise. Human nature, under these intense exercises and affections, is all that need be brought into the account. If it may be well accounted for that persons under a true sense of the glorious and wonderful greatness and excellency of divine things and soul-ravishing views of the beauty and love of Christ should have the strength of nature overpowered, as I have already shown that it may, then I think it is not at all strange that among great numbers that are thus affected and overborne, there should be some persons of particular constitutions that should have their imaginations thus affected. The effect is no other than what bears a proportion and analogy to other effects of the strong exercise of their minds. It is no wonder, when the thoughts are so fixed and the affections so strong— and the whole soul so engaged, ravished, and swallowed up—that all other parts of the body are so affected as to be deprived of their strength and the whole frame ready to dissolve. Is it any wonder that, in such a case, the brain in particular (especially in some constitutions), which we know is most especially affected by intense contemplations and exercises of mind, should be so affected that its strength and spirits should for a season be diverted and taken off from impressions made on the organs of external sense, and be wholly employed in a train of pleasing delightful imaginations corresponding with the present frame of the mind? Some are ready to interpret such things wrong and to lay too much weight on them, such as prophetical visions, divine revelations, and sometimes significations from heaven of what shall come to pass, which the issue, in some instances I have known, has shown to be otherwise. But yet, it appears to me that such things are evidently sometimes from the Spirit of God, though indirectly; that is, their extraordinary frame of mind, and that strong and lively sense of divine things which is the occasion of them, is from his Spirit; and also as the mind continues in its holy frame and retains a divine sense of the excellency of spiritual things even in its rapture, which holy frame and sense is from the Spirit of God, though the imaginations that attend it are but accidental, and therefore there is commonly something or other in them that is confused, improper, and false.

V. It is no sign that a work is not from the Spirit of God if example is a great means of it. It is surely no argument that an effect is not from God if means are used in producing it; for we know that it is God's manner to make use of means in carrying on his work in the world, and it is no more an argument against the divinity of an effect that this means is made use of than if it was by any other means. It is agreeable to Scripture that persons should be influenced by one another's good example. The Scripture directs us to set good examples to that end (Matt. 5:16; 1 Peter 3:1; 1 Tim. 4:12; Titus 2:7) and also directs us to be influenced by the good examples of others and to follow them (2 Cor. 8:1–7; Heb. 6:12; Phil. 3:17; 1 Cor. 4:16; 11:1; 2 Thess. 3:9; 1 Thess. 1:7). By this it appears that example is one of God's means, and certainly it is no argument that a work is not of God if his own means are made use of to effect it.

And as it is a *scriptural* way of carrying on God's work by example, so it is a *reasonable* way. It is no argument that men are not influenced by reason, that they are influenced by example. This way of persons holding forth truth to one another has a tendency to enlighten the mind and to convince reason. None will deny but that for persons to signify things one to another by words may rationally be supposed to tend to enlighten each other's minds; but the same thing may be signified by actions, and signified much more fully and effectually. Words are of no use otherwise than as they convey our own ideas to others, but actions in some cases may do it much more fully. There is a language in actions—in some cases, much more clear and convincing than in words. It is therefore no argument against the goodness of the effect if persons are greatly affected by seeing others so, though the impression is made only by seeing the tokens of great and extraordinary affection in others in their behavior, taking for granted what they are affected with, without hearing them say one word. There may be language sufficient in such a case in their behavior only to convey their minds to others and to signify to them their sense of things more than can possibly be done by words only. If a person should see another under extreme bodily torment, he might receive much clearer ideas, and more convincing evidence of what he suffered by his actions in his misery, than he could do only by the words of an unaffected indifferent relater. In like manner he might receive a greater idea of anything that is excellent and very delightful from the behavior of one that is in actual enjoyment than by the dull narration of one which is inexperienced and insensible himself. I desire that this matter may be examined by the strictest reason. Is it not manifest that effects produced in persons' minds are rational, since not only weak and ignorant people are much influenced by example, but also those that make the greatest boast of strength of reason are more influenced by reason held forth in this way than almost any other way? Indeed, the religious affections of many when raised by this means, as by hearing the Word preached or any other means, may prove flashy and soon vanish, as Christ represents the stony-ground hearers; but the affections of some thus moved by example are abiding and prove to be of saving issue.

There never yet was a time of remarkable pouring out of the Spirit and great revival of religion but that example had a main hand. So it was at the Reformation, and in the apostles' days in Jerusalem, Samaria, Ephesus, and other parts of the world, as will be most manifest to anyone that attends to the accounts we have in the Acts of the Apostles. As in those days one person was moved by another, so one city or town was influenced by the example of another: "So that you were examples to all that believe in Macedonia and Achaia, for from you sounded out the Word of the Lord, not only in Macedonia and Achaia, but also in every place your faith to God-ward is spread abroad" (1 Thess. 1:7–8).

It is no valid objection against examples being so much used, that the Scripture speaks of the Word as the principal means of carrying on God's work; for the Word of God is the principal means, nevertheless, by which other means operate and are made effectual. Even the sacraments have no effect but by the Word; and so it is that example becomes effectual, for all that is visible to the eye is unintelligible and vain without the Word of God to instruct and guide the mind. It is the Word of God that is indeed held forth and applied by example, as the Word of the Lord sounded forth to other towns in Macedonia and Achaia by the example of those that believed in Thessalonica.

That example should be a great means of propagating the church of God seems to be several ways signified in Scripture: it is signified by Ruth's following Naomi out of the land of Moab into the land of Israel, when she resolved that she would not leave her, but would go where she went and would lodge where she lodged, and that Naomi's people should be her people and Naomi's God her God. Ruth, who was the ancestral mother of David and of Christ, was undoubtedly a great type of the church, upon which account her history is inserted in the canon of Scripture. In her leaving the land of Moab and its gods to come and put her trust under the shadow of the wings of the God of Israel, we have a type of the conversion not only of the Gentile church but of every sinner that is naturally an alien and stranger, but in his conversion forgets his own people and father's house and becomes a fellow-citizen with the saints and a true Israelite. The same seems to be signified in the effect that the example of the spouse, when she was sick of love, has on the daughters of Jerusalem, i.e., visible Christians, who are first awakened by seeing the spouse in such extraordinary circumstances and then converted. See Song of Solomon 5:8–9; 6:1. And this is undoubtedly one way that "the Spirit and the bride say, Come" (Rev. 22:17), i.e., the Spirit in the bride. It is foretold that the work of God should be very much carried on by this means in the last great outpouring of the Spirit that should introduce the glorious day of the church so often spoken of in Scripture: "And the inhabitants of one city shall go to another, saying, Let us go speedily to pray before the Lord, and to seek the Lord of hosts: I will go also. Yea, many people, and strong nations, shall come to seek the Lord of hosts in Jerusalem, and to pray before the Lord. Thus says the Lord of hosts, In those days it shall come to pass that ten men shall take hold out of all languages of the nations, even shall take hold of the skirt of him that is a Jew, saying, We will go with you, for we have heard that God is with you" (Zech. 8:21–23).

VI. It is no sign that a work is not from the Spirit of God if many who seem to be the subjects of it are guilty of great imprudences and irregularities in their conduct. We are to consider that the end for which God pours out his Spirit is to make men holy, and not to make them politicians. It is no wonder that, in a mixed multitude of all sorts—wise and unwise, young and old, of weak and strong natural abilities, under strong impressions of mind—there are many who behave themselves imprudently. There are but few that know how to conduct themselves under vehement affections of any kind, whether of a temporal or spiritual nature; to do so requires a great deal of discretion, strength, and steadiness of mind. A thousand imprudences will not prove a work to be not of the Spirit of God if there are not only imprudences, but many things prevailing that are irregular and really contrary to the rules of God's holy Word. That it should be thus may be well accounted for from the exceeding weakness of human nature, together with the remaining darkness and corruption of those that are yet the subjects of the saving influences of God's Spirit and have a real zeal for God.

We have a remarkable instance in the New Testament of a people that partook largely of that great effusion of the Spirit in the apostles' days, among whom there nevertheless abounded imprudences and great irregularities: the church at Corinth. There is scarcely any church more celebrated in the New Testament for being blessed with large measures of the Spirit of God, both in his ordinary influences in convincing and converting sinners and also in his extraordinary and miraculous gifts; yet what manifold imprudences, great and sinful irregularities, and strange confusion did they run into at the Lord's supper and in the exercise of church discipline! To this may be added their indecent manner of attending other parts of public worship, their jarring and contention about their teachers, and even the exercise of their extraordinary gifts of prophecy, speaking with tongues, and the like, wherein they spoke and acted by the immediate inspiration of the Spirit of God.

And if we see great imprudences, and even sinful irregularities, in some who are great instruments to carry on the work, it will not prove it not to be the work of God. The apostle Peter himself, who was a great, eminently holy, and inspired apostle—and one of the chief instruments of setting up the Christian church in the world—when he was actually engaged in this work, was guilty of a great and sinful error in his conduct, of which the apostle Paul speaks in Galatians 2:11–13: "But when Peter was come to Antioch, I withstood him to the face, because he was to be blamed; for before that certain came from James, he did eat with the Gentiles, but when they were come, he withdrew and separated himself, fearing them that were of the circumcision; and the other Jews dissembled likewise with him; insomuch that Barnabas also was carried away with their dissimulation." If a great pillar of the Christian church—one of the chief of those who are the very foundations on which, next to Christ, the whole church is said to be built—was guilty of such an irregularity, is it any wonder if other lesser instruments, who have not that extraordinary conduct of the divine Spirit he had, should be guilty of many irregularities?

And in particular, it is no evidence that a work is not of God if many who are either the subjects or the instrument of it are guilty of too great forwardness to censure others as unconverted. For this may be through mistakes they have embraced concerning the marks by which they are to judge of the hypocrisy and carnality of others, or from not duly apprehending the latitude the Spirit of God uses in the methods of his operations, or from want of making due allowance for that infirmity and corruption that may be left in the hearts of the saints, as well as through want of a due sense of their own blindness, weakness, and remaining corruption, whereby spiritual pride may have a secret vent this way under some disguise and not be discovered. If we allow that truly pious men may have a great deal of remaining blindness and corruption and may be liable to mistakes about the marks of hypocrisy, as undoubtedly all will allow, then it is not unaccountable that they should sometimes run into such errors as these. It is as easy, and upon some accounts more easy, to account for why the remaining corruption of good men should sometimes have an unobserved vent this way than most other ways, and without doubt (however lamentable) many holy men have erred in this way.

Lukewarmness in religion is abominable and zeal an excellent grace; yet above all other Christian virtues, this needs to be strictly watched and searched, for it is that with which corruption, and particularly pride and human passion, is exceedingly apt to mix unobserved. And it is observable that there never was a time of great reformation to cause a revival of zeal in the church of God but that it has been attended, in some notable instances, with irregularity and a running out some way or other into an undue severity. Thus in the apostles' days, a great deal of zeal was spent about unclean meats, with heat of spirit in Christians one against another, both parties condemning and censuring one another as not being true Christians. But the apostle had charity for both, as influenced by a spirit of real piety: "He that eats, says he, to the Lord he eats and gives God thanks; and he that eats not, to the Lord he eats not and gives God thanks." So in the church of Corinth, they had got into a way of extolling some ministers and censuring others, and were puffed up one against another; but yet these things were no sign that the work then so wonderfully carried on was not the work of God. And after this, when religion was still greatly flourishing in the world and a spirit of eminent holiness and zeal prevailed in the Christian church, the zeal of Christians ran out into a very improper and undue severity in the exercise of church discipline towards delinquents. In some cases they would by no means admit them into their charity and communion though they appeared never so humble and penitent. And in the days of Constantine the Great, the zeal of Christians against heathenism ran out into a degree of persecution. So in that glorious revival of religion at the Reformation, zeal in many instances appeared in a very improper severity and even a degree of persecution in some of the most eminent Reformers, the great Calvin in particular. And many in those days of the flourishing of vital religion were guilty of severely censuring others that differed from them in opinion in some points of divinity.

VII. Nor are many errors in judgment and some delusions of Satan intermixed with the work any argument that the work in general is not of the Spirit of God. However great a spiritual influence may be, it is not to be expected that the Spirit of God should be given now in the same manner as to the apostles infallibly to guide them in points of Christian doctrine, so that what they taught might be relied on as a rule to the Christian church. And if many delusions of Satan appear at the same time that a great religious concern prevails, it is not an argument that the work in general is not the work of God any more than it was an argument in Egypt that there were no true miracles wrought there by the hand of God because Jannes and Jambres wrought false miracles at the same time by the hand of the devil.

Yea, the same persons may be the subjects of much of the influences of the Spirit of God and yet in some things be led away by the delusions of Satan, and this be no more a paradox than many other things that are true of real saints in the present state, where grace dwells with so much corruption and the new man and the old man subsist together in the same person, and the kingdom of God and the kingdom of the devil remain for a while together in the same heart. Many godly persons have undoubtedly, in this and other ages, exposed themselves to woeful delusions by an aptness to lay too much weight on impulses and impressions, as if they were immediate revelations from God to signify something future or to direct them where to go and what to do.

VIII. If some who were thought to be wrought upon fall away into gross errors or scandalous practices, it is no argument that the work in general is not the work of the Spirit of God. That there are some counterfeits is no argument that nothing is true; such things are always expected in a time of reformation. If we look into church history, we shall find no instance of any great revival of religion but what has been attended with many such things. Instances of this nature in the apostles' days were innumerable; some fell away into gross heresies, others into vile practices, though they seemed to be the subjects of a work of the Spirit—and were accepted for a while among those that were truly so, as their brethren and companions—and were not suspected till they went out from them. And some of these were teachers and officers—and eminent persons in the Christian church—whom God had endowed with miraculous gifts of the Holy Ghost, as appears by the beginning of the sixth chapter of the Hebrews. An instance of these was Judas, who was one of the twelve apostles and had long been constantly united to and intimately conversant with a company of truly experienced disciples without being discovered or suspected till he revealed himself by his scandalous practice. He had been treated by Jesus himself in all external things as if he had truly been a disciple, even investing him with the character of apostle, sending him forth to preach the gospel, and enduing him with miraculous gifts of the Spirit. For though Christ knew him, yet he did not then clothe himself with the character of omniscient Judge and searcher of hearts, but acted the part of a minister of the visible church (for he was his Father's minister), and therefore rejected him not till he had revealed himself by his scandalous practice, thereby giving an example to guides and rulers of the visible church not to take it upon themselves to act the part of searcher of hearts, but to be influenced in their administrations by what is visible and open. There were some instances then of such apostates as were esteemed eminently full of the grace of God's Spirit. An instance of this nature probably was Nicolas, one of the seven deacons, who was looked upon by the Christians in Jerusalem in the time of that extraordinary pouring out of the Spirit as a man full of the Holy Ghost, and was chosen out of the multitude of Christians to that office for that reason, as you may see in Acts 6:3, 5. Yet he afterwards fell away and became the head of a sect of vile heretics, of gross practices, called from his name the sect of the Nicolaitans[2] (Rev. 2:6, 15).

So in the time of the Reformation from popery, how great was the number of those who for a while seemed to join with the Reformers, yet fell away into the grossest and most absurd errors and abominable practices. And it is particularly observable that in times of great pouring out of the Spirit to revive religion in the world, a number of those who for a while seemed to partake in it have fallen off into whimsical and extravagant errors and gross enthusiasm, boasting of high degrees of spirituality and perfection, censuring and condemning others as carnal. Thus it was with the Gnostics in the apostles' times, and thus it was with several sects at the Reformation, as Anthony Burgess observes in his book called *Spiritual Refinings*, Part I, Sermon 23, p. 132:

> The first worthy Reformers and glorious instruments of God found a bitter conflict herein, so that they were exercised not only with formalists and traditionary papists on the one side, but men that pretended themselves to be more enlightened than the Reformers were on the other side. Hence they called those that did adhere to the Scripture, and would try revelations by it, Literists and Vowelists, as men acquainted with the words and vowels of the Scripture, having nothing of the Spirit of God; and wherever in any town the true doctrine of the gospel broke forth to the displacing of popery, presently such opinions arose, like tares that came up among the good wheat, whereby great divisions were raised and the Reformation made abominable and odious to the world, as if that had been the sun to give heat and

---

2. But though these heretics assumed his name, it does not follow that he countenanced their enormities. See Calmet's Dict. Nicolas.

warmth to those worms and serpents to crawl out of the ground. Hence they inveighed against Luther and said he had only promulgated a carnal gospel. Some of the leaders of those wild enthusiasts had been for a while highly esteemed by the first Reformers and peculiarly dear to them. Thus also in England, at the time when vital religion much prevailed in the days of King Charles I, the interregnum, and Oliver Cromwell, such things as these abounded. And so in New England, in her purest days, when vital piety flourished, such kind of things as these broke out. Therefore, the devil's sowing such tares is no proof that a true work of the Spirit of God is not gloriously carried on.

IX. It is no argument that a work is not from the Spirit of God if it seems to be promoted by ministers insisting very much on the terrors of God's holy law with a great deal of pathos and earnestness. If there is really a hell of such dreadful and never-ending torments as is generally supposed, of which multitudes are in great danger—and into which the greater part of men in Christian countries do actually from generation to generation fall, for want of a sense of its terribleness and so for want of taking due care to avoid it—then why is it not proper for those who have the care of souls to take great pains to make men sensible of it? Why should they not be told as much of the truth as can be? If I am in danger of going to hell, I should be glad to know as much as possibly I can of the dreadfulness of it. If I am very prone to neglect due care to avoid it, he does me the best kindness who does most to represent to me the truth of the case that sets forth my misery and danger in the liveliest manner.

I appeal to everyone: is this not the very course they would take in case of exposedness to any great temporal calamity? If any of you who are heads of families saw one of your children in a house all on fire and in imminent danger of being soon consumed in the flames, yet seemed to be very insensible of its danger and neglected to escape after you had often called to it—would you go on to speak to it only in a cold and indifferent manner? Would not you cry aloud and call earnestly to it and represent the danger it was in, and its own folly in delaying, in the most lively manner of which you were capable? If you should continue to speak to it only in a cold manner, as you are wont to do in ordinary conversation about indifferent matters, would not those about you begin to think you were bereft of reason yourself? This is not the way of mankind in temporal affairs of great moment that require earnest heed and great haste and about which they are greatly concerned. They are not wont to speak to each other of their danger and warn them but a little or in a cold and indifferent manner. Nature teaches men otherwise. If we who have the care of souls knew what hell was, had seen the state of the damned, or by any other means had become sensible how dreadful their case was—and at the same time knew that the greater part of men went there, and saw our hearers not sensible of their danger—it would be morally impossible for us to avoid most earnestly setting before them the dreadfulness of that misery and their great exposedness to it, and even to cry aloud to them.

When ministers preach of hell and warn sinners to avoid it in a cold manner—though they may say in words that it is infinitely terrible—they contradict themselves. For actions, as I observed before, have a language as well as words. If a preacher's words represent the sinner's state as infinitely dreadful, while his behavior and manner of speaking contradict it—showing that the preacher does not think so—he defeats his own purpose, for the language of his actions in such a case is much more effectual than the bare signification of his words. Not that I think that the law only should be preached: ministers may preach other things too little. The gospel is to be preached as well as the law, and the law is to be preached only to make way for the gospel and in order that it may be preached more effectually. The main work of ministers is to preach the gospel: *Christ is the end of the law for righteousness.* So that a minister would miss it very much if he should insist so much on the terrors of the law as to forget his Lord and neglect to preach the gospel; but yet the law is very much to be insisted on, and the preaching of the gospel is like to be in vain without it.

And certainly such earnestness and affection in speaking is beautiful, as becomes the nature and importance of the subject. Not but that there may be such a thing as an indecent boisterousness in a preacher, something besides what naturally arises from the nature of his subject, and in which the matter and manner do not well agree together. Some talk of it as an unreasonable thing to fright persons to heaven, but I think it is a reasonable thing to endeavor to fright persons away from hell. They stand upon its brink and are just ready to fall into it, and are senseless of their danger. Is it not a reasonable thing to fright a person out of a house on fire? The word *fright* is commonly used for sudden, causeless fear or groundless surprise; but surely a just fear, for which there is good reason, is not to be spoken against under any such name.

SECTION 2

What are distinguishing Scripture evidences of a work of the Spirit of God?

Having shown, in some instances, what are not evidences that a work wrought among a people is not a work of the Spirit of God, I now proceed in the second place, as was proposed, to show positively what are the sure, distinguishing Scripture evidences and marks of a work of the Spirit of God, by which we may proceed in judging of any operation we find in ourselves or see among a people without danger of being misled. And in this, as I said before, I shall confine myself wholly to those marks which are given us by the apostle in the chapter wherein is my text, where this matter is particularly handled, and more plainly and fully than anywhere else in the Bible. And in speaking to these marks, I shall take them in the order in which I find them in the chapter.

I. When the operation is such as to raise their esteem of that Jesus who was born of the virgin and was crucified without the gates of Jerusalem, and seems more to confirm and establish their minds in the truth of what the gospel declares to us of his being the Son of God and the Savior of men, that is a sure sign that it is from the Spirit of God. This sign the apostle gives us in the second and third verses: "Hereby you know the Spirit of God; and every spirit that confesses that Jesus Christ is come in the flesh is of God; and every spirit that confesses not that Jesus Christ is come in the flesh is not of God." This implies a confessing not only that there was such a person who appeared in Palestine and did and suffered those things that are recorded of him, but that he was Christ, i.e., the Son of God, anointed to be Lord and Savior, as the name Jesus Christ implies. That thus much is implied in the apostle's meaning is confirmed by the fifteenth verse, where the apostle is still on the same subject of signs of the true Spirit: "Whoever shall confess that Jesus is the Son of God, God dwells in him, and he in God." And it is to be observed that the word *confess*, as it is often used in the New Testament, signifies more than merely allowing; it implies an establishing and confirming of a thing by testimony and declaring it with manifestation of esteem and affection: "Whoever therefore shall confess me before men, him will I confess also before my Father which is in heaven" (Matt. 10:32); "I will confess you among the Gentiles, and sing unto your name" (Rom. 15:9); "that every tongue shall confess that Jesus Christ is Lord, to the glory of God the Father" (Phil. 2:11). And that this is the force of the expression, as the apostle John uses it in the place, is confirmed in the next chapter, verse 1: "Whoever believes that Jesus is the Christ is born of God, and everyone that loves him that begat loves him also that is begotten of him." And by that parallel place of the apostle Paul, where we have the same rule given to distinguish the true Spirit from all counterfeits: "Wherefore I give you to understand that no man speaking by the Spirit of God calls Jesus accursed (or will show an ill or mean esteem of him) and that no man can say that Jesus is the Lord but by the Holy Ghost "(1 Cor. 12:3).

So that if the spirit that is at work among a people is plainly observed to work so as to convince them of Christ and lead them to him—to confirm their minds in the belief of the history of Christ as he appeared in the flesh—and that he is the Son of God and was sent of God to save sinners, that he is the only Savior, and that they stand in great need of him; and if he seems to beget in them higher and more honorable thoughts of him than they used to have, and to incline their affections more to him, it is a sure sign that it is the true and right Spirit, however incapable we may be to determine whether that conviction and affection are in that manner or to that degree as to be saving or not.

But the words of the apostle are remarkable; the person to whom the Spirit gives testimony and for whom he raises their esteem must be that Jesus who appeared in the flesh, and not another Christ in his stead, nor any mystical, fantastical Christ, such as the light within. This the spirit of Quakers extols, while it diminishes their esteem of and dependence upon an outward Christ—or Jesus as he came in the flesh—and leads them off from him; but the Spirit that gives testimony for that Jesus and leads to him can be no other than the Spirit of God.

The devil has the most bitter and implacable enmity against that person, especially in his character of the Savior of men; he mortally hates the story and doctrine of his redemption; he never would go about to beget in men more honorable thoughts of him and lay greater weight on his instructions and commands. The Spirit that inclines men's hearts to the seed of the woman is not the spirit of the serpent that has such an irreconcilable enmity against him. He that heightens men's esteem of the glorious Michael, that prince of angels, is not the spirit of the dragon that is at war with him.

II. When the spirit that is at work operates against the interests of Satan's kingdom, which lies in encouraging and establishing sin and cherishing men's worldly lusts, this is a sure sign that it is a true and not a false spirit. This sign we have given us in the fourth and fifth verses: "You are of God, little children, and have overcome them, because greater is he that is in you than he that is in the world. They are of the world; therefore, they speak of the world, and the world hears them." Here is a plain antithesis: it is evident that the apostle is still comparing those that are influenced by the two opposite kinds of spirits, the true and the false, and showing the difference; the one is of God, and overcomes the spirit of the world; the other is of the world, and speaks and savors of the things of the world. The spirit of the devil is here called "he that is in the world." Christ says, "My kingdom is not of this world." But it is otherwise with Satan's kingdom; he is the god of this world.

What the apostle means by "the world," or "the things that are of the world," we learn by his own words in 1 John 2:15–16: "Love not the world, neither the things that are in the world: if any man love the world, the love of the Father is not in him: for all that is in the world, the lust of the flesh, and the lust of the eyes, and the pride of life, is not of the Father, but is of the world." So that by the world the apostle evidently means everything that appertains to the interest of sin and comprehends all the corruptions and lusts of men, and all those acts and objects by which they are gratified.

So we may safely determine from what the apostle says that the spirit that is at work among a people after such a manner as to lessen men's esteem of the pleasures, profits, and honors of the world, and to take off their hearts from an eager pursuit after these things, and to engage them in a deep concern about a future state and eternal happiness which the gospel reveals—and puts them upon earnestly seeking the kingdom of God and his righteousness—and the spirit that convinces them of the dreadfulness of sin, the guilt it brings, and the misery to which it exposes must needs be the Spirit of God.

It is not to be supposed that Satan would convince men of sin and awaken the conscience; it can no way serve his end to make that candle of the Lord shine the brighter and to open the mouth of that vicegerent of God in the soul. It is for his interest, whatever he does, to lull conscience asleep and keep it quiet. To have that, with its eyes and mouth open in the soul, will tend to clog and hinder all his designs of darkness and evermore to disturb his affairs, to cross his interest, and disquiet him, so that he can manage nothing to his mind without molestation. Would the devil, when he is about to establish men in sin, take such a course in the first place, to enlighten and awaken the conscience to see the dreadfulness of sin and make them exceedingly afraid of it, and sensible of their misery by reason of their past sins and their great need of deliverance from their guilt? Would he make them more careful, inquisitive, and watchful to discern what is sinful and to avoid future sins, and so more afraid of the devil's temptations and more careful to guard against them? What do those men do with their reason that suppose that the Spirit that operates thus is the spirit of the devil?

Possibly some may say that the devil may even awaken men's consciences to deceive them and make them think they have been the subjects of a saving work of the Spirit of God, while they are indeed still in the gall of bitterness. But to this it may be replied that the man who has an awakened conscience is the least likely to be deceived of any man in the world; it is the drowsy, insensible, stupid conscience that is most easily blinded. The more sensible conscience is in a diseased soul, the less easily is it quieted without a real healing. The more sensible conscience is made of the dreadfulness of sin and of the greatness of a man's own guilt, the less likely is he to rest in his own righteousness or to be pacified with nothing but shadows. A man that has been thoroughly terrified with a sense of his own danger and misery is not easily flattered and made to believe himself safe, without any good grounds. To awaken conscience and convince it of the evil of sin cannot tend to establish it, but certainly tends to make way for sin and Satan's being cut out. Therefore, this is a good argument that the Spirit that operates thus cannot be the spirit of the devil, unless we suppose that Christ knew not how to argue, who told the Pharisees—who supposed that the Spirit by which he wrought was the spirit of the devil—"that Satan would not cast out Satan" (Matt. 12:25–26). And therefore, if we see persons made sensible of the dreadful nature of sin and of the displeasure of God against it, of their own miserable condition as they are in themselves by reason of sin, and earnestly concerned for their eternal salvation—and sensible of their need of God's pity and help, and engaged to seek it in the use of the means that God has appointed—we may certainly conclude that it is from the Spirit of God, whatever effects this concern has on their bodies, though it cause them to cry out aloud, or to shriek, or to faint, or though it throw them into convulsions, or whatever other way the blood and spirits are moved.

The influence of the Spirit of God is yet more abundantly manifest if persons have their hearts drawn off from the world, weaned from the objects of their worldly lusts, and taken off from worldly pursuits by the sense they have of the excellency of divine things and the affection they have to those spiritual enjoyments of another world that are promised in the gospel.

III. The spirit that operates in such a manner as to cause in men a greater regard to the Holy Scriptures and establishes them more in their truth and divinity is certainly the Spirit of God. This rule the apostle gives us in 1 John 4:6: "We are of God; he that knows God hears us; he that is not of God hears not us: hereby know we the spirit of truth and the spirit of error. We are of God"; that is, "We the apostles are sent forth of God and appointed by him to teach the world and to deliver those doctrines and instructions which are to be their rule; he that knows God hears us," etc. The apostle's argument here equally reaches all that in the same sense are *of God;* that is, all those that God has appointed and inspired to deliver to his church its rule of faith and practice: all the prophets and apostles, whose doctrine God has made the foundation on which he has built his church, as in Ephesians 2:20—in a word, all the penmen of the Holy Scriptures. The devil never would attempt to beget in persons a regard to that divine Word which God has given to be the great and standing rule for the direction of his church in all religious matters, and all concerns of their souls, in all ages. A spirit of delusion will not incline persons to seek direction at the mouth of God. *To the law and to the testimony* is never the cry of those evil spirits that have no light in them, for it is God's own direction to discover their delusions. "And when they shall say unto you, Seek unto them that have familiar spirits, and unto wizards that peep and that mutter: should not a people seek unto their God? for the living to the dead? To the law and to the testimony; if they speak not according to this word, it is because there is no light in them" (Isa. 8:19–20). The devil does not say the same as Abraham did, "They have Moses and the prophets, let them hear them"; nor the same that the voice from heaven did concerning Christ, *Hear him.* Would the spirit of error, in order to deceive men, beget in them a high opinion of the infallible rule and incline them to think much of it and be very conversant with it? Would the prince of darkness, in order to promote his kingdom of darkness, lead men to the sun? The devil has ever shown a mortal spite and hatred towards that holy book the Bible: he has done all in his power to extinguish that light and to draw men off from it; he knows it to be that light by which his kingdom of darkness is to be overthrown. He has had for many ages experience of its power to defeat his purposes and baffle his designs; it is his constant plague. It is the main weapon which Michael uses in his war with him; it is the sword of the Spirit that pierces him and conquers him. It is that great and strong sword with which God punishes Leviathan, that crooked serpent. It is that sharp sword that we read of in Revelation 14:15 that proceeds out of the mouth of him that sat on the horse, with which he smites his enemies. Every text is a dart to torment the old serpent. He has felt the stinging smart thousands of times; therefore, he is engaged against the Bible and hates every word in it, and we may be sure that he never will attempt to raise persons' esteem of it or affection to it. And accordingly we see it common in enthusiasts that they depreciate this written rule and set up the light within or some other rule above it.

IV. Another rule to judge spirits may be drawn from those compellations given to the opposite spirits in the last words of verse 6: "the spirit of truth and the spirit of error." These words exhibit the two opposite characters of the Spirit of God and other spirits that counterfeit his operations. And therefore, if by observing the manner of the operation of a spirit that is at work among a people we see that it operates as a spirit of truth, leading persons to truth, convincing them of those things that are true, we may safely determine that it is a right and true spirit. For instance, if we observe that the spirit at work makes men more sensible than they used to be, that there is a God, and that he is a great and sin-hating God, that life is short and very uncertain, that there is another world, that they have immortal souls and must give account of themselves to God, that they are exceedingly sinful by nature and practice, that they are helpless in themselves—and confirms them in other things that are agreeable to some sound doctrine—the spirit that works thus operates as a spirit of truth; he represents things as they truly are. He brings men to the light; for whatever makes truth manifest is light, as the apostle Paul observes in Ephesians 5:13–14: "But all things that are reproved (or discovered, as it is in the margin) are made manifest by the light; for whatever makes manifest is light." And therefore we may conclude that it is not the spirit of darkness that thus discovers and makes manifest the truth. Christ tells us that Satan is a liar and the father of lies, and his kingdom is a kingdom of darkness. It is upheld and promoted only by darkness and error. Satan has all his power of dominion by darkness. Hence we read of the power of darkness in Luke 22:53 and Colossians 1:13. And devils are called "the rulers of the darkness of this world." Whatever spirit removes our darkness and brings us to the light undeceives us and, by convincing us of the truth, does us a kindness. If I am brought to a sight of truth and am made sensible of things as they really are, my duty is immediately to thank God for it, without standing first to inquire by what means I have such a benefit.

V. If the spirit that is at work among a people operates as a spirit of love to God and man, it is a sure sign that it is the Spirit of God. This sign the apostle insists upon from the sixth verse to the end of the chapter: "Beloved, let us love one another, for love is of God, and everyone that loves is born of God and knows God. He that loves not knows not God, for God is love. . . ." Here it is evident that the apostle is still comparing those two sorts of persons that are influenced by the opposite kinds of spirits and mentions love as a mark by which we may know who has the true spirit; but this is especially evident by verses 12 and 13: "If we love one another, God dwells in us, and his love is perfected in us: hereby know we that we dwell in him and he in us, because he has given us of his Spirit." In these verses love is spoken of as if it were that wherein the very nature of the Holy Spirit consisted, or as if divine love dwelling in us and the Spirit of God dwelling in us were the same thing, as it is also in the last two verses of the foregoing chapter and in the 16th verse of this chapter. Therefore, this last mark which the apostle gives of the true Spirit he seems to speak of as the most eminent, and so insists much more largely upon it than upon all the rest, and speaks expressly of both love to God and men—of "love to men" in verses 7, 11, and 12; of "love to God" in verses 17–19; of both together in the last two verses; and of love to men, as arising from love to God, in these last two verses.

Therefore, when the spirit that is at work among the people tends this way and brings many of them to high and exalting thoughts of the Divine Being and his glorious perfections and works in them an admiring, delightful sense of the excellency of Jesus Christ, representing him as the chief among ten thousand and altogether lovely, and makes him precious to the soul, winning and drawing the heart with those motives and incitements to love of which the apostle speaks in that passage of Scripture we are upon, that is, the wonderful, free love of God in giving his only-begotten Son to die for us, and the wonderful dying love of Christ to us, who had no love to him but were his enemies—this must needs be the Spirit of God: "In this was manifested the love of God towards us, because God sent his only-begotten Son into the world, that we might live through him. Herein is love: not that we loved God, but that he loved us, and sent his Son to be the propitiation for our sins" (vv. 9–10). "And we have known, and believed, the love that God has to us" (v. 16). "We love him because he first loved us" (v. 19). The spirit that excites to love on these motives, makes the attributes of God as revealed in the gospel and manifested in Christ delightful objects of contemplation, and makes the soul to long after God and Christ—after their presence and communion, acquaintance with them, and conformity to them—and to live so as to please and honor them; the spirit that quells contentions among men and gives a spirit of peace and goodwill, excites to acts of outward kindness and earnest desires of the salvation of souls, and causes a delight in those that appear as the children of God and followers of Christ—I say, when a spirit operates after this manner among a people, there is the highest kind of evidence of the influence of a true and divine spirit.

Indeed, there is a counterfeit love that often appears among those who are led by a spirit of delusion. There is commonly in the wildest enthusiasts a kind of union and affection arising from self-love, occasioned by their agreeing in those things wherein they greatly differ from all others and from which they are objects of the ridicule of all the rest of mankind. This naturally will cause them so much the more to prize those peculiarities that make them the objects of others' contempt. Thus the ancient Gnostics, and the wild fanatics that appeared at the beginning of the Reformation, boasted of their great love one to another—one sect of them, in particular, calling themselves the family of love. But this is quite another thing than that Christian love I have just described; it is only the working of a natural self-love and no true benevolence, any more than the union and friendship which may be among a company of pirates that are at war with all the rest of the world. There is enough said in this passage of the nature of a truly Christian love thoroughly to distinguish it from all such counterfeits. It is love that arises from apprehension of the wonderful riches of the free grace and sovereignty of God's love to us in Christ Jesus, being attended with a sense of our own utter unworthiness, as in ourselves the enemies and haters of God and Christ, and with a renunciation of all our own excellency and righteousness. See verses 9, 10, 11, and 19. The surest character of true divine supernatural love—distinguishing it from counterfeits that arise from a natural self-love—is that the Christian virtue of humility shines in it: that which above all others renounces, abases, and annihilates what we term self. Christian love, or true charity, is a humble love: "Charity vaunts not itself, is not puffed up, does not behave itself unseemly, seeks not her own, is not easily provoked" (1 Cor. 13:4–5). When therefore we see love in persons attended with a sense of their own littleness, vileness, weakness, and utter insufficiency, and so with self-diffidence, self-emptiness, self-renunciation, and poverty of spirit, these are the manifest tokens of the Spirit of God. He that thus dwells in love dwells in God, and God in him. What the apostle speaks of as a great evidence of the true Spirit is God's love or Christ's love: "his love is perfected in us" (v. 12). What kind of love that is we may see best in what appeared in Christ's example. The love that appeared in that Lamb of God was not only a love to friends but to enemies, and a love attended with a meek and humble spirit. "Learn of me," says he, "for I am meek and lowly in heart." Love and humility are two things the most contrary to the spirit of the devil of anything in the world, for the character of that evil spirit, above all things, consists in pride and malice.

Thus I have spoken particularly to the several marks the apostle gives us of a work of the true Spirit. There are some of these things which the devil would not do if he could; thus he would not awaken the conscience and make men sensible of their miserable state by reason of sin and sensible of their great need of a Savior; and he would not confirm men in the belief that Jesus is the Son of God and the Savior of sinners, or raise men's value and esteem of him; he would not beget in men's minds an opinion of the necessity, usefulness, and truth of the Holy Scriptures or incline them to make much use of them; nor would he show men the truth in things that concern their souls' interest, to undeceive them and lead them out of darkness into light, and give them a view of things as they really are. And there are other things that the devil neither can nor will do; he will not give men a spirit of divine love or Christian humility and poverty of spirit, nor could he if he would. He cannot give those things he has not himself; these things are as contrary as possible to his nature. And therefore when there is an extraordinary influence or operation appearing on the minds of a people, if these things are found in it, we are safe in determining that it is the work of God, whatever other circumstances it may be attended with, whatever instruments are used, whatever methods are taken to promote it, whatever means a sovereign God, whose judgments are a great deep, employs to carry it on, and whatever motion there may be of the animal spirits, whatever effects may be wrought on men's bodies. These marks that the apostle has given us are sufficient to stand alone and support themselves. They plainly show the finger of God and are sufficient to outweigh a thousand such little objections as many make from oddities, irregularities, errors in conduct, and the delusions and scandals of some professors.

But here some may object to the sufficiency of the marks given, because of what the apostle Paul says in 2 Corinthians 11:13–14: "For such are false apostles, deceitful workers, transforming themselves into the apostles of Christ; and no marvel, for Satan himself is transformed into an angel of light."

To which I answer that this can be no objection against the sufficiency of these marks to distinguish the true from the false spirit in those false apostles and prophets in whom the devil was transformed into an angel of light, because it is principally with a view to them that the apostle gives these marks, as appears by the words of the text: "Believe not every spirit, but try the spirits, whether they are of God"; and this is the reason he gives, because many false prophets are gone out into the world: "There are many gone out into the world who are the ministers of the devil, who transform themselves into the prophets of God, in whom the spirit of the devil is transformed into an angel of light; therefore, try the spirits by these rules that I shall give you, that you may be able to distinguish the true spirit from the false, under such a crafty disguise." Those false prophets the apostle John speaks of are doubtless the same sort of men with those false apostles and deceitful workers that the apostle Paul speaks of, in whom the devil was transformed into an angel of light; and therefore we may be sure that these marks are especially adapted to distinguish between the true Spirit and the devil transformed into an angel of light, because they are given especially for that end, that is, the apostle's declared purpose and design, to give marks by which the true Spirit may be distinguished from those sorts of counterfeits.

And if we look over what is said about these false prophets and false apostles (as there is much said about them in the New Testament) and take notice in what manner the devil was transformed into an angel of light in them, we shall not find anything that in the least injures the sufficiency of these marks to distinguish the true Spirit from such counterfeits. The devil transformed himself into an angel of light, as there was in them a show and great boast of extraordinary knowledge in divine things (Col. 2:8; 1 Tim. 1:6–7; 6:3–5; 2 Tim. 2:14–18; Titus 1:10, 16). Hence their followers called themselves Gnostics, from their great pretended knowledge; and the devil in them mimicked the miraculous gifts of the Holy Spirit in visions, revelations, prophecies, miracles, etc. Hence they are called false apostles and false prophets (see Matt. 24:24). Again, there was a false show of and lying pretensions to great holiness and devotion in words (Rom. 16:17–18; Eph. 4:14). Hence they are called deceitful workers and wells and clouds without water (2 Cor. 11:13; 2 Peter 2:17; Jude 12). There was also in them a show of extraordinary piety and righteousness in their superstitious worship (Col. 2:16–23). So they had a false, proud, and bitter zeal (Gal. 4:17–18; 1 Tim. 1:6; 6:4–5). And they had likewise a false show of humility in affecting an extraordinary outward meanness and dejection, when indeed they were vainly puffed up in their fleshly mind, and made a righteousness of their humility and were exceedingly lifted up with their eminent piety (Col. 2:18, 23). But how do such things as these in the least injure those things that have been mentioned as the distinguishing evidences of the true Spirit? Besides such vain shows which may be from the devil, there are common influences of the Spirit which are often mistaken for saving grace, but these are out of the question because, though they are not saving, they yet are the work of the true Spirit.

Having thus fulfilled what I at first proposed in considering what are the certain distinguishing marks by which we may safely proceed in judging whether any work that falls under our observation is the work of the Spirit of God or not, I now proceed to the application.

SECTION 3

Practical Inferences

I. From what has been said, I will venture to draw this inference: *that the extraordinary influence that has lately appeared, causing an uncommon concern and engagedness of mind about the things of religion, is undoubtedly in general from the Spirit of God.* There are but two things that need to be known in order to such a work's being judged of: *facts* and *rules*. The *rules* of the Word of God we have had laid before us; and as to *facts*, there are but two ways that we can come at them so as to be in a capacity to compare them with the rules, either by our own observation or by information from others who have had opportunity to observe them.

As to this work, there are many things concerning it that are notorious and which, unless the apostle John was out in his rules, are sufficient to determine it to be in general the work of God. The Spirit that is at work takes off persons' minds from the vanities of the world, engages them in a deep concern about eternal happiness, puts them upon earnestly seeking their salvation, and convinces them of the dreadfulness of sin and of their own guilty and miserable state as they are by nature. It awakens men's consciences, makes them sensible of the dreadfulness of God's anger, and causes in them a great desire and earnest care and endeavor to obtain his favor. It puts them upon a more diligent improvement of the means of grace which God has appointed, accompanied with a greater regard to the Word of God, a desire of hearing and reading it, and of being more conversant with it than they used to be. And it is notoriously manifest that the spirit that is at work in general operates as a spirit of truth, making persons more sensible of what is really true in those things that concern their eternal salvation, such as that they must die, that life is very short and uncertain, that there is a great sin-hating God to whom they are accountable and who will fix them in an eternal state in another world, and that they stand in great need of a Savior. It makes persons more sensible of the value of Jesus who was crucified and their need of him and that it puts them upon earnestly seeking an interest in him. It cannot be but that these things should be apparent to people in general through the land, for these things are not done in a corner; the work has not been confined to a few towns in some remoter parts, but has been carried on in many places all over the land and in most of the principal, populous, and public places in it. Christ in this respect has wrought among us in the same manner that he wrought his miracles in Judea. It has now been continued for a considerable time, so that there has been a great opportunity to observe the manner of the work. And all such as have been very conversant with the subjects of it see a great deal more that, by the rules of the apostle, does clearly and certainly show it to be the work of God.

And here I would observe that the nature and tendency of a spirit that is at work may be determined with much greater certainty, and less danger of being imposed upon, when it is observed in a great multitude of people of all sorts and in various places than when it is only seen in a few in some particular place that have been much conversant one with another. A few particular persons may agree to put a cheat upon others by a false pretense and professing things of which they never were conscious. But when the work is spread over great parts of a country, in places distant from one another, among people of all sorts and of all ages, and in multitudes possessed of a sound mind, good understanding, and known integrity, there would be the greatest absurdity in supposing, from all the observation that can be made by all that is heard from and seen in them—for many months together, and by those who are most intimate with them in these affairs and have long been acquainted with them—that yet it cannot be determined what kind of influence the operation they are under has upon people's minds, can it not be determined whether it tends to awaken their consciences or to stupefy them; whether it inclines them more to seek their salvation or neglect it; whether it seems to confirm them in a belief of the Scriptures or to lead them to Deism; whether it makes them have more regard for the great truths of religion or less?

And here it is to be observed that for persons to profess that they are so convinced of certain divine truths as to esteem and love them in a saving manner, and for them to profess that they are more convinced or confirmed in the truth of them than they used to be, and find that they have a greater regard to them than they had before, are two very different things. Persons of honesty and common sense have much greater right to demand credit to be given to the latter profession than to the former. Indeed, in the former, it is less likely that a people in general should be deceived than some particular persons. But whether persons' convictions, and the alteration in their dispositions and affections, are in a degree and manner that is saving is beside the present question. If there are such effects on people's judgments, dispositions, and affections as have been spoken of, whether they are in a degree and manner that is saving or not, it is nevertheless a sign of the influence of the Spirit of God. Scripture rules serve to distinguish the common influences of the Spirit of God, as well as those that are saving, from the influence of other causes.

And as, by the providence of God, I have for some months past been much among those who have been the subjects of the work in question, and particularly have been in the way of seeing and observing those extraordinary things with which many persons have been offended—such as persons' crying out aloud, shrieking, being put into great agonies of body, etc.—and have seen the manner and issue of such operations and the fruits of them for several months together, many of them being persons with whom I have been intimately acquainted in soul concerns, before and since, so I look upon myself called on this occasion to give my testimony that— so far as the nature and tendency of such a work is capable of falling under the observation of a bystander to whom those that have been the subjects of it have endeavored to open their hearts, or can be come at by diligent and particular inquiry—this work has all those marks that have been pointed out. And this has been the case in very many instances in every article; and in many others, all those marks have appeared in a very great degree.

The subjects of these uncommon appearances have been of two sorts: either those who have been in great distress from an apprehension of their sin and misery; or those who have been overcome with a sweet sense of the greatness, wonderfulness, and excellency of divine things. Of the multitude of those of the former sort that I have had opportunity to observe, there have been very few, but their distress has arisen apparently from real proper conviction and being in a degree sensible of that which was the truth. And though I do not suppose, when such things were observed to be common, that persons have laid themselves under those violent restraints to avoid outward manifestations of their distress that perhaps they otherwise would have done, yet there have been very few in whom there has been any appearance of feigning or affecting such manifestations, and very many for whom it would have been undoubtedly utterly impossible for them to avoid them. Generally, in these agonies they have appeared to be in the perfect exercise of their reason; and those of them who could speak have been well able to give an account of the circumstances of their mind and the cause of their distress at the time, and were able to remember and give an account of it afterwards. I have known a very few instances of those who, in their great extremity, have for a short space been deprived in some measure of the use of reason; but among the many hundreds, and it may be thousands, that have lately been brought to such agonies, I never yet knew one lastingly deprived of their reason. In some that I have known, melancholy has evidently been mixed, and when it is so the difference is very apparent; their distresses are of another kind, and operate quite after another manner, than when their distress is from mere conviction. It is not truth only that distresses them, but many vain shadows and notions that will not give place either to Scripture or reason. Some in their great distress have not been well able to give an account of themselves or to declare the sense they have of things or to explain the manner and cause of their trouble to others that yet I have had no reason to think were not under proper convictions and in whom there has been manifested a good issue. But this will not be at all wondered at by those who have had much to do with souls under spiritual difficulties: some things of which they are sensible are altogether new to them; their ideas and inward sensations are new, and they therefore know not how to express them in words. Some who, on first inquiry, said they knew not what was the matter with them have on being particularly examined and interrogated been able to represent their case, though of themselves they could not find expressions and forms of speech to do it.

Some suppose that terrors producing such effects are only a fright. But certainly there ought to be a distinction made between a very great fear or extreme distress arising from an apprehension of some dreadful truth—a cause fully proportionable to such an effect—and a needless, causeless fright. The latter is of two kinds; either, first, when persons are terrified with that which is not the truth (of which I have seen very few instances unless in case of melancholy); or, secondly, when they are in a fright from some terrible outward appearance and noise and a general notion thence arising. These apprehend that there is something or other terrible, they know not what, without having in their minds any particular truth whatever. Of such a kind of fright I have seen very little appearance among either old or young.

Those who are in such extremity commonly express a great sense of their exceeding wickedness: the multitude and aggravations of their actual sins; their dreadful pollution, enmity, and perverseness; their obstinacy and hardness of heart; a sense of their great guilt in the sight of God; and the dreadfulness of the punishment due to sin. Very often they have a lively idea of the horrible pit of eternal misery; and at the same time it appears to them that the great God who has them in his hands is exceedingly angry, and his wrath appears amazingly terrible to them. God appears to them so much provoked, and his great wrath so increased, that they are apprehensive of great danger, and that he will not bear with them any longer but will now forthwith cut them off and send them down to the dreadful pit they have in view, at the same time seeing no refuge. They see more and more of the vanity of everything they used to trust to and with which they flattered themselves, till they are brought wholly to despair in all and to see that they are at the disposal of the mere will of the God who is so angry with them. Very many, in the midst of their extremity, have been brought to an extraordinary sense of their fully deserving that wrath and the destruction which was then before their eyes. They feared every moment that it would be executed upon them; they have been greatly convinced that this would be altogether just and that God is indeed absolutely sovereign. Very often, some text of Scripture expressing God's sovereignty has been set home upon their minds, whereby they have been calmed. They have been brought, as it were, to lie at God's feet; and after great agonies, a little before light has arisen, they have been composed and quiet, in submission to a just and sovereign God, but their bodily strength much spent. Sometimes their lives, to appearance, were almost gone; and then light has appeared, and a glorious Redeemer, with his wonderful, all-sufficient grace, has been represented to them often in some sweet invitation of Scripture. Sometimes the light comes in suddenly, sometimes more gradually, filling their souls with love, admiration, joy, and self-abasement, drawing forth their hearts after the excellent lovely Redeemer, and longings to lie in the dust before him and that others might behold, embrace, and be delivered by him. They had longings to live to his glory, but were sensible that they can do nothing of themselves, appearing vile in their own eyes and having much jealousy over their own hearts. And all the appearances of a real change of heart have followed, and grace has acted, from time to time, after the same manner that it used to act in those that were converted formerly, with the like difficulties, temptations, buffetings, and comforts—excepting that in many, the light and comfort have been in higher degrees than ordinary. Many very young children have been thus wrought upon. There have been some instances very much like those of Mark 1:26 and 9:26, of whom we read that "when the devil had cried with a loud voice, and rent them sore, he came out of them." And probably those instances were designed for a type of such things as these. Some have several turns of great agonies before they are delivered, and others have been in such distress which has passed off, and no deliverance at all has followed.

Some object against it as great confusion when there is a number together in such circumstances making a noise, and say, God cannot be the author of it because he is the God of order, not of confusion. But let it be considered what is the proper notion of confusion but the breaking that order of things whereby they are properly disposed and duly directed to their end so that, the order and due connection of means being broken, they fail of their end. Now the conviction of sinners for their conversion is the obtaining of the end of religious means. Not but that I think the persons thus extraordinarily moved should endeavor to refrain from such outward manifestations what they well can, and should refrain to their utmost, at the time of their solemn worship. But if God is pleased to convince the consciences of persons so that they cannot avoid great outward manifestations, even to interrupting and breaking off those public means they were attending, I do not think this is confusion or an unhappy interruption, any more than if a company should meet on the field to pray for rain, and should be broken off from their exercise by a plentiful shower. Would to God that all the public assemblies in the land were broken off from their public exercises with such confusion as this the next Sabbath day! We need not be sorry for breaking the order of means by obtaining the end to which that order is directed. He who is going to fetch a treasure need not be sorry that he is stopped by meeting the treasure in the midst of his journey.

Besides those who are overcome with conviction and distress, I have seen many of late who have had their bodily strength taken away with a sense of the glorious excellency of the Redeemer and the wonders of his dying love, with a very uncommon sense of their own littleness and exceeding vileness attending it, with all expressions and appearances of the greatest abasement and abhorrence of themselves. Not only new converts, but many who were, as we hope, formerly converted have had their love and joy attended with a flood of tears and a great appearance of contrition and humiliation, especially for their having lived no more to God's glory since their conversion. These have had a far greater sight of their vileness and the evil of their hearts than ever they had, with an exceeding earnestness of desire to live better for the time to come, but attended with greater self-diffidence than ever; and many have been overcome with pity to the souls of others and longing for their salvation. And many other things I might mention in this extraordinary work, answering to every one of those marks which have been insisted on. So that if the apostle John knew how to give signs of a work of the true Spirit, this is such a work.

Providence has cast my lot in a place where the work of God has formerly been carried on. I had the happiness to be settled in that place two years with the venerable Stoddard and was then acquainted with a number who, during that season, were wrought upon under his ministry. I have been intimately acquainted with the experiences of many others who were wrought upon under his ministry before that period in a manner agreeable to the doctrine of all orthodox divines. And of late, a work has been carried on there with very much of uncommon operations, but it is evidently the same work that was carried on there in different periods, though attended with some new circumstances. And certainly we must throw by all talk of conversion and Christian experience, and not only so, but we must throw by our Bibles and give up revealed religion, if this is not in general the work of God. Not that I suppose the degree of the Spirit's influence is to be determined by the degree of effect on men's bodies or that those are always the best experiences which have the greatest influence on the body.

JONATHAN EDWARDS

And as to the imprudences, irregularities, and mixture of delusion that has been observed, it is not at all to be wondered at that a reformation after a long-continued and almost universal deadness should at first, when the revival is new, be attended with such things. In the first creation God did not make a complete world at once, but there was a great deal of imperfection, darkness, and mixture of chaos and confusion after God first said, "Let there be light," before the whole stood forth in perfect form. When God at first began his great work for the deliverance of his people after their long-continued bondage in Egypt, there were false wonders mixed with the true for a while, which hardened the unbelieving Egyptians and made them to doubt the divinity of the whole work. When the children of Israel first went to bring up the ark of God after it had been neglected and had been long absent, they sought not the Lord after the due order (1 Chron. 15:13). At the time when the sons of God came to present themselves before the Lord, Satan came also among them. And Solomon's ships, when they brought gold, silver, and pearls, also brought apes and peacocks. When daylight first appears after a night of darkness, we must expect to have darkness mixed with light for a while, and not have perfect day and the sun risen at once. The fruits of the earth are first green before they are ripe, and come to their proper perfection gradually; and so, Christ tells us, is the kingdom of God: "So is the kingdom of God: as if a man should cast seed into the ground and should sleep and rise night and day, and the seed should spring and grow up, he knows not how; for the earth brings forth fruit of herself—first the blade, then the ear, after that the full corn in the ear"(Mark 4:26–28).

The imprudences and errors that have attended this work are the less to be wondered at if it is considered that chiefly young persons have been the subjects of it, who have less steadiness and experience and, being in the heat of youth, are much more ready to run to extremes. Satan will keep men secure as long as he can, but when he can do that no longer, he often endeavors to drive them to extremes, and so to dishonor God and wound religion in that way. And doubtless it has been one occasion of much misconduct that in many places, people see plainly that their ministers have an ill opinion of the work and therefore, with just reason, dare not apply themselves to them as their guides in it, and so are without guides. No wonder then that when a people are as sheep without a shepherd, they wander out of the way. A people in such circumstances stand in great and continual need of guides, and their guides stand in continual need of much more wisdom than they have of their own. And if a people have ministers that favor the work and rejoice in it, yet it is not to be expected that either the people or ministers should know so well how to conduct themselves in such an extraordinary state of things—while it is new, and what they never had any experience of before, and time to see their tendency, consequences, and issue. The happy influence of experience is very manifest at this day in the people among whom God has settled my abode. The work which has been carried on there this year has been much purer than that which was wrought there six years before: it has seemed to be more purely spiritual, free from natural and corrupt mixtures and anything savoring of enthusiastic wildness and extravagance. It has wrought more by deep humiliation and abasement before God and men, and they have been much freer from imprudences and irregularities. And particularly there has been a remarkable difference in this respect: that whereas many before, in their comforts and rejoicings, did too much forget their distance from God and were ready in their conversation together of the things of God, and of their own experiences, to talk with too much lightness, now they seem to have no disposition that way, but rejoice with a more solemn, reverential, humble joy, as God directs (Ps. 2:11). Not because the joy is not as great, and in many instances much greater. Many among us who were wrought upon in that former season have now had much greater communications from heaven than they had then. Their rejoicing operates in another manner: it abases them, breaks their hearts, and brings them into the dust. When they speak of their joys, it is not with laughter, but a flood of tears. Thus those that laughed before weep now, and yet by their united testimony, their joy is vastly purer and sweeter than that which before did more raise their animal spirits. They are now more like Jacob, when God appeared to him at Bethel, when he saw the ladder that reached to heaven and said, "How dreadful is this place!" And like Moses, when God showed him his glory on the mount, when he made haste and bowed himself unto the earth.

II. Let us all be hence warned *by no means to oppose or do anything in the least to clog or hinder the work; but, on the contrary, do our utmost to promote it.* Now that Christ is come down from heaven in a remarkable and wonderful work of his Spirit, it becomes all his professed disciples to acknowledge him and give him honor.

The example of the Jews in Christ's and the apostles' times is enough to beget in those who do not acknowledge this work a great jealousy of themselves, and to make them exceedingly cautious of what they say or do. Christ then was in the world, and the world knew him not; he came to his own professing people, and his own received him not. That coming of Christ had been much spoken of in the prophecies of Scripture which they had in their hands, and it had been long expected; and yet because Christ came in a manner they did not expect, and which was not agreeable to their carnal reason, they would not own him. Nay, they opposed him, counted him a madman, and pronounced the spirit that he wrought by to be the spirit of the devil. They stood and wondered at the great things done and knew not what to make of them, but yet they met with so many stumbling-blocks that they finally could not acknowledge him. And when the Spirit of God came to be poured out so wonderfully in the apostles' days, they looked upon it as confusion and distraction. They were *astonished* by what they saw and heard, but not *convinced*. And especially was the work of God then rejected by those that were most conceited of their own understanding and knowledge, agreeable to Isaiah 29:14: "Therefore, behold, I will proceed to do a marvelous work among this people, even a marvelous work and a wonder; for the wisdom of their wise men shall perish, and the understanding of their prudent men shall be hid." And many who had been in reputation for religion and piety had a great spite against the work because they saw it tended to diminish their honor and to reproach their formality and lukewarmness. Some, upon these accounts, maliciously and openly opposed and reproached the work of the Spirit of God and called it the work of the devil, against inward conviction, and so were guilty of the unpardonable sin against the Holy Ghost.

There is another, a spiritual coming of Christ to set up his kingdom in the world that is as much spoken of in Scripture prophecy as that first coming, and which has long been expected by the church of God. We have reason to think from what is said of this that it will be, in many respects, parallel with the other. And certainly, that low state into which the visible church of God has lately been sunk is very parallel with the state of the Jewish church when Christ came and therefore no wonder at all that when

Christ comes, his work should appear a strange work to most; yea, it would be a wonder if it should be otherwise. Whether the present work is the beginning of that great and frequently predicted coming of Christ to set up his kingdom or not, it is evident from what has been said that it is a work of the same Spirit and of the same nature. And there is no reason to doubt but that the conduct of persons who continue long to refuse acknowledging Christ in the work—especially those who are set to be teachers in his church—will be in like manner provoking to God as it was in the Jews of old while refusing to acknowledge Christ, notwithstanding what they may plead of the great stumbling-blocks that are in the way and the cause they have to doubt of the work. The teachers of the Jewish church found innumerable stumbling-blocks that were to them insuperable. Many things appeared in Christ, and in the work of the Spirit after his ascension, which were exceedingly strange to them; they seemed assured that they had just cause for their scruples. Christ and his work were to the Jews a stumbling-block; "but blessed is he," says Christ, "who shall not be offended in me." As strange and as unexpected as the manner of Christ's appearance was, yet he had not been long in Judea working miracles before all those who had opportunity to observe and yet refused to acknowledge him brought fearful guilt upon themselves in the sight of God; and Christ condemned them, that though they "could discern the face of the sky and of the earth, yet they could not discern the signs of those times; and why, says he, even of yourselves, you judge not what is right?" (Luke 12:56–57).

It is not to be supposed that the great Jehovah had bowed the heavens and appeared here now for so long a time in such a glorious work of his power and grace—in so extensive a manner, in the most public places of the land, and in almost all parts of it—without giving such evidences of his presence that great numbers, and even many teachers in his church, can remain guiltless in his sight without ever receiving and acknowledging him and giving him honor and appearing to rejoice in his gracious presence, or without so much as once giving him thanks for so glorious and blessed a work of his grace wherein his goodness does more appear than if he had bestowed on us all the temporal blessings that the world affords. A long-continued silence in such a case is undoubtedly provoking to God, especially in ministers. It is a secret kind of opposition that really tends to hinder the work. Such silent ministers stand in the way of the work of God, as Christ said of old: "He that is not with us is against us." Those who stand wondering at this strange work, not knowing what to make of it and refusing to receive it—and ready it may be sometimes to speak contemptibly of it, as was the case with the Jews of old—would do well to consider and to tremble at St. Paul's words to them in Acts 13:40–41: "Beware therefore lest that come upon you which is spoken of in the prophets: Behold, you despisers, and wonder and perish; for I work a work in your days which you shall in no wise believe, though a man declare it unto you." Those who cannot believe the work to be true because of the extraordinary degree and manner of it should consider how it was with the unbelieving lord in Samaria, who said, "Behold, if the Lord should make windows in heaven, might this thing be?" To whom Elisha said, "Behold, you shall see it with your eyes, but shall not eat thereof." Let all to whom this work is a cloud and darkness—as the pillar of cloud and fire was to the Egyptians—take heed that it be not their destruction while it gives light to God's Israel.

I would entreat those who quiet themselves that they proceed on a principle of prudence and are waiting to see the issue of things—and what fruits those that are the subjects of this work will bring forth in their lives and conversations—to consider whether this will justify a long refraining from acknowledging Christ when he appears so wonderfully and graciously present in the land. It is probable that many of those who are thus waiting know not for what they are waiting. If they wait to see a work of God without difficulties and stumbling-blocks, it will be like the fool's waiting at the riverside to have the water all run by. A work of God without stumbling-blocks is never to be expected. *It must need be that offenses come.* There never yet was any great manifestation that God made of himself to the world without many difficulties attending it. It is with the works of God as with his Word: they seem at first full of things that are strange, inconsistent, and difficult to the carnal unbelieving hearts of men. Christ and his work always was, and always will be, a stone of stumbling and rock of offense, a gin and a snare to many. The prophet Hosea, speaking of a glorious revival of religion in God's church—when God would be as the dew unto Israel, who should grow as the lily and cast forth his roots as Lebanon, whose branches should spread, etc.—concludes all thus: "Who is wise, and he shall understand these things? prudent, and he shall know them? For the ways of the

Lord are right, and the just shall walk in them, but the transgressors shall fall therein" (Hos. 14:9).

It is probable that the stumbling-blocks that now attend this work will in some respects be increased and not diminished. We probably shall see more instances of apostasy and gross iniquity among professors. And if one kind of stumbling-block is removed, it is to be expected that others will come. It is with Christ's works as it was with his parables: things that are difficult to men's dark minds are ordered of purpose for the trial of their dispositions and spiritual sense and that those of corrupt minds and of an unbelieving, perverse, caviling spirit, "seeing might see and not understand." Those who are now waiting to see the issue of this work think they shall be better able to determine by and by, but probably many of them are mistaken. The Jews that saw Christ's miracles waited to see better evidences of his being the Messiah. They wanted a sign from heaven, but they waited in vain; their stumbling-blocks did not diminish, but increased. They found no end to them, and so were more and more hardened in unbelief. Many have been praying for that glorious reformation spoken of in Scripture, who knew not what they have been praying for (as it was with the Jews when they prayed for the coming of Christ) and who, if it should come, would not acknowledge or receive it.

This pretended prudence in persons waiting so long before they acknowledged this work will probably in the end prove the greatest imprudence. Hereby they will fail of any share of so great a blessing and will miss the most precious opportunity of obtaining divine light, grace, and comfort, heavenly and eternal benefits that God ever gave in New England. While the glorious fountain is set open in so wonderful a manner and multitudes flock to it and receive a rich supply for the wants of their souls, they stand at a distance, doubting, wondering, and receiving nothing, and are like to continue thus till the precious season is past. It is indeed to be wondered at that those who have doubted the work which has been attended with such uncommon external appearances should be easy in their doubts without taking thorough pains to inform themselves by going where such things have been to be seen, narrowly observing and diligently inquiring into them, not contenting themselves with observing two or three instances, nor resting till they were fully informed by their own observation. I do not doubt but that if this course had been taken, it would have convinced all whose minds are not shut up against conviction. How greatly have they erred who only from the uncertain reproofs of others have ventured to speak slightly of these things! That caution of an unbelieving Jew might teach them more prudence: "Refrain from these men and let them alone; for if this counsel or this work is of men, it will come to naught, but if it is of God, you cannot overthrow it, lest you are found to fight against God" (Acts 5:38–39). Whether what has been said in this discourse is enough to produce conviction that this is the work of God or not, I hope that for the future they will at least hearken to the caution of Gamaliel now mentioned so as not to oppose it or say anything which has even an indirect tendency to bring it into discredit, lest they should be found opposers of the Holy Ghost. There are no kinds of sins so hurtful and dangerous to the souls of men as those committed against the Holy Ghost. We had better speak against God the Father or the Son than to speak against the Holy Spirit in his gracious operations on the hearts of men. Nothing will so much tend forever to prevent our having any benefit of his operations on our own souls.

If there are any who still resolutely go on to speak contemptibly of these things, I would beg of them to take heed that they be not guilty of the unpardonable sin. When the Holy Spirit is much poured out and men's lusts, lukewarmness, and hypocrisy are reproached by its powerful operations, then is the most likely time of any for this sin to be committed. If the work goes on, it is well if among the many that show an enmity against it some be not guilty of this sin, if none have been already. Those who maliciously oppose and reproach this work and call it the work of the devil want but one thing of the unpardonable sin, that is, doing it against inward conviction. And though some are so prudent as not openly to oppose and reproach this work, yet it is to be feared—at this day, when the Lord is going forth so gloriously against his enemies—that many who are silent and inactive, especially ministers, will bring this curse of the angel of the Lord upon themselves: "Curse Meroz, said the angel of the Lord, curse bitterly the inhabitants thereof, because they came not to the help of the Lord, to the help of the Lord against the mighty" (Judg. 5:23).

Since the great God has come down from heaven and manifested himself in so wonderful a manner in this land, it is vain for any of us to expect any other than to be greatly affected by it in our spiritual state and circumstances respecting the favor of God one way or other. Those who do not become more happy by it will become far more guilty and miserable. It is always so; such a season as proves an acceptable year and a time of great favor to those who accept and improve it proves a day of vengeance to others (Isa. 59:2). When God sends forth his Word, it shall not return to him void, much less his Spirit. When Christ was upon earth in Judea, many slighted and rejected him; but it proved in the issue to be no matter of indifference to them. God made all that people to feel that Christ had been among them; those who did not feel it to their comfort felt it to their great sorrow. When God only sent the prophet Ezekiel to the children of Israel, he declared that whether they would hear or whether they would forbear, they should know that there had been a prophet among them; how much more may we suppose that when God has appeared so wonderfully in this land, he will make everyone to know that the great Jehovah had been in New England.

III. I come now, in the last place, to apply myself to those who are the friends of this work, who have been partakers of it and are zealous to promote it. Let me earnestly exhort them to give diligent heed to themselves to avoid all errors and misconduct and whatever may darken and obscure the work, and to give no occasion to those who stand ready to reproach it. The apostle was careful to cut off occasion from those that desired occasion. The same apostle exhorts Titus to maintain a strict care and watch over himself, that both his preaching and behavior might be such as "could not be condemned; that he who was of the contrary part might be ashamed, having no evil thing to say of them" (Titus 2:7–8). We had need to be wise as serpents and harmless as doves. It is of no small consequence that we should at this day behave ourselves innocently and prudently. We must expect that the great enemy of this work will especially try his utmost with us, and he will especially triumph if he can prevail in anything to blind and mislead us. He knows it will do more to further his purpose and interest than if he prevailed against a hundred others. We had need to watch and pray, for we are but little children; this roaring lion is too strong for us, and this old serpent too subtle for us.

Humility and self-diffidence and an entire dependence on our Lord Jesus Christ will be our best defense. Let us therefore maintain the strictest watch against spiritual pride or being lifted up with extraordinary experiences and comforts and the high favors of heaven that any of us may have received.

JONATHAN EDWARDS

We need, after such favors, in a special manner to keep a strict and jealous eye upon our own hearts, lest there should arise self-exalting reflections upon what we have received and high thoughts of ourselves as being now some of the most eminent of saints and peculiar favorites of heaven, and that the secret of the Lord is especially with us. Let us not presume that we above all are fit to be advanced as the great instructors and censors of this evil generation and, in a high conceit of our own wisdom and discerning, assume to ourselves the airs of prophets or extraordinary ambassadors of heaven. When we have great discoveries of God made to our souls, we should not shine bright in our own eyes. Moses, when he had been conversing with God in the mount, though his face shone so as to dazzle the eyes of Aaron and the people, yet he did not shine in his own eyes; he knew not that his face shone. Let none think themselves out of danger of this spiritual pride, even in their best frames. God saw that the apostle Paul (though probably the most eminent saint that ever lived) was not out of danger of it—no, not when he had just been conversing with God in the third heaven (see 2 Cor. 12:7). Pride is the worst viper in the heart; it is the first sin that ever entered into the universe, lies lowest of all in the foundation of the whole building of sin, and is the most secret, deceitful, and unsearchable in its ways of working of any lusts whatever. It is ready to mix with everything, and nothing is so hateful to God, contrary to the spirit of the gospel, or of so dangerous consequence; and there is no one sin that does so much let the devil into the hearts of the saints and expose them to his delusions. I have seen it in many instances, even in eminent saints. The devil has come in at this door presently after some eminent experience and extraordinary communion with God and has woefully deluded and led them astray till God has mercifully opened their eyes and delivered them, and they themselves have afterwards been made sensible that it was pride that betrayed them.

Some of the true friends of the work of God's Spirit have erred in giving too much heed to impulses and strong impressions on their minds, as though they were immediate significations from heaven to them of something that should come to pass, or something that it was the mind and will of God that they should do, which was not signified or revealed anywhere in the Bible without those impulses. These impressions, if they are truly from the Spirit of God, are of a quite different nature from his gracious influences on the hearts of the saints: they are of the nature of the extraordinary *gifts* of the Spirit and are properly inspiration, such as the prophets and apostles and others had of old, which the apostle distinguishes from the *grace* of the Spirit in 1 Corinthians 13.

One reason why some have been ready to lay weight on such impulses is an opinion they have had that the glory of the approaching happy days of the church would partly consist in restoring those extraordinary gifts of the Spirit. This opinion, I believe, arises partly through want of duly considering and comparing the nature and value of those two kinds of influences of the Spirit, that is, those that are ordinary and gracious and those that are extraordinary and miraculous. The former are by far the most excellent and glorious, as the apostle largely shows in 1 Corinthians 12:31, etc. Speaking of the extraordinary gifts of the Spirit, he says, "But covet earnestly the best gifts; and yet I show you a more excellent way"; i.e., a more excellent way of the influence of the Spirit. And then he goes on in the next chapter to show what that more excellent way is: the grace of the Spirit, which summarily consists in charity, or divine love. And throughout that chapter he shows the great preference of that above inspiration. God communicates his own nature to the soul in saving *grace* in the heart more than in all miraculous *gifts*. The blessed image of God consists in *that* and not in *these*. The excellency, happiness, and glory of the soul immediately consists in the former. That is a root which bears infinitely more excellent fruit. Salvation and the eternal enjoyment of God is promised to divine grace, but not to inspiration. A man may have those extraordinary gifts and yet be abominable to God and go to hell. The spiritual and eternal life of the soul consists in the grace of the Spirit, which God bestows only on his favorites and dear children. He has sometimes thrown out the other, as it were, to dogs and swine, as he did to Balaam, Saul, and Judas, and some who, in the primitive times of the Christian church, committed the unpardonable sin (Heb. 6). Many wicked men at the day of the judgment will plead, "Have we not prophesied in your name, and in your name cast out devils, and in your name done many wonderful works?" The greatest privilege of the prophets and apostles was not their being inspired and working miracles, but their eminent holiness. The grace that was in their hearts was a thousand times more their dignity and honor than their miraculous gifts. The things in which we find David comforting himself are not his being a king or a prophet, but the holy influences of the Spirit of God in his heart, communicating to him divine light, love, and joy. The apostle Paul abounded in visions, revelations, and miraculous gifts above all the apostles, but yet he esteems all things but loss for the excellency of the spiritual knowledge of Christ. It was not the gifts but the grace of the apostles that was the proper evidence of their names' being written in heaven, in which Christ directs them to rejoice much more than in the devil's being subject to them. To have grace in the heart is a higher privilege than the blessed virgin herself had in having the body of the second person in the Trinity conceived in her womb by the power of the Highest overshadowing her: "And it came to pass as he spoke these things that a certain woman of the company lifted up her voice and said unto him: Blessed is the womb that bore you and the breasts that nursed you! But he said, Yea, rather, blessed are they that hear the Word of God and keep it" (Luke 11:27–28). See also to the same purpose Matthew 12:47, etc. The influence of the Holy Spirit, or divine charity in the heart, is the greatest privilege and glory of the highest archangel in heaven; yea, this is the very thing by which the creature has fellowship with God himself, with the Father and the Son, in their beauty and happiness. Hereby the saints are made partakers of the divine nature and have Christ's joy fulfilled in themselves.

The ordinary sanctifying influences of the Spirit of God are the *end* of all extraordinary gifts, as the apostle shows (Eph. 4:11–13). They are good for nothing any further than as they are subordinate to this end; they will be so far from profiting any without it that they will only aggravate their misery. This is, as the apostle observes, the most excellent way of God's communicating his Spirit to his church; it is the greatest glory of the church in all ages. This glory is what makes the church on earth most like the church in heaven, when prophecy, tongues, and other miraculous gifts cease. And God communicates his Spirit only in that more excellent way of which the apostle speaks: *charity* or divine love, *which never fails*. Therefore, the glory of the approaching happy state of the church does not at all require these extraordinary gifts. As that state of the church will be nearest of any to its perfect state in heaven, so I believe it will be like it in this: that all extraordinary gifts shall have ceased and vanished away; and all those stars and the moon with the reflected light they gave in the night or in a dark season shall be swallowed up in the sun of divine love. The apostle speaks

of these gifts of inspiration as childish things in comparison of the influence of the Spirit in divine love, things given to the church only to support it in its minority till the church should have a complete standing rule
established and all the ordinary means of grace should be settled, but as
things that should cease as the church advanced to the state of manhood.
"When I was a child, I spoke as a child, I understood as a child, I thought
as a child; but when I became a man, I put away childish things" (1 Cor.
13:11; compare the three preceding verses).

When the apostle in this chapter speaks of prophecies, tongues, and revelations ceasing and vanishing away in the church—when the Christian
church should be advanced from a state of minority to a state of manhood—
he seems to have respect to its coming to an adult state in this world as well
as in heaven, for he speaks of such a state of manhood wherein the three
things faith, hope, and charity should remain after miracles and revelation
had ceased, as in the last verse, and "now abide faith, hope, and charity,
these three." *The* apostle's manner of speaking here shows an evident reference to what he had just been saying before, and here is a manifest *antithesis* between *remaining* and that *failing, ceasing,* and *vanishing away* spoken of in verse 8. The apostle had been showing how all those gifts of
inspiration, which were the leading-strings of the Christian church in its
infancy, should vanish away when the church came to a state of manhood.
Then he returns to observe what things remain after those had failed and
ceased, and he observes that those three things shall remain in the church:
faith, hope, and charity. And therefore the adult state of the church he
speaks of is the more perfect one at which it shall arrive on earth, especially
in the latter ages of the world. And this was the more properly observed to
the church at Corinth upon two accounts: because the apostle had before
observed to that church that they were in a state of infancy (1 Cor. 3:1–2)
and because that church seems above all others to have abounded with
miraculous gifts. When the expected glorious state of the church comes,
the increase of light shall be so great that it will in some respect answer
what is said in verse 12 of "seeing face to face" (see Isa. 24:23; 25:7).

Therefore, I do not expect a restoration of these miraculous gifts in the
approaching glorious times of the church, nor do I desire it. It appears to
me that it would add nothing to the glory of those times, but rather diminish from it. For my part, I would rather enjoy the sweet influences of

the Spirit, showing Christ's spiritual divine beauty, infinite grace, and dying love, drawing forth the holy exercises of faith, divine love, sweet complacence, and humble joy in God, one quarter of an hour than to have prophetical visions and revelations the whole year. It appears to me much more probable that God should give immediate revelation to his saints in the dark times of prophecy than now in the approach of the most glorious and perfect state of his church on earth. It does not appear to me that there is any need of those extraordinary gifts to introduce this happy state and set up the kingdom of God through the world; I have seen so much of the power of God in a more excellent way as to convince me that God can easily do it without.

I would therefore entreat the people of God to be very cautious how they give heed to such things. I have seen them fail in very many instances, and know by experience that impressions being made with great power and upon the minds of true, yea eminent, saints—even in the midst of extraordinary exercises of grace and sweet communion with God, and attended with texts of Scripture strongly impressed on the mind—are no sure signs of their being revelations from heaven. I have known such impressions to fail, in some instances, attended with all these circumstances. Those who leave the sure word of prophecy—which God has given us as a light shining in a dark place—to follow such impressions and impulses leave the guidance of the polar star to follow a Jack with a lantern. No wonder, therefore, that sometimes they are led into woeful extravagances.

Moreover, seeing that inspiration is not to be expected, let us not despise human learning. They who assert that human learning is of little or no use in the work of the ministry do not well consider what they say; if they did, they would not say it. By human learning I mean, and suppose others mean, the improvement of common knowledge by human and outward means. And therefore to say that human learning is of no use is as much as to say that the education of a child, or that the common knowledge which a grown man has more than a little child, is of no use. At this rate, a child of four years old is as fit for a teacher in the church of God, with the same degree of grace—and capable of doing as much to advance the kingdom of Christ by his instruction—as a very knowing man of thirty years of age. If adult persons have greater ability and advantage to do service because they have more knowledge than a little child, then doubtless if they have more human knowledge still, with the same degree of grace, they would have still greater ability and advantage to do service. An increase of knowledge, without doubt, increases a man's advantage either to do good or hurt, according as he is disposed. It is too manifest to be denied that God made great use of human learning in the apostle Paul, as he also did in Moses and Solomon.

And if knowledge obtained by human means is not to be despised, then it will follow that the means of obtaining it are not to be neglected—study— and that this is of great use in order to prepare for publicly instructing others. And though having the heart full of the powerful influences of the Spirit of God may at some time enable persons to speak profitably, yea, very excellently, without study, yet this will not warrant us needlessly to cast ourselves down from the pinnacle of the temple, depending upon it that the angel of the Lord will bear us up and keep us from dashing our foot against a stone when there is another way to go down, though it is not so quick. And I would pray that *method* in public discourses which tends greatly to help both the understanding and memory may not be wholly neglected.

Another thing I would beg the dear children of God more fully to consider is how far, and upon what grounds, the rules of the Holy Scriptures will truly justify their passing censures upon other professing Christians as hypocrites and ignorant of real religion. We all know that there is a judging and censuring of some sort or other that the Scripture very often and very strictly forbids. I desire that those rules of Scripture may be looked into and thoroughly weighed and that it may be considered whether our taking it upon us to discern the state of others—and to pass sentence upon them as wicked men, though professing Christians and of a good visible conversation—is not really forbidden by Christ in the New Testament. If it is, then doubtless the disciples of Christ ought to avoid this practice, however sufficient they may think themselves for it, or however needful or of good tendency they may think it. It is plain that the sort of judgment which God claims as his prerogative, whatever that is, is forbidden. We know that a certain judging of the hearts of the children of men is often spoken of as the great prerogative of God and which belongs only to him, as in 1 Kings 8:39: "Forgive, and do, and give unto every man according to his ways, whose heart you know; for you, even you only, know the hearts of all the children of men." And if we examine, we shall find that the judging of hearts which is spoken of as God's prerogative relates not only to the aims and dispositions of men's hearts in particular actions, but chiefly to the state of their hearts as the professors of religion with regard to that profession. This will appear very manifest by looking over the following Scriptures: 1 Chronicles 28:9; Psalm 7:9–11; Psalm 26 throughout; Proverbs 16:2; 17:3; 21:2; John 2:23–25; Revelation 2:22–23. That sort of judging which is God's proper business is forbidden: "Who are you that judges another man's servant? To his own master he stands or falls" (Rom. 14:4); "There is one lawgiver that is able to save or destroy; who are you that judges another?" (James 4:12); "But with me it is a very small thing that I should be judged of you or of man's judgment; yea, I judge not my own self, but he that judges me is the Lord" (1 Cor. 4:3–4).

Again, whatever kind of judging is the proper work and business of the day of judgment is what we are forbidden, as in 1 Corinthians 4:5: "Therefore, judge nothing before the time until the Lord comes, who both will bring to light the hidden things of darkness and will make manifest the counsels of the heart, and then shall every man have praise of God." But to distinguish hypocrites that have the form of godliness and the visible conversation of godly men from true saints or to separate the sheep from the goats is the proper business of the day of judgment; yea, it is represented as the main business and end of that day. They therefore do greatly err who take it upon themselves positively to determine who are sincere and who are not—to draw the dividing line between true saints and hypocrites and to separate between sheep and goats, setting the one on the right hand and the other on the left—and to distinguish and gather out the tares from among the wheat. Many of the servants of the owner of the field are very ready to think themselves sufficient for this and are forward to offer their service to this end, but their Lord says, "Nay, lest while you gather up the tares, you root up also the wheat with them. Let both grow together until the harvest"; and in the time of the harvest he will take care to see a thorough separation made (Matt. 13:28–30). This is agreeable to that aforementioned prohibition of the apostle: "Judge nothing before the time" (1 Cor. 4:5). In this parable, by the servants who have the care of the fruit of the field is doubtless meant the same with the servants who have the care of the fruit of the vineyard (Luke 20) and who are elsewhere represented as servants of the Lord of the harvest, appointed as laborers in his harvest. These we know are ministers of the gospel. Now is that parable in the 13th chapter of Matthew fulfilled: "While men sleep (during a long sleepy, dead time in the church), the enemy has sowed tares; now is the time when the blade is sprung up" and religion is reviving; and now some of the servants who have the care of the field say, Let us go and gather up the tares. I know there is a great aptness in men who suppose they have had some experience of the power of religion to think themselves sufficient to discern and determine the state of others by a little conversation with them; and experience has taught me that this is an error. I once did not imagine that the heart of man had been so unsearchable as it is. I am less charitable and less uncharitable than once I was. I find more things in wicked men that may counterfeit and make a fair show of piety, and more ways that the remaining corruption of the godly may make them appear like carnal men, formalists, and dead hypocrites, than once I knew of. The longer I live, the less I wonder that God challenges it as his prerogative to try the hearts of the children of men and directs that this business should be let alone till harvest. I desire to adore the wisdom of God and his goodness to me and my fellow-creatures that he has not committed this great business into the hands of such a poor, weak, and dim-sighted creature—one of so much blindness, pride, partiality, prejudice, and deceitfulness of heart—but has committed it into the hands of one infinitely fitter for it, and has made it his prerogative.

The talk of some persons and the account they give of their experiences is exceedingly satisfying, and such as forbids and banishes the thought of their being any other than the precious children of God. It obliges and, as it were, forces full charity; but yet we must allow the Scriptures to stand good that speak of everything in the saint belonging to the spiritual and divine life as hidden (Col. 3:3–4). Their food is the hidden manna; they have meat to eat that others know not of; a stranger intermeddles not with their joys. The heart in which they possess their divine distinguishing ornaments is the hidden man in the sight of God only (1 Peter 3:4). Their new name which Christ has given them no man knows but he that receives it (Rev. 2:17). The praise of the true Israelites, whose circumcision is that of the heart, is not of men but of God (Rom. 2:29); that is, they can be certainly known and discerned to be Israelites so as to have the honor that belongs to such only of God, as appears by the use of the like expression by the same apostle in 1 Corinthians 4:5. Here he speaks of its being God's prerogative to judge who are upright Christians and what he will do at the day of judgment, adding, and then shall every man have praise of God."

The instance of Judas is remarkable. Though he had been so much among the rest of the disciples, all persons of true experience, yet his associates never seemed to have entertained a thought of his being any other than a true disciple till he revealed himself by his scandalous practice. And the instance of Ahitophel is also very remarkable; David did not suspect him, though so wise and holy a man, so great a divine, who had such a great acquaintance with Scripture. He knew more than all his teachers, more than the ancients, was grown old in experience, and was in the greatest ripeness of his judgment. He was a great prophet and was intimately acquainted with Ahitophel, he being his familiar friend and most intimate companion in religious and spiritual concerns. Yet David not only never discovered him to be a hypocrite, but relied upon him as a true saint. He relished his religious discourse; it was sweet to him, and he counted him an eminent saint, so that he made him above any other man his guide and counselor in soul matters. But yet he was not only no saint, but a notoriously wicked man, a murderous, vile wretch: "Wickedness is in the midst thereof; deceit and guile depart not from her streets: for it was not an open enemy that reproached me, then I could have borne it; neither was it he that hated me that did magnify himself against me, then I would have hid myself from him: but it was you, a man my equal, my guide and my acquaintance; we took sweet counsel together, and walked unto the house of God in company" (Ps. 55:11–14).

To suppose that men have ability and right to determine the state of the souls of visible Christians, and so to make an open separation between saints and hypocrites such that true saints may be of one visible company and hypocrites of another, separated by a partition that men make, carries in it an inconsistency, for it supposes that God has given men power to make another visible church within his visible church; for by visible Christians or visible saints is meant persons who have a right to be received as such in the eye of a public charity. None can have a right to exclude anyone of this visible church but in the way of that regular ecclesiastical proceeding which God has established in his visible church. I beg of those who have a true zeal for promoting this work of God well to consider these things. I am persuaded that as many of them as have much to do with souls, if they do not hearken to me now, will be of the same mind when they have had more experience.

And another thing that I would entreat the zealous friends of this glorious work of God to avoid is managing the controversy with opposers with too much heat and appearance of an angry zeal, and particularly insisting very much in public prayer and preaching on the persecution of opposers. If their persecution were ten times so great as it is, methinks it would not be best to say so much about it. If it becomes Christians to be like lambs, not apt to complain and cry when they are hurt, it becomes them to be dumb and not to open their mouth, after the example of our dear Redeemer, and not to be like swine that are apt to scream aloud when they are touched. We should not be ready presently to think and speak of fire from heaven when the Samaritans oppose us and will not receive us into their villages. God's zealous ministers would do well to think of the direction the apostle Paul gave to a zealous minister in 2 Timothy 2:24–26: "And the servant of the Lord must not strive, but be gentle unto all men, apt to teach, patient, in meekness instructing those that oppose themselves; if God peradventure will give them repentance, to the acknowledging of the truth; and that they may recover themselves out of the snare of the devil, who are taken captive by him at his will."

I would humbly recommend to those that love the Lord Jesus Christ and would advance his kingdom a good attendance to that excellent rule of prudence which Christ has left us in Matthew 9:16–17: "No man puts a piece of new cloth into an old garment; for that which is put in to fill it up takes from the garment, and the rent is made worse. Neither do men put new wine into old bottles; else the bottles break and the wine runs out, and the bottles perish. But they put new wine into new bottles, and both are preserved." I am afraid the wine is now running out in some part of this land for want of attending to this rule. For though I believe we have confined ourselves too much to a certain stated method and form in the management of our religious affairs, which has had a tendency to cause all our religion to degenerate into mere formality, yet whatever has the appearance of a great innovation—that tends much to shock and surprise people's minds, and to set them a-talking and disputing—tends greatly to hinder the progress of the power of religion. It raises the opposition of some, diverts the mind of others, and perplexes many with doubts and scruples. It causes people to swerve from their great business and turn aside to vain jangling. Therefore that which is very much beside the common practice, unless it is a thing in its own nature of considerable importance, had better be avoided. Herein we shall follow the example of one who had the greatest success in propagating the power of religion: "Unto the Jews I became as a Jew, that I might gain the Jews; to those that are under the law, as under the law, that I might gain those that are under the law; to those that are without law, as without law (being not without law to God, but under to Christ), that I might gain those that are without law. To the weak became I as weak, that I might gain the weak. I am made all things to all men, that I might by all means save some. And this I do for the gospel's sake, that I might be partaker thereof with you" (1 Cor. 9:20–23).

5

The Danger of an Unconverted Ministry

Mark 6:34

GILBERT TENNENT

Strictly speaking, this sermon is misplaced in the present volume. It was preached some two and a half years earlier than Edwards's "Distinguishing Marks." But Tennent (1703–64) was roughly contemporaneous with Edwards, and this sermon, like Edwards's, played a key role in the Great Awakening.

Further, placing the Tennent sermon here, after Edwards, makes it possible to use some of Edwards's categories to evaluate what Tennent did. And that may be helpful to readers of both sermons.

The ecclesiastical background of Tennent's sermon is even more complex than that of Edwards's sermon, though revival was common to both. The first American presbytery had been formed in 1706 in Philadelphia, and in that presbytery had been ministers representing both major strands of New World Presbyterianism—New England Congregationalists and Scotch-Irish Presbyterians. Much—perhaps too much—has been made of the differing emphases of these two groups: the New Englanders on Christian experience and the Scotch-Irish on orthodox doctrine.

To whatever degree these emphases were associated with the differing ethnic backgrounds of Middle Colony Presbyterians, it is true that, as in recent years in the Presbyterian Church in America and the Orthodox Presbyterian Church, these emphases did lead to slightly differing views on what was most important in safeguarding the specific identity of the young denomination. Was it the requirement of precise doctrinal orthodoxy or was it the requirement of a credible profession of personal faith in Christ? Granted that both were important, where should the church focus its most rigorous attention in order to ensure the spiritual health of the church?

Discussions and debates consumed many church meetings in the second and third decades of the eighteenth century and eventually led to the Adopting Act in 1729. The precise force of the Adopting Act, particularly with reference to the different actions taken during the morning and afternoon sessions of the synod that approved the Act, continues to be fodder for twenty-first-century discussion and debate.

Regardless of how (if at all) those matters are resolved, it is critical for us to recognize that these were issues dominating the church both before and after 1729. Far from being "settled" by the 1729 action, they became more and more intensively divisive in the Presbyterian church in the Middle Colonies during the 1730s. And one reason for this was that for much of the 1730s, revival was breaking out in the Middle Colonies just as it was in New England. In fact, at almost exactly the same time as the Northampton revival in 1734, John Cross, a Scot, was leading a major revival in Basking Ridge, New Jersey, during which at least three hundred conversions were reported.[1]

Both Cross and the Tennents, father William and son Gilbert, seem to belie the neat categories that have been used to explain the early tensions in the Presbyterian church. All three were Scotch or Scotch-Irish, and yet all three were fervent supporters of the revivals. In other words, while there is no evidence whatsoever to suggest that either of the Tennents or Cross had any specific doctrinal deficiencies, it is clear that their emphasis was strongly on the critical importance of personal conversion and piety. This emphasis dominated their preaching and dominated the curriculum of the Log College, which William Tennent founded in 1726 in Neshaminy, Pennsylvania.

---

1. Charles Maxson, *The Great Awakening in the Middle Colonies* (Gloucester, Mass.: Peter Smith, 1958), 33.

Men emerging from the Log College in the early 1730s shared their teacher's interests and priorities. Thus, increasing numbers of pro-revival individuals presented themselves for ordination in the fourth decade of the eighteenth century. There were also increasing objections to the qualifications of those individuals. Whether these objections were valid or not is a matter of some dispute, but the result was that the Synod of 1738 passed a new rule stipulating that presbyteries could not consider for ordination any individual who did not possess a degree from a New England college or a European university.

This rule and the debate surrounding its adoption (both leading up to and following 1738) is a fascinating anticipation of so many issues that have faced Presbyterian and Reformed bodies since 1738. What are the minimum requirements for ministerial ordination in the church? How can or should those requirements be met, and even more significantly, how can or should they be measured? Even if we grant that both head and heart must be right, where should be the focus of Presbyterian examination of ministerial candidates? Should those with slight deviations in doctrine be treated differently from those with slight deviations in personal piety? Should the *lives* of candidates receive the same scrutiny as or even greater scrutiny than the *beliefs* of candidates? Presbyteries normally instruct successful candidates that if they, in the future, find themselves out of accord with the doctrinal standards of the church, they must notify the presbytery of the change. Should presbyteries give similar instructions regarding the candidate's personal love for Jesus?

These are fairly fundamental questions. They were in 1738, and they still are in the early twenty-first century. And this is one reason why "Danger" is such an important sermon. Read carefully, that sermon insists that the minister's personal relationship with Christ is far and away the most important aspect of his ministerial credential. Take that away or dilute it or even fail to give it first priority, and the ministry itself is, at best, questionable.

But we must also note the larger issue that Tennent is addressing in this sermon. He is seeking to answer the very question that Edwards posed at the Yale commencement in 1741: How can we tell what is genuine and what is counterfeit? How can we tell what are the essential characteristics of a genuinely gracious ministry? Comparison of the Edwards sermon with the Tennent sermon on this exact point is most instructive. Which of the two would serve better as guidelines for ordination examinations today? Which of the two, appropriately adapted, would serve better as guidelines for church membership inquiries? Which of the two would best serve as guidelines for the church as a whole as it seeks to maintain its mission and ministry?

But there is another reason why "Danger" is such an important sermon, and this reason might help in answering the questions posed immediately above. Stated simply, "The Danger of an Unconverted Ministry" was a main contributor to the first schism in the American Presbyterian Church. Two years after Tennent preached "Danger" in Nottingham, Pennsylvania, the Presbyterian church split into the Presbytery of New York and the Presbytery of Philadelphia. Was Tennent responsible for this split or were his opponents responsible for the split? And the answer is "Yes!"

Both sides were responsible for this rending of the Body of Christ. Both sides spoke harshly about the other. Neither side lived in full obedience to what the Westminster Larger Catechism says are the requirements and the prohibitions of the Ninth Commandment. But no single statement was as damaging to the cause of church unity as Tennent's "Danger" sermon.

Thankfully, after Tennent set the example of biblical repentance in his *Irenicum* in 1749, reunion was possible and was effected in 1758. As he had done in inflaming a difficult situation, Tennent led the way in bringing reconciliation. And in recognition of his extraordinarily important role in bringing the Presbyterian church back together, the reunited church elected Tennent its first moderator in 1758.

As much as the issues raised by Tennent remain prominent in Presbyterian and Reformed ecclesiastical discussions today, so unfortunately does the negative tone of Tennent's sermon seem to dominate those discussions. So often, we who live and work within that tradition seem to have read and taken as our model how Tennent said what he said in "Danger." We seem to have forgotten both Tennent's 1748 Philadelphia sermon on brotherly love and his *Irenicum* published the very next year. We also seem to have forgotten those magnificent comments made by Edwards when describing Christian humility as one of the chief signs of truly gracious affections. Listen again to what Edwards says, both in the context of Tennent's sermon and in the context of our own twenty-first-century ecclesiastical battles:

There is a pretended boldness for Christ that arises from no better principle than pride.... Gracious affections are of a quite contrary tendency—they turn a heart of stone more and more into a heart of flesh. . . . As he [the true Christian] has more holy boldness, so he has less of self-confidence, or a forward-assuming boldness, and more modesty. As he is more sure than others of deliverance from hell, so he has a greater sense of its desert. He is less apt than others to be shaken in faith; but more apt to be moved with solemn warnings, with God's frowns, and with the calamities of others. He has the firmest comfort, but the softest heart; richer than others, but poorest of all in spirit. He is the tallest and strongest saint, but the least and tenderest child among them.[2]

Tennent's "Danger" and Edwards's "Distinguishing Marks" thus need to be read together. The former states the problem in sharp dichotomies, almost as Tennent felt his opponents were doing with their insistence on super-precise theology. The latter considers the nuances of biblical teaching and Christian experience, just as Edwards's opponents claimed to be doing. In the end, of course, Tennent and Edwards were "on the same page." Lives founded on the sovereign, regenerative work of God's Spirit and totally focused on his glory are, in the final analysis, "the distinguishing marks of a converted ministry."

THE DANGER OF AN UNCONVERTED MINISTRY

GILBERT TENNENT

And Jesus, when he came out, saw many people, and was moved with compassion towards them, because they were as sheep not having a shepherd. (Mark 6:34)

2. Jonathan Edwards, *A Treatise Concerning Religious Affections*, in *The Works of Jonathan Edwards*, vol. 1 (Edinburgh: Banner of Truth Trust, 1974), 305–07.

As a faithful ministry is a great ornament, blessing, and comfort to the church of God, and even the feet of such messengers are beautiful, so on the contrary an ungodly ministry is a great curse and judgment. These caterpillars labor to devour every green thing.

There is nothing that may more justly call forth our saddest sorrows and make all our powers and passions mourn in the most doleful accents, the most incessant, insatiable, and deploring agonies, than the melancholy case of such who have no faithful ministry! This truth is set before our minds in a strong light in the words that I have chosen now to insist upon, in which we have an account of our Lord's grief with the causes of it.

We are informed that our dear Redeemer was moved with compassion towards them. The original word signifies the strongest and most vehement pity issuing from the innermost bowels.

But what was the cause of this great and compassionate commotion in the heart of Christ? It was because he saw many people as sheep having no shepherd. Why, had the people then no teachers? O yes! They had heaps of Pharisee-teachers that came out, no doubt after they had been at the feet of Gamaliel the usual time, and according to the acts, canons, and traditions of the Jewish church. But notwithstanding the great crowds of these orthodox, letter-learned, and regular Pharisees, our Lord laments the unhappy case of that great number of people who, in the days of his flesh, had no better guides because those were as good as none (in many respects), in our Savior's judgment. For all of them, the people were as sheep without a shepherd.

From the words of our text, the following proposition offers itself to our consideration: That the case of those who have no other but Pharisee-shepherds or unconverted teachers is much to be pitied.

In discoursing upon this subject, I would:

1. Inquire into the characters of the old Pharisee-teachers.

2. Show why the case of such people who have no better should be pitied.

3. Show how pity should be expressed upon this mournful occasion!

First I am to inquire into the characters of the old Pharisee-teachers. Now, I think the most notorious branches of their character were these: pride, policy, malice, ignorance, covetousness, and bigotry to human inventions in religious matters.

The old Pharisees were very proud and conceited; they loved the uppermost seats in the synagogues and to be called *Rabbi, Rabbi;* they were masterly and positive in their assertions, as if forsooth knowledge must die with them; they looked upon others that differed from them, and the common people, with an air of disdain, and especially any who had a respect for Jesus and his doctrine, and disliked them; they judged such accursed.

The old Pharisee-shepherds were as crafty as foxes; they tried by all means to ensnare our Lord by their captious questions and to expose him to the displeasure of the state, while in the meantime, by sly and sneaking methods, they tried to secure for themselves the favor of the grandees and the people's applause; and this they obtained to their satisfaction (John 7:48).

But while they exerted the craft of foxes, they did not forget to breathe forth the cruelty of wolves in a malicious aspersing the person of Christ and in a violent opposing of the truths, people, and power of his religion. Yea, the most stern and strict of them were the ringleaders of the party: Witness Saul's journey to Damascus, with letters from the chief priest to bring bound to Jerusalem all that he could find of that Way. It's true the Pharisees did not proceed to violent measures with our Savior and his disciples just at first. But that was not owing to their good nature, but their policy, for they feared the people. They must keep the people in their interests. Ay, that was the main chance, the compass that directed all their proceedings; and therefore such sly, cautious methods must be pursued as might consist herewith. They wanted to root vital religion out of the world, but they found it beyond their thumb.

Although some of the old Pharisee-shepherds had a very fair and strict outside, yet they were ignorant of the new birth: Witness Rabbi Nicodemus, who talked like a fool about it. Hear how our Lord cursed those plaistered hypocrites: "Woe unto you, scribes and Pharisees, hypocrites; for you are like whited sepulchres, which indeed appear beautiful outward, but are within full of dead bones and of all uncleanness. Even so you also appear righteous unto men, but within you are full of hypocrisy and iniquity" (Matt. 23:27–28). Ay, if they had but a little of the learning then in fashion, and a fair outside, they were presently put into the priest's office, though they had no experience of the new birth. O sad!

The old Pharisees, for all their long prayers and other pious pretenses, had their eyes, with Judas, fixed upon the bag. Why, they came into the priest's office for a piece of bread; they took it up as a trade and therefore endeavored to make the best market of it they could. O shame!

It may be further observed that the Pharisee-teachers in Christ's time were great bigots to small matters in religion. "Woe unto you, scribes and Pharisees, hypocrites; for you pay tithe of mint and anise and cumin and have omitted the weightier matters of the law, judgment, mercy, and faith" (Matt. 23:23). The Pharisees were fired with a party-zeal; they compassed sea and land to make a proselyte, and yet when he was made, they made him twofold more the child of hell than themselves. They were also bigoted to human inventions in religious matters: Paul himself, while he was a natural man, was wonderfully zealous for the traditions of the fathers. Ay, those poor blind guides, as our Lord testifies, strained at a gnat and swallowed a camel.

And what a mighty respect had they for the Sabbath-day forsooth! inasmuch that Christ and his disciples must be charged with the breach thereof, for doing works of mercy and necessity. Ah, the rottenness of these hypocrites! It was not so much respect to the Sabbath as malice against Christ that was the occasion of the charge; they wanted some plausible pretense to offer against him, in order to blacken his character.

And what a great love had they in pretense to those pious prophets, who were dead before they were born, while in the meantime they were persecuting the Prince of Prophets! Hear how the King of the church speaks to them, upon this head: "Woe unto you, scribes and Pharisees, hypocrites; because you build the tombs of the prophets, and garnish the sepulchres of the righteous, and say, If we had been in the days of our fathers, we would not have been partakers with them in the blood of the prophets. You serpents, you generations of vipers, how can you escape the damnation of hell?" (Matt. 23:29–33).

The second general head of discourse is to show why such people who have no better than the old Pharisee-teachers are to be pitied.

1. Natural men have no call of God to the ministerial work under the gospel-dispensation.

Isn't it a principal part of the ordinary call of God to the ministerial work to aim at the glory of God and, in subordination thereto, the good of souls as their chief marks in their undertaking that work? And can any natural man on earth do this? No! no! Every skin of them has an evil eye; for no cause can produce effects above its own power. Are not wicked men forbidden to meddle in things sacred? According to Psalm 50:16: "But unto the wicked God says, What have you to do to declare my statutes, or that you should take my covenant in your mouth?" Now, are not all unconverted men wicked men? Does not the Lord Jesus inform us in John 10:1 that "he who enters not by the door into the sheepfold, but climbs up some other way, the same is a thief and a robber"? In the ninth verse Christ tells us that he is the Door; and that if any man enter in by him, he shall be saved by him, i.e., by faith in him (says Henry). Hence we read of a door of faith being opened to the Gentiles in Acts 14:27. It confirms this gloss: that salvation is annexed to the entrance before-mentioned. Remarkable is that saying of our Savior in Matthew 4:19: "Follow me, and I will make you fishers of men." See, our Lord will not make men ministers till they follow him. Men that do not follow Christ may fish faithfully for a good name and for worldly pelf, but not for the conversion of sinners to God. Is it reasonable to suppose that they will be earnestly concerned for others' salvation when they slight their own? Our Lord reproved Nicodemus for taking upon himself the office of instructing others while he himself was a stranger to the new birth: "Are you a master of Israel and know not these things?" (John 3:10). The apostle Paul (in 1 Timothy 1:12) thanks God for counting him faithful and putting him into the ministry, which plainly supposes that God Almighty does not send Pharisees and natural men into the ministry. For how can these men be faithful that have no faith? It's true that men may put them into the ministry through unfaithfulness or mistake; or credit and money may draw them, and the devil may drive them into it, knowing by long experience of what special service they might be to his kingdom in that office. But God sends not such hypocritical varlets. Hence Timothy was directed by the apostle Paul to commit the ministerial work to faithful men (2 Tim. 2:2). And do not these qualifications necessary for church officers specified in 1 Timothy 3:7–9, 11 and Titus 1:7–8 plainly suppose converting grace? How else can they avoid being greedy of filthy lucre? How else can they hold the mystery of faith in a pure conscience and be faithful in all things? How else can they be lovers of good, sober, just, holy, temperate?

2. The ministry of natural men is uncomfortable.

The enmity that is put between the seed of the woman and the seed of the serpent will now and then be creating jars: And no wonder; for as it was of old, so it is now: "He that was born after the flesh persecuted him that was born after the Spirit." This enmity is not one grain less in unconverted ministers than in others, though possibly it may be better polished with wit and rhetoric and gilded with the specious names of zeal, fidelity, peace, good order, and unity.

The discourses of natural men, not having true love to Christ and the souls of their fellow creatures, are cold and sapless and, as it were, freeze between their lips. And not being sent of God, they want that divine authority with which the faithful ambassadors of Christ are clothed, who herein resemble their blessed Master, of whom it is said that "he taught as one having authority, and not as the scribes" (Matt. 7:29).

And Pharisee-teachers, having no experience of a special work of the Holy Ghost upon their own souls, are therefore neither inclined to nor fitted for discoursing, frequently, clearly, and pathetically, upon such important subjects. The application of their discourses is either short or indistinct and general. They differentiate not the precious from the vile, and divide not to every man his portion, according to the apostolic direction to Timothy. No! they carelessly offer a common mess to their people, and leave it to them to divide it among themselves as they see fit. This is indeed their general practice, which is bad enough. But sometimes they do worse by misapplying the Word through ignorance or anger. They often strengthen the hands of the wicked by promising him life. They comfort people before they convince them, sow before they plow, and are busy in raising a fabric before they lay a foundation. These foolish builders do but strengthen men's carnal security by their soft, selfish, cowardly discourses. They have not the courage or honesty to thrust the nail of terror into sleeping souls; nay, sometimes they strive with all their might to fasten terror into the hearts of the righteous, and so to make those sad whom God would not have made sad! And this happens when pious people begin to suspect their hypocrisy, for which they have good reason. I may add that inasmuch as Pharisee-teachers seek after righteousness, as it were, by the works of the law themselves, they therefore do not distinguish, as they ought, between law and gospel in their discourses to others. They keep driving, driving, to duty, duty, under this notion: that it will recommend natural men to the favor of God, or entitle them to the promises of grace and salvation. And thus those blind guides fix a deluded world upon the false foundation of their own righteousness, and so exclude them from the dear Redeemer. All the doings of unconverted men, not proceeding from the principles of faith, love, and a new nature, nor being directed to the divine glory as their highest end, but flowing from and tending to self as their principle and end are doubtless damnably wicked in their manner of performance, and do deserve the wrath and curse of a sin-avenging God; neither can any other encouragement be justly given them but this: that in the way of duty, there is a peradventure or probability of obtaining mercy.

And natural men want the experience of those spiritual difficulties which pious souls are exposed to in this vale of tears; they know not how to speak a word to the weary in season. Their prayers are also cold; little childlike love to God or pity to poor perishing souls runs through their veins. Their conversation has nothing of the savor of Christ, neither is it perfumed with the spices of heaven. They seem to make as little distinction in their practice as preaching. They love those unbelievers that are kind to them better than many Christians, and choose them for companions, contrary to Psalm 15:4, Psalm 119:115, and Galatians 6:10. Poor Christians are stunted and starved who are put to feed on such bare pastures and such dry nurses, as the Rev. Mr. Hildersham justly calls them. It's only when the wise virgins sleep that they can bear with those dead dogs that can't bark; but when the Lord revives his people, they can't but abhor them. O! it is ready to break their very hearts with grief, to see how lukewarm those Pharisee-teachers are in their public discourses, while sinners are sinking into damnation in multitudes!

3. The ministry of natural men is for the most part unprofitable, which is confirmed by a threefold evidence: Scripture, reason, and experience. Such as the Lord sends not, he himself assures us, shall not profit the people at all (Jer. 23:32). Mr. Pool justly glosses upon this passage of sacred Scripture thus:

That none can expect God's blessing upon their ministry that are not called and sent of God into the ministry. And right reason will inform us how unfit instruments they are to negotiate that work they pretend to. Is a blind man fit to be a guide in a very dangerous way? Is a dead man fit to bring others to life? A madman fit to give counsel in a matter of life and death? Is a possessed man fit to cast out devils? A rebel, an enemy to God, fit to be sent on an embassy of peace to bring rebels into a state of friendship with God? A captive bound in the massy chains of darkness and guilt a proper person to set others at liberty? A leper, or one that has plague-sores upon him, fit to be a good physician? Is an ignorant rustic that has never been at sea in his life fit to be a pilot, to keep vessels from being dashed to pieces upon rocks and sandbanks? Isn't an unconverted minister like a man who would teach others to swim before he has learned it himself, and so is drowned in the act and dies like a fool?

I may add that sad experience verifies what has been now observed concerning the unprofitableness of the ministry of unconverted men. Look into the congregations of unconverted ministers, and see what a sad security reigns there; not a soul convinced that can be heard of for many years together. And yet the ministers are easy, for they say they do their duty! Ay, a small matter will satisfy us in the want of that which we have no great desire after. But when persons have their eyes opened and their hearts set upon the work of God, they are not so soon satisfied with their doings and with want of success for a time. O! they mourn with Micah that they are as those that gather the summer-fruits, as the grape-gleaning of the vintage. Mr. Baxter justly observes that "those who speak about their doings in the aforesaid manner are like to do little good to the church of God. But many ministers (as Mr. Bracel [sic] observes) think the gospel flourishes among them when the people are in peace, and many come to hear the Word and to the sacrament." If with the other they get their salaries well paid, O then it is fine times indeed! in their opinion. O sad! And they are full of hopes that they do good, though they know nothing about it. But what comfort can a conscientious man who travels in birth, that Christ may be formed in his hearers' hearts, take from what he knows not? Will a hungry stomach be satisfied with dreams about meat? I believe not; though I confess a full one may.

What if some instances could be shown of unconverted ministers' being instrumental in convincing persons of their lost state? The thing is very rare and extraordinary. And for what I know, as many instances may be given of Satan's convincing persons by his temptations. Indeed, it's a kind of chance-medley, both in respect of the Father and his children, when any such event happens. And isn't this the reason why a work of conviction and conversion has been so rarely heard of for a long time in the churches till of late: that the bulk of her spiritual guides were stone-blind and stone-dead?

4. The ministry of natural men is dangerous both in respect of the doctrines and practice of piety. The doctrines of original sin, justification by faith alone, and the other points of Calvinism are very cross to the grain of unrenewed nature. And though men, by the influence of a good education and hopes of preferment, may have the edge of their natural enmity against them blunted, yet it's far from being broken or removed: It's only the saving grace of God that can give us a true relish for those nature-humbling doctrines and so effectually secure us from being infected by the contrary. Is not the carnality of the ministry one great cause of the general spread of Arminianism, Socinianism, Arianism, and Deism at this day through the world?

And alas! what poor guides are natural ministers to those who are under spiritual trouble? They either slight such distress altogether, and call it melancholy or madness, and daub those who are under it with untempered mortar. Our Lord assures us that the salt which has lost its savor is good for nothing; some say, It genders worms and vermin. Now, what savor have Pharisee-ministers? In truth, a very stinking one, both in the nostrils of God and good men. . . . Hence is that threatening of our Lord against them in Matthew 23:3: "Woe unto you, scribes and Pharisees, hypocrites; for you shut up the kingdom of heaven against men, for you neither go in yourselves nor suffer those that are entering to go in." Pharisee-teachers will with the utmost hate oppose the very work of God's Spirit upon the souls of men and labor by all means to blacken it, as well as the instruments, which the Almighty improves to promote the same, if it comes near their borders and interferes with their credit or interest. Thus did the Pharisees deal with our Savior.

If it is objected against what has been offered under this general head of discourse that Judas was sent by Christ, I answer (1) that Judas's ministry was partly legal, inasmuch as during that period the disciples were subject to Jewish observances and sent only to the house of Israel (Matt. 10:5–6) and in that they waited after Christ's resurrection for another mission (Acts 1:4), which we find they obtained, and that different from the former (Matt. 28:19). (2) Judas's ministry was extraordinarily necessary in order to fulfill some ancient prophecies concerning him (Acts 1:16–18, 20; John 13:18). I fear that the abuse of this instance has brought many Judases into the ministry, whose chief desire, like their great-grandfather, is to finger the pence and carry the bag. But let such hireling murderous hypocrites take care that they don't feel the force of a halter in this world and an aggravated damnation in the next.

Again, if it is objected that Paul rejoiced that the gospel was preached, though of contention and not sincerely, I answer that the expression signifies the apostle's great self-denial. Some labored to eclipse his fame and character by contentious preaching, thinking thereby to afflict him; but they were mistaken—as to that, he was easy: For he had long before learned to die to his own reputation. The apostle's rejoicing was comparative only: He would rather that Christ should be preached out of envy than not at all, especially considering the gross ignorance of the doctrinal knowledge of the gospel, which prevailed almost universally in that age of the world. Besides, the apostle knew that that trial should be sanctified to him, to promote his spiritual progress in goodness, and perhaps prove a means of procuring his temporal freedom; and therefore he would rejoice. It is certain that we may both rejoice and mourn in relation to the same thing upon different accounts without any contradiction.

But the third general head was to show how pity should be expressed upon this mournful occasion!

My brethren, we should mourn over those that are destitute of faithful ministers, and sympathize with them. Our bowels should be moved with the most compassionate tenderness over those dear fainting souls that are as sheep having no shepherd, after the example of our blessed Lord.

Dear Sirs! we should also most earnestly pray for them, that the compassionate Savior may preserve them by his mighty power through faith unto salvation; support their sinking spirits under the melancholy uneasinesses of a dead ministry; sanctify and sweeten to them the dry morsels they get under such blind men, when they have none better to repair to.

And more especially, my brethren, we should pray to the Lord of the harvest to send forth faithful laborers into his harvest, seeing that the harvest truly is plenteous, but the laborers are few. And O Sirs! how humble, believing, and importunate should we be in this petition! O! Let us follow the Lord, day and night, with cries, tears, pleadings, and groanings upon this account! For God knows there is a great necessity of it. O! Fountain of Mercy and Father of Pity, pour forth upon your poor children a spirit of prayer for the obtaining of this important mercy! Help, help, O Eternal God and Father, for Christ's sake!

And indeed, my brethren, we should join our endeavors to our prayers. The most likely method to stock the church with a faithful ministry, in the present situation of things (the public academies being so much corrupted and abused generally), is to encourage private schools or seminaries of learning which are under the care of skillful and experienced Christians, in which those only should be admitted who, upon strict examination, have in the judgment of a reasonable charity the plain evidences of experimental religion. Pious and experienced youths who have a good natural capacity and great desires after the ministerial work from good motives might be sought for and found up and down in the country, and put to private schools of the prophets, especially in such places where the public ones are not. This method, in my opinion, has a noble tendency to build up the church of God. And those who have any love to Christ or desire after the coming of his kingdom should be ready, according to their ability, to give something, from time to time, for the support of such poor youths who have nothing of their own. And truly, brethren, this charity to the souls of men is the most noble kind of charity. O! if the love of God be in you, it will constrain you to do something to promote so noble and necessary a work. It looks hypocritical to go no further when other things are required than cheap prayer. Don't think it much if the Pharisees should be offended at such a proposal; these subtle, selfish hypocrites are wont to be afraid about their credit and their kingdom, and truly they are both of little worth, for all the bustle they make about them. If they could help it, they wouldn't let one faithful man come into the ministry; and therefore their opposition is an encouraging sign. Let all the followers of the Lamb stand up and act for God against all opposers: Who is upon God's side—who?

The improvement of this subject remains. And:

1. If it is so that the case of those who have no other or no better than the Pharisee-teachers is to be pitied, then what a scroll and scene of mourning and lamentation and woe is opened because of the swarms of locusts, the crowds of Pharisees, that have as covetously as cruelly crept into the ministry in this adulterous generation! They as nearly resemble the character given of the old Pharisees in the doctrinal part of this discourse as one crow's egg does another. It is true that some of the modern Pharisees have learned to prate a little more orthodoxly about the new birth than their predecessor Nicodemus, while being in the meantime as great strangers to the feeling and experience of it as he. They are blind who see not this to be the case of the body of the clergy of this generation. And O! that our heads were waters and our eyes a fountain of tears, that we could day and night lament with the utmost bitterness the doleful case of the poor church of God upon this account.

2. From what has been said, we may learn that such who are contented under a dead ministry have not in them the temper of that Savior they profess. It's an awful sign that they are as blind as moles and as dead as stones, without any spiritual taste and relish. And alas! isn't this the case of multitudes? If they can get one that has the name of a minister with a band and a black coat or gown to carry on Sabbath-days among them, although never so coldly and unsuccessfully; if he is free from gross crimes in practice, takes good care to keep at a due distance from their consciences, and is never troubled about his unsuccessfulness—O! Think the poor fools, that is a fine man indeed; our minister is a prudent, charitable man; he is not always harping upon terror and sounding damnation in our ears like some rash-headed preachers who by their uncharitable methods are ready to put poor people out of their wits or to run them into despair. O! How terrible a thing is that despair! Ay, our minister, honest man, gives us good caution against it. Poor, silly souls! Consider seriously these passages of the prophet Jeremiah: chapters 5, 30, 31.

3. We may learn the mercy and duty of those that enjoy a faithful ministry. Let such glorify God for so distinguishing a privilege and labor to walk

worthy of it, to all well-pleasing, lest for their abuse thereof they are exposed to a greater damnation.

4. If the ministry of natural men is as it has been represented, then it is both lawful and expedient to go from them to hear godly persons. Yea, it's so far from being sinful to do this that for one who lives under a pious minister of lesser gifts, after having honestly endeavored to get benefit by his ministry and yet gets little or none, but finds real benefit and more benefit elsewhere, I say that he may lawfully go frequently where he gets most good to his precious soul after regular application to the pastor where he lives for his consent, and proposing the reasons thereof, when this is done in the spirit of love and meekness, without contempt of any, as also without rash anger or vain curiosity.

Natural reason will inform us that good is desirable for its own sake. Now, as Dr. Voetius observes, good added to good makes it a greater good, and so more desirable; and therefore evil as evil, or a lesser good, which is comparatively evil, cannot be the object of desire.

There is a natural instinct put even into the irrational creatures by the Author of their being to seek after the greater natural good, as far as they know it. Hence the birds of the air fly to the warmer climates in order to shun the winter cold, and also doubtless to get better food; for where the carcass is, there the eagles will be gathered together. The beasts of the field seek the best pastures, and the fishes of the ocean seek after the food they like best.

But the written Word of God confirms the aforesaid proposition, while God by it enjoins us "to covet earnestly the best gifts"; also "to prove all things and hold fast that which is good" (1 Cor. 12:31; 1 Thess. 5:21). And is it not the command of God that we should grow in grace? (2 Peter 3:18; 1 Peter 2:2). Now, does not every positive command enjoin the use of such means as have the most direct tendency to answer the end designed, namely, the duty commanded? If there are a variety of means, is not the best to be chosen? Else how can the choice be called rational, and becoming to an intelligent creature? To choose otherwise knowingly—is it not contrary to common sense, as well as religion, and daily confuted by the common practice of all the rational creation about things of far less moment and consequence?

That there is a difference and variety in preachers' gifts and graces is undeniably evident from the united testimony of Scripture and reason.

And that there is a great difference in the degrees of hearers' edification under the hearing of these different gifts is as evident to the feeling of experienced Christians as anything can be to sight.

It is also an unquestionable truth that ordinarily God blesses most the best gifts for the hearers' edification, as by the best food he gives the best nourishment. Otherwise, the best gifts would not be desirable, and God Almighty in the ordinary course of his providence, by not acting according to the nature of things, would be carrying on a series of unnecessary miracles, which to suppose is unreasonable. The following places of holy Scripture confirm what has been last observed: 1 Corinthians 14:12; 1 Timothy 4:14–16; 2 Timothy 1:6; Acts 11:24.

If God's people have a right to the gifts of all God's ministers, pray, why mayn't they use them as they have opportunity? And if they should go a few miles farther than ordinary to enjoy those which they profit most by, who do they wrong? Now, our Lord does inform his people in 1 Corinthians 3:22 that whether Paul, or Apollos, or Cephas, all was theirs.

But the example of our dear Redeemer will give further light in this argument. Though many of the hearers, not only of the Pharisees but of John the Baptist, came to hear our Savior, not only upon weekdays but upon Sabbath-days, in great numbers and from very distant places, yet he reproved them not: And did not our Lord love the apostle John more than the rest, and took him with him, before others, with Peter and James, to Mount Tabor and Gethsemane? (Matt. 17, 26).

To bind men to a particular minister against their judgment and inclinations, when they are more edified elsewhere, is carnal with a witness, a cruel oppression of tender consciences, a compelling of men to sin. For he that doubts is damned if he eats, and whatever is not of faith is sin.

Besides, it is an unscriptural infringement on Christian liberty (1 Cor. 3:22). It's a yoke worse than that of Rome itself. Dr. Voetius asserts that "even among the Papists, as to hearing of sermons, the people are not deprived of the liberty of choice." It's a yoke like that of Egypt, which cruel Pharaoh formed for the necks of the oppressed Israelites when he obliged them to make up their stated task of brick, but allowed them no straw. So we must grow in grace and knowledge, but in the meantime, according to the notion of some, we are confined from using the likeliest means to attain that end.

If the great ends of hearing may be attained as well and better by hearing of another minister than our own, then I see not why we should be under a fatal necessity of hearing our parish-minister perpetually or generally. Now, what are, or ought to be, the ends of hearing but the getting of grace and growing in it? (Rom. 10:14). As 1 Peter 2:2 asserts: "As babes desire the sincere milk of the Word, that you may grow thereby." (Poor babes like not dry breasts, and living men like not dead pools.) Well, then, and may not these ends be obtained out of our parish-line? Faith is said to come by hearing in Romans 10. But the apostle doesn't add your "parish-minister." Isn't the same Word preached out of our parish, and is there any restriction in the promises of blessing the Word to only those who keep within their parish-line ordinarily? If there is, I have not yet met with it; yea, I can affirm that so far as knowledge can be had in such cases, I have known persons to get saving good to their souls by hearing over their parish-line, and this makes me earnest in defense of it.

That which ought to be the main motive of hearing any, that is, our soul's good or greater good, will excite us, if we regard our own eternal interest, to hear there where we attain it; and he that hears with lesser views acts like a fool and a hypocrite.

Now, if it is lawful to withdraw from the ministry of a pious man in the case aforesaid, how much more from the ministry of a natural man? Surely it is both lawful and expedient, for the reasons offered in the doctrinal part of this discourse—to which let me add a few words more.

To trust the care of our souls to those who have little or no care for their own, to those who are both unskillful and unfaithful, is contrary to the common practice of considerate mankind relating to the affairs of their bodies and estates and would signify that we set light by our souls, and did not care what became of them. For if the blind lead the blind, will they not both fall into the ditch?

Is it a strange thing to think that God does not ordinarily use the ministry of his enemies to turn others to be his friends, seeing he works by suitable means?

I cannot think that God has given any promise that he will be with and bless the labors of natural ministers. For if he had, he would be surely as good as his word. But I can neither see nor hear of any blessing upon these men's labors—unless it is a rare and wonderful instance of chance-medley!—

whereas the ministry of faithful men blossoms and bears fruit, as the rod of Aaron. "But if they had stood in my counsel, and had caused my people to hear my words, then they should have turned them from their evil way and from the evil of their doings" (Jer. 23:22).

From such as have a form of godliness, and deny the power thereof, we are enjoined to turn away (2 Tim. 3:5). And are there not many such?

Our Lord advised his disciples to beware of the leaven of the Pharisees in Matthew 16:6, by which he shows that he meant their doctrine and hypocrisy (Mark 8:15; Luke 12:1), which were both sour enough.

Memorable is the answer of our Lord to his disciples in Matthew 15:12–14: "Then came his disciples and said unto him, 'Do you know that the Pharisees were offended?' And he answered and said, 'Every plant which my Heavenly Father has not planted shall be rooted up. Let them alone; they are blind leaders of the blind: And if the blind lead the blind, both shall fall into the ditch.' "

If it is objected that we are bid to go to hear those that sit in Moses' chair (Matt. 23:2–3), I would answer this, in the words of a body of dissenting ministers: That sitting in Moses' chair signifies a succeeding of Moses in the ordinary part of his office and authority; so did Joshua and the 70 elders (Ex. 18:21–26). Now, Moses was no priest (say they), though of Levi's tribe, but king in Jeshurun, a civil ruler and judge, chosen by God (Ex. 18:13). Therefore, no more is meant by the Scripture in the objection but that it is the duty of people to hear and obey the lawful commands of the civil magistrate, according to Romans 13:5.

If it is opposed to the preceding reasonings that such an opinion and practice would be apt to cause heats and contentions among people, I answer that the aforesaid practice, accompanied with love, meekness, and humility, is not the proper cause of those divisions, but the occasion only, or the cause by accident, and not by itself. If a person exercising modesty and love in his carriage to his minister and neighbors, through uprightness of heart, designing nothing but his own greater good, repairs there frequently where he attains it, is this any reasonable cause of anger? Will any be offended with him because he loves his soul and seeks the greater good thereof, and is not like a senseless stone without choice, sense, and taste? Pray, must we leave off every duty that is the occasion of contention or division? Then we must quit powerful religion altogether. For he that will live godly in

Christ Jesus shall suffer persecution. And particularly we must carefully avoid faithful preaching, for that is wont to occasion disturbances and divisions, especially when accompanied with divine power. "Our gospel came not unto you in word only, but in power"; and then it is added that they "received the Word in much affliction" (1 Thess. 1:5, 6). And the apostle Paul informs us in 1 Corinthians 16:9 that a great and effectual door was opened unto him and that there were many adversaries. Blessed Paul was accounted a common disturber of the peace, as well as Elijah long before him, and yet he left not off preaching for all that. Yea, our blessed Lord informs us that he came not to send peace on earth, but rather a sword, variance, fire, and division, even among relations (Matt. 10:34–36; Luke 12:49, 51–53). He also tells us that while the strong man armed keeps the house, all the goods are in peace. It is true that the power of the gospel is not the proper cause of those divisions, but the innocent occasion only. No, the proper cause of sinful divisions is that enmity against God and holiness which is in the hearts of natural men of every order; being stirred up by the devil, and their own proud and selfish lusts. And very often natural men, who are the proper causes of the divisions aforesaid, are wont to deal with God's servants as Potiphar's wife did by Joseph; they lay all the blame of their own wickedness at their doors, and make a loud cry!

Those who confine opposition and division as following upon living godliness and successful preaching to the first ages of Christianity, it is much to be feared, neither know themselves nor the gospel of Christ. For surely the nature of true religion, as well as of men and devils, is the same in every age.

Is not the visible church composed of persons of the most contrary characters? While some are sincere servants of God, are not many servants of Satan under a religious mask, and have not these a fixed enmity against the other? How is it then possible that a harmony should subsist between such till their nature be changed? Can light dwell with darkness?

Undoubtedly it is a great duty to avoid giving just cause of offense to any; and it is also highly necessary that pious souls should maintain union and harmony among themselves, notwithstanding their different opinions in lesser things. And no doubt this is the drift of the many exhortations which we have to peace and unity in Scripture.

Surely it cannot be reasonably supposed that we are exhorted to a unity in anything that is wicked or inconsistent with the good or greater good of our poor souls. For that would be like the unity of the devils, a legion of which dwelt peaceably in one man; or like the unity of Ahab's false prophets. All these four hundred daubers were very peaceable and much united, and all harped on the pleasing string. Ay, they were moderate men, and had the majority on their side.

But possibly some may again object against persons' going to hear others besides their own ministers, using the Scripture about Paul and Apollos (1 Cor. 1:12), and say that it is carnal. Dr. Voetius answers the aforesaid objection as follows: "The apostle reproves (says he) such as made sects, saying, 'I am of Paul,' and 'I of Apollos'—and we with him reprove them. But this is far from being against the choice which one has of sermons and preachers; seeing at one time we cannot hear all, neither does the explication and application of all equally suit such a person in such a time or condition, or equally quicken and subserve the increase of knowledge."

Because the apostle in the aforesaid place reproves an excessive love to or admiration of particular ministers, accompanied with a sinful contention, slighting, and disdaining of others who are truly godly, and with sect-making, to say that from hence it necessarily follows that we must make no difference in our choice or in the degrees of our esteem of different ministers according to their different gifts and graces is an argument of as great a force as to say that because gluttony and drunkenness are forbidden, therefore we must neither eat nor drink, or make any choice in drinks or victuals, let our constitution be what it will.

Surely the very nature of Christian love inclines those that are possessed of it to love others chiefly for their goodness, and therefore in proportion thereto. Now, seeing that the inference in the objection is secretly built upon the supposition that we should love all good men alike, it strikes at the foundations of that love to the brethren which is laid down in Scripture as a mark of true Christianity (1 John 5) and so is carnal, with a witness.

Again it may be objected that the aforesaid practice tends to grieve our parish-minister and to break congregations in pieces.

I answer: If our parish-minister is grieved at our greater good, or prefers his credit before it, then he has good cause to grieve over his own rottenness and hypocrisy. And as for breaking of congregations to pieces upon the account of people's going from place to place to hear the Word with a view to get greater good, that spiritual blindness and death that so generally prevails will put this out of danger. It is but a very few that have got any spiritual relish; the most will venture their souls with any formalist and be well satisfied with the sapless discourses of such dead drones.

Well, doesn't the apostle assert that Paul and Apollos are nothing? Yes, it is true, they and all others are nothing as efficient causes; they could not change men's hearts. But were they nothing as instruments? The objection insinuates one of these two things: either that there is no difference in means as to their suitableness or that there is no reason to expect a greater blessing upon the most suitable means—both which are equally absurd, and before confuted.

But it may be further objected, with great appearance of zeal, that what has been said about people's getting of good or greater good over their parish-line is a mere fiction, for they are out of God's way.

I answer that there are three monstrous ingredients in the objection, namely, a begging of the question in debate, rash judging, and limiting of God.

It is a mean thing in reasoning to beg or suppose that which should be proved, and then to reason from it. Let it be proved that they are out of God's way, and then I will freely yield. But till this is done, bold say-sos will not have much weight with any but dupes or dunces. And for those who cry out against others for uncharitableness, to be guilty of it themselves in the meantime in a very great degree is very inconsistent. Isn't it rash to judge of things they have never heard? But those that have received benefit and are sensible of their own uprightness will think it a light thing to be judged of man's judgment. Let Tertullus ascend the theater and gild the objection with the most mellifluous Ciceronean eloquence—it will no more persuade them that what they have felt is but a fancy (unless they are under strong temptations of Satan, or scared out of their wits by frightful expressions) than to tell a man in proper language who sees that it is but a notion; he does not see. Or to tell a man who feels pleasure or pain that it's but a deluded fancy; he is quite mistaken.

Besides, there is a limiting of the Holy One of Israel in the aforesaid objection, which sinful sin the Hebrews were reproved for. It is a piece of daring presumption to pretend by our finite line to fathom the infinite depths that are in the being and works of God. The query of Zophar is just and reasonable in Job 11:7–8: "Can you by searching find out God?" The humble apostle with astonishment acknowledged that the ways of God were past finding out (Rom. 11:33). Surely the wind blows where it wishes, and we cannot tell from whence it comes, nor where it goes. Doesn't Jehovah ride upon a gloomy cloud and make darkness his pavilion, and isn't his path in the great waters? (Ps. 18; 77:19).

I would conclude my present meditations upon this subject by exhorting all those who enjoy a faithful ministry to a speedy and sincere improvement of so rare and valuable a privilege, lest by their foolish ingratitude the righteous God be provoked to remove the means they enjoy, or his blessing from them, and so at last to expose them in another state to enduring and greater miseries. For surely these sins which are committed against greater light and mercy are more presumptuous, ungrateful, and inexcusable; there is in them a greater contempt of God's authority and slight of his mercy; those evils do awfully violate the conscience and declare a love to sin as sin; such transgressors do rush upon the bosses of God's buckler, court destruction without a covering, and embrace their own ruin with open arms. And therefore, according to the nature of justice, which proportions sinners' pains according to the number and heinousness of their crimes and the declaration of divine truth, you must expect an inflamed damnation. Surely it shall be more tolerable for Sodom and Gomorrah in the Day of the Lord than for you, unless you repent.

And let gracious souls be exhorted to express the most tender pity over such as have none but Pharisee-teachers in the manner here described, to which let the example of our Lord in the text before us be an inducing and effectual incitement, as well as the gracious and immense rewards which follow upon so generous and noble a charity in this and the next state.

And let those who live under the ministry of dead men, whether they have got the form of religion or not, repair to the living, where they may be edified. Let those who will oppose it. What famous Mr. Jenner observes upon this head is most just: "That if there is any godly soul, or any that desires the salvation of his soul, and lives under a blind guide, he cannot go out (of his parish) without giving very great offense; it will be thought a giddiness and a slighting of his own minister at home. When people came out of every parish round about to John, no question but this bred heart-burning against John, ay, and ill-will against those people that would not be satisfied with that teaching they had in their own synagogues." But though your neighbors growl against you and reproach you for doing your duty in seeking your soul's good, bear their unjust censures with Christian meekness and persevere, knowing that suffering is the lot of Christ's followers and that spiritual benefits do infinitely overbalance all temporal difficulties.

And O! that vacant congregations would take due care in the choice of their ministers! Here indeed they should hasten slowly. The church of Ephesus is commended for trying those who said they were apostles and were not, and for finding them liars. Hypocrites are against all knowing of others and judging, in order to hide their own filthiness; like thieves they flee a search because of their stolen goods. But the more they endeavor to hide, the more they expose their shame. Does not the spiritual man judge all things? Though he cannot know the states of subtle hypocrites infallibly, yet may he not give a near guess who are the sons of Sceva by their manner of praying, preaching, and living? Many Pharisee-teachers have got a long fine string of prayer by heart, so that they are never at a loss about it; their prayers and preaching are generally of a length, and both as dead as a stone and without all savor. I beseech you, my dear brethren, to consider that there is no probability of your getting good by the ministry of Pharisees. For they are no shepherds (no faithful ones) in Christ's account. They are as good as none—nay, worse than none, upon some accounts. For take them first and last, and they generally do more hurt than good. They serve to keep better out of the places where they live; nay, when the life of piety comes near their quarters, they rise up in arms against it, consult, contrive, and combine in their conclaves against it, as a common enemy that discovers and condemns their craft and hypocrisy. And with what art, rhetoric, and appearances of piety will they varnish their opposition of Christ's kingdom? As the magicians imitated the works of Moses, so do false apostles and deceitful workers imitate the apostles of Christ.

I shall conclude this discourse with the words of the apostle Paul in 2 Corinthians 11:14–15: "And no marvel; for Satan himself is transformed into an angel of light. Therefore, it is no great thing if his ministers also are transformed as the ministers of righteousness, whose end shall be according to their works."

6

Discourse Concerning Unlimited Submission and Non-Resistance to the Higher Powers

Romans 13:1−7

JONATHAN MAYHEW

Should Jonathan Mayhew (1720–66) really be included in this collection?[1] After all, many, in both his day and ours, would regard him as a liberal, perhaps even outside the bounds of orthodoxy in the direction of Unitarianism. Mayhew was born on Martha's Vineyard, the son of a missionary to the Indians, and graduated from Harvard in 1744. When he was ordained at West Church in Boston in 1747, only two other ministers attended the service, probably because of widespread concern about his theology.

---

1. Sermon Pamphlet. Boston, printed and sold by D. Fowle in Queen-Street; and by D. Gookin over against the South Meeting-House, 1750. Published at the request of the hearers. The substance of which was delivered in a sermon preached in the West Meeting-House in Boston the Lord's Day after the 30th of January, 1749/50.

I make no brief for Mayhew's theology. What I do claim is that Mayhew preached within a tradition that was professedly Reformed and that many individuals and churches for whose theology I would want to make a brief have adopted Mayhew's ideas regarding the role of the Christian in civil affairs. Indeed, I can think of no single homiletical source that has more profoundly influenced the shape of modern Reformed civic involvement, both liberal and conservative. I grant that that influence has been indirect and has been mediated through many other sources. And I grant that liberal and conservative actions are often poles apart. But Mayhew's approach to Romans 13 really does lie at the heart of thoughtful justifications for both Christian pro-life rallies and Christian pro-choice rallies.

More important historically, of course, Mayhew's approach to Romans 13 lay at the heart of thoughtful justifications for Christian support for the American Revolution, and that is the context on which I will focus here. Indeed, that is the context that provided the primary mediation through which Mayhew's ideas have made it to the twenty-first century in the United States. In a word, Mayhew provided a theological justification for the American Revolution, and most Christian Americans, to this day, tend to argue for their form of Christian political involvement on the basis of what was done in the Revolution (or in the Civil War, whose advocates and opponents both cited the Revolution in defense of their positions).

But like all the rest of us, Mayhew had a context as well, and to a significant degree, that context has already been outlined in the introduction to Cotton Mather's sermon earlier in this volume. A brief review: Early New England theologians and politicians had been able to seek to structure the colony in the way they thought biblically appropriate because of an anomaly in the original charter granted to the organizers of the endeavor. When that original charter was finally revoked in 1684, a strong tradition of ministerial leadership in asserting the "rights" of the colonies over against English "tyranny" was born. While the new (1692) charter granted to the colonies muted those discussions for a while, the sentiments did not disappear. They remained lying just below the surface, ready to reappear if and when English interference in colonial life was perceived again to threaten.

By the fourth decade of the eighteenth century, the very same decade in which revival broke forth in Northampton and the Middle Colonies, ministerial radar had begun picking up new evidences of this threat. And ironically, there were ideological linkages between the Awakening and the perceived threat of English interference in colonial affairs. Numerous secondary sources detail the nature of that linkage; perhaps the two most helpful are Alan Heimert's *Religion and the American Mind: From the Great Awakening to the Revolution* and Bernard Bailyn's *The Ideological Origins of the American Revolution*.

There were at least two ways in which the Awakening contributed to the cultural ethos that produced Mayhew's sermon. First, the Awakening solidified the sense of theological legitimacy in "casting off shackles" that were perceived to be hindrances to appropriate living. Among the many things that the Great Awakening meant in the development of American life was the destruction of the parish system. During the height of the Awakening, many Christians, perceiving that their own pastors were not fervent (or fervent *enough*) in supporting the Awakening, simply left their churches and started others. These new churches were, in many cases, geographically quite close to those that had been left behind, and most often they were regarded to be of the same denomination as the original churches (though the language of denominationalism is somewhat anachronistic when applied to mid-eighteenth-century America). It was this very phenomenon that so disturbed Rector Timothy Clap at Yale with respect to the visit to New Haven of George Whitefield, Gilbert Tennent, and James Davenport in 1741.

The point is that before the Awakening, simply leaving a church and starting a new one was a relatively rare phenomenon. One might compare the difference between pre- and post-Awakening churches in this area to the difference one sees today between committed evangelical Christians in the Church of England and committed evangelical Christians in one of the theologically conservative American Presbyterian churches. The former seem not to think of leaving and starting a new church as a genuine possibility even though major theological problems are perceived in their church. The latter, especially in light of the history of the groups that trace their ecclesiastical identity back to the mainline Presbyterian church of Princeton Theological Seminary, seem to regard leaving as a viable option whenever significant theological or ethical disputes arise.

The latter attitude toward ecclesiastical authority and church unity, at least in America, may be traced in large measure to the time of the Great

Awakening. Certainly this point can be overstated, but it can just as easily be overlooked. To be sure, the Pilgrims who settled Plymouth were Separatists. They proclaimed that they had left the Church of England. Not so the Puritans of Massachusetts Bay. They, and the huge influence they exerted on early American culture, were much more committed to staying within and working to change the system. This is why John Winthrop and those he led to Boston regarded themselves as continuing members of the Church of England. This is why the charter was so important to them—it gave them the official legitimacy to work, as loyal Englishmen and Englishwomen, to bring about the necessary change in England and in the Church of England.

But the Great Awakening changed things. It began to be more widely perceived than ever before that challenges to an establishment (ecclesiastical or political) could be the legitimate, even the *necessary*, expression of obedience to God. The Awakening simply bred in American Christians a new spirit of separatism, and Jonathan Mayhew capitalized on this new spirit mightily. He also gave it a sort of exegetical defense that was taken up and used over and over again by other American preachers both in the eighteenth century and ever since.

But there is another, and even more direct, linkage between the Awakening and the ideas expressed in "Unlimited Submission." Mayhew himself was actually an opponent of the Awakening, much in the tradition of Charles Chauncy, against whom Jonathan Edwards wrote so powerfully. But Mayhew tapped into a subtle but growing religious sentiment among Awakening supporters. While not precisely accurate and while belied by George Whitefield's own ecclesiastical affiliation, many of the supporters of the Awakening perceived that opposition to this great work of God emanated largely and most influentially from the established Anglican church.

Mayhew chose to preach his sermon on January 30, 1750, the hundred and first anniversary of the execution of King Charles I of England. Indeed, Mayhew himself points this out in the epilogue to the sermon. It is not just *any* authority to which the Scriptures may direct disobedience. It is specifically *English* authority, in both church and state, that thoughtful Christians may be called to disobey. Mayhew, like any other good preacher, was very aware of the situation into which he was preaching. He knew how to build upon both the historical occasion and the developing cultural consensus. And even with his questionable theology, he was able—and he remains able—to touch the hearts and minds of many American Christians.

John Adams, the second President of the United States, in a letter to Hezekiah Niles in 1818, made this powerful statement:

> What do we mean by the American Revolution? Do we mean the American War? The Revolution was effected before the War commenced. The Revolution was in the hearts and minds of the people; a change in their religious sentiments. . . . This radical change in the principles, opinions, sentiments, and affections of the people was the real American Revolution.[2]

Many eighteenth-century Christians who might have rejected Mayhew's theology nevertheless embraced his interpretation of Romans 13, and this fact helps to explain the "real" American Revolution (at least as defined by John Adams). Many twenty-first-century Christians who might also reject Mayhew's theology seem likewise to have embraced his handling of Romans 13, and one can only wonder what all this might help to explain. While it is true, as Edwards pointed out, that "we need not reject all truth which is demonstrated by clear evidence merely because it was once held by some bad man,"[3] still there are possible linkages that might raise real problems.

Here, as with Tennent's sermon but for entirely different reasons, one might apply the principles of Edwards's "distinguishing marks." To what degree, in his exegesis, is Mayhew genuinely God-centered? To what degree does he seem to be allowing his passion for liberty to predetermine his conclusions about the biblical text? These are questions that should probably be asked of *any* Reformed sermon, but they certainly must be asked of a sermon like this, which really did help to shape America.

---

2. Quoted by Sydney Ahlstrom in *A Religious History of the American People* (New Haven: Yale University Press, 1972), 262.

3. Jonathan Edwards, *A Careful and Strict Inquiry into the Modern Prevailing Notions of That Freedom of the Will Which Is Supposed to Be Essential to Moral Agency, Virtue and Vice, Reward and Punishment, Praise and Blame*, in *The Works of Jonathan Edwards*, vol. 1 (Edinburgh: Banner of Truth Trust, 1974), 69.

Discourse Concerning Unlimited Submission and Non-Resistance to the Higher Powers

Jonathan Mayhew

Let every soul be subject unto the higher powers. For there is no power but of God; the powers that be are ordained of God. Whoever therefore resists the power resists the ordinance of God, and they that resist shall receive to themselves damnation. For rulers are not a terror to good works, but to the evil. Will you then not be afraid of the power? Do that which is good, and you shall have praise of the same: For he is the minister of God to you for good. But if you do that which is evil, be afraid, for he bears not the sword in vain, for he is the minister of God, a revenger to execute wrath upon him that does evil. Therefore, you must needs be subject not only for wrath, but also for conscience' sake.

For this cause pay you tribute also, for they are God's ministers, attending continually upon this very thing. Render therefore to all their dues: tribute to whom tribute is due, custom to whom custom, fear to whom fear, honor to whom honor.
(Rom. 13:1–7)

I t is evident that the affair of civil government may properly fall under a moral and religious consideration, at least so far forth as it relates to the general nature and end of magistracy and to the grounds and extent of that submission which persons of a private character ought to yield to those who are vested with authority. This must be allowed by all who acknowledge the divine original of Christianity. For although there is a sense, and a very plain and important sense, in which Christ's "kingdom is not of this world" (John 18:36), his inspired apostles have nevertheless laid down some general principles concerning the office of civil rulers and the duty of subjects, together with the reason and obligation of that duty. And from hence it follows that it is proper for all who acknowledge the authority of Jesus Christ and the inspiration of his apostles to endeavor to understand what is in fact the doctrine which they have delivered concerning this matter. It is the duty of Christian magistrates to inform themselves what it is which their religion teaches concerning the nature and design of their office. And it is equally the duty of all Christian people to inform themselves what it is which their religion teaches concerning the subjection which they owe to the higher powers. It is for these reasons that I have attempted to examine into the Scripture account of this matter in order to lay it before you with the same freedom which I constantly use with relation to other doctrines and precepts of Christianity, not doubting that you will judge upon everything offered to your consideration with the same spirit of freedom and liberty with which it is spoken.

The passage read is the most full and express of any in the New Testament relating to rulers and subjects. And therefore I thought it proper to ground upon it what I had to propose to you with reference to the authority of the civil magistrate and the subjection which is due him. But before I enter upon an explanation of the several parts of this passage, it will be proper to observe one thing which may serve as a key to the whole of it.

It is to be observed, then, that there were some persons amongst the Christians of the apostolic age, and particularly those at Rome, to whom St. Paul is here writing, who seditiously disclaimed all subjection to civil authority, refusing to pay taxes and the duties laid upon their traffic and merchandise, and who scrupled not to speak of their rulers without any due regard to their office and character. Some of these turbulent Christians were converts from Judaism, and others from paganism. The Jews in general had long before this time taken up a strange conceit that, being the peculiar and elect people of God, they were therefore exempted from the jurisdiction of any heathen princes or governors. Upon this ground it was that some of them, during the public ministry of our blessed Savior, came to him with the question: Is it lawful to give tribute unto Caesar or not (see Matt. 22:17)? And this notion many of them retained after they were proselyted to the Christian faith. As to the Gentile converts, some of them grossly mistook the nature of that liberty which the gospel promised and thought that by virtue of their subjection to Christ, the only King and Head of his church, they were wholly freed from subjection to any other prince—as though Christ's kingdom had been of this world in such a sense as to interfere with the civil powers of the earth and to deliver their subjects from that allegiance and duty which they before owed to them. Of these visionary Christians in general who disowned subjection to the civil powers in being where they respectively lived, there is mention made in several places in the New Testament. The apostle Peter in particular characterizes them in this manner: "them that . . . despise government—presumptuous are they, self-willed; they are not afraid to speak evil of dignities" (2 Peter 2:10). Now it is with reference to these doting Christians that the apostle speaks in the passage before us. And I shall now give you the sense of it in a paraphrase upon each verse in its order, desiring you to keep in mind the character of the persons for whom it is designed, so that, as I go along, you may see how just and natural this address is and how well suited to the circumstances of those against whom it is leveled.

The apostle begins thus: "Let every soul[4] be subject unto the higher powers.[5] For there is no power[6] but of God; the powers that be[7] are ordained of

---

4. *Every soul.* This is a Hebraism which signifies *every man,* so that the apostle does not exempt the clergy who were endowed with the gift of prophecy or any other miraculous powers which subsisted in the church at that day. And by his using the Hebrew idiom, it seems that he had the Jewish converts principally in his eye.

5. *The higher powers:* more literally, the *ruling powers.* This term extends to all civil rulers in common.

6. By *power,* the apostle intends not lawless strength and brutal force, without regulation or proper direction, but just authority; for so the word here used properly signifies. There may be power where there is no authority. No man has any authority to do what is wrong and injurious, though he may have power to do it.

7. *The powers that be:* those persons who are in fact vested with authority; those who are

God[8]" (Rom. 13:1). Whereas some professed Christians vainly imagine that they are wholly excused from all manner of duty and subjection to civil authority, refusing to honor their rulers and to pay taxes (which opinion is not only unreasonable in itself, but also tends to fix a lasting reproach upon the Christian name and profession), I now as an apostle and ambassador of Christ exhort every one of you, be he who he will, to pay all dutiful submission to those who are vested with any civil office. For there is, properly speaking, no authority but what is derived from God, as it is only by his permission and providence that any possess it. Yea, I may add that all civil magistrates, as such, although they may be heathens, are appointed and ordained of God. For it is certainly God's will that so useful an institution as that of magistracy should take place in the world for the good of civil society.

The apostle proceeds: "Whoever therefore resists the power resists the ordinance of God, and they that resist shall receive to themselves damnation" (v. 2). Think not, therefore, that you are guiltless of any crime or sin against God when you factiously disobey and resist the civil authority. For magistracy and government being, as I have said, the ordinance and appointment of God, it follows that to resist magistrates in the execution of their offices is really to resist the will and ordinance of God himself. And they who thus resist will accordingly be punished by God for this sin in common with others.

The apostle goes on: "For rulers are not a terror to good works, but to the evil.[9] Will you then not be afraid of the power? Do that which is good, and

---

in possession. And who those are the apostle leaves Christians to determine for themselves; but whoever they are, they are to be obeyed.

8. *Ordained of God:* it is not without God's providence and permission that any are clothed with authority, and it is agreeable to the positive will and purpose of God that there should be some persons vested with authority for the good of society—not that any rulers have their commission immediately from God the supreme Lord of the universe. If any assert that kings or any other rulers are ordained of God in the latter sense, it is incumbent upon them to show the commission which they speak of under the broad seal of heaven. And when they do this, they will no doubt be believed.

9. *For rulers are not a terror to good works, but to the evil.* It cannot be supposed that the apostle designs here, or in any of the succeeding verses, to give the true character of Nero or any other civil powers then in being as if they were in fact such persons as he describes, a terror to evil works only and not to the good. For such a character did not belong to them;

you shall have praise of the same. For he is the minister of God to you for good" (vv. 3–4a). That you may see the truth and justness of what I assert (that magistracy is the ordinance of God, and that you sin against him in opposing it), consider that even pagan rulers are not, by the nature and design of their office, enemies and a terror to the good and virtuous actions of men, but only to the injurious and mischievous to society. Will you not, then, reverence and honor magistracy when you see the good end and intention of it? How can you be so unreasonable? Only mind to do your duty as members of society, and this will gain you the applause and favor of all good rulers. For while you do thus, they are, by their office as ministers of God, obliged to encourage and protect you; it is for this very purpose that they are clothed with power.

The apostle subjoins: "But if you do that which is evil, be afraid, for he bears not the sword in vain, for he is the minister of God, a revenger to execute wrath upon him that does evil"[10] (v. 4b). But upon the other hand, if you refuse to do your duty as members of society, if you refuse to bear your part in the support of government, if you are disorderly and do things which merit civil chastisement, then indeed you have reason to be afraid. For it is not in vain that rulers are vested with the power of inflicting punishment. They are, by their office, not only the ministers of God for good to

---

and the apostle was no sycophant or parasite of power, whatever some of his pretended successors have been. He only tells what rulers would be, provided they acted up to their character and office.

10. It is manifest that when the apostle speaks of it as the office of civil rulers to encourage what is good and to punish what is evil, he speaks only of civil good and evil. They are to consult the good of society as such, not to dictate in religious concerns, not to make laws for the government of men's consciences and to inflict civil penalties for religious crimes. It is sufficient to overthrow the doctrine of the authority of the civil magistrate in affairs of the spiritual nature (so far as it is built upon anything which is here said by St. Paul, or upon anything else in the New Testament) only to observe that all the magistrates then in the world were heathen, implacable enemies to Christianity, so that to give them authority in religious matters would have been, in effect, to give them authority to extirpate the Christian religion and to establish the idolatries and superstitions of paganism. And can anyone reasonably suppose that the apostle had any intention to extend the authority of rulers beyond concerns merely civil and political to the overthrowing of that religion which he himself was so zealous in propagating! But it is natural for those whose religion cannot be supported upon the footing of reason and argument to have recourse to power and force, which will serve a bad cause as well as a good one, and indeed much better.

JONATHAN MAYHEW

those that do well, but also his ministers to revenge, to discountenance and punish those that are unruly and injurious to their neighbors.

The apostle proceeds: "Therefore, you must needs be subject not only for wrath, but also for conscience' sake" (v. 5). Since, therefore, magistracy is the ordinance of God, and since rulers are, by their office, benefactors to society by discouraging what is bad and encouraging what is good, and so preserving peace and order among men, it is evident that you ought to pay a willing subjection to them, not to obey merely for a fear of exposing your-selves to their wrath and displeasure, but also in point of reason, duty, and conscience. You are under an indispensable obligation, as Christians, to honor their office and to submit to them in the execution of it.

The apostle goes on: "For this cause pay you tribute also, for they are God's ministers, attending continually upon this very thing" (v. 6). And here is a plain reason also why you should pay tribute to them, for they are God's ministers, exalted above the common level of mankind—not that they may indulge themselves in softness and luxury and be entitled to the servile homage of their fellow men, but that they may execute an office no less laborious than honorable and attend continually upon the public wel-fare. This being their business and duty, it is but reasonable that they should be requited for their care and diligence in performing it and enabled, by taxes levied upon the subject, effectually to prosecute the great end of their institution: the good of society.

The apostle sums all up in the following words: "Render therefore to all their dues: tribute to whom tribute is due, custom[11] to whom custom, fear to whom fear, honor to whom honor" (v. 7). Let it not, therefore, be said of any of you hereafter that you contemn government, to the reproach of yourselves and of the Christian religion. Neither your being Jews by nation nor your becoming the subjects of Christ's kingdom gives you any dispen-sation for making disturbances in the government under which you live. Approve yourselves, therefore, as peaceable and dutiful subjects. Be ready to pay to your rulers all that they may, in respect of their office, justly de-

---

11. Grotius observes that the Greek words here used [*tribute* and *custom*] answer to the *tributum* and *vectigal* of the Romans. The former was the money paid for the soil and poll; the latter, the duties laid upon some sorts of merchandise. And what the apostle here says deserves to be seriously considered by all Christians concerned in that common practice of carrying on an illicit trade and running of goods.

mand of you. Render tribute and custom to those of your governors to whom tribute and custom belong, and cheerfully honor and reverence all who are vested with civil authority, according to their deserts.

The apostle's doctrine in the passage thus explained concerning the office of civil rulers and the duty of subjects may be summed up in the following observations:[12]

That the end of magistracy is the good of civil society, as such;

That civil rulers, as such, are the ordinance and ministers of God, it being by his permission and providence that any bear rule and agreeable to his will that there should be some persons vested with authority in society for the well-being of it;

That which is here said concerning civil rulers extends to all of them in common: it relates indifferently to monarchical, republican, and aristocratical government; to all other forms which truly answer the sole end of government, the happiness of society; and to all the different degrees of authority in any particular state, to inferior officers no less than to the supreme;

That disobedience to civil rulers in the due exercise of their authority is not merely a political sin, but a heinous offense against God and religion;

That the true ground and reason[13] of our obligation to be subject to the higher powers is the usefulness of magistracy (when properly exercised) to human society, and its subserviency to the general welfare;

---

12. The several observations here only mentioned were handled at large in two preceding discourses upon this subject.

13. Some suppose the apostle in this passage enforces the duty of submission with two arguments quite distinct from each other, one taken from the consideration that rulers are the ordinance and the ministers of God (vv. 1, 2, 4) and the other from the benefits that accrue to society from civil government (vv. 3, 4, 6). And indeed these may be distinct motives and arguments for submission as they may be separately viewed and contemplated. But when we consider that rulers are the ordinance and the ministers of God only so far forth as they perform God's will by acting up to their office and character, and so by being benefactors to society, these make these arguments coincide and run up into one at last, at least so far that the former of them cannot hold good for submission where the latter fails. Put the supposition that any man bearing the title of a magistrate should exercise his power in such a manner as to have no claim to obedience by virtue of that argument which is founded upon the usefulness of magistracy, and you equally take off the force of the other argument also, which is founded upon his being the ordinance and the minister of God. For he is no longer God's ordinance and minister than he acts up to his office and character by exercis-

That obedience to civil rulers is here equally required under all forms of government which answer the sole end of government (the good of society) and to every degree of authority in any state, whether supreme or subordinate (from whence it follows that if unlimited obedience and non-resistance is here required as a duty under any one form of government, it is also required as a duty under all other forms, and as a duty to subordinate rulers as well as to the supreme);

And lastly, that those civil rulers to whom the apostle enjoins subjection are the persons in possession, the powers that be, those who are actually vested with authority.[14]

There is one very important and interesting point which remains to be inquired into; namely, the extent of that subjection to the higher powers which is here enjoined as a duty upon all Christians. Some have thought it warrantable and glorious to disobey the civil powers in certain circumstances and in cases of very great and general oppression, when humble remonstrances fail to have any effect; and, when the public welfare cannot be otherwise provided for and secured, to rise unanimously even against the sovereign himself in order to redress their grievances; to vindicate their natural and legal rights to break the yoke of tyranny and free themselves and posterity from inglorious servitude and ruin. It is upon this principle that many royal oppressors have been driven from their thrones into banishment and many slain by the hands of their subjects. It was upon this

---

ing his power for the good of society. This is, in brief, the reason why it is said above, in the singular number, *the true ground and reason*, etc. The use and propriety of this remark may possibly be more apparent in the progress of the argument concerning resistance.

14. This must be understood with this proviso: that they do not grossly abuse their power and trust, but exercise it for the good of those that are governed. Who these persons were, whether Nero, etc. or not, the apostle does not say, but leaves it to be determined by those to whom he writes. God does not interpose, in a miraculous way, to point out the persons who shall bear rule and to whom subjection is due. And as to the unalienable, indefeasible right of primogeniture, the Scriptures are entirely silent, or rather plainly contradict it, Saul being the first king among the Israelites and appointed to the royal dignity during his own father's lifetime, and he was succeeded, or rather superseded, by David, the last-born among many brethren. Now if God has not invariably determined this matter, it must, of course, be determined by men. And if it is determined by men, it must be determined either in the way of force or of compact. And which of these is the most equitable can be no question.

principle that Tarquin was expelled from Rome and Julius Caesar, the conqueror of the world and the tyrant of his country, cut off in the senate house. It was upon this principle that King Charles I was beheaded before his own banqueting house. It was upon this principle that King James II was made to fly that country which he aimed at enslaving. And upon this principle was the revolution brought about which has been so fruitful of happy consequences to Great Britain. But in opposition to this principle, it has often been asserted that the Scripture in general (and the passage under consideration in particular) makes all resistance to princes a crime in any case whatever. If they turn tyrants and become the common oppressors of those whose welfare they ought to regard with a paternal affection, we must not pretend to right ourselves, unless it is by prayers and tears and humble entreaties. And if these methods fail to procure redress, we must not have recourse to any other, but all suffer ourselves to be robbed and butchered at the pleasure of the Lord's anointed, lest we should incur the sin of rebellion and the punishment of damnation. For he has God's authority and commission to bear him out in the worst of crimes, so far that he may not be withstood or controlled. Now whether we are obliged to yield such an absolute submission to our prince or whether disobedience and resistance may not be justifiable in some cases, notwithstanding anything in the passage before us, is an inquiry in which we are all concerned; and this is the inquiry which is the main design of the present discourse.

Now there does not seem to be any necessity of supposing that an absolute, unlimited obedience, whether active or passive, is here enjoined merely for this reason: that the precept is delivered in absolute terms, without any exception or limitation expressly mentioned. We are enjoined in verse 1 to be "subject to the higher powers" and in verse 5 to be "subject for conscience' sake." And because these expressions are absolute and unlimited (or, more properly, general), some have inferred that the subjection required in them must be absolute and unlimited also, at least so far forth as to make passive obedience and non-resistance a duty in all cases whatever, if not active obedience likewise. Though, by the way, there is here no distinction made between active and passive obedience, and if either of them is required in an unlimited sense, the other must be required in the same sense also by virtue of the present argument, because the expressions are equally absolute with respect to both. But that unlimited obedience of any sort cannot be argued merely from the indefinite expressions in which obedience is enjoined appears from hence: that expressions of the same nature frequently occur in Scripture, upon which it is confessed on all hands that no such absolute and unlimited sense ought to be put. For example, "Love not the world, neither the things that are in the world (1 John 2:15); "Lay not up for yourselves treasures upon earth" (Matt. 6:19); "Take therefore no thought for the morrow" (Matt. 6:34) are precepts expressed in at least equally absolute and unlimited terms; but it is generally allowed that they are to be understood with certain restrictions and limitations, some degree of love to the world and the things of it being allowed. Nor, indeed, do the Right Reverend Fathers in God and other dignified clergymen of the established church seem to be altogether averse to admitting to restrictions in the latter case, however warm any of them may be against restrictions and limitations in the case of submission to authority, whether civil or ecclesiastical. It is worth remarking also that patience and submission under private injuries are enjoined in much more peremptory and absolute terms than any that are used with regard to submission to the injustice and oppression of civil rulers. Thus, "I say unto you that you resist not evil; but whoever shall smite you on the right cheek, turn to him the other also. And if any man will sue you at the law and take away your coat, let him have your cloak also. And whoever shall compel you to go a mile with him, go with him two" (Matt. 5:39–41). Any man may be defied to produce such strong expressions in favor of a passive and tame submission to unjust, tyrannical rulers as are here used to enforce submission to private injuries. But how few are there that understand those expressions literally? And the reason why they do not is because (with submission to the Quakers) common sense shows that they were not intended to so be understood.

But to give some Scripture precepts which are more directly to the point in hand: Children are commanded to obey their parents, and servants their masters, in as absolute and unlimited terms as subjects are here commanded to obey their civil rulers. Thus says this same apostle: "Children, obey your parents in the Lord, for this is right. Honor your father and mother (which is the first commandment with promise). . . . Servants, be obedient to them that are your masters according to the flesh, with fear and trembling, with singleness of your heart as unto Christ" (Eph. 6:1–2, 5). Thus also wives are commanded to be obedient to their husbands: "Wives, submit your-selves unto your own husbands as unto the Lord. For the husband is the head of the wife, even as Christ is the head of the church. . . . Therefore, as the church is subject unto Christ, so let the wives be to their own hus-bands in everything" (Eph. 5:22–24). In all these cases, submission is re-quired in terms at least as absolute and universal as are ever used with re-spect to rulers and subjects. But who supposes that the apostle ever intended to teach that children, servants, and wives should in all cases whatever obey their parents, masters, and husbands, respectively, never making any op-position to their will, even though they should require them to break the commandments of God or should causelessly make an attempt upon their lives? No one puts such a sense upon the expressions, however absolute and unlimited. Why then should it be supposed that the apostle designed to teach universal obedience, whether active or passive, to the higher pow-ers merely because his precepts are delivered in absolute and unlimited terms? And if this is a good argument in one case, why is it not in others also? If it is said that resistance and disobedience to the higher powers is here said positively to be a sin, so also is the disobedience of children to parents, servants to masters, and wives to husbands in other places of Scrip-ture. But the question still remains whether in all these cases there are not some exceptions. In the three latter, it is allowed there are. And from hence it follows that barely the use of absolute expressions is no proof that obe-dience to civil rulers is in all cases a duty or that resistance is in all cases a sin. I should not have thought it worthwhile to take any notice at all of this argument had it not been much insisted upon by some of the advo-cates for passive obedience and non-resistance. For it is, in itself, perfectly trifling and rendered considerable only by the stress that has been laid upon it for want of better.

There is, indeed, one passage in the New Testament where it may seem, at first view, that an unlimited submission to civil rulers is enjoined: "Sub-mit yourselves to every ordinance of man for the Lord's sake" (1 Peter 2:13). "To every ordinance of man," however, is no stronger than that before taken notice of with relation to the duty of wives: "So let the wives be subject to their own husbands in everything." But the true solution of this difficulty (if it is one) is this: by "every ordinance of man" is not meant every com-mand of the civil magistrate without exception, but "every order of magistrates appointed by man," whether superior or inferior. For so the apostle explains himself in the very next words: "Whether it be to the king as supreme, or to governors, as unto them that are sent, etc." But although the apostle had not subjoined any such explanation, the reason of the thing itself would have obliged us to limit the expression [every ordinance of man] to such human ordinances and commands as are not inconsistent with the ordinances and commands of God, the supreme lawgiver; or with any other higher, and antecedent, obligations.

It is to be observed in the next place that as the duty of universal obedience and non-resistance to the higher powers cannot be argued from the absolute unlimited expressions which the apostle here uses, so neither can it be argued from the scope and drift of his reasoning considered with relation to the persons he was here opposing. As was observed above, there were some professed Christians in the apostolic age who disclaimed all magistracy and civil authority in general, despising government and speaking evil of dignities, some under a notion that Jews ought not to be under the jurisdiction of Gentile rulers and others that they were set free from the temporal powers by Christ. Now it is with persons of this licentious opinion and character that the apostle is concerned. And all that was directly to his point was to show that they were bound to submit to magistracy in general. This is a circumstance very material to be taken notice of in order to ascertain the sense of the apostle. For this being considered, it is sufficient to account for all that he says concerning the duty of subjection and the sin of resistance to the higher powers without having recourse to the doctrine of unlimited submission and passive obedience in all cases whatever. Were it known that those in opposition to whom the apostle wrote allowed of civil authority in general, and only asserted that there were some cases in which obedience and non-resistance were not a duty, there would then indeed be reason for interpreting this passage as containing the doctrine of unlimited obedience and non-resistance, as it must in this case be supposed to have been leveled against such as denied that doctrine. But since it is certain that there were persons who vainly imagined that civil government in general was not to be regarded by them, it is most reasonable to suppose that the apostle designed his discourse only against them. And agreeably to this supposition, we find that he argues the usefulness of civil magistracy in general, its agreeableness to the will and purpose of God, who is over all, and so deduces from hence the obligation of submission to it. But it will not follow that because civil government is, in general, a good institution and necessary to the peace and happiness of human society, therefore there are no supposable cases in which resistance to it can be innocent. So the duty of unlimited obedience, whether active or passive, can be argued neither from the manner of expression here used nor from the general scope and design of the passage.

And if we attend to the nature of the argument with which the apostle here enforces the duty of submission to the higher powers, we shall find it to be such a one as concludes not in favor of submission to all who bear the title of rulers in common, but only to those who actually perform the duty of rulers by exercising a reasonable and just authority for the good of human society. This is a point which it will be proper to enlarge upon, because the question before us turns very much upon the truth or falsehood of this position. It is obvious, then, in general that the civil rulers whom the apostle here speaks of, and the obedience to whom he presses upon Christians as a duty, are good rulers,[15] such as are, in the exercise of their office and power, benefactors to society. Such they are described to be throughout this passage. Thus it is said that they are not "a terror to good works, but to the evil"; that they are "God's ministers for good, revengers to execute wrath upon him that does evil"; and that "they attend continually upon this very thing." St. Peter gives the same account of rulers: They are "for a praise to them that do well, and the punishment of evildoers" (1 John 2:15).[16] It is manifest that this character and description of rulers agrees only to such as are rulers in fact as well as in name: to such as govern well and act agreeably to their office. And the apostle's argument for submission to rulers is wholly built and grounded upon a presumption that they do in fact answer this character, and is of no force at all upon supposition of the contrary. If "rulers are a terror to good works, and not to the evil"; if they are not "ministers for good to society," but for evil and distress, by violence and oppression; if they execute wrath upon sober, peaceable persons who do their duty as members of society, and suffer rich and honorable knaves to escape with

---

15. By good rulers are not intended such as are good in a moral or religious, but only in a political, sense: those who perform their duty so far as their office extends and so far as civil society, as such, is concerned in their actions.

16. Reference should be 1 Peter 2:14. Also, see note 14.

impunity; if, instead of attending continually upon the good work of advancing the public welfare, they attend only upon the gratification of their own lust and pride and ambition, to the destruction of the public welfare—if this is the case, it is plain that the apostle's argument for submission does not reach them; they are not the same, but different persons from those whom he characterizes and who must be obeyed according to his reasoning. Let me illustrate the apostle's argument by the following similitude (it is no matter how far it is from anything which has, in fact, happened in the world): Suppose, then, that it were allowed in general that the clergy were a useful order of men, that they ought to be "esteemed very highly in love for their work's sake" (1 Thess. 5:13) and to be decently supported by those whom they serve, "the laborer being worthy of his reward" (1 Tim. 5:18). Suppose further that a number of Reverend and Right Reverend Drones who worked not, who preached perhaps but once a year, and then not the gospel of Jesus Christ but the divine right of tithes, the dignity of their office as ambassadors of Christ, the equity of sinecures, and a plurality of benefices, the excellency of the devotions in that prayer book which some of them hired chaplains to use for them, or some favorite point of church tyranny and anti-Christian usurpation—suppose such men as these, spending their lives in effeminacy, luxury, and idleness (or, when they were not idle, doing that which is worse than idleness), should, merely by the merit of ordination and consecration and a peculiar, odd habit, claim great respect and reverence from those whom they civilly called the "beasts of the laity"[17] and demand thousands per annum for that good service which they never performed and for which, if they had performed it, this would be much more than a *quantum meruit*. Suppose this should be the case (it is only by way of simile, and surely it will give no offense); would not everybody be astonished at such insolence, injustice, and impiety? And ought not such men to be told plainly that they could not reasonably expect the esteem and reward due to the ministers of the gospel unless they did the duties of their office? Should they not be told that their title and habit claimed no regard, reverence, or pay separate from the care and work and various duties of their function? And that while they neglected the latter, the former served only to render them the more ridiculous and contemptible? The application of this similitude to the case in hand is very

---

17. Mr. Leslie.

easy. If those who bear the title of civil rulers do not perform the duty of civil rulers, but act directly counter to the sole end and design of their office, if they injure and oppress their subjects instead of defending their rights and doing them good, they have not the least pretense to be honored, obeyed, and rewarded, according to the apostle's argument. For his reasoning, in order to show the duty of subjection to the higher powers, is, as was before observed, built wholly upon the supposition that they do in fact perform the duty of rulers.

If it is said that the apostle here uses another argument for submission to the higher powers besides that which is taken from the usefulness of their office to civil society when properly discharged and executed—namely, that their power is from God, that they are ordained of God, and that they are God's ministers—and if it is said that this argument for submission to them will hold good although they do not exercise their power for the benefit but for the ruin and destruction of human society, this objection was obviated, in part, before (see Matt. 5:39–41). Rulers have no authority from God to do mischief. They are not God's ordinance or God's ministers in any other sense than as it is by his permission and providence that they are exalted to bear rule, and as magistracy duly exercised and authority rightly applied in the enacting and executing good laws. Laws tempered and accommodated to the common welfare of the subjects must be supposed to be agreeable to the will of the beneficent author and supreme Lord of the universe, whose "kingdom rules over all" (Ps. 103:19) and whose "tender mercies are over all his works" (Ps. 145:9). It is blasphemy to call tyrants and oppressors God's ministers. They are more properly called "the messengers of Satan to buffet us" (2 Cor. 12:7). No rulers are properly God's ministers but such as are "just, ruling in the fear of God" (2 Sam. 23:3). When once magistrates act contrary to their office and the end of their institution, when they rob and ruin the public instead of being guardians of its peace and welfare, they immediately cease to be the ordinance and ministers of God and no more deserve that glorious character than common pirates and highwaymen. So that whenever that argument for submission fails, which is grounded upon the usefulness of magistracy to civil society (as it always does when magistrates do hurt to society instead of good), the other argument, which is taken from their being the ordinance of God, must necessarily fail also, no person of a civil character being God's minister, in the sense of the apostle, any further than he performs God's will by exercising a just and reasonable authority and ruling for the good of the subject.

This is in general. Let us now trace the apostle's reasoning in favor of submission to the higher powers a little more particularly and exactly. For by this it will appear, on one hand, how good and conclusive it is for submission to those rulers who exercise their power in a proper manner and, on the other, how weak and trifling and unconnected it is if it is supposed to be meant by the apostle to show the obligation and duty of obedience to tyrannical, oppressive rulers in common with others of a different character.

The apostle enters upon his subject thus: "Let every soul be subject unto the higher powers. For there is no power but of God; the powers that be are ordained of God" (Rom. 13:1). Here he urges the duty of obedience from this topic of argument: that civil rulers, as they are supposed to fulfill the pleasure of God, are the ordinance of God. But how is this an argument for obedience to such rulers as do not perform the pleasure of God by doing good, but the pleasure of the devil by doing evil, and such as are not, therefore, God's ministers but the devil's! "Whoever therefore resists the power resists the ordinance of God, and they that resist shall receive to themselves damnation"(Rom. 13:2). Here the apostle argues that those who resist a reasonable and just authority, which is agreeable to the will of God, do really resist the will of God himself and will therefore be punished by him. But how does this prove that those who resist a lawless, unreasonable power, which is contrary to the will of God, do therein resist the will and ordinance of God? Is resisting those who resist God's will the same thing as resisting God? Or shall those who do so "receive to themselves damnation? For rulers are not a terror to good works, but to the evil. Will you then not be afraid of the power? Do that which is good, and you shall have praise of the same: For he is the minister of God to you for good"(Rom. 13:3–4a). Here the apostle argues more explicitly than he had before done for revering and submitting to magistracy from this consideration: that such as really performed the duty of magistrates would be enemies only to the evil actions of men and would befriend and encourage the good, and so be a common blessing to society. But how is this an argument: that we must honor and submit to such magistrates as are not enemies to the evil actions of men but to the good, and such as are not a common blessing but a common curse to society! "But if you do that which is evil, be afraid, for he bears not the sword in vain, for he is the minister of God, a revenger to execute wrath upon him that does evil" (Rom. 13:4b). Here the apostle argues from the nature and end of magistracy that such as did evil (and such only) had reason to be afraid of the higher powers, it being part of their office to punish evildoers no less than to defend and encourage such as do well. But if magistrates are unrighteous, if they are respecters of persons, if they are partial in their administration of justice, then those who do well have as much reason to be afraid as those that do evil; there can be no safety for the good nor any peculiar ground of terror to the unruly and injurious. So that in this case, the main end of civil government will be frustrated. And what reason is there for submitting to that government which does by no means answer the design of government? "Therefore, you must needs be subject not only for wrath, but also for conscience' sake" (Rom. 13:5). Here the apostle argues the duty of a cheerful and conscientious submission to civil government from the nature and end of magistracy as he had before laid it down, i.e., as the design of it was to punish evildoers and to support and encourage such as do well, and as it must, if so exercised, be agreeable to the will of God. But how does what he here says prove the duty of a cheerful and conscientious subjection to those who forfeit the character of rules, to those who encourage the bad and discourage the good? The argument here used no more proves it to be a sin to resist such rulers than it does to resist the devil, that he may "flee from us" (James 4:7). For one is as truly the minister of God as the other. "For this cause pay you tribute also, for they are God's ministers, attending continually upon this very thing" (Rom. 13:6). Here the apostle argues the duty of paying taxes from this consideration: that those who perform the duty of rulers are continually attending upon the public welfare. But how does this argument conclude for paying taxes to such princes as are continually endeavoring to ruin the public? And especially when such payment would facilitate and promote this wicked design! "Render therefore to all their dues: tribute to whom tribute is due, custom to whom custom, fear to whom fear, honor to whom honor" (Rom. 13:7). Here the apostle sums up what he had been saying concerning the duty of subjects to rulers. And his argument stands thus: Since magistrates who execute their office well are common benefactors to society and may in that respect be properly styled the "ministers and ordinance of

God," and since they are constantly employed in the service of the public, it becomes you to pay them tribute and custom and to reverence, honor, and submit to them in the execution of their respective offices. This is apparently good reasoning. But does this argument conclude for the duty of paying tribute, custom, reverence, honor, and obedience to such persons as (although they bear the title of rulers) use all their power to hurt and injure the public? Such as are not God's ministers, but Satan's? Such as do not take care of and attend upon the public interest, but their own, to the ruin of the public? That is, in short, to such as have no natural and just claim at all to tribute, custom, reverence, honor, and obedience? It is to be hoped that those who have any regard to the apostle's character as an inspired writer, or even as a man of common understanding, will not represent him as reasoning in such a loose, incoherent manner, and drawing conclusions which have not the least relation to his premises. For what can be more absurd than an argument thus framed: "Rulers are, by their office, bound to consult the public welfare and the good of society; therefore, you are bound to pay them tribute, to honor and to submit to them, even when they destroy the public welfare and are a common pest to society by acting in direct contradiction to the nature and end of their office."

Thus, upon a careful review of the apostle's reasoning in this passage, it appears that his arguments to enforce submission are of such a nature as to conclude only in favor of submission to such rulers as he himself describes; i.e., such as rule for the good of society, which is the only end of their institution. Common tyrants and public oppressors are not entitled to obedience by virtue of anything here laid down by the inspired apostle.

I now add, further, that the apostle's argument is so far from proving it to be the duty of people to obey and submit to such rulers as act in contradiction to the public good,[18] and so to the design of their office, that it proves the direct contrary. For, please observe, if the end of all civil government is the good of society, if this is the thing that is aimed at in constituting civil rulers, and if the motive and argument for submission to government is taken from the apparent usefulness of civil authority, it follows that when no such

---

18. This does not intend their acting so in *a few particular instances*, which the best of rulers may do through mistake, etc., but their acting so habitually and in a manner which plainly shows that they aim at making themselves great by the ruin of their subjects.

good end can be answered by submission, there remains no argument or motive to enforce it. If, instead of this good end's being brought about by submission, a contrary end is brought about, and the ruin and misery of society effected by it, here is a plain and positive reason against submission in all such cases, should they ever happen. And therefore, in such cases, a regard to the public welfare ought to make us withhold from our rulers that obedience and subjection which it would otherwise be our duty to render to them. If it is our duty, for example, to obey our king merely because he rules for the public welfare (which is the only argument the apostle makes use of), it follows by a parity of reason that when he turns tyrant and makes his subjects his prey to devour and to destroy instead of his charge to defend and cherish, we are bound to throw off our allegiance to him and to resist, according to the tenor of the apostle's argument in this passage. Not to discontinue our allegiance in this case would be to join with the sovereign in promoting the slavery and misery of that society, the welfare of which we ourselves as well as our sovereign are indispensably obliged to secure and promote as far as in us lies. It is true that the apostle puts no case of such a tyrannical prince, but by his grounding his argument for submission wholly upon the good of civil society, it is plain he implicitly authorizes and even requires us to make resistance whenever this shall be necessary to the public safety and happiness. Let me make use of this easy and familiar similitude to illustrate the point in hand: Suppose God requires a family of children to obey their father and not to resist him and enforces his command with this argument: that the superintendence and care and authority of a just and kind parent will contribute to the happiness of the whole family, so that they ought to obey him for their own sakes more than for his. Suppose this parent at length runs distracted and attempts, in his mad fit, to cut all his children's throats. Now, in this case, is not the reason before assigned why these children should obey their parent while he continued of a sound mind, namely, their common good, a reason equally conclusive for disobeying and resisting him, since he is become delirious and attempts their ruin? It makes no alteration in the argument whether this parent, properly speaking, loses his reason or does, while he retains his understanding, that which is as fatal in its consequences as anything he could do, were he really deprived of it. This similitude needs no formal application.

But it ought to be remembered that if the duty of universal obedience and non-resistance to our king or prince can be argued from this passage, the same unlimited submission under a republican or any other form of government, and even to all the subordinate powers in any particular state, can be proved by it as well, which is more than those who allege it for the mentioned purpose would be willing should be inferred from it. So that this passage does not answer their purpose, but really overthrows and confuses it. This matter deserves to be more particularly considered. The advocates for unlimited submission and passive obedience do, if I mistake not, always speak with reference to kingly or monarchical government as distinguished from all other forms, and with reference to submitting to the will of the king in distinction from all subordinate officers acting beyond their commission and the authority which they have received from the Crown. It is not pretended that any persons besides kings have a divine right to do what they please so that no one may resist them without incurring the guilt of factiousness and rebellion. If any other supreme powers oppress the people, it is generally allowed that the people may get redress by resistance, if other methods prove ineffectual. And if any officers in a kingly government go beyond the limits of that power which they have derived from the Crown (the supposed original source of all power and authority in the state) and attempt, illegally, to take away the properties and lives of their fellow subjects, they may be forcibly resisted, at least till application can be made to the Crown. But as to the sovereign himself, he may not be resisted in any case, nor any of his officers, while they confine themselves within the bounds which he has prescribed to them. This is, I think, a true sketch of the principles of those who defend the doctrine of passive obedience and non-resistance. Now there is nothing in Scripture which supports this scheme of political principles. As to the passage under consideration, the apostle here speaks of civil rulers in general, of all persons in common vested with authority for the good of society, without any particular reference to one form of government more than to another, or to the supreme power in any particular state more than to subordinate powers. The apostle does not concern himself with the different forms of government.[19] This he supposes left entirely to human prudence and dis-

---

19. The essence of government (I mean good government; and this is the only government which the apostle treats in this passage) consists in the making and executing of good laws—laws tempered to the common felicity of the governed. And if this is in fact done, it

cretion. Now the consequence of this is that unlimited and passive obedience is no more enjoined in this passage under monarchical government or to the supreme power in any state than under all other species of government which answer the end of government, or to all the subordinate degrees of civil authority, from the highest to the lowest. Those, therefore, who would from this passage infer the guilt of resisting kings in all cases whatever, though acting ever so contrary to the design of their office, must, if they will be consistent, go much further and infer from it the guilt of resistance under all other forms of government and of resisting any petty officer in the state, though acting beyond his commission in the most arbitrary, illegal manner possible. The argument holds equally strong in both cases. All civil rulers, as such, are the ordinance and ministers of God; and they are all, by the nature of their office and in their respective spheres and stations, bound to consult the public welfare. With the same reason, therefore, that any deny unlimited and passive obedience to be here enjoined under a republic, aristocracy, or any other established form of civil government, or to subordinate powers acting in an illegal and oppressive manner (with the same reason), others may deny that such obedience is enjoined to a king, monarch, or any civil power whatever. For the apostle says nothing that is peculiar to kings; what he says extends equally to all other persons whatever, vested with any civil office. They are all, in exactly the same sense, the ordinance of God and the ministers of God, and obedience is equally enjoined to be paid to them all. For, as the apostle expresses it, "there is no power but of God," and we are required to "render to all their dues," and not more than their dues. And what these dues are, and to whom they are to be

---

is evidently, in itself, a thing of no consequence at all what the particular form of government is: whether the legislative and executive power is lodged in one and the same person or in different persons; whether in one person, whom we call an absolute monarch; whether in a few, so as to constitute an aristocracy; whether in many, so as to constitute a republic; or whether in three coordinate branches, in such manner as to make the government partake something of each of these forms and to be, at the same time, essentially different from them all. If the end is attained, it is enough. But no form of government seems to be so unlikely to accomplish this end as absolute monarchy. Nor is there anyone that has so little pretense to a divine original, unless it is in this sense: that God first introduced it into, and thereby overturned, the commonwealth of Israel as a curse upon that people for their folly and wickedness particularly in desiring such a government. (See 1 Sam. 8.) Just so God before sent quails among them as a plague and a curse, and not as a blessing (Num. 11).

rendered, the apostle says not, but leaves to the reason and consciences of men to determine.

Thus it appears that the common argument grounded upon this passage in favor of universal and passive obedience really overthrows itself by proving too much, if it proves anything at all; namely, that no civil officer is, in any case whatever, to be resisted, though acting in expressed contradiction to the design of his office—which no man in his senses ever did or can assert.

If we calmly consider the nature of the thing itself, nothing can well be imagined more directly contrary to common sense than to suppose that millions of people should be subjected to the arbitrary, precarious pleasure of one single man (who has naturally no superiority over them in point of authority) so that their estates and everything that is valuable in life, and even their lives also, shall be absolutely at his disposal if he happens to be wanton and capricious enough to demand them. What unprejudiced man can think that God made all to be thus subservient to the lawless pleasure and frenzy of one, so that it shall always be a sin to resist him! Nothing but the most plain and express revelation from heaven could make a sober, impartial man believe such a monstrous, unaccountable doctrine, and indeed the thing itself appears so shocking, so out of all proportion, that it may be questioned whether all the miracles that ever were wrought could make it credible that this doctrine really came from God. At present, there is not the least syllable in Scripture which gives any countenance to it. The hereditary, indefeasible, divine right of kings and the doctrine of non-resistance, which is built upon the supposition of such a right, are altogether as fabulous and chimerical as transubstantiation or any of the most absurd reveries of ancient or modern visionaries. These notions are fetched neither from divine revelation nor human reason; and if they are derived from neither of those sources, it is not much matter from whence they come or whither they go. Only it is a pity that such doctrines should be propagated in society to raise factions and rebellions, as we see they have in fact been both in the last and in the present reign.

But then, if unlimited submission and passive obedience to the higher powers in all possible cases is not a duty, it will be asked, "How far are we obliged to submit? If we may innocently disobey and resist in some cases, why not in all? Where shall we stop? What is the measure of our duty? This doctrine tends to the total dissolution of civil government and to introduce such scenes of wild anarchy and confusion as are more fatal to society than the worst of tyranny."

After this manner, some men object; and indeed, this is the most plausible thing that can be said in favor of such an absolute submission as they plead for. But the worst (or rather the best) of it is that there is very little strength or solidity in it. For similar difficulties may be raised with respect to almost every duty of natural and revealed religion. To instance only in two, both of which are near akin, and indeed exactly parallel, to the case before us: It is unquestionably the duty of children to submit to their parents, and of servants to their masters. But no one asserts that it is their duty to obey and submit to them in all supposable cases, or universally a sin to resist them. Now does this tend to subvert the just authority of parents and masters? Or to introduce confusion and anarchy into private families? No. How then does the same principle tend to unhinge the government of that larger family, the body politic? We know, in general, that children and servants are obliged to obey their parents and masters, respectively. We know also, with equal certainty, that they are not obliged to submit to them in all things without exception, but may in some cases reasonably, and therefore innocently, resist them. These principles are acknowledged upon all hands, whatever difficulty there may be in fixing the exact limits of submission. Now there is at least as much difficulty in stating the measure of duty in these two cases as in the cases of rulers and subjects. So this is really no objection, at least no reasonable one, against resistance to the higher powers. Or, if it is one, it will hold equally against resistance in the other cases mentioned. It is indeed true that turbulent, vicious-minded men may take occasion from the principle that their rulers may, in some cases, be lawfully resisted to raise factions and disturbances in the state and to make resistance where resistance is needless, and therefore sinful. But is it not equally true that children and servants of turbulent, vicious minds may take occasion from the principle that parents and masters may in some cases be lawfully resisted to resist when resistance is unnecessary, and therefore criminal? Is the principle in either case false in itself merely because it may be abused and applied to legitimate disobedience and resistance in those instances to which it ought not to be applied? According to this way of arguing, there will be no true principles in the world; for there are not but what may be wrested and perverted to serve bad purposes, either through the weakness or wickedness of men.[20]

A people really oppressed to a great degree by their sovereign cannot well be insensible when they are so oppressed. And such a people (if I may allude to an ancient fable) have, like the hesperian fruit, a dragon for their

---

20. We may very safely assert these two things in general, without undermining government: One is that no civil rulers are to be obeyed when they enjoin things that are inconsistent with the commands of God. All such disobedience is lawful and glorious, particularly if persons refuse to comply with any legal establishment of religion because it is a gross perversion and corruption (as to doctrine, worship, and discipline) of a pure and divine religion brought from heaven to earth by the Son of God (the only King and Head of the Christian church) and propagated through the world by his inspired apostles. All commands running counter to the declared will of the supreme legislator of heaven and earth are null and void, and therefore disobedience to them is a duty, not a crime. (See note 18.) Another thing that may be asserted with equal truth and safety is that no government is to be submitted to at the expense of that which is the sole end of all government—the common good and safety of society—because to submit in this case, if it should ever happen, would evidently be to set up the means as more valuable and above the end, than which there cannot be a greater solecism and contradiction. The only reason of the institution of civil government, and the only rational ground of submission to it, is the common safety and utility. If, therefore, in any case the common safety and utility would not be promoted by submission to government, but the contrary, there is no ground or motive for obedience and submission, but for the contrary.

Whoever considers the nature of civil government must indeed be sensible that a great degree of implicit confidence must unavoidably be placed in those that bear rule. This is implied in the very notion of authority's being originally a trust committed by the people to those who are vested with it, as all just and righteous authority is; all besides is mere lawless force and usurpation, neither God nor nature having given any man a right of dominion over any society independently of that society's approbation and consent to be governed by him. Now as all men are fallible, it cannot be supposed that the public affairs of any state should be always administered in the best manner possible, even by persons of the greatest wisdom and integrity. Nor is it sufficient to legitimate disobedience to the higher powers that they are not so administered or that they are in some instances very ill-managed, for upon this principle it is scarcely supposable that any government at all could be supported or subsist. Such a principle manifestly tends to the dissolution of government and to throw all things into confusion and anarchy. But it is equally evident, upon the other hand, that those in authority may abuse their trust and power to such a degree that neither the law of reason nor of religion requires that any obedience or submission should be paid

protector and guardian. Nor would they have any reason to mourn if some Hercules should appear to dispatch him. For a nation thus abused to arise unanimously and to resist their prince, even to the dethroning him, is not criminal, but a reasonable way of vindicating their liberties and just rights; it is making use of the means, and the only means, which God has put into their power for mutual and self-defense. And it would be highly criminal in them not to make use of this means. It would be stupid tameness and unaccountable folly for whole nations to suffer one unreasonable, ambitious, and cruel man to wanton and riot in their misery. And in such a case

to them; but, on the contrary, that they should be totally discarded and the authority which they were before vested with transferred to others, who may exercise it more to those good purposes to which it was given. Nor is this principle (that resistance to the higher powers is, in some extraordinary cases, justifiable) so liable to abuse as many persons seem to apprehend it. For although there will be always some petulant, querulous men in every state—men of factious, turbulent, and carping dispositions, glad to lay hold of any trifle to justify and legitimate their caballing against their rulers, and other seditious practices—yet there are, comparatively speaking, but few men of this contemptible character. It does not appear but that mankind, in general, have a disposition to be as submissive and passive and tame under government as they ought to be. Witness a great, if not the greatest, part of the known world, who are now groaning but not murmuring under the heavy yoke of tyranny! While those who govern do it with any tolerable degree of moderation and justice, and in any good measure act up to their office and character by being public benefactors, the people will generally be easy and peaceable and be rather inclined to flatter and adore than to insult and resist them. Nor was there ever any general complaint against any administration which lasted long but what there was good reason for. Till people find themselves greatly abused and oppressed by their governors, they are not apt to complain; and whenever they do, in fact, find themselves thus abused and oppressed, they must be stupid not to complain. To say that subjects in general are not proper judges when their governors oppress them and play the tyrant, and when they defend their rights, administer justice impartially, and promote the public welfare, is as great treason as ever man uttered—'tis treason, not against one single man, but the state, against the whole body politic; 'tis treason against mankind; 'tis treason against common sense; 'tis treason against God. And this impious principle lays the foundation for justifying all the tyranny and oppression that ever any prince was guilty of. The people know for what end they set up and maintain their governors, and they are the proper judges when they execute their trust as they ought to do it; when their prince exercises an equitable and paternal authority over them; when from a prince and common father he exalts himself into a tyrant; when from subjects and children he degrades them into the class of slaves, plunders them, makes them his prey, and unnaturally sports himself with their lives and fortunes.

Jonathan Mayhew

it would, of the two, be more rational to suppose that they that did *not* resist than that they who did would receive to themselves damnation.

OF KING CHARLES'S SAINTSHIP AND MARTYRDOM

And this naturally brings us to make some reflections upon the resistance which was made about a century since to that unhappy prince, King Charles I, and upon the anniversary of his death. This is a point which I should not have concerned myself about were it not that some men continue to speak of it, even to this day, with a great deal of warmth and zeal and in such a manner as to undermine all the principles of liberty, whether civil or religious, and to introduce the most abject slavery both in church and state, so that it is become a matter of universal concern. What I have to offer upon this subject will be comprised in a short answer to the following queries:

For what reason was the resistance to King Charles I made?

By whom was it made?

Was this resistance rebellion[21] or not?

How did the anniversary of King Charles's death come at first to be solemnized as a day of fasting and humiliation?

And lastly, why do those of the Episcopal clergy who are very high in the principles of ecclesiastical authority continue to speak of this unhappy man as a great saint and martyr?

For what reason, then, was the resistance to King Charles made? The general answer to this inquiry is that it was on account of the tyranny and oppression of his reign. Not a great while after his ascension to the throne, he married a French Catholic, and with her seemed to have wedded the politics if not the religion of France also. For afterwards, during a reign— or rather a tyranny—of many years, he governed in a perfectly wild and arbitrary manner, paying no regard to the constitution and laws of the kingdom, by which the power of the Crown was limited, or to the solemn oath which he had taken at his coronation. It would be endless, as well as need-

---

21. I speak of rebellion, treason, saintship, martyrdom, etc. throughout this discourse only in the scriptural and theological sense. I know not how the law defines them, the study of that not being my employment.

less, to give a particular account of all the illegal and despotic measures which he took in his administration—partly from his own natural lust of power, and partly from the influence of wicked councilors and ministers. He committed many illustrious members of both houses of Parliament to the tower for opposing his arbitrary schemes. He levied many taxes upon the people without consent of Parliament, and then imprisoned great numbers of the principal merchants and gentry for not paying them. He erected, or at least revived, several new and arbitrary courts, in which the most unheard-of barbarities were committed with his knowledge and approbation. He supported that more than fiend, Archbishop Laud and the clergy of his stamp, in all their church-tyranny and hellish cruelties. He authorized a book in favor of sports upon the Lord's Day, and several clergymen were persecuted by him and the mentioned pious bishop for not reading it to the people after divine service. When the Parliament complained to him of the arbitrary proceedings of his corrupt ministers, he told that august body, in a rough, domineering, unprincely manner, that he wondered how anyone should be so foolish and insolent as to think that he would part with the meanest of his servants upon their account. He refused to call any Parliament at all for the space of twelve years together, during all of which time he governed in an absolutely lawless and despotic manner. He took all opportunities to encourage the papists and to promote them to the highest offices of honor and trust. He (probably) abetted the horrid massacre in Ireland, in which two hundred thousand Protestants were butchered by the Roman Catholics. He sent a large sum of money, which he had raised by his arbitrary taxes, into Germany to raise foreign troops, in order to force more arbitrary taxes upon his subjects. He not only by a long series of actions, but also in plain terms, asserted an absolutely uncontrollable power, saying even in one of his speeches to Parliament that as it was blasphemy to dispute what God might do, so it was sedition in subjects to dispute what the king might do. Towards the end of his tyranny, he came to the House of Commons with an armed force[22] and demanded five of its principal members to be delivered up to him. And this was a prelude to that unnatural war which he soon after levied against his own dutiful subjects, whom

---

22. Historians are not agreed on what number of soldiers attended him in this monstrous invasion of the privileges of Parliament. Some say 300, some 400, and the author of *The History of the Kings of Scotland* says 500.

he was bound by all the laws of honor, humanity, piety, and, I might add, of interest also to defend and cherish with a paternal affection. I have only time to hint at these facts in a general way, all of which, and many more of the same tenor, may be proved by good authorities. So that the figurative language which St. John uses concerning the just and beneficent deeds of our blessed Savior may be applied to the unrighteous and execrable deeds of this prince: "And there are also many other things which King Charles did, the which, if they should be written every one, I suppose that even the world itself could not contain the books that should be written" (John 21:25). Now it was on account of King Charles's thus assuming a power above the laws, in direct contradiction to his coronation-oath and governing the greatest part of his time in the most arbitrary, oppressive manner—it was upon this account that the resistance was made to him which, at length, issued in the loss of his crown and of that head which was worthy to wear it.

But by whom was this resistance made? Not by a private junto; not by a small seditious party; not by a few desperadoes who, to mend their fortunes, would embroil the state; but by the lords and commons of England. It was they that almost unanimously opposed the king's measures for overturning the constitution and changing that free and happy government into a wretched, absolute monarchy. It was they that, when the king was about levying forces against his subjects in order to make himself absolute, commissioned officers, raised an army to defend themselves and the public. And it was they that maintained the war against him all along, till he was made prisoner. This is indisputable. Though it was not, properly speaking, the Parliament but the army which put him to death afterwards. And it ought to be freely acknowledged that most of their proceeding in order to get this matter effected, and particularly the court by which the king was at last tried and condemned, was little better than a mere mockery of justice.

The next question which naturally arises is whether this resistance which was made to the king by the Parliament was proper rebellion or not. The answer to this is plain, that it was not, but a most righteous and glorious stand, made in defense of the natural and legal rights of the people against the unnatural and illegal encroachments of arbitrary power. Nor was this a rash and too-sudden opposition. The nation had been patient under the oppressions of the Crown even to long suffering for a course of many years, and there was no rational hope of redress in any other way. Resistance was absolutely necessary in order to preserve the nation from slavery, misery, and ruin. And who so proper to make this resistance than the lords and commons: the whole representative body of the people, guardians of the public welfare, each of which was, in point of legislation, vested with an equal, coordinate power with that of the Crown?[23] Here were two branches of the legislature against one: two which had law and equity and the constitution on their side against one which was impiously attempting to overturn law and equity and the constitution and to exercise a licentious sov-

---

23. The English constitution is essentially free. The character which J. Caesar and Tacitus both give of the ancient Britons so long ago is that they were extremely jealous of their liberties, as well as a people of a martial spirit. Nor have there been wanting frequent instances and proofs of the same glorious spirit (in both respects) remaining in their posterity ever since in the struggles they have made for liberty, both against foreign and domestic tyrants. Their kings hold the title to the throne solely by grant of Parliament, i.e., in other words, by the voluntary consent of the people. And, agreeably hereto, the prerogative and rights of the Crown are stated, defined, and limited by law, and that as truly and strictly as the rights of any inferior officer in the state or, indeed, of any private subject. And it is only in this respect that it can be said that "the king can do no wrong." Being restrained by the law, he cannot, while he confines himself within those just limits which the law prescribes to him as the just measure of his authority, injure and oppress the subject. The king, in his coronation-oath, swears to exercise only such a power as the constitution gives him. And the subject, in the oath of allegiance, swears only to obey him in the exercise of such a power. The king is as much bound by his oath not to infringe the legal rights of the people as the people are bound to yield subjection to him. From this it follows that as soon as the prince sets himself up above the law, he loses the king in the tyrant; he does, to all intents and purposes, unking himself by acting out of and beyond that sphere which the constitution allows him to move in. And in such cases, he has no more right to be obeyed than any inferior officer who acts beyond his commission. The subject's obligation to allegiance then ceases, of course, and to resist him is no more rebellion than to resist any foreign invader. There is an essential difference between government and tyranny, at least under such a constitution as the English. The former conflicts in ruling according to law and equity, the latter in ruling contrary to law and equity. So also there is an essential difference between resisting a tyrant and rebellion. The former is a just and reasonable self-defense; the latter conflicts in resisting a prince whose administration is just and legal—and this is what denominates it a crime. Now it is evident that King Charles's government was illegal, and very oppressive, through the greatest part of his reign. And therefore, to resist him was no more rebellion than to oppose any foreign invader or any other domestic oppressor.

JONATHAN MAYHEW

ereignty over the properties, consciences, and lives of all the people, such a sovereignty as some inconsiderately ascribe to the Governor of the world. I say inconsiderately because God himself does not govern in an absolutely arbitrary and despotic manner. The power of this Almighty King (I speak not without caution and reverence; the power of this Almighty King) is limited by law; not, indeed, by acts of Parliament, but by the eternal laws of truth, wisdom, and equity and the everlasting tables of right reason— tables that cannot be repealed, or thrown down and broken like those of Moses. But King Charles set himself up above all these as much as he did above the written laws of the realm and made mere humor and caprice, which are no rule at all, the only rule and measure of his administration. And now, is it not perfectly ridiculous to call resistance to such a tyrant by the name of rebellion—the grand rebellion? Even that Parliament which brought King Charles II to the throne, and which ran loyally mad, severely reproved one of their own members for condemning the proceedings of that Parliament which first took up arms against the former king. And upon the same principles that the proceedings of this Parliament may be censured as wicked and rebellious, the proceedings of those who, since, opposed King James II and brought the prince of Orange to the throne may be censured as wicked and rebellious also. The cases are parallel. But whatever some men may think, it is to be hoped that, for their own sakes, they will not dare to speak against the revolution, upon the justice and legality of which depends (in part) his present majesty's right to the throne.

If it is said that although the Parliament which first opposed King Charles's measures and at length took up arms against him were not guilty of rebellion, yet certainly those persons were who condemned and put him to death, even this perhaps is not true. For he had, in fact, unkinged himself long before and had forfeited his title to the allegiance of the people. So those who put him to death were at most only guilty of murder, which, indeed, is bad enough, if they were really guilty of that (which is at least disputable). Cromwell and those who were principally concerned in the (nominal) king's death might possibly have been very wicked and designing men. Nor shall I say anything in vindication of the reigning hypocrisy of those times, or of Cromwell's maladministration during the interregnum (for it is truth, and not a party, that I am speaking for). But still it may be said that Cromwell and his adherents were not, properly speaking, guilty of rebellion because he whom they beheaded was not, properly speaking, their king but a lawless tyrant. Much less are the whole body of the nation at that time to be charged with rebellion on that account, for it was no national act; it was not done by a free Parliament. And much less still is the nation at present to be charged with the great sin of rebellion for what their ancestors did (or rather did not) a century ago.

But how came the anniversary of King Charles's death to be solemnized as a day of fasting and humiliation? The true answer in brief to that inquiry is that this fast was instituted by way of court and compliment to King Charles II upon the restoration. All were desirous of making their court to him, of integrating themselves, and of making him forget what had been done in opposition to his father, so as not to revenge it. To effect this, they ran into the most extravagant professions of affection and loyalty to him, insomuch as he himself said that it was a mad and harebrained loyalty which they professed. And among other strange things which his first Parliament did, they ordered the thirtieth of January (the day on which his father was beheaded) to be kept as a day of solemn humiliation, to deprecate the judgments of heaven for the rebellion which the nation had been guilty of, in that which was no national thing and which was not rebellion in them that did it. Thus they soothed and flattered their new king, at the expense of their liberties, and were ready to yield up freely to Charles II all that enormous power which they had justly resisted Charles I for usurping to himself.

The last query mentioned was why those of the Episcopal clergy who are very high in the principles of ecclesiastical authority continue to speak of this unhappy prince as a great saint and martyr? This, we know, is what they constantly do, especially upon the thirtieth of January, a day sacred to the extolling of him and to the reproaching of those who are not of the established church. "Out of the same mouth on this day proceed blessing and cursing" (James 3:8–10); "therewith bless they their God, even Charles, and therewith curse they the dissenters"; and their "tongue can no man tame; it is an unruly evil, full of deadly poison." King Charles is, upon this solemnity, frequently compared to our Lord Jesus Christ, both in respect of the holiness of his life and the greatness and injustice of his sufferings; and it is a wonder they do not add something concerning the merits of his death also. But *blessed saint* and *royal martyr* are as humble titles as any that are thought worthy of him.

Now this may, at first view, well appear to be a very strange phenomenon. For King Charles was really a man black with guilt and "laden with iniquity" (Isa. 1:4), as appears by his crimes before mentioned. He lived a tyrant, and it was the oppression and violence of his reign that brought him to his untimely and violent end at last. Now what of saintship or martyrdom is there in all this! What of saintship is there in encouraging people to profane the Lord's Day? What of saintship in falsehood and perjury? What of saintship in repeated robberies and depredations? What of saintship in throwing real saints and glorious patriots into goals? What of saintship in overturning an excellent civil constitution and proudly grasping at an illegal and monstrous power? What of saintship in the murder of thousands of innocent people and involving a nation in all the calamities of a civil war? And what of martyrdom is there in a man's bringing an immature and violent death upon himself by "being wicked overmuch" (Eccl. 7:17)? Is there any such thing as grace without goodness? As being a follower of Christ without following him? As being a disciple without learning of him to be just and beneficent? Or as saintship without sanctity?[24] If not, I fear it will be hard to prove this man a saint. And verily one would be apt to suspect that the church must be but poorly stocked with saints and martyrs which is forced to adopt such enormous sinners into her calendar in order to swell the number.

But to unravel this mystery of iniquity (as well as of nonsense), which has already worked for a long time among us (see 2 Thess. 2:7), or at least to give the most probable solution of it, it is to be remembered that King

---

24. Is it any wonder that even persons who do not *walk after their own lusts should scoff at such saints* as this, both in the *first* and in the *last days*, even *from everlasting to everlasting*? (2 Peter 3:3–4). But perhaps it will be said that these things are mysteries which (although very true in themselves) lay understandings cannot comprehend—or, indeed, any other persons among us, besides those who, being inwardly moved by the Holy Ghost, have taken a trip across the Atlantic to obtain Episcopal ordination and the indelible character. However, if these consecrated gentlemen do not quite despair of us, it is hoped that in the abundance of their charity, they will endeavor to elucidate these dark points and, at the same time, explain the creed of another of their eminent saints, which we are told that unless we believe faithfully (i.e., believingly) we cannot be saved—which creed (or rather riddle), notwithstanding all the labors of the pious and metaphysical Dr. Waterland, remains somewhat enigmatic still.

Charles, this burlesque upon saintship and martyrdom, though so great an oppressor, was a true friend to the church—so true a friend to her that he was very well affected towards the Roman Catholics and would probably have been very willing to unite Lambeth and Rome. This appears by his marrying a true daughter of that true "mother of harlots" (Rev. 17:5), which he did with a dispensation from the Pope, that supreme bishop, to whom when he wrote he gave the title of Most Holy Father. His queen was extremely bigoted to all the follies and superstitions and to the hierarchy of Rome and had a prodigious ascendancy over him all his life. It was in part owing to this that he (probably) abetted the massacre of the Protestants in Ireland; that he afflicted in extirpating the French Protestants at Rochelle; that he all along encouraged papists, and popishly effected clergymen, in preference to all other persons; and that he upheld that monster of wickedness, Archbishop Laud, and the bishops of his stamp, in all their church-tyranny and diabolical cruelties. In return to his kindness and indulgence in that respect, they caused many of the pulpits throughout the nation to ring with the divine absolute, indefeasible right of kings; with the praises of Charles and his reign; and with the damnable sin of resisting the Lord's anointed, let him do what he would. So that not Christ, but Charles, was commonly preached to the people. In plain English, there seems to have been an impious bargain struck up between the scepter and the surplice for enslaving both the bodies and souls of men. The king appeared to be willing that the clergy should do what they would—set up a monstrous hierarchy like that of Rome, a monstrous inquisition like that of Spain or Portugal, or anything else which their own pride and the devil's malice could prompt them to—provided always that the clergy would be tools to the Crown; that they would make the people believe that kings had God's authority for breaking God's law; that they had a commission from heaven to seize the estates and lives of their subjects at their pleasure; and that it was a damnable sin to resist them, even when they did such things as deserved more than damnation. This appears to be the true key for explaining the mysterious doctrine of King Charles's saintship and martyrdom. He was a saint not because he was in his life a good man, but a good churchman; not because he was a lover of holiness, but the hierarchy; not because he was a friend to Christ, but the Craft. And he was a martyr in his death not because he bravely suffered death in the cause of truth and righteousness, but because he died an enemy to liberty and the rights of conscience; i.e., not because he died an enemy to sin, but dissenters. For these reasons it is that all bigoted clergymen and friends to church-power paint this man as a saint in his life, though he was such a mighty, such a royal sinner; and as a martyr in his death, though he fell a sacrifice only to his own ambition, avarice, and unbounded lust of power. And from prostituting their praise upon King Charles, and offering him that incense which is not his due, it is natural for them to make a transition to the dissenters (as they commonly do) and to load them with that reproach which they do not deserve, they being generally professed enemies both to civil and ecclesiastical tyranny. We are commonly charged (upon the thirtieth of January) with the guilt of putting the king to death, under a notion that it was our ancestors that did it; and so we are represented in the blackest of colors, not only as schismatics, but also as traitors and rebels and all that is bad. And these lofty gentlemen usually rail upon this head in such a manner as plainly shows that they are either grossly ignorant of the history of those times which they speak of or, which is worse, that they are guilty of the most shameful prevarication, slander, and falsehood. But every petty priest with a roll and a gown thinks he must do something in imitation of his betters, in lawn, and show himself a true son of the church. And thus, through a foolish ambition to appear considerable, they only render themselves contemptible.

But suppose our forefathers did kill their mock saint and martyr a century ago; what is that to us now? If I mistake not, these gentlemen generally preach down the doctrine of the imputation of Adam's sin to his posterity as absurd and unreasonable, notwithstanding they have solemnly subscribed what is equivalent to it in their own articles of religion. And therefore one would hardly expect that they lay the guilt of the king's death upon us, although our forefathers had been the only authors of it. But this conduct is much more surprising when it does not appear that our ancestors had any more hand in it than their own. However, bigotry is sufficient to account for this and many other phenomena which cannot be accounted for in any other way.

Although the observation of this anniversary seems to have been (at least) superstitious in its original, and although it is often abused to very bad purposes by the established clergy as they serve themselves of it to perpetuate strife, a party spirit, and divisions in the Christian church, yet it is to be hoped that one good end will be answered by it, quite contrary to their intention: It is to be hoped that it will prove a standing memento that Britons will not be slaves, and a warning to all corrupt councilors and ministers not to go too far in advising to arbitrary, despotic measures.

To conclude: Let us learn to be free and to be loyal. Let us not profess ourselves vassals to the lawless pleasure of any man on earth. But let us remember, at the same time, government is sacred and not to be trifled with. It is our happiness to live under a government of a prince who is satisfied with ruling according to law, as every other good prince will. We enjoy under his administration all the liberty that is proper and expedient for us. It becomes us, therefore, to be contented and dutiful subjects. Let us prize our freedom, but not "use our liberty for a cloak of maliciousness" (1 Peter 2:16). There are men who strike at liberty under the term *licentiousness*. There are others who aim at popularity under the disguise of patriotism. Be aware of those. Extremes are dangerous. There is at present among us perhaps more danger of the latter than of the former. For that reason I would exhort you to pay all due regard to the government over us, to the king and all in authority, and to "lead a quiet and peaceable life" (1 Tim. 2:2). And while I am speaking of loyalty to our earthly prince, suffer me just to put you in mind to be loyal also to the supreme Ruler of the universe, "by whom kings reign and princes decree justice" (Prov. 8:15). To which eternal immortal, invisible, even to the only Wise God (1 Tim. 1:17) be all honor and praise, dominion and thanksgiving, through Jesus Christ our Lord. Amen.

7

The United States Elevated to Glory and Honor

Deuteronomy 26:19

EZRA STILES

Ezra Stiles (1727–95) was arguably the most famous American preacher of the latter half of the eighteenth century. He was clearly the most influential. The sense that the America presented in the Declaration of Independence and the United States Constitution is special among nations and has a manifest destiny can largely be traced to him and those whom he directly influenced.

In one sense, Stiles is the heir of John Cotton and John Winthrop—he interprets the American nation in terms that are clearly and intentionally religious. But he would have disagreed with many of the fundamentals of the theology of those two earlier preachers. He certainly did not envision America as a "Holy Commonwealth" in the ways or for the reasons that those Puritans did. In the body of his theology and in the essence of this sermon, he is much closer to Jonathan Mayhew.

Indeed, it was in providing a theological rationale for the American Revolution that Stiles made his reputation. Possibly his most famous sermon,

"A Discourse on the Christian Union," was preached in Bristol, Rhode Island, on April 23, 1760. Listen to the charge he gave to that congregation:

> The right of conscience and private judgment is unalienable, and it is truly the interest of all mankind to unite themselves into one body for the liberty, free exercise, and unmolested enjoyment of this right, especially in religion. . . . You are very sensible that there is a formal attempt on the chastity and order of our churches which is vigilantly to be guarded against, at present, till our churches grow into one. . . . Our cause is one, and a cause not in decline, not in disrepute, but in honor and a most flourishing prosperity. Let us be cemented together by forbearance, fellowship, union. . . . Let the grand errand into America never be forgotten.[1]

The liberty, free exercise, and unmolested enjoyment of the exercise of conscience and private judgment was clearly Stiles's highest theological priority. To achieve this goal, he thought war with England to be both biblically justifiable and probably necessary. He came to this conclusion because of many of the things that had so disturbed Jonathan Mayhew. But, that we may be clear on the background of these beliefs, a summary of some of the danger signs of the earlier eighteenth century might be helpful.

In 1715, the Church of England presented to King George I a petition for the establishment of an American bishop, whose responsibility would include the Anglicanization of the Colonies. The petition was rejected, but the church continued its efforts. In 1722, the rector and the entire faculty of Yale renounced the Congregational way and became Episcopalians. All were summarily fired, and this became known as the "Great Apostasy" at Yale.

In 1742, seven Anglican clergy in Connecticut petitioned the Bishop of London for an American bishop, citing reasons very similar to those contained in the 1715 petition. Responding to these and similar events, Noah Hobart preached powerfully in 1746 in Stamford, Connecticut, on the topic: "Episcopalianism: A Sign of the Evil of Times." Then there was the Mayhew sermon in 1750 and the Stiles sermon in 1760. Both Carl Bridenbaugh in *Mitre and Sceptre* and Alan Heimert in *Religion and the American*

---

1. Quoted by Carl Bridenbaugh in *Mitre and Sceptre: Transatlantic Faiths, Ideas, Personalities, and Politics, 1689–1775* (London: Oxford University Press, 1962), 3.

Mind provide extensive discussions of further ways in which fears of the *Church* of England became fodder for sermons about the increasing dangers posed to the Colonies by the *nation* of England.

In light of this kind of rhetoric, all that would be needed to produce specific ministerial calls for rebellion was a single action that could be interpreted as proof of the malicious, anti-Christian intentions of the English. That event occurred on March 22, 1765, when the English Parliament passed the Stamp Act. There was now no hesitancy on the part of preachers such as Mayhew and Stiles to counsel rebellion. As Bridenbaugh puts it, "In the eyes of the dissenting ministers, no distinction between religious and civil liberties any longer existed; liberty itself faced extinction, and they rushed to its defense."[2]

One historical fact and one interpretative suggestion should be made here. Factually, we simply need to remember that not all evangelical or Reformed ministers agreed with the position being taken by Mayhew and Stiles. Mark Noll, in his excellent study *Christians in the American Revolution*, argues that in point of fact, about a third of colonial ministers supported the Revolution, a third actively opposed the Revolution, and a third remained officially neutral.[3] Further, there appears to be no ground for arguing that these three groups were theologically homogeneous. That is, each of the groups would have contained significant numbers of both conservatives and liberals.

Asking why this was the case leads to the interpretative suggestion. Is it possible that those ministers who preached in support of the Revolution had come to confuse "desirable means" with "required ends"? While no one (at least in the latter part of the eighteenth century) would argue that liberty was not useful in living lives of religious obedience, some (Mayhew and Stiles among them) came to regard political liberty as essential to the Christian enterprise. Once liberty became an *end* rather than merely a *means* to an end, a fundamental change in the very definition of Christianity had occurred.

This change is suggested above in the move from the preaching of John Cotton and John Winthrop to the preaching of Cotton Mather. And this

---

2. Ibid., 257.

3. Mark Noll, *Christians in the American Revolution* (Grand Rapids: Christian University Press, 1977).

change is analyzed in powerful detail in the most philosophical work of the greatest preacher in the present collection. Jonathan Edwards, in his treatise on "Freedom of the Will," provides profound biblical insight into the lure of the notion of freedom and a superb biblical response to that lure. If only Mayhew and Stiles had listened! (If only we would listen today!)

But it was the voice of Mayhew and the voice of Stiles and the voices of other such preachers that carried the day in the seventh and eighth decades of the eighteenth century. They carried the day to such a degree that Bernard Bailyn, in his Bancroft Prize–winning and Pulitzer Prize–winning *The Ideological Origins of the American Revolution*, can talk about "the contagion of liberty" with which the Colonies were swept before, during, and after the American Revolution.[4]

And it was that "contagion of liberty" that Stiles essentially celebrates in the following sermon. The threat to liberty is what led to the Revolution, and the establishment and protection of liberty is that which now defines "The United States Elevated to Glory and Honor." Preached on May 8, 1783, these are Stiles's own words:

> We once thought Britain our friend and gloried in her protection. But some demon whispered folly into the present reign, and Britain forced upon America the tremendous alternative of the loss of liberty or the last appeal—either of which instantly alienated and dissolved our affection; it was impossible to hesitate—and the affection is dissolved, never, nevermore to be recovered. Like that between Syracuse and Athens, it is lost forever.

So what, according to this preacher who claimed to be Reformed in his theology, is the essence of the American nation? What is now the nature of the light that shines from the hill that is America? How would the answers to these questions, asked of Stiles's sermon, compare with answers to similar questions that might be asked of the sermons of Cotton and Winthrop and Edwards?

We have much to learn, in both positive and negative directions, from these Reformed sermons, all of which shaped America.

---

4. Bernard Bailyn, *The Ideological Origins of the American Revolution* (Cambridge, Mass.: Harvard University Press, 1967), 230–319.

The United States
Elevated to Glory
and Honor

Ezra Stiles

*And to make you high above all nations which he has made in
praise and in name and in honor, and that you may be a holy
people unto the Lord your God. (Deut. 26:19)*

Taught by the omniscient Deity, Moses foresaw and predicted the
capital events relative to Israel through the successive changes of
depression and glory until their final elevation to the first dignity
and eminence among the empires of the world. These events have been so
ordered as to become a display of retribution and sovereignty, for while the
good and evil hitherto felt by this people have been dispensed in the way
of exact national retribution, their ultimate glory and honor will be of the
divine sovereignty, with a "not for your sakes do I this, says the Lord, be it
known unto you—but for my holy name's sake."

However it may be doubted whether political communities are rewarded
and punished in this world only and whether the prosperity and decline of
other empires have corresponded with their moral state as to virtue and
vice, yet the history of the Hebrew theocracy shows that the secular welfare of God's ancient people depended upon their virtue, their religion,
their observance of that holy covenant which Israel entered into with God
on the plains at the foot of Nebo on the other side of the Jordan. Here
Moses, the man of God, assembled three million people, the number of the
United States, and recapitulated and gave them a second publication of

the sacred jural institute delivered thirty-eight years before with the most awful solemnity at Mount Sinai. A Law dictated with sovereign authority by the Most High to a people, a world, a universe, becomes of invincible force and obligation without any reference to the consent of the governed. It is obligatory for three reasons: its original justice and unerring equity, the omnipotent Authority by which it is enforced, and the sanctions of rewards and punishments. But in the case of Israel, he condescended to a mutual covenant and by the hand of Moses led his people to avouch the Lord Jehovah to be their God, and in the most public and explicit manner voluntarily to engage and covenant with God to keep and obey his Law. Thereupon this great prophet, whom God had raised up for so solemn a transaction, declared in the name of the Lord that the Most High avouched, acknowledged, and took them for a peculiar people to himself, promising to be their God and Protector and, upon their obedience, to make them prosperous and happy (Deut. 29:10, 14; 30:9, 19). He foresaw indeed their rejection of God and predicted the judicial chastisement of apostasy, a chastisement involving the righteous with the wicked. But to comfort and support the righteous in every age and under every calamity, and to make his power known among all nations, God determined that a remnant should be saved. Thus Moses and the Prophets by divine direction interspersed their writings with promises that when the ends of God's moral government should be answered in a series of national punishments, inflicted for a succession of ages, he would by his irresistible power and sovereign grace subdue the hearts of his people to a free, willing, joyful obedience; turn their captivity; and recover and gather them from all the nations whither the Lord had scattered them in his fierce anger—bring them into the land which their fathers possessed—and multiply them above their fathers— and rejoice over them for good, as he rejoiced over their fathers (see Deut. 30:3–9). Then the words of Moses, hitherto accomplished but in part, will be literally fulfilled when this branch of the posterity of Abraham shall be nationally collected and become a very distinguished and glorious people under the Great Messiah the Prince of Peace. He will then make them high above all nations which he has made in praise and in name and in honor, and they shall become a holy people unto the Lord their God.

I shall enlarge no further upon the primary sense and literal accomplishments of this and numerous other prophecies respecting both Jews and

Gentiles in the latter-day glory of the church. For I have assumed the text only as introductory to a discourse upon the political welfare of God's American Israel and as allusively prophetic of the future prosperity and splendor of the United States. We may then consider:

I. What reason we have to expect that, by the blessing of God, these states may prosper and flourish into a great American republic and ascend into high and distinguished honor among the nations of the earth. "To make you high above all nations which he has made in praise and in name and in honor."

II. That our system of dominion and civil polity would be imperfect without the true religion or that from the diffusion of virtue among the people of any community would rise their greatest secular happiness, which will terminate in the conclusion that holiness ought to be the end of all civil government, "that you may be a holy people unto the Lord your God."

I. The first of these propositions will divide itself into two branches and lead us to show:

1. Wherein consists the true political welfare and prosperity, and what civil administration is necessary for the elevation and advancement, of a people to the highest secular glory.

2. The reasons rendering it probable that the United States will, by the ordering of heaven, eventually become this people. But I shall combine these together as I go along.

Dominion is founded in property and resides where that is, whether in the hands of the few or many. The dominion founded in the feudal tenure of estate is suited to hold a conquered country in subjection, but is not adapted to the circumstances of free citizens. Large territorial property vested in individuals is pernicious to society. Civilians, in contemplating the principles of government, have judged superior and inferior partition of property necessary in order to preserve the subordination of society and establish a permanent system of dominion. This makes the public defense the interest of a few landholders only.

A free tenure of lands, an equable distribution of property, enters into the foundation of a happy state; by this I mean that the body of the people may have it in their power, by industry, to become possessed of real freehold fee simple estate. For connected with this will be a general spirit and principle of self-defense—defense of our property, liberty, country. This has been singularly verified in New England, where we have realized the capital ideas of Harrington's Oceana.

But numerous population, as well as industry, is necessary towards giving value to land, to judiciously partitioned territory. The public weal requires the encouragement of both. A very inconsiderable value arose from the spare, thin settlement of the American aboriginals, of whom there are not fifty thousand souls on this side of the Mississippi. The Protestant Europeans have generally bought the native right of soil as far as they have settled and paid the value tenfold, and are daily increasing the value of the remaining Indian territory a thousandfold. And in this manner we are a constant increasing revenue to the sachems and original lords of the soil. How much must the value of lands reserved to the natives of North and South America be increased to remaining Indians by the inhabitation of two or three hundred million Europeans?

Heaven has provided this country, not indeed derelict, but only partially settled and consequently open, for the reception of a new enlargement of Japheth. Europe was settled by Japheth; America is settling from Europe. And perhaps this second enlargement bids fair to surpass the first, for we are to consider all the European settlements of America collectively as springing from and transfused with the blood of Japheth. Already for ages has Europe arrived to a plenary, if not declining, population of a hundred million. In two or three hundred years this second enlargement may cover America with three times that number, if the present ratio of increase continues with the enterprising spirit of Americans for colonization and removing out into the wilderness and settling new countries. And if Spain and Portugal should adopt that wise regulation respecting the connection of the sexes, which would give a spring to population within the tropics equal to that without, there may now be three or four million whites, or Europeans, in North and South America, of which one-half are in rapid increase and the rest scarcely keeping their number good without supplies from the parent states. The number of French, Spaniards, Dutch, and Portuguese may be one million souls in all America, and they have transfused their blood into a great number of Indians. The United States may be two million souls, whites, which have been an increase upon perhaps fewer than twenty or thirty thousand families from Europe. Can we contemplate their present and anticipate their future increase and not be struck with astonishment to find ourselves in the midst of the fulfillment of the prophecy of Noah? May we not see that we are the object which the Holy Ghost had in view four thousand years ago when he inspired the venerable patriarch with the visions respecting his posterity? How wonderful the accomplishments in distant and disconnected ages! While the principal increase was first in Europe, westward from Scythia, the residence of the family of Japheth, a branch of the original enlargement extending eastward into Asia and spreading round to the southward of the Caspian, became the ancient kingdoms of Media and Persia.[5] And thus he dwelt in the tents of Shem. Hence the singular and almost identical affinity between the Persian and Teutonic languages through all ages to this day. And now the other part of the prophecy is fulfilling in a new enlargement, not in the tents of Shem, but in a country where Canaan shall be his servant, at least unto tribute.

I rather consider the American Indians as Canaanites of the expulsion of Joshua, some of which in Phœnician ships coasted the Mediterranean to its mouth, as appears from an inscription which they left there. Procopius, who was born in Palestine, a master of the Phœnician and other oriental languages and the historiographer of the great Belisarius, tells us that at Tangier he saw and read an inscription upon two marble pillars there, in the ancient Phœnician (not the then modern Punic) letter, "We are they who have fled from the face of Joshua the robber, the son of Nun." Bochart and Selden conjecture the very Punic itself. Plato, Ælian, and Diodorus Siculus narrate voyages into the Atlantic Ocean thirty days west from the pillars of Hercules to the island of Atlas. This inscription examined by Procopius suggests that the Canaanites, in coasting along from Tangier, might soon get into the trade winds and be undesignedly wafted across the Atlantic to land in the tropical regions and commence the settlements of Mexico and Peru. Another branch of the Canaanitish expulsions might take the resolution of the ten tribes, travel northeastward to where never man dwelt, become the Tchuschi and Tungusi Tartars about Kamschatka and Tscukotskionoss in the northeast of Asia, and thence, by water, pass over from island to island through the northern archipelago to America, and become the scattered sachemdoms of these northern regions. It is now known that Asia is separated by water from America, as certainly appears from the Baron Dulfeldt's voyage round the north of Europe into the Pa-

---

5. Jos. ant. lib. I. C. 6.

cific Ocean, A.D. 1769. Amid all the variety of national dialects, there reigns a similitude in their language, as there is also in complexion and beardless features, from Greenland to Del Fuego, and from the Antilles to Otaheite, which show them to be one people. . . .

It is certainly for the benefit of every community that it be transfused with the efficacious motives of universal industry. This will take place if everyone can enjoy the fruits of his labor and activity unmolested. All the variety of labor in a well-regulated state will be so ordered and encouraged as that all will be employed in a just proportion in agriculture, mechanical arts, commerce, and the literary professions. It has been a question whether agriculture or commerce needs most encouragement in these states. But the motives for both seem abundantly sufficient. Never did they operate more strongly than at present. The whole continent is in activity, and in the lively, vigorous exertion of industry. Several other things call for encouragement, such as the planting of vineyards, olive yards, and cotton walks; the raising of wool, planting mulberry trees, and the culture of silk; and, I add, establishing manufactories. This last is necessary, very necessary, far more necessary indeed than is thought by many deep politicians. Let us have all the means possible of subsistence and elegance among ourselves if we would be a flourishing republic of real independent dignity and glory.

Another thing tending to the public welfare is removing causes of political animosities and civil dissension, promoting harmony, and strengthening the union among the several parts of this extended community. In the memorable *bellum sociale* among the Romans, 300,000 of Roman blood fought 700,000 brethren of the Italian blood. After a loss of 60,000 in disputing a trifling point of national honor, they pacificated the whole by an amnesty and giving the city to the Italians. We may find it a wise policy a few years hence, under certain exceptions, to settle an amnesty and circulate a brotherly affection among all the inhabitants of this glorious republic. We should live henceforward in amity, as brothers inspired with and cultivating a certain national benevolence, unitedly glorying in the name of a Columbian or American and in the distinguished honor and aggrandizement of our country, like that ancient national affection which we once had for the parent state, while we gloried in being a part of the British empire and when our attachment and fidelity grew to an unexampled vigor and strength. This appeared in the tender distress we felt at the first thoughts of the dissolution of this ancient friendship. We once thought Britain our friend and gloried in her protection. But some demon whispered folly into the present reign, and Britain forced upon America the tremendous alternative of the loss of liberty or the last appeal—either of which instantly alienated and dissolved our affection; it was impossible to hesitate—and the affection is dissolved, never, nevermore to be recovered. Like that between Syracuse and Athens, it is lost forever. A political earthquake through the continent has shaken off America from Great Britain. O! how painful and distressing the separation and dismemberment! Witness all you patriotic breasts, all you lovers of your country, once lovers of Great Britain; witness the tender sensations and heartfelt violence, the reluctant distress and sorrow with which you were penetrated when spurned from a parent's love, when you felt the conviction of the dire necessity of an everlasting parting, to meet no more, never to be united again!

Oh, England! How did I once love you! How did I once glory in you! How did I once boast of springing from your bowels, though at four descents ago, and the nineteenth from Sir Adam of Knapton! In the rapturous anticipation of your enlargement and reflourishing in this western world, how have I been wont to glory in the future honor of having you for the head of the Britannico-American empire for the many ages until the millennium—when your great national glory should have been advanced in then becoming a member of the universal empire of the Prince of Peace. And if perchance, in some future period, danger should have arisen to you from European states, how I would have flown on the wings of prophecy, with the numerous hardy hosts of your American sons, inheriting your ancient principles of liberty and valor, to rescue and reenthrone the hoary, venerable head of the most glorious empire on earth! But now farewell—a long farewell—to all this greatness! And yet even now methinks, in such an exigency, I could leap the Atlantic, not into your bosom but to rescue an aged parent from destruction, and then return on the wings of triumph to this asylum of the world and rest in the bosom of liberty.

Moreover, as we have seen the wisdom of our ancestors in instituting a militia, so it is necessary to continue it. The Game Act, in the time of James I, insidiously disarmed the people of England. Let us not be insidiously disarmed. In all our enlargements of colonization, in all our increasing millions, let the main body be exercised annually to military discipline, whether in war or peace. This will defend us against ourselves and against surrounding states. Let this be known in Europe in every future age, and we shall never again be invaded from the other side of the Atlantic. "The militia of this country," says General Washington, "must be considered as the palladium of our security, and the first effectual resort in case of hostility."

Another thing necessary is a vigilance against corruption in purchasing elections and in designations to offices in the Legislatures and Congress, instituting such efficacious provisions against corruption as shall preclude the possibility of its rising to any great height before it shall be controlled and corrected. Although in every political administration the appointment to offices will ever be considerably influenced by the sinister, private, personal motives either of interest or friendship, yet the safety of the state requires that this should not go too far. An administration may indeed proceed tolerably when the officers of a well-arranged system are in general ordinary characters, provided there is a pretty good sprinkling of men of wisdom interspersed among them. How much more illustrious would it be if three-quarters of the offices of government were filled with men of ability, understanding, and patriotism? What an animation would it diffuse through a community if men of real merit in every branch of business were sure of receiving the rewards and honors of the state? That great and wise monarch Olam Fodhla, the Alfred of Ireland, 1,000 years before Christ, instituted an annual review and examination of all the achievements and illustrious characters in the realm; and being approved by himself and the annual assembly of the nobles, he ordered their names and achievements to be enrolled in a public register of merit. This continued 2,000 years, to the time of that illustrious chieftan Brien O'Boroihme. This had an amazing effect. By this animation, the heroic, military, and political virtues with civilization (and, I add, science and literature) ascended to an almost unexampled and incredible perfection in Ireland ages before they figured in other parts of Europe, not excepting even Athens and Rome. I have a very great opinion of Hibernian merit, literary as well as civil and military, even in the ages before St. Patrick.

But to return: The cultivation of literature will greatly promote the public welfare. In every community, while provision is made that all should be taught to read the Scriptures and the very useful parts of common education, a good proportion should be carried through the higher branches of literature. Effectual measures should be taken for preserving and diffusing knowledge among a people. The voluntary institution of libraries in different vicinities will give those who have not a liberal education an opportunity of gaining that knowledge which will qualify them for usefulness. Travels, biography, and history, the knowledge of the policies, jurisprudence, and scientific improvements among all nations, ancient and modern, will form the civilian, the judge, the senator, the patrician, the man of useful eminence in society. The colleges have been of singular advantage in the present day. When Britain withdrew all her wisdom from America, this revolution found above two thousand in New England only who had been educated in the colleges, intermixed among the people, and communicating knowledge among them. Almost all of them have approved themselves useful, and there have been some characters among us of the first eminence for literature. It would be for the public emolument should there always be found a sufficient number of men in the community at large of vast and profound erudition and perfect acquaintance with the whole system of public affairs to illuminate the public councils, as well as to fill the three learned professions with dignity and honor.

I have thus shown wherein consists the true political welfare of a civil community or sovereignty. The foundation is laid in a judicious distribution of property and in a good system of polity and jurisprudence, on which will arise, under a truly patriotic, upright, and firm administration, the beautiful superstructure of a well-governed and prosperous empire.

Already does the new constellation of the United States begin to realize this glory. It has already risen to an acknowledged sovereignty among the republics and kingdoms of the world. And we have reason to hope, and I believe to expect, that God has still greater blessings in store for this vine which his own right hand has planted to make us high among the nations in praise and in name and in honor. The reasons are very numerous, weighty, and conclusive.

In our civil constitutions, those impediments are removed which obstruct the progress of society towards perfection, such as the tenure of estates and arbitrary government. The vassalage of dependent tenures, the tokens of ancient conquests by Goths and Tartars, still remain all over Asia and Europe. In this respect, as well as others, the world begins to open its eyes. One grand experiment in particular has lately been made. The present Empress of Russia, by granting lands in freehold in her vast wildernesses of Volkouskile, together with religious liberty, has allured and already drafted from Poland and Germany a colonization of six hundred thousand souls in six years only, from 1762 to 1768.

Liberty, civil and religious, has sweet and attractive charms. The enjoyment of this, with property, has filled the English settlers in America with a most amazing spirit, which has operated and still will operate with great energy. Never before has the experiment been so effectually tried of every man's reaping the fruits of his labor and feeling his share in the aggregate system of power. The ancient republics did not stand on the, people at large, and therefore no example or precedent can be taken from them. Even men of arbitrary principles will be obliged, if they would figure in these states, to assume the patriot so long that they will at length become charmed with the sweets of liberty.

Our degree of population is such as to give us reason to expect that this will become a great people. It is probable that within a century from our independence the sun will shine on fifty million inhabitants in the United States. This will be a great, a very great nation, nearly equal to half Europe. Already has our colonization extended down the Ohio and to Koskaseah on the Mississippi. And if the present ratio of increase should be rather diminished in some of the elder settlements, yet an accelerated multiplication will attend our general propagation and overspread the whole territory westward for ages. So that before the millennium, the English settlements in America may become more numerous millions than the greatest dominion on earth, the Chinese empire. Should this prove a future fact, how applicable would be the text when the Lord shall have made his American Israel high above all nations which he has made in numbers and in praise and in name and in honor!

I am sensible some will consider these as visionary Utopian ideas. And so they would have judged, had they lived in the apostolic age and been told that by the time of Constantine the empire would have become Christian. As visionary that the twenty thousand souls which first settled New England should be multiplied to near a million in a century and a half. As visionary that the Ottoman empire must fall by the Russian. As visionary to the Catholics is the certain downfall of the Pontificate. As Utopian would it have been to the loyalists at the battle of Lexington that in less than eight years, the independence and sovereignty of the United States should be acknowledged by four European sovereignties, one of which should be Britain herself. How wonderful the revolutions, the events of Providence! We live in an age of wonders. We have lived an age in a few years. We have seen more wonders accomplished in eight years than are usually unfolded in a century.

God be thanked, we have lived to see peace restored to this bleeding land, at least a general cessation of hostilities among the belligerent powers. And on this occasion, does it not become us to reflect how wonderful, how gracious, how glorious has been the good hand of our God upon us in carrying us through so tremendous a warfare! . . .

Let there be a tranquil period for the unmolested accomplishment of the *Magnalia Dei*, the great events in God's moral government, designed from eternal ages to be displayed in these ends of the earth.

And here I beg leave to congratulate my country upon the termination of this cruel and unnatural war, the cessation of hostilities, and the prospect of peace. May this great event excite and elevate our first, our highest acknowledgments to the Sovereign Monarch of universal nature, to the Supreme Disposer and Controller of all events; let this our pious, sincere, and devout gratitude ascend in one general effusion of heartfelt praise and hallelujah in one united cloud of incense, the incense of universal joy and thanksgiving to God, from the collective body of the United States.

And while we render our supreme honors to the Most High, the God of armies, let us recollect with affectionate honor the bold and brave sons of freedom who willingly offered themselves and bled in the defense of their country. Our fellow citizens, the officers and soldiers of the patriot army, who, with the Manlys, the Joneses, and other gallant commanders and brave seamen of the American navy have heroically fought the war by sea and by land, merit of their once bleeding but now triumphant country laurels, crowns, rewards, and the highest honors. Never was the profession of arms used with more glory or in a better cause since the days of Joshua the son of Nun. O Washington! How do I love thy name! How have I often adored and blessed your God for creating and forming you the great ornament of humankind! Upheld and protected by the Omnipotent, by the Lord of Hosts, you have been sustained and carried through one of the most arduous and most important wars in all history. The world and posterity will, with admiration, contemplate your deliberate, cool, and stable judgment, your virtues, and your valor and heroic achievements as far surpassing those of Cyrus, whom the world loved and adored. The sound of your name shall go out into all the earth and extend to distant ages. . . .

Providence has ordered that at the Reformation, the English translation of the Bible should be made with very great accuracy—with greater accuracy, it is presumed, than any other translation. This is said while allowing that some texts admit of correction. I have compared it throughout with the originals, Hebrew, Greek, and Syriac, and beg leave to judge and testify it to be a very excellent translation. Nor do I believe a better is ever to be expected in this imperfect state. It sustained a revision of numerous translators from Tyndale to the last review by the bishops and other learned divines in the time of James I 180 years ago, and has never been altered since. It may have been designed by Providence for the future perusal of more millions of the human race than ever were able to read one book, and for their use to the millennial ages.

This great American revolution, this recent political phenomenon of a new sovereignty arising among the sovereign powers of the earth, will be attended to and contemplated by all nations. Navigation will carry the American flag around the globe itself and display the Thirteen Stripes and New Constellation at Bengal and Canton, on the Indus and Ganges, on the Whang-ho and Yang-tse-kiang; and with commerce will import the wisdom and literature of the east. That prophecy of Daniel is now literally fulfilling . . . there shall be a universal traveling to and fro, and knowledge shall be increased. This knowledge will be brought home and treasured up in America and, being here digested and carried to the highest perfection, may reblaze back from America to Europe, Asia, and Africa, and illumine the world with truth and liberty.

That great civilian Dr. John Adams, the learned and illustrious American ambassador, observes thus: "But the great designs of Providence must be accomplished—great indeed! The progress of society will be accelerated by centuries by this revolution. The emperor of Germany is adopting, as fast as he can, American ideas of toleration and religious liberty, and it will become the fashionable system of Europe very soon. Light spreads from the dayspring in the west; and may it shine more and more until the perfect day." So widespread may be the spirit for the restoration and recovery of long-lost national rights that even the Cortes of Spain may re-exist and re-sume their ancient splendor, authority, and control of royalty. The same principles of wisdom and enlightened politics may establish rectitude in public government throughout the world.

The most ample religious liberty will also probably obtain among all nations. Benevolence and religious lenity is increasing among the nations. The Reformed in France, who were formerly oppressed with heavy perse-cution, at present enjoy a good degree of religious liberty, though by silent indulgence only. A reestablishment of the edict of Nantz would honor the grand monarch by doing public justice to a large body of his best and most loyal subjects. The emperor of Germany, last year, published an imperial decree granting liberty for the free and unmolested exercise of the Protes-tant religion within the Austrian territories and dominions. The Inquisi-tion has been, in effect, this year suppressed in Spain, where the king, by an edict of November 3, 1782, proclaimed liberty for inhabitants of all re-ligions; and by a happily conceived plan for literary reformation, the au-rora of science will speedily blaze into meridian splendor in that kingdom. An emulation for liberty and science is enkindled among the nations, and will doubtless produce something very liberal and glorious in this age of sci-ence, this period of the empire of reason.

The United States will embosom all the religious sects or denominations in Christendom. Here they may all enjoy their whole respective systems of worship and church government, complete. Of these, next to the Presbyte-rians, the Church of England will hold a distinguished and principal figure. They will soon furnish themselves with a bishop in Virginia and Maryland, and perhaps another to the northward, to ordain their clergy, give confir-mation, and superintend and govern their churches, the main body of which will be in Virginia and Maryland, besides a diaspora or interspersion in all the other states. The *Unitas Fratrum*, for above thirty years past, have had Moravian bishops in America, and I think they have three at present, though not of local or diocesan jurisdiction, their pastorate being the whole unity throughout the world. In this there ever was a distinction between the Bohemian episcopacy and that of the eastern and western churches, for in a body of 2,000 ancient Bohemian churches, they seldom had above two or three bishops. The Baptists, the Friends, the Lutherans, the Romanists are all considerable bodies in all their dispersions through the states. The Dutch, Gallic, and German Reformed or Calvinistic churches among us I consider as Presbyterian, differing from us in nothing of moment, save in language. There is a considerable body of these in the states of New York, Jersey, Pennsylvania, and at Ebenezer in Georgia. There is a Greek church brought from Smyrna, but I think it falls below these states. There are Wesleyans, Mennonists, and others, all of which make a very considerable amount in comparison with those who will give the religious complexion to America, which for the southern parts will be Episcopal, the northern Presbyterian. All religious denominations will be independent of one another, as much as the Greek and Armenian Patriarchates in east; and having on account of religion no superiority as to secular powers and civil immunities, they will cohabit together in harmony. . . .

It was of the Lord to send Joseph into Egypt to save many people and to show forth his praise. It is of the Lord that a woman clothed with the sun, and the moon under her feet, and upon her head a crown of twelve stars, should flee into the wilderness, where she has a place prepared of God and where she might be the repository of wisdom and keep the commandments of God and have the testimony of Jesus. It may have been of the Lord that Christianity is to be found in such great purity in this church exiled into the wildernesses of America, and that its purest body should be evidently advancing forward by an augmented natural increase and spiritual edification into a singular superiority, with the ultimate subserviency to the glory of God, in converting the world.

When we look forward and see this country increased to forty or fifty million, while we see all the religious sects increased into respectable bodies, we shall doubtless find the united body of the Congregational, consociated, and Presbyterian churches making an equal figure with any of them—or to say the least, to be of such magnitude as to number that it will be to no purpose for other sects to meditate their eversion. This, indeed, is enterprised, but it will end in a Sisyphean labor. There is the greatest prospect that we shall become thirty out of forty million. And while the avenues to civil improvement and public honors will here be equally open to all sects, so it will be no dishonor hereafter to be a Presbyterian or of the religious denomination which will probably ever make the most distinguished figure in this great republic. And hereafter when the world shall behold us a respectable part of Christendom, they may be induced by curiosity with calmness and candor to examine whether something of Christianity may not really be found among us. And while we have to lament our Laodiceanism, deficient morals, and incidental errors, yet the collective system of evangelical doctrines, the instituted ordinances, and the true ecclesiastical polity may be found here in a great degree of purity. Europeans, and some among us, have habituated themselves to a most contemptible idea of the New England churches—conceiving us to be only a colluvies of error, fanaticism, irregularity, and confusion. They have taken this idea in part from our brethren in Britain, who have viewed us very much also in the same light to this day. This on the contrary is the truth: that, allowing for offenses unavoidable, for imperfections and controversies incident to the churches in their most regular state, our churches are as completely Reformed and as well modeled according to the Scripture plan as can be expected until the millennium. Particularly these essential things may be found among them upon examination: that the churches or particular congregations are regularly formed and duly uphold public worship every Lord's Day, and this ordinarily in a very decent, solemn manner, that the preaching of the Word, baptism, and the Lord's Supper are regularly and duly administered by the pastors and that the pastors are orderly and regularly set apart to the ministry by the laying on of the hands of the presbytery or of those who have regularly derived office power, in lineal succession, from the apostles and Jesus Christ. We have no classical or synodical tribunals, yet we have ecclesiastical councils. And our church discipline, although not sufficiently attended to, is such that persons of evident scandal and immorality and vicious ministers (of which, God be thanked, there have been but few, very few indeed) cannot live long in our churches. With all our humbling imperfections, I know of no amendments necessary as to our general system of church polity. Nothing of moment, unless it be grace, no doctrine, no ordinance or institution of the primitive churches, but may be found in general reception and observance among us. If we are condemned for having no tribunals or judicatories out of the church (which, however, is not true), let it be remembered that neither Christ nor his apostles ever instituted any and that in this respect, we are just in the same state with regard to ecclesiastical polity as the hundred and fifty churches of the apostolic age,[6] and particularly the seven churches of Asia in the time of St. John.

The invalidity of our ordinations is objected against us, and so of consequence the invalidity of all our official administrations. And now that we are upon the matter, give me leave to exhibit a true, though summary, state of it as the result of a very full, laborious, and thorough inquiry. It was the mistaken opinion of some of our first ministers in New England (than whom there never was a more learned collection, for they embosomed all the theological and ecclesiastical erudition of all ages) that the power of ordination of all church officers was in the church. They well knew from ecclesiastical and Scripture antiquity that the power of election was there, and they judged ordination the lesser act; but their great reason was that the church might not be controlled by any exterior authority, whether episcopal or presbyterian, and so no more be harassed by bishops' courts or any other similar tribunals. Our fathers held to an eldership, for they saw it in all antiquity, as well as the Bible, and it was their judgment that elders should be ordained by elders of the same church. The most of the first forty churches had ruling elders; a few had not. These few created an early difficulty, on which our fathers early made a mistaken decision: that where there were no elders in the church, ordination might be done by the laying on of hands of delegated brethren. The introduction of ministers already ordained into the pastoral charge of a particular church was at first done by lay brethren, and this was from the beginning improperly called *ordination*, however often repeated. A repetition of ordinations or baptisms does not nullify the first regular administrations. All the first New England ministers were ordained before. Thus Mr. Wilson was first ordained by a bishop in England; then in 1630, by Governor Winthrop and others, he was ordained a teacher in Boston; he was then ordained an elder. And upon the accession of Mr. Cotton in 1633, he was, by this Elder and Governor Winthrop, again a third time ordained and constituted pastor. So the learned and courtly Mr. Davenport was ordained by a bishop, then by the

---

6. It has been computed that the churches of the apostolic age did not exceed one hundred and fifty or two hundred congregations in the whole world.

brethren, pastor of the church in New Haven in 1639; and in 1668, he was again ordained pastor of the first church in Boston by Elder Penn. Mr. Hooker was ordained a presbyter by a bishop in England, and then again in 1633 by the brethren at Newtown. . . .

Although St. Patrick was born in Wales, yet he was educated and ordained in Gaul and borrowed from thence the model of his churches. This shows that the Gallican churches, before their subjugation to Rome, as well as the Church of England in the time of the bishops and monks, of Glassenbury, were similar in their ecclesiastical polity to the churches in Egypt before the council of Nice, to those of Ireland in Patrick's day, to the present *Waldensian reliquiae*, or remnant of the ancient Gallic churches, and to the Calvinistic churches of the Reformation.

If the whole Christian world were to revert back to this original and truly primitive model, how far more simple, uniform, beautiful, and even glorious would the church universal appear than under the mutilated, artificial forms of the pontifical or patriarchal constitutions of the middle and present ages? And how far more agreeable to the ecclesiastical polity instituted and delivered by the holy apostles? May this be exhibited and displayed in the American churches. Of this it gives me joy to believe there is the greatest prospect. The initial revival of this primeval institution is indeed already so well established here, where the Presbyterians hold so great a proportion in the American republic, that there can be but little doubt but that in the ordinary course of events, our increasing and growing interest, without any interference with the other sects, will at length ascend to such a magnitude and become so great and respectable a part of Christendom as to command the attention, contemplation, and fraternal love of our brethren and fellow Christians, of the church universal, and even of the world itself. And when the set time to favor Zion shall come in God's good and holy providence, while Christendom may no longer disdain to adopt a reformation from us, the then newly gospelized heathen may light up their candle at America. In this country, out of sight of miters and the purple, removed from systems of corruption confirmed for ages, supported by the spiritual janissaries of an ecclesiastical hierarchy, and aided and armed by the secular power, religion may be examined with the noble Berean freedom, the freedom of American-born minds; and revelation, both as to the true evangelical doctrines and church polity, may be settled here before they shall have undergone a thorough discussion and been weighed with a calm and unprejudiced candor elsewhere. Great things are to be effected in the world before the millennium, which I do not expect to commence under seven or eight hundred years hence; and perhaps the liberal and candid disquisitions in America are to be rendered extensively subservient to some of the most glorious designs of Providence, and particularly in the propagation and diffusion of religion through the earth, in filling the whole earth with the knowledge of the glory of the Lord. A time will come when six hundred million of the human race shall be ready to drop their idolatry and all false religion when Christianity shall triumph over superstition, as well as Deism, Gentilism, and Mahometism. They will then search all Christendom for the best model, the purest exemplification of the Christian church, with the fewest human mixtures. And when God in his providence shall convert the world, should the newly Christianized nations assume our form of religion, should American missionaries be blessed to succeed in the work of Christianizing the heathen, in which the Romanists and foreign Protestants have very much failed, it would be an unexpected wonder and a great honor to the United States. And thus the American republic, by illuminating the world with truth and liberty, would be exalted and made high among the nations in praise and in name and in honor. I doubt not this is the honor reserved for us; I had almost said, in the spirit of prophecy, the zeal of the Lord of Hosts will accomplish this.

> So, the dread seer in Patmo's waste who trod,
> Led by the visions of the guiding GOD,
> Saw the dim vault of heav'n its folds unbend;
> And gates and spires, and streets and domes, descend
> Far down the skies; with suns and rainbows crown'd,
> The new form'd city lights the world around.[7]

Having shown wherein consists the prosperity of a state and what reason we have to anticipate the glory of the American empire, I proceed to show:

---

7. Vision of Colum. b. 2.

II. That her system of dominion must receive its finishing from religion, or that from the diffusion of virtue among the people of any community would arise their greatest secular happiness, all of which will terminate in the conclusion that holiness ought to be the end of all civil government— "that you may be a holy people unto the Lord your God."

On the subject of religion, we might be concise and transient, if indeed a subject of the highest moment ought to be treated with brevity.

It is readily granted that a state may be very prosperous and flourishing without Christianity: Witness the Egyptian, Assyrian, Roman, and Chinese empires. But if there is a true religion, one would think that it might be at least some additional glory. We must become a holy people in reality in order to exhibit the experiment never yet fully made in this unhallowed part of the universe: whether such a people would be the happiest on earth. It would greatly conduce to this if Moses and Aaron, the magistracy and priesthood, should cooperate and walk together in union and harmony. The political effort of the present day through most of the United States is to disunite, divide, and separate them through fear, lest the United States, like the five viceroyships of New Spain, should be entangled and oppressed with the spiritual domination of European and Asiatic hierarchies—as if by the title of minister or pastor we might not as well be reminded of the ministers of Holland and Geneva, or the mild and peaceable pastors of the primitive church, as of the domineering prelates and other haughty, intriguing dignitaries of the Romish church. Hence Aaron is spurned at a distance, and the Levites are beheld with shy contempt as a useless, burdensome, dangerous tribe; and in some of the states, for the only sin of being priests of the Most High God, they are inhibited all civil officers and to a great degree disenfranchised of their civil immunities and rights of citizenship. I thank my God for this ordering of his holy providence (for I wish the clergy never to be vested with civil power) while I am considering the spirit and disposition of the public towards the church of God, indicated by such events. A general spirit reigns against the most liberal and generous establishments in religion, against the civil magistrates' encouraging or having anything more to do about religion than to keep the civil peace among contending sects, as if this was all that is to be done for religion by the friends of Jesus. And hence, in designating to the magistracy and offices of government, it begins to be a growing idea that it is mighty indifferent, forsooth, not only whether a man is of this or the other religious sect, but whether he is of any religion at all; that truly Deists and men of indifferentism as to all religion are the most suitable persons for civil office and most proper to hold the reins of government; and that to prevent partiality in governors and emulation among the sects, it is wise to consign government over into the hands of those who, Galliolike, have no religion at all. This is Machiavellian wisdom and policy! And hence examples are frequently adduced of men distinguished truly for Deism, perhaps libidinous morals and every vice, yet of great abilities (it is said great civilians, lawyers, physicians, warriors, governors, patriots, politicians), while as great or greater and more numerous characters in the same departments (a Thuanus, a Grotius, a Paul, of Venice, a Sir Henry Wotton, a Sir Peter King, a Selden, a Newton, a Boyle), those miracles of wisdom and friends to religion and virtue, are passed by with transient coolness and neglect. I wish we had not to fear that a neglect of religion was coming to be the road to preferment. It was not so here in our fathers' days.

Shall the Most High send down truth into this world from the world of light and truth, and shall the rulers of this world be afraid of it? Shall there be no intrepid Daniels, great in magistracy, great in religion? How great was that holy man, that learned and pious civilian, when he shone in the supreme triumvirate at the head of an empire of one hundred and twenty provinces, venerable for political wisdom, venerable for religion!

If men, not merely nominally Christians but of real religion and sincere piety, joined with abilities, were advanced and called up to office in every civil department, how would it countenance and recommend virtue? But, alas! is there not too much Laodiceanism in this land? Is not Jesus in danger of being wounded in the house of his friends? Nay, have we gone already such lengths in declension that if even the Holy Redeemer himself and his apostles were to reappear among us, while unknown to be such, and importune the public government and magistracy of these states to become nursing fathers to the church, is it not to be feared that some of the states, through timidity and fearfulness of touching religion, would excuse themselves and dismiss the holy messengers, the heavenly visitants, with coldness and neglect, though importuning the spouse with an "Open to me my beloved, my sister, my dove."

But after the present period of Deism and skeptical indifference in religion, of timidity and irresolution in the cause of the great Emmanuel, perhaps there may arise a succession of civil magistrates who will not be ashamed of the cross of Christ, nor of patronizing his holy religion, with a generous catholicism and expanded benevolence towards all of every denomination who love our Lord Jesus Christ in sincerity and truth—patronizing it, I repeat, not with the insidious views of a Hutchinsonian policy, but from a rational and firm belief and love of evangelical truth. Zion's friends will rejoice in Zion's welfare, and the religious as well as civil patriot will shine in the faces of the future Moseses and Joshuas of this land. So shone it in the first Governor Winthrop, and so shines it in a Washington. Yea, I glory in believing and knowing that there are many now in the public magistracy of this and the other states who feel with that illustrious and most excellent governor, upon whom rested much of the spirit of Samuel and David, and of Jehoshaphat, Hezekiah, and Josiah, I mean Nehemiah the Tirshata, who, with Moses, esteemed the reproaches of Christ greater riches than the treasures of Egypt, who was of so pious, so noble, so patriotic a spirit, such a lover of his country and the true religion, that he preferred the very dust of Zion to the gardens of Persia, and the broken walls of Jerusalem to the palaces of Shushan.

Whenever religion is erected on the ruins of civil government, and when civil government is built on the ruins of religion, both are so far essentially wrong. The church has never been of any political detriment here, for it has never been vested with any civil or secular power in New England, although it is certain that civil dominion was but the second motive, religion the primary one, with our ancestors in coming hither and settling this land. It was not so much their design to establish religion for the benefit of the state as civil government for the benefit of religion, and as subservient and even necessary towards the peaceable enjoyment and unmolested exercise of religion—of that religion for which they fled to these ends of the earth. An institution is not made for the laws, but the laws for the institution. I am narrating a historical fact, not giving a position or principle, which by shrewd politicians may be abused to justify spiritual tyranny and to support the claims of the pontificate over all the civil states, kingdoms, and empires in Christendom.

The American Nehemiah, the opulent and pious Governor Winthrop I, and the other first magistrates of the several New England republics were men of singular wisdom and exemplary piety. And, God be thanked, the senatorial assembly of this happiest of all the United States still embosoms so many Phinehases and Zerubbabels, so many religious patriots, the friends of Jesus and his holy religion, and the Messiah's cause is here accompanied with civil government and the priesthood—allusively, "the two olive trees upon the right of the candlestick [the churches] and upon the left, the two golden branches, which through the two golden pipes, Moses and Aaron, empty the golden oil out of themselves" (Zech. 4:11) and diffuse their salutary influence of order and happiness through the community.

As to nominal Christianity, I have no doubt but that it will be upheld for ages in these states. Through the liberty enjoyed here, all religious sects will grow up into large and respectable bodies. But the Congregational and Presbyterian denomination, however hitherto despised, will, by the blessing of heaven, continue to hold the greatest figure in America and, notwithstanding all the fruitless labors and exertions to proselyte us to other communions, become more numerous than the whole collective body of our fellow Protestants in Europe. The whole proselytism of New England in particular, for sixty or seventy years past, has not exceeded a few thousands, while our augment in that term, by natural increase, has been half a million. The future difference in our favor will be far greater, even admitting a tenfold increase of proselytism. We anticipate with pleasure the growth and multiplication of our churches. God grant that we may not, like the seven churches of Asia, have a name to live while we are dead. Happy will it be for us should we become a holy people, zealous of good works. For it is undoubtedly the will of heaven, and especially after the recent salvations of the Most High, that we should be a holy people unto the Lord our God.

It is greatly to be wished that these principles of our common Christianity might be found in general reception among all the churches of these states:

The Trinity in unity, in the one undivided essence of the great Jehovah.

The sacred Scriptures are of divine inspiration.

In the immense universe, two little systems of intelligences, or orders of being, have lapsed; and unhappily we have the dishonor of being one of them.

The second person of the co-eternal Trinity, having assumed human nature, made a real atonement for sin, and by his vicarious obedience and sufferings exhibited that righteousness and vicarious merit by which alone we are forgiven and justified.

The Holy Ghost is equally a divine person with the Father and the Son, sharing with them divine, supreme, equal, and undivided honors.

True virtue consists in a conformity of heart and life to the divine law, which is as obligatory upon Christians as if eternal life were suspended on perfect obedience.

The internal principle of holiness essentially consists in divine love, a disinterested affection for moral excellency, a delight in the beauty and glory of the divine character, that is, the supreme love of God. And connected with and issuing from this is a joyful acquiescence in his will, a rejoicing in his sovereignty and universal dominion.

While salvation and pardon is of free grace, the retributions of eternity will be according to our works.

Whenever I find these principles, with others connected with them, and the real belief of them evinced by an amiable life, there I judge the essentials of Christianity to be found, and thither my charity and benevolence extends with equal ardor and sincerity, be the religious denomination as it may. Of these, the doctrines of the divinity of the Lord Jesus and his real vicarious atonement are the most important, the Jachin and Boaz, the pillar truths of the gospel, the *articuli stantis et cadentis ecclesiae*.

This was the system of theology brought over from the other side of the flood by our pious forefathers, now with God. The more this is realized in a state, the more will its felicity be advanced. For certainly the morals of Christianity are excellent. It enjoins obedience to magistracy, justice, harmony, and benevolence among fellow citizens; and what is more, it points out immortality to man. Politicians, indeed, usually consider religion only as it may affect and subserve civil purposes, and hence it is mighty indifferent to them what the state of religion may be, provided they can ride in the whirlwind and direct the storm. Nothing is more common than to see them in every country making use of sects for their own ends, whom they in their hearts despise and ridicule with supreme contempt. Not so the Christian patriot, who from his heart wishes the advancement of Christianity much less for the civil good than for the eternal welfare of immortal souls.

We err much if we think the only or chief end of civil government is secular happiness. Shall immortals, illuminated by revelation, entertain such an opinion? God forbid! Let us model civil society with the adoption of divine institutions, so as shall best subserve the training up and disciplining innumerable millions for the more glorious society of the church of the firstborn! Animated with the sublime ideas which Christianity infuses into a people, we shall be led to consider the true religion as the highest glory of a civil polity. The Christian institution so excelled in glory that the Mosaic lost all its glory. So the most perfect secular polity, though very excellent, would lose all its glory when compared with a "kingdom wherein dwells righteousness," a community wherein the religion of the divine Jesus reigns in vigor and perfection. . . .

While we have to confess and lament the vice rampant in Christendom, we have reason to believe that the more Christianity prevails in a country, civil society will be more advanced; ferocious manners will give way to the more mild, liberal, just, and amiable manners of the gospel.

Be it granted that in all countries are to be found men of integrity, honor, benevolence, and excellent morals, even where vice has a prevalent reign, to the greatest excesses of a general licentiousness; yet supposing a community, a kingdom, a world overspread with such characters with the finest morals of a Socrates, or a Confucius—what would be the moral state of such a country, in comparison with one overspread with the reign of the Christian morals? I mean in perfection.

However much we may admire the morals of Plato or Epictetus, they are not to be compared with those taught by Moses and the divine Jesus. Nor are we to conceive that civil virtue is the only end of civil government. As the end of God's government is his declarative glory in the holiness and happiness of the universe, so all civil government ought to subserve the same end. The most essential interests of rational beings are neglected when their secular welfare only is consulted. If therefore we defend and plead for Christianity from its secular and civil utility only, and leave it there, we dishonor religion by robbing it of half—nay, its greatest glories. It serves a higher purpose. For although it subserves the civil welfare infinitely beyond the morals of Deism and idolatry, yet it also provides for the interests of eternity, which no other religion does. It opens to us the most grand and sublime discoveries concerning God, reconciliation with him, and the reunion of this lapsed world with the immense universe. Discoveries momentous and interesting beyond conception! Without them we are left to perfect incertitude, if not totally in the dark, with respect to eternity and its vast concerns.

Should we have recourse to the goodness of God—yet of all beings, angels would think that man should be the last to reason from the benevolence and goodness of the universal parent to the impossibility of his offspring being involved in future ill, when from thence we might equally reason against the existence of present ill. If some distant seraph who never knew nor heard of ill should reason thus, it would be no marvel, perhaps; but that we, with all our sins and sufferings about us, should go into such reasonings is the height of folly, the absurdity of absurdities! And why should that infinite goodness preserve the numerous millions that die in finished, though half-punished vice, who did not preserve the lives of those upon whom the tower of Siloam fell, who did not avert the desolations of Lisbon, Naples, Herculaneum, and Palermo? Cast your eyes thither, O man, "remember the battle, and do no more" (Job 41:8).

If instead of reasoning from the works and Word of God, and thus ascending upwards into deity, "we take the high priori road, and reason downwards until we doubt of God,"[8] if by inductive reasonings from the perfections of God to what can and what cannot be, we should among other things boldly conclude a Trinity and the incarnation of the eternal Word absurd nullities, and yet it should appear in another state that a crucified Jesus sits at the right hand of the Majesty on high, how would these mighty sensible characters, these fine geniuses, these sublime, these foolish reasoners be disappointed? May I be forgiven a very earnest solicitude here, having myself passed through the cloudy, darksome valley of skepticism and stood on the precipice from whence I was in danger of taking a juvenile leap into the irrecoverable depths of Deism? For so rare are the Forbses and the Jenninges, the instances of emancipated real infidels, that *nulla vestigia retrorsum*[9] may be inscribed on the temple of Deism. Knowing these dangers, I

8. Pope.
9. No return from hence.

pity from my heart, and almost bleed at every pore, for those who are caught in the vortex and are captivated with the wily, satirical, delusory, and deficient reasonings of Deism. Elevated with the pride of mental enlargement, of a supposedly untrammeled understanding, they ascend aloft above the clouds of prejudices into the Pisgah heights, from whence they fancy that they see all religions the same, that is, equally nothing but priestcraft and artificial error. Whereupon they compliment themselves as endowed with a superiority of discernment in morals, with high sensibility, sentimental and liberal ideas, and charm themselves with other fine self-applied diction, which in truth only clothes the *taedium*, the weariness of half-discussed unfinished inquiries, or perhaps the hope that at worst the want of certain knowledge may pass with God, if there is any, as a sufficient excuse for some of the doubtful levities of life.

But errors in judgment, it is said, will be of no account with God. In ten thousand matters they may not. We may trifle on many things, but on the things that respect eternity, the things of religion, it is too solemn, too dangerous to trifle. Although most religions are false and ridiculous, there may, however, be one which we must renounce or trifle with at our peril. For if revelation is true, as most assuredly it is, it is in Jesus only that we have eternal life. Infidels and those excessively benevolent Christians who consider all religions alike and equally ridiculous do well in their calmer moments to ponder these words of the eternal Judge: "He that believes on the Son has everlasting life, and he that believes not on the Son shall not see life, but the wrath of God abides on him" (John 3:36). And also these words: "Whoever shall deny me before men, him will I also deny before my Father which is in heaven" (Matt. 10:33). Where then will a Judas and a Beadle appear? Step forth, you Herbert, the father of Deism; come hither, you Bolingbrokes, Tindals, Collinses, Humes, Voltaires, with all your shining abilities; and that disappointed group of self-opinionated deniers of the Lord that bought them, with that cloud of deluded followers, who would not that I should reign over them—vanish from my presence, with all the light of your boasted wisdom, into the blackness of darkness forever and ever! On what principles can the despised, the amiable Jesus withhold or recede from so awful a sentence, so tremendous a denunciation!

How infinitely happier those who, believing the record which God gives of his Son, have received him and have become the sons of God? Is it nothing, is it a small thing, to be initiated into the glorious idea of God and the Trinity revealed in the Scriptures, to contemplate the hierarchy and government of the universe and the high dignity of that most illustrious personage who is our Intercessor, Advocate, and Sovereign? Shall this light come into the world and we neglect it? And shall it be said that these views do not animate a sublimer virtue than the motives taken from civil society? Shall the consideration of being citizens of a little secular kingdom or community be equally animating with those taken from our being citizens of the august monarchical republic of the universe? But I must desist, with only observing that the United States are under peculiar obligations to become a holy people unto the Lord our God on account of the late eminent deliverance, salvation, peace, and glory with which he has now crowned our new sovereignty (Deut. 4:34).

8

A Sermon Delivered at the Opening of the General Assembly of the Presbyterian Church in the United States

1 Corinthians 14:12

ARCHIBALD ALEXANDER

At the opening of the nineteenth century, the Presbyterian church was well positioned to serve the new republic of the United States of America. With bases in both the north and south, it was prepared to minister to the growing westward movement by means of the 1801 Plan of Union with the Congregational church, a cooperative arrangement that resulted in more Presbyterian than Congregational churches being formed on the frontier, but that also opened a door to the more progressive theology of New England. Revivals of the "Second Awakening," occurring on the Kentucky–Tennessee frontier (where the Cumberland Presbyterian schism would be one result) and on the Yale College campus of Jonathan Edwards's grandson, Timothy Dwight, signaled a need for more and better-educated ministers.

Ashbel Green (1762–1848), pastor of Philadelphia's Second Presbyterian Church, had begun corresponding with Samuel Miller (1769–1850), one of the ministers of First Presbyterian Church in New York City, about the need for a theological seminary to train Presbyterian ministers. Princeton College, which had earlier served this purpose, now had too broad a curriculum and lacked the needed focus on spiritual formation. Andover Seminary had been established in Massachusetts in 1801 by Trinitarian Congregationalists concerned over Harvard's hiring of a Unitarian on its faculty. The idea of an educational institution purely for the preparation of ministers, preceded by a liberal-arts college education, was a new thing on the American scene. The need for more ministers for the burgeoning American population, the threat of Unitarianism and increasingly liberal theology, and the excesses of some revivalistic enthusiasm all seemed to call for such a school.

The trigger for the establishment of a Presbyterian seminary, which turned out to be the Theological Seminary of the denomination at Princeton, New Jersey, was a sermon at the opening of the 1808 General Assembly by its retiring moderator, Archibald Alexander (1772–1851), then pastor of the Third Presbyterian Church of Philadelphia (also known as Pine Street Presbyterian Church). The sermon actually called for such a seminary in every presbytery, "or at least every synod." The 1809 General Assembly, responding to an overture from the Philadelphia Presbytery, appointed a committee of eight ministers and three laymen, chaired by the Congregational delegate to the Assembly, Timothy Dwight, to consider the possibility of establishing "a theological school." The committee reported back that it had considered three possibilities—one great school centrally located, two schools situated to serve north and south, and a school within each synod—but that it favored the first option of one great school. The 1810 General Assembly concluded that the presbyteries had approved this option, and a committee composed of Ashbel Green, Samuel Miller, Archibald Alexander, and four other ministers was appointed to draw up a "Plan of the Seminary." In 1811 the Assembly adopted that plan, and by that time enough money had been raised to establish the seminary. The 1812 Assembly voted to locate the seminary at Princeton, elected a board of directors, and chose Archibald Alexander to be the first professor. He was inaugurated on August 12, 1812.[1] He would be joined in 1813 by Samuel Miller and in 1820 by the young Charles Hodge (1797–1878) to form the early faculty. Other Presbyterian seminaries would later be formed, but the "Princeton Theology," shaped particularly by Hodge, his son Archibald Alexander Hodge (1823–86), Benjamin Breckinridge Warfield (1851–1921), and J. Gresham Machen (1881–1937), would have pervasive and long-standing influence in conservative Presbyterian circles.

The foundation for this Princeton Theology was laid in the life and character of Archibald Alexander. Born on April 17, 1772 in the Great Valley of Virginia, seven miles east of Lexington, he learned the Westminster Shorter Catechism by age 7 and studied under his pastor, William Graham, at Liberty Hall Academy. At age 16 he became a private tutor in a family near Fredericksburg, where he was invited to read to an elderly woman from the writings of the Puritan John Flavel. Observance of the effects of revival in southern Virginia combined with the reading of Flavel to give him assurance of salvation by 1789. Resuming his studies with Graham, he found fluency in speech when asked to exhort the congregation in a church service in 1790. Under care of Lexington Presbytery, he attended a General Assembly in Philadelphia as a ruling elder in 1791 and was licensed that year at age 19. As an itinerant preacher, he learned to speak effectively without notes. Ordained in 1794, he served as pastor of two Virginia churches, then as president of the struggling Hampden-Sydney College from 1797 to 1801 and, after a tour of New England, again in 1802 to 1807. From 1807 to 1812 he was pastor of Pine Street Presbyterian Church in Philadelphia before being called to serve at Princeton Seminary, where he

---

1. See David B. Calhoun, *Princeton Seminary*, 2 vols. (1994, 1996), vol. 1: *Faith and Learning, 1812–1868* (Edinburgh and Carlisle, Pa.: Banner of Truth Trust), 29–36; and also Lefferts A. Loetscher, *Facing the Enlightenment and Pietism: Archibald Alexander and the Founding of Princeton Theological Seminary* (Westport, Conn. and London: Greenwood Press, 1983), 94–97, 121–38.

would continue until his death on October 22, 1851. David Calhoun has described Alexander:

> About five feet, seven inches tall, Alexander was a small, slender man. He was never arrogant or domineering, but he was an outstanding leader. . . . He was a firm Calvinist, a scholar of note, a preacher of real power, an effective counselor, and a quiet leader. In his own life he combined strong convictions with such mildness and fairness that contemporaries often designated him a "moderate man," and a modern writer calls him a "winsome conservative." . . .
>
> Dr. Alexander created and shaped Princeton Seminary. He impressed his viewpoint and personality upon it as few men have ever stamped an institution. He modeled both "piety" and "solid learning"—and he would not let the seminary lose sight of either.[2]

Charles Hodge, who was his student and colleague for many years and almost like a son, said toward the end of his own life:

> There was something sublime and beautiful in the humility of old Dr. Alexander, when he found himself at the feet of Jesus. There was no questioning of the reason, no opposition of the heart. The words of Scripture were received as the revelation of what is true and right from the highest source of truth and goodness.[3]

Alexander's sermon before the General Assembly of 1808 reflects many of the qualities of the "Princeton Theology" that would develop over the last forty years of his life. Speaking on 1 Corinthians 14:12, "Seek that you may excel to the edifying of the church," he addresses "first, wherein the edification of the church consists; and secondly, to mention some of those qualifications which will be most useful to the ministers of the gospel in promoting this object." In regard to the edification of the church, he sees it as consisting in the maintenance and advancement of "truth, unity, purity, and felicity."

His discussion of truth reflects the Scottish Common Sense philosophy that would characterize the Princeton approach to epistemology. He sees

---

2. Calhoun, *Princeton Seminary*, 1:346.

3. Quoted in Calhoun, *Princeton Seminary*, 1:348–49.

dangers from two directions: rational Christianity as represented by Unitarianism and enthusiasm as manifested in some of revivalism's excesses. The answer to either one is the authority of Scripture. Unity of the church does not have to mean agreement on every interpretation of Scripture, but only on those truths that are fundamental. Differences in forms of worship also need not destroy unity, but the highest excellence should be maintained in the performance of every part of divine service for the sake of purity in worship.

It is in the context of discipline of the church for the sake of purity that he introduces his plea for the establishment of seminaries. This leads him into discussion of the qualifications for ministry. First of all is "profound and accurate knowledge of the sacred Scriptures," which entails knowledge of the original languages. Joined with this must be a "friendly pacific spirit." Also essential is the gift of preaching, which is not a matter of oratorical gifts, nor can the goal be to please men, but rather to glorify God and seek the salvation of men. Finally, the minister must be characterized by a spirit of prayer.

Alexander's own style of preaching is described by David Calhoun:

> Dr. Alexander's voice was clear and high pitched and his gestures restrained. He had the habit of placing his forefinger under his chin, and sometimes against his nose in a peculiar manner. He always began quietly, avoiding "all that brings the speaker's personality before the hearer." When he got into his sermon, however, "his eye kindled, his face was radiant," as he was carried along by the "operation of the Holy Spirit" working through his thoughts and words. Listeners often commented that Dr. Alexander preached as though he were speaking to each person in the audience individually.[4]

His own example, reinforced through almost forty years of teaching at Princeton Seminary, helped fulfill the vision provided in his sermon before the General Assembly in 1808.

---

4. Calhoun, *Princeton Seminary*, 1:93–94. For more on Alexander's preaching, see pp. 49–50, 95–96, 132, 342.

A Sermon Delivered at the Opening of the General Assembly of the Presbyterian Church in the United States

Archibald Alexander

Seek that you may excel to the edifying of the church.
(1 Cor. 14:12)

The cessation of those miraculous gifts with which the Christian church was endowed in the beginning is an event of which there is no clear intimation in the New Testament, but there are several weighty reasons which may be assigned to account for it.

When the Christian religion was fully established by the evidence of miracles, there was no longer any necessity for their continuance; or this evidence, having been once exhibited, must ever remain sufficient and by means of authentic testimony may serve for the conviction of all succeeding generations.

The frequency and long continuance of miracles would destroy their effect, and in time they would cease to furnish any conclusive argument in favor of revelation, or rather would cease to be miracles; for if it were as common for men to rise from the dead as to be born, there would be nothing miraculous in the one event more than in the other.

But a third reason is the abuse to which these spiritual gifts were subject. We might have supposed that if anything could have passed through the hands of men without being perverted, it would have been these supernatural endowments, which were given by the immediate operation of the Holy Spirit; but we learn from the sacred Scriptures, especially from this epistle, that they were as much, and perhaps more, subject to abuse as the talents possessed by nature or acquired by industry.

The Corinthian church was favored with a rich variety of these gifts, but in the exercise of them their spiritual men fell into great disorder. Instead of using them for the edification of the church according to their original destination, they seemed disposed to pervert them to the purposes of ambition and vainglory. They were more desirous of possessing these gifts than of excelling in charity, and courted rather such as distinguished and exalted the individual than such as tended to the edification and comfort of the church of God.

The apostle expresses his sentiments fully on this subject, in this and the two succeeding chapters, and having corrected their errors and reproved them for their abuses, he advises them, since they were ambitious of spiritual gifts, to seek to excel or abound (as the word should be translated) to the edifying of the church; that is, in those gifts which would enable them to be most useful in promoting the glory of God and the edification of the church.

Now, although the gifts to which the apostle refers have ceased, yet the exhortation in the text is as applicable to common as to supernatural endowments; for every qualification should be earnestly sought which tends to the edification of the church, and talents should be desired by the ministers of the gospel only with this view. I purpose, therefore, in this discourse to consider, first, wherein the edification of the church consists; and secondly, to mention some of those qualifications which will be most useful to the ministers of the gospel in promoting this object.

I. The word *edification* is borrowed from architecture, and literally signifies the progress of a building. This appears to be a favorite allusion with the apostle Paul when speaking of the increase of the church, and the figure is very beautiful and comprehensive. The structure of an elegant building, especially of a magnificent temple, is among the highest efforts of human skill. It is a work which requires the aid of almost every art and cannot be accomplished without the application of much wisdom and power.

The principal things in the erection of an edifice which deserve attention are the foundation, the plan, the materials, and the decoration. The foundation is an essential thing. The most beautiful building may be brought to a speedy dissolution by a want of solidity in its basis, and it should not only be solid, but sufficiently extensive to receive the whole pile which is designed to be erected on it.

The plan of the work is also of primary importance. As a large house must consist of a variety of parts, and as a multitude of workmen must be employed, if everyone should pursue his own plan, or if they should divide themselves into separate parties and proceed without respect to a uniform plan and without regarding the design and labors of one another, the consequence would be that the different parts of the building would not only grow out of all just proportion, but might interfere with and destroy one another, until at length the whole edifice would fall into ruins or stand in an unshapely and useless pile, the derision of every spectator.

The materials of a building should be of good quality and should be arranged in due order, every part occupying its own place, and not heaped promiscuously together. If an architect should build on a good foundation fragile or perishable materials; if, for example, he should pile up "wood, hay, or stubble" instead of employing solid mineral substances, he would deservedly suffer great loss of reputation in the estimation of all who might be acquainted with the fact. Or if a workman should put the weakest materials in the place of the strongest, or cement them together with untempered mortar, he would gain but little credit or emolument by his labor.

Finally, a building is incomplete until it receives its decorations and is furnished with everything necessary for the accommodation of its inhabitants or for the performance of the service for which it was designed.

The application to the church of these ideas which occur in contemplating the progress of a building is so natural and obvious that it would be tedious to run the parallel in detail. With only a general reference to these particulars, therefore, I will proceed to state that the edification of the church consists in the maintenance and advancement of truth, unity, purity, and felicity. These four words include everything which enters into the idea of the increase and perfection of the church.

1. Truth is the foundation on which the whole building rests. Take this away and religion will be mere superstition; morality, a matter of convenience; and the most fervent devotion, enthusiasm.

Truth is the subject of knowledge. It is the object of faith and furnishes the proper motives to all pious and benevolent affections. It delineates the path of duty and shows us with certainty the kind and degree of happiness which is attainable. It is a clear and heavenly light, deprived of which the understanding would be as useless and inconvenient as the eyes without the natural light.

This, however, is a word of very extensive signification. It embraces the universe. Substances and qualities, facts and propositions, ideas and declarations are all included under this comprehensive term. But we are not called to explore the whole circle of truths in the universe. This infinite object is only within the grasp of the divine Intellect, which surveys, with one comprehensive view, all possible and actual existences. Our situation with respect to truth resembles our condition in relation to the light of the sun. Although infinite rays are scattered from this luminous orb in all directions, yet we are only concerned with those which come near to us, and of these it is only a small portion which we have occasion to use; so the number of truths which can be known by man is comparatively small, and of attainable truths there are few which are absolutely necessary.

Of these some are discoverable by the light of nature, for although I admit that there are no innate ideas, properly speaking, yet I maintain that there are some first truths or self-evident principles to which every rational mind assents as soon as they are proposed. I believe, moreover, that there are such truths in morals in which all men do as certainly agree as in any mathematical axioms and which no man retaining his reason can by any art or effort disbelieve. These are the stock on which all others must be engrafted. If there were no such thing as the light of nature or a discernment of some evident moral truths, a revelation might be addressed with as much reason to a brute as to a man. All argument and every species of proof and illustration would be to him useless on this subject. This, however, does not imply that all men do actually contemplate these truths any more than they do those necessary truths which lie at the foundation of the science of number and quantity; nor does it imply that the knowledge of the Deity, which is so general in the world, is the result of reasoning or the discovery of natural light. The contrary of both of these I believe to be the fact. Uncivilized men think of little beyond the immediate objects of their senses and appetites; and as to such a process of reasoning as that which proves the existence of God, they are as much strangers to it as they are to the most abstruse demonstrations in mathematics. All that I maintain is that there are some truths so evident that all men are under the necessity of assenting to them from the very constitution of their nature as soon as they are distinctly proposed to the mind, and that there are others so obviously deducible from these that the reasoning by which they are established produces conviction in every person who attends to it. Thus far does the light of nature go in all; and we ought not to disparage it, for it is as much the gift of God as inspiration itself.

Revelation proceeds upon the principle that men do possess some knowledge of moral subjects and a feeling of moral obligation. This is as much taken for granted in every part of the Scriptures as that they are possessed of an instinctive desire of happiness and aversion to misery.

But if we were left to nature's light, dark and wretched would be our condition. Even if reason were cultivated, and we should deduce by logical inference every truth for which there are data in nature, our situation would not be mended. So far is it from being true that the light of reason is sufficient that the more clearly this light shines, the more distinctly would man perceive that his situation was miserable and, as far as he could judge, hopeless.

The truths most important to the peace and salvation of men are revealed only in the sacred Scriptures. The plan of redemption is here gradually unfolded from the first dawn of light in paradise until the Sun of Righteousness arose with all his splendor on a benighted world.

Christ himself is the truth. He has not only revealed the truth, but all the rays of this divine light are concentrated in him. From his face the divine glory beams forth with its brightest luster. The wisdom, power, justice, purity, love, and faithfulness of God are here clearly exhibited. In his actions and sufferings, the spirituality and extent of the law of God and the nature and just deserts of sin are set forth in a stronger light than any words could represent them. So completely does the character of Jesus Christ as Mediator involve all important truth that no dangerous error can be conceived which does not affect our views of his personal dignity or mediatorial work.

This, therefore, is said to be "eternal life," or all that is necessary to obtain eternal life: to "know the only true God and Jesus Christ whom he has sent." To "preach Jesus Christ and him crucified" includes the whole range of doctrines taught by the apostle Paul. The aspect of every dispensation, of every institution, of every leading fact and principal prediction in the whole system of revelation is turned toward the incarnate Son of God. In him is contained that mystery of godliness which through eternity will be developing for the instruction and entertainment of saints and angels.

In proportion as the doctrines which relate to Christ the Redeemer are understood, received, and reduced to practice does the edifice of the church stand firmly on its basis; and in proportion as these are extended and propagated, the glorious building is enlarged. The prophets and apostles who speak of the Messiah may on that account be called the foundation; but "Jesus Christ himself is the chief cornerstone, in whom all the building, fitly framed together, grows into a holy temple in the Lord."

Both in ancient and modern times, the assaults of the enemies of the church have been directed against this cornerstone; and although the gates of hell have failed of success in their attempts to shake this rock on which the church is built, yet as the malice of Satan is incapable of being extinguished or mitigated, we may expect renewed attacks until the time of his confinement shall arrive. In our own times, infidelity has come in like a flood and threatened to inundate the church with a horrible species of philosophical atheism. The torrent swelled high and raged with fearful impetuosity, but its violence has now abated, and the danger from this source appears to be in a good measure over. But the watchmen on the walls of Zion ought not to lie supinely down or nod upon their posts, but should endeavor to observe the motions of the enemy so successfully that they may be able to give seasonable warning of the kind of assault which may next be expected.

From the signs of the times, I apprehend the danger to evangelical truth which will now arise will be from two opposite points: from what is called rational Christianity and enthusiasm.

Most of those speculative men who were lately inclined to Deism will now fill the ranks of Socinianism—or Unitarianism, as they choose to denominate their religion. The errors of idolized reason are very dangerous because they have for their abetters the learned and powerful of this world, and the influence of their example is very extensive.

These opinions, however, are not likely to spread very widely among the common people, as they divest religion of all its awful and interesting attributes, so that the more sincerely and fully any person becomes a convert to this system, the more indifferent he will become to all religion. But no religion will engage the attention of people generally unless it is calculated to interest their feelings. It appears to me, therefore, that enthusiasm is likely to spread more extensive mischief among the unlearned than any species of free-thinking. The passions excited by enthusiasm, it is true, are too violent to be lasting, but the evil produced is nevertheless often permanent. Enthusiasm and superstition have commonly been represented as the two extremes in religion, but to me it appears that they are near akin and succeed each other as cause and effect. The wild ebullitions of enthusiasm when they subside leave their subjects under the fatal influence of some absurd opinions which become the creed of a new sect, and almost invariably such superstitious customs are adopted as are effectual to shield them from every approach of truth. Thus, these errors are often perpetuated for many generations, and at last only die with the extinction of the people who held them.

It is curious to observe how nearly extremes sometimes approach each other in their ultimate effects. No two things appear more opposite in their origin and operation than Unitarianism and enthusiasm: the one proceeding from the pride of reason, the other from the exuberance of the imagination; the one renouncing all pretensions to divine assistance, the other professing to be guided by inspiration at every step. Yet in this they agree: that they equally tend to discredit and set aside the authority of the Scriptures of truth. The rationalist will not receive many of the doctrines of revelation because they do not accord with his preconceived notions, which he calls the dictates of reason. The enthusiast will not submit to the authority of Scripture because he imagines that he is under the direction of a superior guide. The one makes his own reason the judge of what he will receive as true from the volume of revelation; the other determines everything, whether it relates to opinion or practice, by the suggestions of his fancied inspiration.

On the errors which arise from both these quarters we should keep a watchful eye, and against them we should make a firm and faithful stand. On the one hand, we must unequivocally deny to reason the high office of deciding at her bar what doctrines of Scripture are to be received and what not; and on the other, we must insist that all opinions, pretensions, experiences, and practices must be judged by the standard of the Word of God.

"To the law and to the testimony" let us make our appeal against every species of error; "if they speak not according to these, it is because there is no light in them."

2. The second thing included in the edification of the church is unity.

That the church of Christ is catholic and ought to form one undivided body is too evident, and too generally admitted, to need any demonstration. As there is but "one Lord, but one faith, but one baptism, but one Father of all, one Spirit, one hope of our calling," certainly there should be but one body; and all the members of that body are bound "to keep the unity of the Spirit in the bond of peace. Christ, when he ascended up on high, led captivity captive, and gave gifts unto men—some apostles, and some prophets, and some evangelists, and some pastors and teachers—for the perfecting of the saints for the work of the ministry, for the edifying of the body of Christ, till we all come in the unity of the faith and the knowledge of the Son of God unto a perfect man, unto the measure of the stature of the fullness of Christ, who is the head from whom the whole body, fitly joined together and compacted by that which every joint supplies, according to the effectual working in the measure of every part, makes increase of the body unto the edifying of itself in love." "For as the body is one, and has many members, and all the members of that one body, being many, are one body, so also is Christ. For by one Spirit are we all baptized into one body, whether we be Jews or Gentiles, whether we be bond or free, and have all been made to drink into one Spirit."

But although there is an agreement among Christians about the propriety and obligation of church unity, yet it is a matter of dispute wherein this unity consists and by what it is broken. Perhaps a better definition of it cannot be given than in these words of the apostle Paul: "to walk by the same rule, to mind the same thing." Unity without agreement is a solecism. If all the professed Christians in the world should adopt the same name and submit to the same ecclesiastical government, it would not come up to the Scripture idea of unity. Those attempts, therefore, which have for their object the bringing into the same society and under the same denomination people of widely different sentiments are deserving of little commendation. The nearer such jarring materials are brought together, the greater will be the discord. Truth and an agreement in the acknowledgment of truth are the only solid foundation of Christian unity and peace. But here the great difficulty occurs. Is it to be expected that perfect uniformity of opinion and practice can exist consistently with free inquiry? The doctrines, the inferences, the reasonings and incidental questions which may arise out of the Scriptures are infinite. To suppose that an agreement in all these, or in as many of them as may happen to be brought under consideration, is essential to the unity of the church is indeed to make it an unattainable object; for probably there are no two men, nor ever were, who agreed in every question which related to religion. I take it for granted, therefore, that such a uniformity is not required, as we ought not to suppose that the exalted Head of the church would prescribe and enjoin a kind of unity which is impracticable. I would not, however, be understood to intimate that there is a radical difference in the structure of the minds of men, for I am of the opinion that if every film of ignorance and mist of prejudice could be removed, and the same evidence of truth be exhibited to the understandings of all men, their judgments would in all cases be as much alike as their perceptions of colors of objects by the eye. But nothing, except inspiration of the highest kind, could place men in such a situation.

That which seems necessary to the solution of this difficulty is to determine how far this agreement must extend. What truths shall we require others to acknowledge before we will unite with them? I answer: only such as are fundamental. And if the question is proposed: What truths are fundamental? I answer: only such as are necessary to be known and received in order to constitute a person a sincere disciple of Jesus Christ. For if every error or imperfection in knowledge is made a bar to our acknowledgment of one another as members of Christ's body, then there is an end not only of catholic unity, but of all Christian society. Upon these principles every man in the world would be cast out of the church, for perfect freedom from error is as little to be expected in this life as perfect freedom from sin. I see no other leading mark to guide us in drawing the line but the one already mentioned. Still, however, the difficulty remains undiminished, and the question returns: What truths are essential to the constitution of a real Christian? To this question I confess I find it impossible to give a definite answer which will be applicable to all cases; for to a man in one situation that knowledge may be essential, which to another differently situated may be less important. An error may be fundamental to a man educated under favorable circumstances, which would not be so to a person just converted to Christianity from a savage state. But although the exact limits between truths which are essential to salvation and those which are not cannot be defined with accuracy, yet we may keep on the safe side of this line without ensnaring the consciences of sincere Christians or producing schism in the body of Christ. In the beginning, creeds and formulas of doctrine were short and general. The abstruse and naughty questions which have since filled the Christian world with contention were not thought of, and happy would it have been for the church if this primitive simplicity had continued. But the application of a vain philosophy and subtle logic to divine truth multiplied articles of faith and engendered endless contentions. This is a matter of deep regret, but the blame does not so properly belong to the orthodox church, which increased from time to time her articles of faith, as to the heretics who, by starting and propagating new errors continually, rendered it necessary that the opposite truths should be distinctly stated and defended.[5]

---

5. The evil which attends the multiplication of articles of faith is that dogmas come to be included in them which are either not contained in the word of God or not explicitly stated and determinately fixed by that infallible standard. When one unqualified assent is required by a church to things of this kind, it lays the foundation of schism. For supposing that all the propositions required to be believed are true, yet if they are such as real Christians, in the honest pursuit of truth, may differ about, they ought not to be made articles of faith or terms of communion, for the reasons which have already been offered. And it often happens that propositions which have been received into the creed of a church in order to oppose some prevailing error in the course of time become intelligible or liable to misconstruction with all those who do not know the particular opinions against which they were leveled and the history of the times when the error sprang up and was opposed. It would seem very proper when a false doctrine which caused the introduction of a particular article of belief has fallen into oblivion that the article

But there is another obstacle in the way of unity which seems to be of great magnitude. Those who may agree in fundamentals, and who may acknowledge each other as members of the catholic church, may yet differ in so many minor points that they cannot harmoniously worship together, nor join in church communion with mutual edification.

Perhaps this difficulty will not be found so insuperable on close examination as it appears on the first glance. Christian unity does not require all the members of the catholic body to worship in one assembly or to join in communion at the same table. As this in its full extent is naturally impossible, so as far as it is practicable it may not be expedient. Among people of the same denomination and under the same rules of government and discipline, it often happens that there is such a diversity in some modes of worship, and also in opinion about circumstantial matters, that the members of the same body cannot worship or commune together with harmony. But nobody supposes that these trivial differences break or disturb the unity of the church. And if a number of churches united together should hold some peculiar opinion, or adopt some peculiar practice in worship, or even if they should regulate their church government upon a different plan from others, why should this be considered as an infraction of unity any more than in the other case, as long as their peculiarities do not affect fundamentals in doctrine or essentials in worship? If indeed this section of the church should denounce all other Christians as heretics and anathematize all who differed ever so little from them, or if they should consider all the ministrations in other churches as unauthorized and invalid so that they would think it necessary to rebaptize their members upon their coming to join them or, if ministers, to re-ordain them, this would be a direct violation of the unity of the church, and all those who proceed in this way are chargeable with making a schism in the body of Christ. It is not every separation which amounts to schism. Christians may differ in opinion about matters of comparatively small importance, and in consequence may find it convenient to form different associations, while they still keep the unity of the Spirit in the bond of peace. There are at pres-

itself should be rescinded, were it not that the alteration or abolition of articles of religion has the appearance of renouncing the doctrines contained in them, and therefore ought not to be ventured upon unless some real inconvenience is found to result from their continuance.

ent several denominations of Christians in this country who manage their own affairs without mutual association or any direct intercommunity, and yet they love each other and acknowledge each other as members of the catholic church. The only thing, in my view, which is wanting to complete the unity of these bodies is some convention or general bond of union which might be considered as a mutual and public acknowledgment of each other.

With respect to this matter, I think I may be permitted to say that our church has manifested a Christian and liberal spirit without losing sight of the great principles on which every firm union must rest.

But that which especially calls for our attention is the duty of preserving peace and unity in that department of the church over which the Lord has made us overseers. Our body is now large and widely extended. Some diversity of opinion and practice may be expected, but the progress of schism (which has already made its appearance) would be a most disastrous event. There is a great difference between a schism of long standing and one of recent date. The former, where there has not been a departure into dangerous error, generally becomes innocuous after the lapse of a certain time. It is like a fracture which, though not well set, is healed again and gives no further pain; but a new schism is like a fresh wound, which must go through the process of inflammation and suppuration before it can be healed at all. Religious controversy among the people at large will ever be the bane of piety and of every social virtue. It enkindles the worst passions and drives men to the greatest extremes. It is not necessary that the points in dispute should be of great magnitude to render religious controversy virulent and malignant; yea, often the more imperceptible the shades of difference, the more furiously do the waters of contention boil. This very thing has already brought indelible disgrace upon the Christian name, and it is a subject which well deserves the attention of the clergy, for whoever heard of a schism which did not originate from the pride, resentment, or misguided zeal of those who were called the ministers of Christ? And it is a lamentable truth that talents, which qualify a man to do little good, enable him to do much mischief. So much easier is it to destroy than to edify. Many architects of the greatest eminence, whose names are now buried in oblivion, must have been for a long time employed in rearing the celebrated temple of Diana at

Ephesus; but one poor miscreant immortalized his name by burning it down in a single night.

Let us therefore be on our guard against the demon of discord, and let us "be of one mind, and live in peace, and the God of love and peace shall be with us."

3. The third thing in order is purity. This respects the worship and the discipline of the church. The purity of worship is corrupted first by paying divine honors to other objects besides the true God. The heathens fell universally into this abominable practice. The Jews also were prone to idolatry, and even the Christian church has been exceedingly corrupted by the introduction of improper objects of worship, such as saints, angels, the virgin Mary, relics, crucifixes, images, and the consecrated host.

But secondly, the worship of God is corrupted by mingling with the instituted rites of religion unmeaning or superstitious ceremonies. The imagination of man has ever been fertile in producing a multiplicity of religious services, but with respect to the whole of them, the challenge of the Almighty is: "Who has required this at your hands?" Some things indeed in the mode of conducting the worship of God must be discretionary, and these should be regulated by the general rules: "Let all things be done decently, and in order." "Let all things be done to edification."

The common pretext for burdening the service of the church with ceremonies is that it is decent and becoming that a Being so august and glorious should be worshiped with pomp and magnificence—but Jehovah "dwells not in temples made with hands." "The heaven is his throne, and the earth his footstool." In vain do we attempt by rites of our own invention to honor him whom the "heaven and heaven of heavens cannot contain." Such attempts are rather indicative of groveling than exalted conceptions of the Supreme Being, for as to the pomp of unmeaning ceremonies, it is infinitely beneath his regard.

The strongest argument for introducing ceremonies into the worship of God is derived from the effect which they are supposed to have in engaging the attention and impressing the heart. But this effect is transient, for when their novelty wears off, these ceremonies answer no other purpose than to conceal the true nature of religion from the inconsiderate mind. The substance is lost by attention to minute forms. The people are generally inclined to look no further than the surface and, having run through the round of ceremony, sit down contented with themselves, while they remain ignorant of the nature or necessity of spiritual worship. Indeed, this argument supposes the worshipers of God to be in a very rude and uncultivated state, who like children can be engaged and pleased with mere ceremony and unmeaning parade. A correct and cultivated mind perceives the greatest sublimity and dignity to be allied to the most perfect simplicity. This is the leading feature in the aspect of nature and also in the finest works of art, especially in architecture. It is observed by a late traveler that the superb columns, arches, domes, etc. which are still visible in upper Egypt are formed with such perfect simplicity that there is no such thing to be seen as any part, figure, or device intended merely for ornament. The taste of those great artists who designed and executed these stupendous works was perfectly correct. And those who undertake to be builders in the spiritual temple of the Lord should be careful not to disfigure the edifice by childish ornament.

It ought, however, to be observed that purity of worship is in no way inconsistent with the highest excellence in the performance of every part of divine service. And on this subject, permit me to observe that in the external worship of our church, I know of nothing which needs improvement more than the music with which we offer up our praises to God. As this is an instituted part of worship, it was certainly intended that it should be performed in such a way as to produce the effects which good music is calculated to produce. But a great part of the singing of our churches is little better than recitation. The kind of music for which I plead is vocal music; of all others the most perfect, the best suited to devotion, and corresponding best with the simplicity of divine worship.

I will now make a few remarks on the subject of purity as it respects the discipline of the church. The first thing here which deserves our attention is the introduction of suitable men into the ministry. If you would have a well-disciplined army, you must begin by appointing good officers. There is no subject which more deserves the attention of our church when met in general assembly than this. The deficiency of preachers is great. Our vacancies are numerous and often continue for years unsupplied, by which means they are broken up or destroyed. Our seminaries of learning, although increasing in literature and numbers, furnish us with few preachers. This state of affairs calls loudly for your attention. Some measures have already been adopted by the recommendation of the general assembly to remedy this evil; but although they promise considerable success, yet they are inadequate to the object. In my opinion, we shall not have a regular and sufficient supply of well-qualified ministers of the gospel until every presbytery, or at least every synod, shall have under its direction a seminary established for the single purpose of educating youth for the ministry, in which the course of education from its commencement shall be directed to this object—for it is much to be doubted whether the system of education pursued in our colleges and universities is the best calculated to prepare a young man for the work of the ministry. The great extension of the physical sciences and the taste and fashion of the age have given such a shape and direction to the academic course that, I confess, it appears to me to be little adapted to introduce a youth to the study of the sacred Scriptures.

The consequence of the deficiency of well-qualified preachers has been that some have been disposed to venture upon the dangerous expedient of introducing men who were destitute of the literary qualifications required of our directory. And here permit me to suggest whether the rule which prescribes the kind and degree of learning which presbyteries shall require of candidates is not susceptible of amendment. As it now stands, it is rather a standard to which we wish to be conformed than a rule with which we strictly comply. I believe it is a fact that no presbytery in our body has been able, uniformly, to obey the letter of this law; and this frequency of violation in all has led some to dispense with it altogether. I think, therefore, if from the circumstances of our churches there is a necessity for deviating from this rule in any degree, it would be better to recommend to the presbyteries such an alteration as would authorize this proceeding.

The end of all our labors, however, should be to promote holiness in the great body of the church. The necessity of purity of heart and life in order to salvation is indispensable. "Blessed are the pure in heart, for they shall see God." "Follow peace with all men and holiness, without which no man shall see the Lord." But on this subject it would be improper for me to enlarge at present.

As our standard of doctrine and discipline declares that all baptized persons are members of the church and under its government, we should endeavor to promote purity by a careful attention to the religious education of children. On this point the doctrine of our church is right, but our practice is generally wrong. We baptize children, but we do not treat them afterwards as members of the church. They are not kept under a wholesome discipline, nor, as they grow up, admonished, exhorted, and restrained as they should be. This species of discipline has been so long relaxed and is so much in opposition to the indolent and corrupt feelings of human nature that to restore it is difficult and must require time. But we should immediately betake ourselves to the work and do what we can. The relinquishment of this principle and the practice arising out of it have produced incalculable evil in our churches, and may be considered as one chief cause why many once-flourishing congregations have dwindled into insignificance. If a general reformation ever takes place, it must begin here. The proper education of children and discipline of youth are the most important of all means in producing purity in the church.

There is another plan of discipline which has gained much credit of late and savors of greater strictness and purity, which considers none as properly members of the visible church but such as exhibit evidences of vital piety. Although it is true that all members of the church are under the most solemn obligations to be truly pious, and all their hopes derived from mere profession, privileges, or external performances are deceitful, yet it ever has been and ever will be found that all attempts of man to draw a visible line between the regenerate and unregenerate are ineffectual. In theory the plan is plausible, but in practice it is seen to be impossible. But perhaps it may be thought that we should endeavor to make the separation as completely as possible. I answer that the thing is not only impracticable but unwarrantable. As we have not the necessary knowledge, so we are not invested with the proper authority. At the same time, I admit that men of scandalous lives and propagators of heretical opinions should be solemnly excluded from the church and that all persons within her pale should be dealt with, when they need it, by the discipline of reproof, admonition, censure and suspension. I also admit that in receiving persons into the church or to its distinguishing privileges, we should examine whether they have the requisite knowledge and are of regular lives, and that we should then and constantly afterwards inform them of the absolute necessity of regeneration, faith, and a holy life, and may with propriety enter into free conversation with them on the subject of experimental religion. But to undertake to determine whether they are regenerate or not is no part of our duty of officers of the church of Christ. This is a prerogative which he has reserved to himself and which he will publicly exercise at the appointed time.[6]

---

6. In reality, this plan of discipline, if it could be carried into complete effect, would contravene one principal end for which the visible church was established, that is, to serve as a school in which disciples might be instructed in the Christian religion from the very rudiments, or as a nursery in which the seeds of genuine piety might be implanted. Can we admit the idea that after the church is established, the most important and the greatest blessings of the gospel covenant must be received without her pale? And I ask, where received? In the world, in the kingdom of darkness! Surely the ordinary birthplace of God's children is his own house, which is the church. It is Zion which brings forth children when she travails. To her appertain the promises, the ordinances of the gospel, the ministers of the word, and all the usual and stated means of grace. But it may be asked what advantage there is in receiving or retaining those in the church who are not regenerate. I answer: *Much every way,* chiefly because they are hereby placed in the situation most favorable to their salvation. But ought not all members of the church to be truly pious? They ought; and that they may become so, they should be continued in her connection. If casting them out would hasten their conversion, then it ought to be done, but how can this be supposed?

The question may arise: Who are then to be admitted into the visible church, and when is it proper to exclude any from this society? I answer: All those who acknowledge Christ to be the anointed prophet of God and Savior of the world, and who profess a desire to be instructed in his religion, may and ought to be received into the visible church; and as we are capable of receiving instructions and deriving benefit from Christ as a teacher and Savior before we are competent to judge and act for ourselves, all infants or minors under the care and tuition of members of the church who are willing to undertake to give them a Christian education ought to be received as disciples into the school of Christ, that from their infancy they may grow up in the nurture and admonition of the Lord. And as to exclusion from the church, it should be regulated by the same principle. When the authority of the Head of the church is denied, or his Word and ordinances openly condemned, or when such a course of conduct is pursued as tends to the dissolution and destruction of the society, then and not till then is it proper to excommunicate a member from the visible church of Christ.

Some may perhaps infer from what has been said on this subject that a foundation is laid for the indiscriminate admission of all baptized persons to the table of the Lord; but this consequence does by no means follow. The admission of a person into a society does not

4. On the fourth particular I shall say nothing at present, as this is not the place of the church's rest and enjoyment, except that the true felicity of the body while here in the wilderness will be most effectually advanced by promoting truth, unity, and purity.

I will now, agreeably to the plan proposed, mention some of those gifts and qualifications by excelling in which the ministers of the gospel may most effectually edify the church.

1. The first attainment which I shall mention is a profound and accurate knowledge of the sacred Scriptures. This knowledge, although very important and indeed indispensably necessary, is very difficult of acquisition. To ascertain what opinions other men have formed of the truths of Scripture, and what controversies have been agitated respecting particular points of doctrine, is not so very difficult. But to study the sacred oracles for ourselves in the midst of the dust of contention and, despite the prejudices of education and of party, to elicit the true meaning of the Holy Ghost requires an ardent love of truth, an unwearied attention, unshaken fortitude, and invincible perseverance in the student of sacred literature.

We who live in this remote age and distant country labor under peculiar disadvantages in the study of the sacred Scriptures. They are written

---

entitle him at once to attend on all the mysteries of that society. Many things may be necessary to be first learned, and many steps to be taken, before the novice is prepared for the higher privileges of the society. In the Christian church, there is no ordinance or duty concerning which there are such solemn cautions left on record as that of the Lord's supper. An unworthy attendance contracts the guilt of "crucifying the Lord afresh," and every man is required "to examine himself" before he approaches the sacred table. This subject, it is probable, has been much misunderstood by many serious people, who have been kept back from this important duty rather by a superstitious dread than godly fear; but still there is great necessity to warn the members of the church not to approach rashly, nor without due preparation. All who are in the church are no doubt under solemn obligations to obey this dying command of their Savior; but there is an order to be observed in the performance of duties, and according to this order, preparation precedes attendance. As in the case of the Passover, the duty was obligatory on all the people of Israel, but if by any means the preparation of the sanctuary was wanting, it was judged expedient to defer the performance of the duty until it could be obtained; so with respect to the Lord's supper, it is a duty incumbent on all, but not always as soon as they become members of the church, but when they are sufficiently instructed and duly prepared to discern the Lord's body.

in languages difficult to be acquired by us, both on account of the scarcity of suitable books and teachers of competent skill and of being hard to be perfectly understood by any in consequence of having for so many centuries remained dead. And in the volume of inspiration, there are continual references to the customs, transactions, and prevailing sentiments of the people to whom they were originally addressed and of those concerning whom they speak, all of which things are now with great difficulty ascertained.

Translations of the Scriptures we have, both in ancient and modern languages, and an excellent one in our own tongue; but surely the expounders of a law ought to be able to read it in the original. The judge of a law which related only to life, liberty, or property would not be tolerated if he depended merely on a translation in making up his opinions. Nothing but absolute necessity should hinder us from studying the Scriptures in the original languages. And although it is a study which will require much labor and time, yet it will richly repay those who persevere in it and will enable them to promote the edification of the church more effectually than literary acquirements of any other kind. I hope that the time is approaching when all other studies will, among theological students, yield the precedence to oriental literature, that is, to the study of the Bible, and that other branches of learning will be prized only as they afford assistance in the elucidation of the inspired volume.

When those who are designed for the ministry shall be acquainted with the Scriptures from their childhood, and when those invested with the sacred office shall with an undivided attention and with an ardent love of truth study the inspired Scriptures, then we may expect that error will be eradicated, the schisms of the church healed, and primitive purity restored.

2. Another quality which is of great importance in the ministers of the gospel, and by abounding in which they will promote the edification of the church, is a pacific spirit. The church of God would never have exhibited the unnatural spectacle of a house divided against itself if all the professed ministers of Jesus had been constantly possessed of a competent portion of the meek and humble spirit of their master.

If we value the peace and unity of the church of Christ which he has purchased with his own blood, if we regard the salvation of our own souls and that of our hearers, let us endeavor to divest ourselves of all pride and ambition, of all envy, jealousy, and un-Christian resentments, and let us be clothed with humility and cultivate that peaceable temper which is so congenial with the religion which we profess and teach.

A friendly pacific spirit among the clergy towards each other is of the utmost importance to the peace and edification of the church. But if, instead of this, they should view each other's conduct with that jaundiced eye which discolors every action, or if they are disposed to pervert to an ill sense every word of a brother which may have the least obliquity when compared with their own rule, or if when convened to transact the business of the church they should ever so far lose sight of the principles which should govern them as to be determined, at all events, upon carrying their own measures and supporting their own opinions and should be disposed to bear down with authority, or repel with acrimony, everything which may not coincide with their own views, then we may bid adieu to unity and concord.

Our office as preachers of the gospel is always important, but we are never loaded with a heavier responsibility than when we are delegated to meet in this Assembly. The wisdom, the moderation, the mutual forbearance, the brotherly love and pure evangelical zeal, and, may I not add, the order and decorum which shall characterize this body will have a great effect on the church's peace. On the contrary, if a spirit of resentment and if dissensions and personal feelings ever are permitted to enter into your deliberations and govern your decisions, the harmony of our churches will be at an end; the cause of truth will suffer; piety will languish; schism will abound; Zion will sit disconsolate in the dust; and all her friends will mourn, while her enemies will triumph and their reproaches and blasphemies be multiplied.

3. The next thing which I shall mention as being of importance to qualify us to promote the edification of the church is the gift of preaching, and a disposition to exercise it with diligence. This is the chief instrument which God has been pleased to select both for the conversion and edification of his people, and although it may appear weak and even foolish to an unbelieving world, yet in all ages it has proved to be "the wisdom of God, and the power of God unto salvation, to all those who believe." As this is a highly important work, so it is a very difficult one; and when we contemplate the nature and consequences of our undertaking, we have reason to cry out with trembling, "Who is sufficient for these things?"

I know of no employment in which the attainment of excellence is more difficult. Rules for our assistance have already been multiplied, and I feel no desire to add to their number. Indeed, rules of rhetoric never were of much service in forming a good preacher. They may correct some trivial mistakes of gesture or utterance into which public speakers are apt to fall, but they cannot make an orator. And it is even doubtful whether oratory itself, as an art, has been of much service to the church. We know that it is one of the most envied and admired attainments which a man can possess. A finished orator will attract numerous hearers, but his audience attends his preaching as they would a show or spectacle, merely for entertainment. The truths which he delivers are no further regarded by them than as they furnish the speaker with an opportunity of being sublime or pathetic. Admiration is the only effect produced in the multitude, and the humble Christian finds that to be entertained and pleased and to be fed and edified are two different things. Pulpit eloquence was never more cultivated, and never attained greater perfection, than on the continent of Europe in some periods of the last century; and yet no important effect seems to have been produced by these splendid exhibitions of oratory. Paul, although ranked with the first of orators by the first of critics, yet disclaims all assistance from this art.

There is indeed a species of eloquence which every man possesses when he delivers anything which deeply affects his own heart, which may be called the eloquence of nature; for it is the simple expression of our sentiments and passions by such tones and gestures as are dictated by nature. It requires no study, is regulated by no rules of art. Those who think the least about oratory, and who are the furthest removed from any design of appearing eloquent, are the persons most likely to succeed in speaking naturally and impressively. Good speaking is more impeded by a too-anxious desire to speak well than by all other causes.[7]

---

7. The above remarks are not intended to refer to the matter, but only to the manner of discourse. It is believed that affectation, or an unnatural manner, is the chief fault of most speakers. With respect to tones, looks, gesture, etc., the best rule is "to follow nature." No art, no rules can teach us how to express significantly and impressively the emotions and feelings of the heart. In all cases nature dictates the proper expression where the emotions are in real exercise, and every attempt to express feelings which do not exist must fail of success with the judicious hearer and indicates such disingenuity as should never be found in a preacher of the gospel.

If these sentiments are correct, the best method which we can pursue will be to lose all attention to and concern about the manner of our speaking in the importance of the subjects on which it is our duty to discourse.

To preach the gospel as ambassadors of God to guilty men, to preach those awful truths which cannot be delivered without being attended with effects of the most momentous importance, to preach as those who must give an account of every one of our hearers, to preach as persons who are fearful every moment of being stained with the "blood of those who perish," to preach with the eternal torments of the damned and the everlasting joys of heaven open to our view—this, my brethren, is difficult; this is too much for mortal man!

It is hard to appear as public speakers and feel no undue concern for our own reputation. However firmly we may resolve, when alone, to consult nothing but the glory of God and the salvation of men, yet we must be divinely assisted, or habitually self-mortified, to an uncommon degree if we are not affected with too strong a desire for the applause of our hearers or too keen an apprehension of their contempt.

But when to please men is the chief object of the speaker, what a spectacle does he exhibit to superior beings! He speaks the truth, it may be, but his only concern is that his discourse may be thought to be handsomely composed or eloquently delivered. He considers not that in every word which he speaks, he is the dispenser of life or death.

Yet this undue anxiety to promote the idol self does not in every case appear by an attention to elegance of composition and eloquence in delivery; it often shows itself in attempts to appear uncommonly warm and zealous in the cause of God. But the fervors of those who affect zeal are divested of all solemnity, and their discourse degenerates into rant and empty vociferation. Instead of the genuine feelings of the heart, there is stirred up a ferment of mere animal passions; and the speaker exhausts himself with incoherent declamation, which may produce some sympathy in the weak and ignorant, but which greatly disgusts the judicious.

But the greatest gifts will answer no end unless they are exercised. Of all men in the world we are under the strongest obligations to be diligent in our calling: in no profession does sloth rise to such a magnitude in the catalogue of vices as in ours.

Archibald Alexander

We have undertaken an awfully important work, and woe be unto us if we preach not the gospel! We must be instant in season and out of season. For while we may be indulging our ease, souls are perishing—yea, perishing from under our ministry. Shall we then devote to amusements, to secular employments, or to unimportant studies those precious moments which, if rightly improved, might rescue some immortal souls from everlasting torments? God forbid. "In the morning let us sow our seed, and in the evening withhold not our hand, for we know not which will prosper, this or that."

4. The last important qualification which I shall mention is a spirit of prayer. If the question were proposed by what means Zion shall be raised from the dust and become the joy of the whole earth, I would answer: By prayer. This is not peculiar to ministers of the gospel, but they should abound and excel in this heavenly gift. Although our profession leads us to be much conversant with religious subjects and to engage in many religious duties, yet there are no Christians who are in more danger of suffering the lively flame of devotion to languish and to sink down into a state of awful declension and deadness than the preachers of the gospel. What the state of our intercourse with our God and Savior is, what nearness of access to a throne of grace we enjoy from day to day, how much of a wrestling importunate spirit of prayer we possess, can be known only to God and our own consciences. But of this one thing we may be certain: that if we are deficient here, we are deficient everywhere else. If we have not confidence to speak to God as a father, how shall we deliver his messages to the people? The minister who approaches nearest to God in prayer may be expected to be most successful in speaking to men; and perhaps one reason why many of us see our labors attended with so little fruit is because we are so little in the habit of frequent, fervent, affectionate prayer. May God endue us all richly with those gifts and graces which will enable us effectually to promote the edification of the church!

And to his name shall be the glory. Amen.

9

Professing Christians, Awake!

Romans 13:11

ASAHEL NETTLETON

The revivals of the eighteenth century in America, known as the "Great Awakening," were led for the most part by Calvinists, such as Jonathan Edwards and George Whitefield. What is often termed the "Second Great Awakening" of the nineteenth century, with its beginnings in the Kentucky–Tennessee frontier and in Yale in Connecticut, is usually best known for the "new measures" of Charles Finney, with the belief that the sinner had it within his power to decide for Christ, and therefore the revivalist preacher did all in his power to bring about such a decision. By the mid-nineteenth century these methods and the accompanying man-centered theology had left their mark on American Protestantism.

244

The beginnings of the Second Awakening were, however, distinctively Calvinistic. A signal example of that is the ministry and preaching of Asahel Nettleton (1783–1844). Born on April 21, 1783 in North Killingworth, Connecticut, Nettleton experienced a conversion in 1801 and entered Yale, where he assisted in counseling students during a revival in 1807 and from which he graduated in 1809 with the aim to become a foreign missionary. Licensed to preach by the Congregational church in 1811, he found effective ministry as an itinerant preacher in Congregational churches of eastern Connecticut. He entered upon this ministry with several convictions: (1) that he must not diminish the effectiveness of the settled pastorate, (2) that he would not seek to stir up emotions where it was not clear that the Holy Spirit had preceded him, and (3) that he would not stay if it appeared that reliance was upon him as the instrument.[1] His preaching tended to be sober and intellectual, often with enactment by him of the sinner under conviction. The characteristic result was not emotional effects, but often silence. His sermons typically concluded with a moving prayer that God would apply the teachings of Scripture to the people who were in need of repentance and faith. Revivals occurred under his preaching not only in Connecticut, but also in Schenectady, New York in 1819, at Yale in 1820, and in other parts of New England. He was particularly diligent in personal counseling and instruction as a following to his revivals.

His friend and fellow revivalist Lyman Beecher described Nettleton's preaching as follows:

> The power of his preaching included many things. It was highly intellectual as opposed to declamation, or oratorical, pathetic appeals to imagination or the emotions. It was discriminatingly doctrinal, giving a clear and strong exhibition of doctrines denominated Calvinistic, explained, defined, proved, and applied, and objections stated and answered. It was deeply experimental in the graphic development of the experience of saint and sinner. It was powerful beyond measure in stating and demolishing objections, and at times terrible and overwhelming in close, pungent, and direct application to the particular circumstances of sinners. . . .

---

1. See Tom Nettles, "An Introduction to Asahel Nettleton," in *Asahel Nettleton: Sermons from the Second Great Awakening* (Ames, Iowa: International Outreach Inc., 1995), v.

But there was another thing which gave accumulating power to his sermons. They were adapted to every state and stage of revival, and condition of individual experience. His revivals usually commenced with the Church in confessions of sin and reformation. He introduced the doctrine of depravity, and made direct assaults on the conscience of sinners, explained regeneration, and cut off self-righteousness, and enforced immediate repentance and faith, and pressed to immediate submission in the earlier stages.[2]

Beecher would eventually support the "New Measures" of Finney and also the "New Haven Theology" of Nathaniel Taylor, both of which Nettleton opposed after 1826. After suffering a decline in health from typhus in 1822 to 1824, Nettleton moved to the south, having effective ministry in Virginia and South Carolina, including with students at Union Seminary and Hampden-Sydney College. In 1833, after a year's ministry in England, Nettleton, with Bennet Tyler and others, established the Theological Institute of Connecticut in East Windsor, which later became the Hartford Theological Seminary, where he lectured on evangelism and counseled students. He died in May 1844 after a long and painful illness.

His sermon "Professing Christians, Awake!" is a characteristic example of his Calvinistic revivalism. It is marked both by the serious urgency of his appeal and also by almost constant scriptural quotations and allusions. There are effectual appeals to parents and family, challenges concerning the zeal of the world's commerce and concerning the spiritual warfare in which we are engaged, appeals for the sake of one impenitent sinner in the congregation and concerning the wasting of the brief time of our lives, a comparison to the attitude of Jesus Christ, and a challenge concerning the reality of heaven and of hell. Aimed at professing believers, it concludes with an appeal to repent, and thus it is a good example of Calvinistic revival preaching in the Second Awakening period.

---

2. Charles Beecher, ed., *Autobiography of Lyman Beecher*, 2 vols. (New York, 1864; Cambridge, Mass.: Harvard University Press, 1961), 2:363–65, as quoted in Iain H. Murray, *Revival & Revivalism: The Making and Marring of American Evangelicalism, 1750–1858* (Edinburgh and Carlisle, Pa.: Banner of Truth Trust, 1994), 199.

Professing Christians, Awake!

Asahel Nettleton

And that knowing the time, that now it is high time to awake out of sleep. (Rom. 13:11)

The text is addressed to Christians. The language is borrowed from natural sleep in which a person is in a great measure insensible to the objects and to what is passing around him, but life remains in the body. And thus it is when there is much insensibility to divine things among Christians—they sleep, but life remains in the soul. Language similar is often addressed to sinners, but then the image is borrowed from the dead who sleep in the dust. Hence the exhortation: "Awake, you that sleep, arise from the dead, and Christ shall give you light."

The wise and the foolish virgins both went forth to meet the bridegroom—and while he tarried they all slumbered and slept. But between the two mark the difference. The one has oil in her vessel, but the other has none. One has life, but the other is dead. Our text then is addressed to the Christian who was dead, but is alive again. To the Christian who is asleep and again bears the image of death. And now it is high time to awake out of sleep.

It is proposed:

I. To inquire when the Christian may be said to sleep.

II. To offer motives which ought to induce him to awake.

I. When does the Christian sleep?

1. In general he desires his own case, and begins to consult that, when it comes in competition with duty. Religion is the great business of his life.

It imposes on him many duties which are painful and crossing to corrupt nature. Thus the fraternal admonition—"Exhort one another daily, lest any be hardened through the deceitfulness of sin. You shall in any way rebuke your neighbor, and not suffer sin upon him"—is the command of God. To neglect this and similar duties for fear of incurring reproach is to indulge in spiritual sloth. You may sit down and rest quietly if you will not disturb your fellow sinners around you with a sight of their sin and danger. This requires no effort. And here thousands resign themselves to rest. Individuals or a church may close their eyes on the conduct of an offender and be silent, and this awful indifference to his soul assumes the name of charity, without lifting a finger to *restore such a one in the spirit of meekness*. The slothful servant will ever consult his own ease by sinful contrivance to shun duty.

2. As one in sleep is insensible of the objects and to what is passing around him, so in a measure is it sometimes with the Christian. Though not wholly lost to a sense of divine things, yet they make but a feeble or slight impression on his soul. In this frame they go to the house of God, and no wonder they soon forget what they have never felt. Once they saw the glory of God in the face of Jesus Christ, but now they walk in darkness. Once they had a feeling sense of the worth of souls and could weep over perishing sinners around them—"I beheld the transgressors and was grieved"—but now they can endure the sight almost without emotion.

This unhappy state of mind is further evident from their conversation. Once they seemed to be dead to this world—they spoke often one to another—their conversation was in heaven. But now their attention is all engrossed with the world; they converse with ease and cheerfulness about the trifles of time, but on the great things of eternity have little or nothing to say. Or perhaps they speak on these high and heavenly themes, but it is in a dull and lifeless manner. They seem to glance over the mind like trifles. They appear not to take an immediate interest in the subject. They feel not the impressive weight of eternal realities. When this is the case, they talk like a person in sleep. He knows not what he says.

3. Another mark of this unhappy state of mind is a reluctance to secret prayer, which very properly has been styled the breath of the Christian. Has anyone continued long without the spirit of prayer, it is a sign that he is asleep. And if not shortly awaked from this breathless state, we shall be compelled to believe that he is dead. How far these and similar remarks

apply to professing Christians present, you will understand me, is best known to themselves. One thing is certain. Sure I am it is not my business to cry peace in the ears of any who are asleep.

But I proceed.

II. What motives ought to induce them to awake? First, consider "the time." My brethren, it is gospel time. Gospel light is risen upon us. And those who do not open their eyes on the glory of this light must remain in eternal darkness and despair. "For if our gospel be hid, it is hid to them that are lost, in whom the god of this world has blinded the minds of them which believe not, lest the light of the glorious gospel of Christ, who is the image of God, should shine unto them."

The light of heaven is shining upon us. And can you sleep? "Behold, now is the accepted time; behold, now is the day of salvation." It is no time to sleep. It is the day that we shall ever witness: the day of salvation. The business of this day will not suffer you to sleep. It calls on you loudly to awake. Think, my brethren, have you nothing to do for yourselves? Have you no sins to repent of, no evil propensities to mortify? Are your evidences of grace bright enough? Do you love God with all your hearts, and are you perfectly conformed to his holy law? In short, are you willing to die as you are? If you have anything to do for yourselves, it is high time to awake out of sleep. "Prepare to meet your God, O Israel."

Have you nothing to do for your brethren? Is no brother or sister wandering from the path of duty? Go and in a feeling, friendly manner tell him his fault between him and you alone. Why hesitate? Delay not. Duty calls. God commands, and love to his soul demands that you go without delay. "If he shall hear you, you have gained your brother."

Parents! Where are your children? Are they all brought securely within the ark of safety? Doubtless you pray with them and for them. But this is not all your duty. Have you ever taught them that they are sinners, that they must be born again, and are you urging them to remember their Creator now in the days of their youth? Were you this day called to part with one of your children, could you rest satisfied that you had done your duty? Have you not one word more of instruction, counsel, or warning for your children before you meet them at the bar of God? If so, then it is high time that parents awake to a sense of their duty: that you set your houses in order and prepare for death.

Again, it is high time to awake because others are up and active about us. The men of this world shame us by their conduct. They rise up early and sit up late. They plan and execute. Labor, fatigue, and hardship are nothing to them if they can but collect a little of this world together before they leave it. They are laying up treasures on earth, which the moth and rust will soon corrupt. And shall you not be as earnest to lay up for yourselves a more enduring substance—a treasure in the heavens? They are laboring for that meat which perishes, but you are called to labor for that which endures unto everlasting life. Do you not feel reproved by their conduct, to think that the children of this world are in their generation wiser than the children of light?

Again, my brethren, you are on the field of battle. And it is high time to awake, for the enemy is up and active about us. The prince of darkness with all the several ranks of evil angels is your enemy. The malice of their legions is directed against the Redeemer's kingdom in this world. War is declared with all saints. And the legions of hell have gone up upon the breadth of the earth. He is already in possession of the hearts of all wicked men. They are his servants. The devil is styled the "prince of this world, the ruler of the darkness of this world; this is the spirit that now works in the children of disobedience." While you sleep, these are all sowing tares and destroying about us. Says the Captain of your salvation, "He that is not with me is against me; he that gathers not with me scatters abroad."

Observe: it is not a feeble foe you have to contend with. You are called to wrestle, not merely with flesh and blood, but before the battle is won you will have to grapple and contend with angelic powers, with principalities and powers. Observe: your enemy is crafty. Snares and temptations are laid thick around you, and unless you are wakeful you will certainly be ignorant of his devices. That moment when you let down your watch, the enemy began to come in upon you like a flood. While you slept, the Philistines were upon you. And I would come to blow the trumpet and sound the alarm. Awake, you that sleep. Cast off the works of darkness and put on the armor of light. Think not to find a bed of sloth in the field of battle. "Awake and put on the whole armor of God, that you may be able to stand against the wiles of the devil. For we wrestle not against flesh and blood, but against principalities, against powers, against spiritual wickedness in high places. Therefore, take unto you the whole armor of God, that you may be able to withstand in the evil day, and having done all, to stand. Stand therefore having your loins girt about with truth, and having on the breastplate of righteousness; and your feet shod with the preparation of the gospel of peace; above all, taking the shield of faith, with which you may be able to quench the fiery darts of the wicked." Awake, then, for your enemies are many, powerful, and crafty.

Another reason why you should awake is that sinners are perishing around you. While you sleep, your example will contribute much to their destruction. Yes, while you sleep the world may now be stumbling over you down to destruction. Little does that ungodly professor of religion think what a train of immortal souls may be following him down to hell. It is a fact not to be concealed that one ungodly professor of religion may do more to prevent the conversion of sinners than many infidels. I know it is most unreasonable that mankind should suffer themselves to be thus forever ruined. It can surely be no consolation to the sinner in hell that he was led there by a hypocrite.

Brethren, is heaven and hell a fable? If so, then let us treat them as such. Or are they eternal realities? Why, then, this silence, this seeming indifference to the souls of men that your fellow sinners should obtain the one and escape the other? Do you verily believe that within a few days you shall be in heaven, singing the song of redeeming love—or in hell with devils and damned spirits forever and ever? Have you ever described your own danger and fled for refuge from the wrath to come, and do you feel no concern for the souls of men? Or are there no sinners in this place? Have they all become righteous? Do all profess to know the Lord from the least to the greatest? Is there no prayerless family in this place, on whom God has declared he will pour out his fury? No prayerless youth to whom God has said, "I will cast you off forever"?

My brethren, if there is one impenitent sinner among us who is in danger of going into that place of eternal torment, can you sleep? One sinner in this house! One inhabitant of hell! Solemn thought! One soul present that will be lost forever. Who can it be? Could you bear to hear the name? Who among us shall dwell with the devouring fire? Who among us shall dwell with everlasting burning? Have you not reason to believe that many are now living "without hope and without God in the world"? "Wide is the gate, and broad is the way, that leads to destruction, and many there are which go in thereat, because strait is the gate, and narrow is the way, which leads unto life, and few there are that find it."

Wherever God designs to pour out his Spirit and to call up the attention of sinners to divine things, he will be inquired of by his children to do it for them. This he has taught us in his Word and often in the language of his providence. It is high time for you to awake out of sleep; for others are awake—sinners at a distance are alarmed—and hundreds are now flocking to Christ. And can you rest? Are there not more souls here to be saved or lost forever? Are they not as precious as ever? And is he not a prayer-hearing God? Has God forgotten to be gracious? Is his mercy clean gone forever? And will he be favorable no more? No, my brethren, "the Lord's hand is not shortened that it cannot save, neither his ear heavy that it cannot hear." Come, then, "you that make mention of the Lord, keep not silence; if you speak not to warn the wicked, the same wicked man shall die in his iniquity, but his blood will I require at your hand."

Brethren, how is your zeal for the salvation of souls compared with that of the Son of God? "He beheld the city and wept over it—O Jerusalem, Jerusalem."

> Did Christ o'er sinners weep?
> And shall our tears be dry?

How is your zeal compared with that of Paul? "I have great heaviness and continual sorrow in my heart for my brethren, my kinsmen according to the flesh. Many walk, of whom I have told you often, and now tell you even weeping, that they are the enemies of the cross of Christ." There is a dreadful storm of divine wrath coming upon the world of the ungodly. It is high time to awake out of sleep, for their damnation slumbers not.

Again, consider how long you have slept and you will see that it is high time to awake. How many months—and of some may we ask, how many years—have you slept in God's vineyard? And still you continue on sleeping away the day of salvation. Let me tell you that your sleep is awfully dangerous. If not shortly awaked, God in anger will say: "Let their eyes be darkened that they may not see."

Further, consider what time of day it is with you and you will see it is *high time to awake*. How long has your sun been up? Your best season is already gone. With some, I perceive, the sun has already passed its meridian.

Yes, it is now hastening its rapid descent. Aged fathers, your sun is now casting its last beams upon the mountains. "Yet a little while is the light with you. Work while it is day; the night comes when no man can work." If then you have any work to do, any word to leave for your brethren, or your children, they are now waiting to hear. Delay not, for while I am speaking night is coming on. "Whatever your hand finds to do, do it with your might; for there is no work, nor device, nor knowledge, nor wisdom in the grave, whither you go."

The believer ought to awake and take a view of the glorious prospect that lies just before him. Come, then, you mourning pilgrim, you who have long traversed the wilderness asking the way to Zion, you who have long labored and prayed and groaned to be delivered from the bondage of sin, your struggles for eternal life shall have an end. "Look up—and lift up your head, for behold, your redemption draws nigh. It is high time to awake out of sleep; for now is your salvation nearer than when you believed." Nearer than it was last year. Nearer than it was the last Sabbath—nearer than ever, on all the wings of time it flies. This night you may wake up amid the song of angels—and a crown of glory, of eternal life, may be placed on your head.

> Short is the passage, short the space
> Between my home and me;
> There, there behold the radiant place—
> How near the mansions be!

Awake then and behold the glorious dawn of a bright new day. "Where your sun shall no more go down: neither shall your moon withdraw itself, for the Lord shall be your everlasting light, and the days of your mourning shall be ended."

Finally, it is high time to awake, for all who do not awake in time will suddenly awake in hell. There is great danger of being deceived and thus only dreaming of heaven. The Christian can never sleep sound, but is always disturbed. I sleep, says the church, but my heart wakes. He cannot sleep long. He will soon be affrighted and wake up awfully alarmed. But others sleep sound. They are at ease in Zion. They neither weep for their sins nor rejoice in hope of the glory of God. Their hope of heaven is a pleasant dream which cannot be broken. And here they sink down into a deep sleep.

The Christian church is a net which gathers every kind. Ten virgins professed to be followers of Christ. Of this number, five only were real Christians. Many are called, but few are chosen. Many will go to the bar of God with hopes no better than the spider's web. Many who now commune together on earth will never meet in heaven. Many who now appear to us to be real Christians will, no doubt to our surprise, be found on the left hand of Christ.

The sinner having professed religion with a false hope can hardly be driven to give it up. "The hope of the hypocrite is like the giving up of the ghost. What mean you, O sleeper!" If you will not now awake, by the worth of your soul, I entreat you to fling away your hope of heaven. "For there shall be weeping and gnashing of teeth when you shall see Abraham, and Isaac, and Jacob, and all the prophets in the kingdom of God and yourselves thrown out. And behold, there are last which shall be first, and there are first which shall be last."

Better fling away your hope and conclude you are lost than to sleep any longer, for then will you awake in earnest to inquire, "What must I do to be saved? Watch, therefore, for you know not when the master of the house comes, lest coming suddenly he find you sleeping. At midnight the cry will be made, Behold, the bridegroom comes." Then will there be great confusion, for thousands will be deceived. "Let him that thinks he stands take heed."

"These things says he that has the seven spirits of God and the seven stars: I know your works, that you have a name that you live, and are dead. Be watchful, and strengthen the things which remain that are ready to die, for I have not found your works perfect before God. Remember, therefore, how you have received and heard, and hold fast, and repent. If, therefore, you shall not watch, I will come on you as a thief, and you shall not know what hour I will come upon you."

And now it is time—it is high time to awake out of sleep, because many will be forced to awake when suddenly they shall lift up their eyes in hell, being in torment.

10

God's Great Love to Us

Romans 8:32

JAMES WADDEL ALEXANDER

An expert on the history of revivals, J. Edwin Orr, concluded that "the Awakening of 1857–58 was the most thorough and most wholesome movement ever known in the Christian church."[1] Often referred to as the "Laymen's Prayer Revival," this was a spiritual awakening that began with weekly noontime prayer meetings at the North Reformed Dutch Church in Lower Manhattan of New York City, growing from six participants the first week, on September 23, 1857, to as many as 3,000 daily in March, with scores of meeting places by April 1858. Eventually this revival spread across the whole nation of the United States.[2] Coming in a decline of revivalism of the "New Measures" type of Charles Finney, this awakening was characterized by a solemn waiting upon the Holy Spirit in prayer.

In the midst of this ministry in New York City, and encouraging it by his preaching, his writing of tracts, and his prayer services, was James Waddel Alexander (1804–59), pastor of Fifth Avenue Presbyterian Church. Alexander was the son of the founding professor at Princeton Seminary, Archibald

---

1. Quotation from an unpublished manuscript in Iain H. Murray, *Revival & Revivalism: The Making and Marring of American Evangelicalism, 1750–1858* (Edinburgh and Carlisle, Pa.: Banner of Truth Trust, 1994), 332.

2. Murray, *Revival & Revivalism*, 342–43, 331.

Alexander, and like his father he was born in Virginia (March 13, 1804), made profession of his faith in his teens and was ordained in his early twenties, and served as pastor of the Charlotte Court House Church in Virginia (1826–28), where his father had served thirty years earlier. Also like his father, James Alexander had to struggle between a pastoral calling and an academic one. After serving as pastor of the First Presbyterian Church of Trenton, New Jersey from 1829 to 1832, he was professor of rhetoric and Latin language and literature at the College of New Jersey in Princeton from 1833 to 1844. During his eleven years at the College he preached over sixty times a year, and for seven of those years he served as pastor of the African-American Presbyterian Church in Witherspoon Street.[3] Alexander then accepted a call to be pastor of the Duane Street Presbyterian Church in New York City, where he served from 1844 to 1849. With the imminent death of Professor Samuel Miller at Princeton Seminary, the General Assembly elected Alexander to be professor of ecclesiastical history and church government there in 1849. In 1851, however, sorely missing pastoral ministry, he accepted a call to the Fifth Avenue Presbyterian Church in New York City, where he served until his death in 1859.

Signs of spiritual awakening were appearing by the spring of 1856. That summer, while his younger brother, Princeton Seminary professor Joseph Addison Alexander, was staying in his New York home and writing his commentary on Acts, James Alexander was giving his midweek lectures on that same book to his church, and they were attended with great interest. Meanwhile, Jeremiah Lanphier from Alexander's church had begun his ministry at the North Dutch Church on Fulton Street, where the Laymen's Prayer Revival began in September 1857. Alexander and his wife took a trip to Europe for his health from May to October of 1857, and when they returned, they found New York in turmoil over a financial panic of October 14. As the prayer revival gathered momentum, Alexander wrote sixteen tracts for distribution at police and fire stations across the city. In one of these, "Pray for the Spirit," Alexander wrote, "In order to mighty and unexampled revival, what we especially need is for the whole church to be down on its knees before God."[4] As conversions multiplied, Alexander commented on

---

3. David B. Calhoun, *Princeton Seminary*, 2 vols. (1994, 1996), vol. 1: *Faith and Learning, 1812–1868* (Edinburgh and Carlisle, Pa.: Banner of Truth Trust), 287.

4. Murray, *Revival & Revivalism*, 343. Calhoun, *Princeton Seminary*, 1:370.

the increased decorum of the prayer meetings and of the openness of thousands to doctrine and reproof. The books of Charles Haddon Spurgeon were being bought by the thousands. Even presbytery meetings were characterized by brothers "flowing together in love." According to Alexander:

> You may rest assured there is a great awakening among us, of which not one word gets into the papers; and that there are meetings of great size, as free from irreverence as any you ever saw. I have never seen sacramental occasions more tender and still than some meetings held daily in our part of the town.[5]

By June it was estimated that there had been 50,000 conversions in New York and 200,000 across the Northeast.

On January 17, 1859, his brother Addison preached for James at Fifth Avenue Presbyterian Church in the morning, and in the afternoon James preached for a still younger brother, Samuel Davies Alexander, at Fifteenth Street Presbyterian Church. Experiencing "the solemnity" of sharing pulpits with his brothers, he wrote that he longed to preach "with more simplicity—less of the conventional, less regard for rule, less care for criticism, less notice of the literary element, less regard for custom, more as Calvin, as Luther, as Paul preached." He continued:

> As life runs on, I feel the seriousness of my situation as a minister, but, oh, how little improvement! Oh, my ascended Lord and Master! Be pleased to anoint me afresh for my ministry, send me some new and special grace, and cast me not aside as a useless instrument: for Christ's sake. Amen.[6]

James Alexander, whose health was never strong, was no doubt further exhausted from the physical demands of the revival. In June 1859 he and his wife journeyed south for his health, and he died in Red Sweet Springs, Virginia on July 31, 1859.

James Alexander had a keen intellect. During his lifetime he contributed more material that was published in the *Biblical Repository and Princeton Review* than any other author, with the exception of Charles Hodge.[7] It was

---

5. Quoted in Murray, *Revival & Revivalism*, 344.

6. Quoted in Calhoun, *Princeton Seminary*, 1:371.

7. Mark A. Noll, ed., *The Princeton Theology, 1812–1921* (Grand Rapids: Baker, 1983), 16.

his words as a 32-year-old man that brought to a harmonious conclusion a crucial meeting on the Princeton Seminary campus that led to the united stand of Old School Presbyterians in 1837.[8] As a scholar, he preached sound doctrine, but it was above all doctrine to be applied to the lives of spiritually needy people. It was the gospel that he preached. Charles Hodge said that it was the combination of natural ability, wide scholarship, eloquence, and Christian devotion that made James Alexander "not the first of orators to hear on rare occasions, but the first of preachers to sit under month after month and year after year."[9]

His sermon "God's Great Love to Us" is a communion sermon. His doctrinal concerns are evident in his opposition to the Deistic and Socinian challenges to the need for a mediator and in his criticism of "popish legalism." But his focal point is the atonement as the fundamental doctrine of Christianity. The final quarter of the sermon deals with experience. The answer to doubts is the preexisting divine veracity, on which faith lays hold. Look to Christ, he urges, and away from self and all deservings. First the Savior, then his gifts; one puts aside the world and awaits the Lord's coming.

At the memorial service at Alexander's church in New York Charles Hodge preached the sermon from Acts 9:20, most appropriately entitled "He Preached Christ."

GOD'S GREAT LOVE TO US

JAMES WADDEL ALEXANDER

He that spared not his own Son, but delivered him up for us all, how shall he not with him also freely give us all things? (Rom. 8:32)

---

8. Murray, *Revival & Revivalism*, 337.

9. Calhoun, *Princeton Seminary*, 1:489 n.53.

With how inadequate a comprehension do any of us read or hear this saying! To know its meaning, one would need to explore the eternity of the past and the eternity of the future. For it tells of bounty having its spring in the counsels of ages, and of bounty which runs on with branching abundance among immortal spirits in glory. Intermediate in this succession come all the good things of this life, which our Heavenly Father condescends to secure to us by promise. But the principal and absorbing object set before the eye in this remarkable passage is the most wonderful upon which any intellect could turn, and yet—such is our privilege, even from infancy—the most familiar to our mind and memory; namely, the love of God to sinful man. Sometimes we are ready to wish it were possible to travel backward on our line of experience to that point in childhood when gospel grace first came to our cognizance, or else to stand in the position of some serious inquiring heathen who opens his ear and heart to the news of a redeeming God, that by either of these ways we might get rid of the dullness and indifference which our worn and jaded souls derive from long hardening of custom. My brethren, the freshness of apprehension and feeling which we desire can be wrought in us only by faith, which the Spirit of God produces by means of the Word. Continued attention to the one topic before us may be blessed to fit us for the enjoyment of ordinances. Devout consideration of the text will cause it to yield us these two thoughts: God's love to us in giving his Son; and God's love to us carrying with it, and certifying to the soul, all subordinate blessings. One points to the cause, the other to the effects, and each may be examined under a twofold view, which will give clearness to the discussion.

I. *God's Love to Us in Giving His Son*. Here is a great and heavenly subject, which may be properly considered under two aspects: God's love to us is the blessing of blessings; and is demonstrated by the greatest of gifts.

1. *God's Love to Us Is the Blessing of Blessings*. As we and all mankind are no better than orphans in the universe if we have no belief in a Divine Creator and Benefactor, so even thus believing we must be miserable unless we are persuaded that he regards us with favor. A Deity who is, or even may be, malignant towards us would inspire no feelings but those of slavish fear and sickening horror, akin to the experience of heathen devil-worshipers,

who grovel in acts of propitiation to the powers they hate. Nor should we derive any comfort or support from maintaining the existence of a Great Supreme who, as Epicurus dreamed, sat in the heavens indifferent to human weal or woe. So soon as we admit a Great First Cause, ever active in preserving and governing all things, we begin to feel an interest in his dispositions towards us; and our inquiries become the more earnest and yearning with every new apprehension of him as infinite in wisdom and power. "How does this glorious God regard me, and what may I reasonably expect at his hands?" These are questions which lie at the bottom of all religions, under every form of theism. Study of Providence, in the obscure and awful volumes of history and experience, where the pages are often marked with tears and blood, does not ease the mind in regard to man's destiny, or that certainty which we would fain have for ourselves. That God governs and that he is just and ever good is seen to be compatible with the existence of horrid miseries—and what is to hinder these from being our own? What assures us that the next stage of existence may not be infernal? What shall make it undeniable that as evils have been, so they shall not continue and increase? Dark doubtings like these, which unassisted reason cannot exorcise, become of a blacker hue when conscience tells us we are sinners and when we behold vindicatory justice seeking amends of transgressors. Some voice, therefore, is hearkened for which may credibly whisper that God is propitious. If he is our enemy, we perish, and perish all the more because we cannot reenter our original nothing. These boding thoughts, which belong to all human beings, are those which predispose men to seek for a revelation, and which when a revelation is offered lead them to inquire wistfully at its oracle. Now the first teachings, even of the Word of God, are not such as to remove all doubt. The law precedes the gospel. Hope is smitten down before it is lifted to the rock of support. And when conscience is thoroughly aroused, and sin makes its motions felt in the heart, the thought of the Almighty One, clad in holiness and judgment, becomes insufferable. Then it is that he who was previously careless as to his Creator begins to comprehend that unless this glorious Jehovah is his friend, it would be better for soul and body that he had never been born. Deep thought, great knowledge, and just reasoning only add to these solicites; and the more the light is thrown on the Scriptures, the more does the inquirer see that if God is against him, his misery is sure forever. These are the conclusions at which many arrive, and at which all would arrive if guided by truth. What would you offer a man to take the place of God's favor or to neutralize his wrath? Accumulate all honors, science, power, modes of delight or exaltation, and what will they do for him on whose soul and destiny the Lord God Omnipotent looks with a steady frown? Let us go further: Suppose it were possible for God to shower all other gifts on the earthly lot of man, yet withholding his love; would not this be mocking torture? On the other hand, give to any soul assurance of God's perpetual love, and you crown that soul with bliss. In cool, impartial moments, therefore, when reason is sound, all other good seems trifling compared with the love of the infinite Jehovah. The immortal creature needs nothing more to make it happy to all eternity. "There are many," cries David, "that say, who will show us any good? Lord, lift up the light of your countenance upon us." Therefore, we justly conclude that God's love to us is the indispensable favor without which we have nothing; in other words, it is the blessing of blessings.

2. *God's Love Is Demonstrated by the Greatest of Gifts.* The greatest gift is this: "He spared not his own Son, but delivered him up for us all." Other, lesser gifts there are, in gracious, yea divine, abundance, on which we might meditate; but all these are branches from this one root, lesser loves from this one love. We have seen the necessity under which fallen humanity lies of having some assuring utterance of God's benevolence to keep it from despair and elevate it in blissful hope. The infinitely benevolent Creator, who is also the Redeemer, chose to vouchsafe such a manifestation; but no human mind, probably no finite spirit, could ever have had a suspicion or conjecture previously to revealing inspiration what shape this utterance would take. When the mystery burst into revelation, all heaven must have been struck mute at so new, so awful a shining forth of the divine majesty. The great method of saving mankind may be looked at on various sides, from many points of observation, and in manifold relations, but we are about to restrict our view to a single aspect of redeeming grace, namely, God's giving his Son. This will be enough, for it reveals the heart of infinite compassion. God is love; and the divine fullness finds no such fit outlet and effluence as in the delivering up of the Word for us all. The due consideration of the act would carry us back into the eternal ages of primeval silence, when as yet no worlds had rolled from the creative hand, when no angelic spirit had gazed into the face of the First Fair and First Good, when

Godhead as yet was all, and the very relation of Creator and creature lay hid in idea; when the Word was with God, yea, "was God," coequal, consubstantial, coeternal. But we must descend from, or rather assume, these high points of theology and fix our thoughts on the simple truth that "God spared not his own Son."

The sonship with which we are familiar on earth is a copy or shadow of that Eternal Sonship existing between God the Father and God the Son and is perhaps intended to enable us more adequately to comprehend the grandeur and tenderness of the gift. When we read that God spared not his "own Son," a number of gushing affections aptly furnish interpretation as they spring in the parental heart. Things heavenly take earthly types, and infinite throbbings of divine love are translated into terms of domestic affection. "The Father loves the Son" is a proposition true in heaven as in earth; but the profundity, the loftiness, the amplitude of such love neither men nor seraphs can comprehend, any more than they can circumnavigate and fathom infinity. Man was made in God's image—partly we conceive that he might have some notion of his spiritual Creator, and hence man's affections afford some key to the awful, inscrutable acts of the Divine Majesty. But these are so far above, out of our sight, that it is unspeakable relief when by the incarnation we find the heart of God beating in a human bosom and the pulses of infinite affection driving their stream through our own flesh. Yet behind all this is the infinite compassion on which the coming of Christ in human nature is founded. "In this was manifested the love of God toward us, because God sent his only begotten Son into the world, that we might live through him" (1 John 4:9). And here it is necessary to lift an obstacle out of the way, which artful enmity sometimes lays down, before the steps of ignorance. Our scheme of salvation by Christ is thus caviled at by Deistic or Socinian unbelief: "You make a mediator necessary, as though God were implacable. You make God a tyrant, thirsting for blood and refusing to be appeased but by the immolation of his more merciful Son." This is a subtle and blasphemous mode of casting opprobrium on the Scriptures and the cross, and with superficial thinkers and bigoted scoffers it finds too ready acceptance. The charge, whether it comes from ignorance or malice, is purely false and has its origin in the Father of Lies, who, having failed to thwart Christ's work, now seeks to defame it. "We do make a mediator necessary"—not, however, because God is implacable, but in order to carry out the benignant intentions of him who seeks how he may be a "just God" and yet "a Savior." That we represent him as "a tyrant thirsting for blood" is a calumny which our souls abhor, and which we fling back to the pit from whose sulphureous smoke it came; for we honor him who desires not the death of the sinner, and who waits to be gracious. Far from holding that our blessed God "thirsts for blood," as these Sadducean slanderers allege, we gather out of the Scriptures every variety of tender comparison to express the divine earnestness to wrest the souls of men from imminent destruction. And when, by a profane burlesque, our enemies stigmatize the God whom we adore and love as "refusing to be appeased save by the immolation of his Son," we reject the diabolic jeer with filial indignation, and would gladly show them, if enmity could allow them to hear reason, that the tremendous sacrifice of Jesus was the means originated by God himself for the expression and manifestation of a love to man which transcends all creature-conception. Know, those of you whose shallow theology would pluck all that is mysterious and all that is sublime from the system of salvation, that God gave his Son, and that in so giving him he affords the greatest possible manifestation of his uncaused love. In other connections, we might show how other perfections than love made this sacrifice necessary to the declarative glory of God.

The passage before us is far from being the only one in which this form of the great truth is set forth. The giving or delivering of the Son is a favorite mode of inspired expression. Those blessed lips had not long been opened at the night interview with Nicodemus before they uttered this immortal sentence, since graven on a million hearts: "For God so loved the world that he gave his only begotten Son, that whoever believes in him should not perish, but have everlasting life" (John 3:16). The gift, according to the Master, is a proof of love. And by a change of figure, in the very next verse: "For God sent not his Son into the world to condemn the world, but that the world through him might be saved." The sending is, in God's intent, a means to salvation, and so a token of love. God "sent his Son to be the propitiation" (1 John 4:10). "The Father sent his Son to be the Savior of the world" (1 John 4:14). "Whom," says Paul, "God has set forth to be a propitiation" (Rom. 3:25). And more strongly: "For he has made him to be sin for us, who knew no sin, that we might be made the righteousness of God in him" (2 Cor. 5:21). And lest opposers should say the sacrificial part was wrested by wicked men out of God's hands in the exercise of their wicked freedom against his design, we are taught that the very murderers, guilty in the act, were unconsciously causing the wrath of man to praise God and working out his decree. For at Pentecost, Peter thus addresses these executioners concerning Jesus: "Him, being delivered by the determinate counsel and foreknowledge of God, you have taken, and by wicked hands have crucified and slain" (Acts 2:23). In all these places, the words "gave," "sent," "set forth," and "delivered" go to show that the mediatorial work originated in the will and purpose of God, and was the demonstration of his love.

It is not merely a doctrine of Christianity; it is the fundamental doctrine. There is no gospel without it. It is the very gospel, or glad-tidings. Everything else in the gospel is but an expansion of this: God loves the world of sinners. To preach "Christ and him crucified" is to preach God's love. The sinking wretch who believes in Jesus and is saved believes in God's love. All the arguments by which we urge sinners to credit God's willingness to receive them run up into this: "Herein is love, not that we loved God, but that he loved us, and sent his Son to be the propitiation for our sins" (1 John 4:10). And this therefore is what the convert to God feels that he has attained—belief that God loves him. Before, he had no knowledge of God but as a legal Avenger. Even when nearest to the kingdom, he was resting on some supposed truth short of this, and was all in darkness. Day broke when he looked up into the clear countenance of God's love to him. The great efficacy of the cross, indeed, towards God is in the way of expiation, but its great efficacy towards us is as proof of love. Whatever is wanting, this is always present in true faith: persuasion of God's love in Christ. And so whenever we see the things that are freely given us of God, we recognize God's love as demonstrated by the greatest of gifts.

II. *God's Love to Us Carrying with It, and Certifying to the Soul, All Subordinate Blessings.* That is to say, he that so loved as not to spare his own Son, but delivered him up for us all, cannot but with him also freely give us all things. And this necessity of love, this certain out-flowing of streams from the fount, this plenitude of gratuitous kindnesses from the full heart of infinite grace, is made sure to the belief of the soul. Or, separately considered:

1. *God's Love Carries with It All Subordinate Blessings,* that is, all other blessings, because all other blessings are subordinated. This comprises all,

as God comprises the universe. He who has God has all; he who has God's love has the world of divine favors. The greater includes the less; or rather, the whole includes the parts. God's love cannot be conceived as greater than when he gives his own Son, from his own bosom, gives him to be man, to be humbled, to be put to death, to bear punishment, to be made a curse. If a king were to give to his feeble bride, whom he had plucked with strong hand out of slavery, all his possessions and a share of all his kingdom, surely she might rely on him for a piece of bread or a drink of water. This is just the argument of grace. God's great gift necessitates his lesser gifts. God's own Son is so transcendent a donation—how shall he not with him also freely give us all things! The reason why some do not enjoy the full force of this divine logic is that they stagger about the premises. If they only comprehended the immense value of the original gift; if they could only catch a glimpse of the glory, beauty, loveliness, and infinite dearness to the Father of him who is in his bosom; if they did only follow him down from heaven to earth, through his life, agony, and bloody sweat, his cross and passion, his burial, resurrection, and ascension; if they only stood amazed, as well they might, at this great love with which God loved us while we were yet dead in sins—why, brethren, they could no more doubt God's love and willingness to bless, in all things else, than the bride folded in the embrace of affection can suspect the husband who has endowed her with his all of plotting her ruin. The entire unbroken chain of covenant love hangs on God's intention, from the first link to the last, from decree to consummation. "Whom he did predestinate, them he also called: and whom he called, them he also justified; and whom he justified, them he also glorified" (Rom. 8:30). How natural, how irresistible the conclusion that immediately follows? "What shall we then say to these things? If God is for us, who can be against us?" And then our text—a text which embosoms all the gospel in all its principle and all its effects, source and flood, center and circumference, love and bliss, from God to the creature, forever and forever.

Seek no longer, then, Christian brethren, to separate the love of the Son from the love of the Father. They are but dimensions of one and the same amazing orb. Seek rather, with all saints, to comprehend what is the breadth and length and depth and height, and to know the love of Christ which passes knowledge, that you might be filled with all the fullness of God. The reason why we do not expatiate on the subordinate gifts is that they are innumerable, comprehending all good which can tend to the happiness and perfection of the creature. In the sublime burst which follows our text, even the Pauline diction reels under the load of benefit, while his wide induction draws within its circle death, life, angels, things present, things to come, height, depth, yea, all creatures—tracing up all to "the love of God which is in Christ Jesus our Lord" (v. 39).

2. *God's Love to Us Certifying to the Soul All Subordinate Blessings.* Here doctrine turns into experience, as the bud becomes a flower. The doctrine was that God's love in the capital article leads by necessary result to his love in every other article; the experience is that I know and feel it to be so; I open my heart to the greater good and to those which are less; I believe and am persuaded that God is for me and that none—that nothing—can be against me. If this is wanting in any of us, it is because we have not faith. And here, my brethren, I am bound to testify, whomever it may startle or offend, that a large number of Christians, even in those which they consider their most profitable moments, go about the work of obtaining peace in their hearts by an inverted process, the very opposite of what is prescribed in the New Testament. When doubts overcloud their confidence, when remaining sin stirs inwardly, when the future looks portentous, when their religion has become all trembling and tears—what is it they do? Perhaps you know this very sacramental hour. They sit down to the work of exclusively scanning and measuring wretched, imperfect self. They turn over the massive books, filled with their own liabilities. They debit themselves with ten thousand items which they can never pay. They hope by this method to find a balance so favorable that they shall be able to rise hoping in God, and therefore to apply to promises made to regenerate persons. I dare boldly pronounce, from God's Word, that genuine evangelical comfort was never produced in this way—never, never, never. This Sinai never yet uttered peace, while it has thundered many a believer into temporary despair. What then is the right way? We need attention, for we are touching the very vital point of difference between old divinity and the new, between the joyful free grace which from the silver trumpets of Luther, Melanchthon, Calvin, Knox, and Cranmer shook and melted Europe in a great portion of its church and that substitute of alleged improvement but real retrocession to popish legalism, which has made the chief part of many experiences to consist in doubting and which, if pursued to legitimate re-

sults, would speedily land us in a scheme of self-salvation. It ought to be clear to any reason that the ground of a sinner's trust in Christ for salvation must be something independent of, and prior to, any exercises of his own soul—yea, something that is the cause of such exercises—and that therefore, when doubts arise, the resort to ultimate support must be to this same pre-existing and divine ground. And what can this be but the divine veracity assuring us that God loves us! Precisely for this reason is faith so often dwelt on as the instrument because faith, as faith, lays hold of God's veracity, and trust is nothing else but faith in a promise. Here then is our experience of God's love, when "the love of God is shed abroad in the heart by the Holy Ghost," and here the way of direct escape out of Satan's legal net. Poor pilgrim, have you like Bunyan's mythic Christian been confronted by Moses and left smarting? Flee to Jesus Christ. All Martin Luther's experience was a wrestling against the demon of legality. God was preparing him to teach a free gospel with a strength of expression which makes his book on the Galatians a golden volume. "But you will say" (says he, on Galatians 5:5), "I feel not myself to have any righteousness, or at the least, I feel but very little. You must not feel, but believe that you have righteousness. And unless you believe that you are righteous, you do great injury unto Christ, who has cleansed you by the washing of water through the Word, who also died upon the cross, condemned sin, and killed death, that through him you might obtain righteousness and everlasting life." O how precious to my recollection is St. Mary's Church Aldermanbury, near which I once lodged, because there it was that Poor Joseph, having a large parcel of yarn hanging over his shoulders, went in and heard the text which saved him: 1 Timothy 1:15. On his dying bed, the happy, simple soul possessed the certitude of God's love to him as a sinner. For (you remember) when some of the religious sort asked, "But what say you of your own heart, Joseph? Is there no token of good about it? No saving change there? Have you closed with Christ by acting faith upon him?" "Ah, no!" replied he. "Joseph can act nothing—Joseph has nothing to say of himself but that he is the chief of sinners; yet seeing that it is a faithful saying that Jesus, he who made all things, came into the world to save sinners, why may not Joseph after all be saved?" We have stood by the dying bed of great and learned Christians, long the guides of others in theology; but their faith was that of Poor Joseph, a divinely wrought persuasion of God's love to them, evidenced by the gift of his own Son. The nearest, safest, truest way to Christ is the direct way. After all your self-examinations, preparations, and conditions, you will have to throw them away, and come thus at last. Come now—and from the opened side behold all blessings issuing in a perpetual, widening, deepening river. What is it that can harm you if you accept God's own Son? Condemnation? "It is God that justifies." Death for your sins? "It is Christ that died, yea rather that is risen again, who is even at the right hand of God, who also makes intercession for us." Can he condemn or punish—such is the meaning—him who died, who rose, who reigns, who intercedes? Look to him, and away with self and all deservings. And if you fear your own weakness, lest you should fall away, know that security against this also is in the grant. Because it would be nugatory and dishonorable to the Scriptures so to interpret verses 35–39 as if they meant that though "tribulation, distress, persecution, etc.," though "angels, principalities, powers," etc., cannot separate us from Christ, yet sin can and may! Shocking nullification of the covenant! For how could any or all of these ever separate except by sin! And what a glorying would that be, or appear to be, if all he meant was, "Thank God, I shall never be separated, unless I sin, and so separate myself!" No, dear fellow believers, you have not so learned Christ, nor has this been the hope you have derived from his Word when you have heard him say: "I give unto them eternal life; and they shall never perish, neither shall any man pluck them out of my hand" (John 10:28). Feeble would be the reliance if eventual salvation hung suspended on the hair of our own will, which might break under satanic temptations in the last hour! But no! "I am persuaded that neither death, nor life, nor angels, nor principalities, nor powers, nor things present nor things to come, nor height, nor depth, nor any other creature, shall be able to separate us from the love of God, which is in Christ Jesus our Lord."

"The love of God"—it is our theme. We have seen it comprehending and certifying all, through the gift of the Son. And hence it is that you have this morning heard so little of merely temporal benefits. Christ gives these indeed out of his immeasurable fullness, but gives them only as appendages to the chief good. "God will give grace and glory; no good thing will he withhold from them that walk uprightly." Have you the greater gift, my suffering brother or sister? Be assured you shall have the less. Whatever is best for your ultimate blessedness and glory will be dispensed to you in due manner, measure, and time. The unreconciled hear this with disgust. A gospel which should offer earthly good is all the gospel they desire; and if they sometimes faintly sigh for religion, it is in hope of increasing selfish earthly good. But you, who have been taught by the Spirit to consider sin the grand evil and Christ the all-comprising good, you will rejoice in this gradation of benefits: first my Savior, then his gifts. For you have learned to look at the things which are not seen, but are eternal. And experience has long since convinced you that you never had so much real enjoyment of worldly things as when you forgot them entirely as a distinct object of pursuit, and that you never really knew what happiness in religion was until you made an entire, unreserved surrender, relinquishing to the world, and to worldly communicants, the race after riches, the contest for place, the miserable rivalry of lineage, dress, equipage, entertainment, and expense, the pride of knowledge, art, and literature, and girded up your loins to await the Lord's coming.

11

The Headship of Christ over the Church

Ephesians 1:22–23

BENJAMIN MORGAN PALMER

The Presbyterian Church, U.S., or "Southern Presbyterian Church," was born as the Presbyterian Church in the Confederate States of America on December 4, 1861 as it opened its First General Assembly in Augusta, Georgia. A year and a half earlier the Old School Presbyterian Church had enjoyed a relatively cordial General Assembly in May of 1860, although the tensions between North and South were already on the rise with the Republican party's nomination for President that month of Abraham Lincoln, who was perceived in the South as radically anti-slavery. Lincoln's election as President of the United States on November 6, 1860 triggered a reaction across the deep South, threatening secession from the Union. The reaction included some of the pulpits of the Presbyterian church. On Wednesday, November 21, a day declared by the government of South Carolina as a day of prayer and fasting, James Henley Thornwell preached in the Presbyterian Church of Columbia a "Sermon on National Sins." On November 29, on a similar occasion in Louisiana, Benjamin Morgan Palmer (1818–1902) preached a "Thanksgiving Sermon" in the First Presbyterian

Church of New Orleans. Both Thornwell and Palmer acknowledged that it was a departure from lifelong commitments not to bring matters of secular politics into the pulpit, but they felt the occasion to be extraordinary, demanding that they bring their understanding of God's will to the national situation. In his stirring address, Palmer expressed the conviction that God assigns to a people a historic trust. Then he made a declaration that is astounding to more modern ears: "If then the South is such a people, what, at this juncture, is their providential trust: I answer, that it is *to conserve and to perpetuate the institution of domestic slavery as now existing.*"[1] He viewed this as a matter of self-preservation, but also as in the best interests of the slaves for whom Southerners were the guardians and for the good of the civilized world that depended on Southern agricultural products. Palmer's oratory had an electric effect on his audience, and thousands of copies of his address were distributed across the South. One contemporary claimed that Palmer had done more than "any other non-combatant in the South to promote rebellion."[2] Later in life Palmer may have regretted preaching that sermon, according to his biographer:

> The time came when the wisdom of his course in preaching that sermon seemed less apparent; indeed, he is said to have repented preaching the discourse, though the day never came when he took an essentially different view of the great subject discussed.[3]

By the time that the Old School Presbyterian General Assembly met in Philadelphia in May of 1861, the nation was already dividing. South Carolina had fired on Fort Sumter on April 12, and President Lincoln had called up troops to quell the rebellion. All the Southern states had withdrawn from the Union except for Tennessee and North Carolina, and the latter seceded during the General Assembly's meeting. On May 28 the As-

---

1. Quoted in Thomas Cary Johnson, *The Life and Letters of Benjamin Morgan Palmer* (Richmond, Va.: Presbyterian Committee of Publication, 1906), 209, italics in the original. The entire address is on pp. 206–18.

2. Ernest Trice Thompson, *Presbyterians in the South*, 3 vols. (Richmond, Va.: John Knox Press, 1963, 1973), vol. 1: *1607–1861*, 557–58.

3. Johnson, *Life of Palmer*, 223.

sembly adopted resolutions offered by Gardiner Spring, pastor of the Brick Presbyterian Church of New York City. The second resolution stated:

> That this General Assembly . . . do hereby acknowledge and declare our obligations to promote and perpetuate, as far as in us lies, the integrity of these United States, and to strengthen, uphold, and encourage, the Federal Government in the exercise of all its functions under our noble Constitution: and to this Constitution in all its provisions, requirements, and principles, we profess our unabated loyalty. . . .[4]

The "Gardiner Spring Resolutions" were adopted 156–66. Charles Hodge of Princeton offered a protest, which was signed by 57 others. The protest claimed that the Assembly's action answered an essentially political question of whether one's allegiance should be primarily to the Union or to the States, a question on which Christian consciences were divided. The Assembly's answer to the protest was vehement:

> Would they [the protestants] have us recognize, as good Presbyterians, men whom our own government, with the approval of Christendom, may soon execute as traitors? . . . What, when "a crime, the heinousness of which can be only imperfectly estimated" . . . is already committed; when thousands of Presbyterians are likely to be seduced from their allegiance by the machinations of wicked men; . . . when armed rebellion joins issue with armed authority on battle-fields, where tens of thousands must perish; when it remains a question, whether our national life survives the conflict . . . is it uncalled for, unnecessary, for this Christian Assembly to renew . . . respect for the majesty of law, and a sense of the obligation of loyalty?[5]

Clearly, in the heat of the circumstances, the North was matching the South in seeing matters in black-and-white terms with no moderate shades of gray in between. Palmer's "Thanksgiving Sermon," identifying abolitionism with the spirit of the French Revolution, had put the Southern case as the defense of God, all religion, and all truth against atheism.[6]

---

4. Quoted in Thompson, *Presbyterians in the South*, 1:564.
5. Quoted in Thompson, *Presbyterians in the South*, 1:566.
6. Johnson, *Life of Palmer*, 212–13.

By August of 1861 all Old School presbyteries of the Southern states (by now including Tennessee) were being summoned to a General Assembly of a newly constituted Presbyterian Church in the Confederate States of America, to meet in Augusta, Georgia on December 4. It was on that date that Benjamin Morgan Palmer preached the opening sermon and then was elected, by acclamation after two other candidates yielded, as moderator of the First Assembly. James Henley Thornwell was generally recognized as the intellectual leader of Southern Presbyterianism; however, his failing health prevented his serving as moderator, and his gifts were best employed from the floor of the Assembly.[7]

Palmer at this point had been pastor of the First Presbyterian Church of New Orleans, one of the largest congregations in the denomination, for five years. His roots were in South Carolina. Born January 25, 1818 in Charleston, he entered Amherst College in Massachusetts at age 14, his parents both having come from New England backgrounds. After two years there, reacting to what he viewed as unfair aspersions on Southern life, he completed his college education at the University of Georgia in 1838 and his seminary education at Columbia Theological Seminary in 1841. While at the latter, he sat under the preaching of Thornwell at the First Presbyterian Church of Columbia, South Carolina. Licensed in 1841, Palmer served at Anderson, South Carolina and then at the First Presbyterian Church of Savannah, Georgia. In 1843 he was called to succeed Thornwell as pastor at Columbia, where he continued to 1854. In that year he was called to serve as professor of ecclesiastical history and polity at Columbia Seminary, but in 1856 he accepted the pastorate of the First Presbyterian Church of New Orleans.[8] In 1860 the Old School Presbyterian General Assembly invited Palmer by a unanimous vote, ironically on a nomination made by Gardiner Spring, to take the chair of Pastoral Theology and Sacred Rhetoric at Princeton Seminary.[9] Palmer was by this time, however, committed to the pastorate, and except for interruptions from the Civil War, he would remain in New Orleans until his death in 1902. During the war he ministered to the Army of the West for two months in the

---

7. Thompson, *Presbyterians in the South*, vol. 2: *1861–1890*, 17.

8. Morton H. Smith, *Studies in Southern Presbyterian Theology* (Jackson, Miss.: Presbyterian Reformation Society and Amsterdam: Jacob Van Campen, 1962), 217–18.

9. Thompson, *Presbyterians in the South*, 1:552–53.

summer of 1862 and to the Army of Tennessee in the summer of 1863. He taught theology at Columbia Seminary from 1862 to 1865 while unable to be in New Orleans.

The First Church of New Orleans was the fourth largest Presbyterian church in the South, with 531 members, when Palmer came as pastor in 1856. In 1866 it had 436 members, but by 1880 it had 749. His preaching attracted 300 to 500 visitors on Sundays in 1870, and in 1885 there was an attendance of 1,500 at a Sunday morning service.[10] He was recognized for his faithful pastoral ministry, comforting the sick and bereaved from all stations of life, but primarily for his oratorical gifts. His voice had great power and versatility. Although somewhat under average height, he often gave the impression of being much taller. He preached normally without notes, and even when he did use a manuscript—as on the occasions of his "Thanksgiving Sermon" and of his opening sermon for the First General Assembly—he spoke with great freedom. He was acknowledged as one of the four greatest orators of the Southern Presbyterian Church and perhaps the most eloquent of all.[11] His preaching tended to be topical, addressing the great doctrines of Scripture, including the distinctive doctrines of Calvinism. As his biographer noted:

> He was a living refutation of the widely current notion that the day of doctrinal preaching is over. For thirteen years in one pulpit and forty-six years in another, he was preeminently a doctrinal preacher, and a preacher of the very marrow of the doctrines of sacred Scriptures. He delighted in preaching the great cardinal doctrines.[12]

His forty-six years of ministry in New Orleans came to an end when he was struck by a streetcar on May 5, 1902, when on his way to a church meeting. With a broken leg and other injuries, he lingered for a few weeks, lapsed into a coma, and died on May 25 at age 84.[13]

---

10. Thompson, *Presbyterians in the South*, 1:426; 2:284–85 n., 379.

11. Thompson, *Presbyterians in the South*, 2:379–80. For other descriptions of Palmer as a preacher, see Johnson, *Life of Palmer*, 650, 660–65, and Smith, *Studies in Southern Presbyterian Theology*, 218–20.

12. Johnson, *Life of Palmer*, 661.

13. Johnson, *Life of Palmer*, 620–24.

Palmer's opening sermon on the historic occasion of the First General Assembly of the Southern Presbyterian Church on December 4, 1861 enunciates several of the distinctive themes of that denomination, including the spiritual nature of the church and the "divine right" nature of Presbyterian polity. The theme is "The Headship of Christ over the Church," set forth as the crucial topic for the historic situation. There is obvious consciousness of the occasion for the church and for the nation. Allusion is made to the Gardiner Spring Resolutions of the Old School General Assembly of the previous May:

> Do we understand, fathers and brethren, the mission of the church given us here to execute? It is to lift up throughout the world our testimony for this headship of Christ. The convocation of this Assembly is in part that testimony. But a little while since, it was attempted in the most august court of our church to place the crown of our Lord upon the head of Caesar—to bind that body, which is Christ's fullness, to the chariot in which that Caesar rides. . . . And now this Parliament of the Lord's freemen solemnly declares that, by the terms of her great charter, none but Jesus may be the King in Zion.

Christ alone is the legislator for the church, and "all power under him is simply ministerial."

But before he reaches these conclusions, Palmer develops the doctrines both of the deity and humanity of Christ as head of the church and then of the doctrine of the church, both as ideal and as actual and visible. Along the way there are numerous oratorical flourishes, of which only one will suffice here as an example: "Bursting from the secret pavilion, the eternal Word leaps forth to execute the stern demand. He unclothes himself of light, lays aside the garments of praise, and takes upon himself the form of a servant, that he may sound the depths of human woe and pay the costly ransom for a guilty soul." Fittingly, the great orator concludes with the cross of Christ and an appeal to carry out the Great Commission. However much Palmer was influenced by the patriotic currents of his situation in the context of the Civil War, even to the point of inconsistency with his own doctrine of the purely spiritual nature of the church, his emphasis fell on the gospel of Jesus Christ.

THE HEADSHIP OF CHRIST
OVER THE CHURCH

BENJAMIN MORGAN PALMER

Fathers and brethren: This Assembly is convened under circumstances of unusual solemnity, and any one of us might well shrink from the responsibility of uttering the first words which are to be spoken here. I see before me venerable men whom the church of God has honored with the highest mark of her confidence—men venerable for their wisdom, no less than for their age—who should, perhaps, as your organ, speak today in the hearing of the nation and of the church. But a Providence which I have had no hand in shaping seems to have devolved upon me this duty, as delicate as it is solemn. It only remains for me to bespeak your sympathy, and to implore the divine blessing upon what I may be able to say from the concluding words of the first chapter of Ephesians: "And gave him to be head over all things to the church, which is his body, the fullness of him that fills all in all" (Eph. 1:22–23).

You have often admired in the epistles of Paul the vigor of his inspired and sanctified logic, driving like a wedge through the complications of the most perplexed reasoning to its very heart. Not less wonderful is that intellectual comprehensiveness which, stretching across the breadth of a zone, gathers up all the indirections of his theme and lays them over upon it in rapid and cumulative utterances, till language begins to break beneath the weight of his thought; and the arguments, set on fire with the ardor of his emotion, reach the goal a perfect pyramid of flame. The passage just recited is a sufficient example of this rare combination of the discursive with the severely logical in writings of this great apostle; for the grand thoughts it presents are nevertheless gathered up by the way, and wrought into the texture of his discourse by incidental illusion. Having first traced the calling and salvation of these Ephesian Christians to its source in the free and gracious love of God, through which they were chosen in Christ, and having unfolded the method of grace, by redemption through his blood, he pauses that he may lift them to some adequate conception of the privileges into which they have been introduced. This, however, he attempts not through cold and didactic exposition, but in the language of prayer, burning throughout with a holy and earnest passion: "that the eyes of their understanding may be enlightened, to know what is the hope of their calling, what are the riches of the glory of their inheritance," and what is the almightiness of the power by which they have been transformed from sinners into saints. Then as if to give some external measure of that power, he points them to the resurrection and exaltation of Christ, in which their own spiritual renovation is implicitly contained. Kindling with the grandeur of his theme growing thus by the accumulation of wayside suggestions, he heaps together in rapid description these phrases burdened with the glory of that headship which belongs to this risen Savior, and the honors of that church standing to him in such august relations; till even Paul, with his inspired logic all on fire, can say nothing more than that she is "his body, the fullness of him that fills all in all." The power of human speech is exhausted in this double utterance, and silence lends its emphasis to the unspoken thoughts which no dialect beneath that of the seraphim may express. Who of us, my brethren, has not been stunned by this holy vehemence of Paul as he piles together his massive words, each bursting with a separate wealth, and revealing the agony of language in uttering the deep things of God? What resource have we but to halt at the articulation of his text—until, stored with their digressive sweets, we return to follow the wheels of his chariot as it bounds along the great highway of his discourse? Such an excursus I now propose to you, for no theme occurs to me more suited to the solemnity of this occasion than the supreme dominion to which Christ is exalted as the head of the church, and the glory of the church in that relation as being at once his body and his fullness.

The testimony of Scripture is given with great largeness to this headship of Christ. In this immediate connection, Paul affirms that he is "set at the Father's own right hand in the heavenly places, far above all principality and power, and might and dominion, and every name that is named, not only in this world, but also in that which is to come; and has put all things under his feet, and gave him to be the head over all things" (Eph. 1:20–23). Again, in Philippians: "Therefore, God also has highly exalted him and given him a name which is above every name, that at the name of Jesus every knee should bow, of things in heaven and things in earth, and things under the earth, and that every tongue should confess that Jesus Christ is Lord, to the glory of God the Father" (Phil. 2:9–11). What enumeration can be more exhaustive, and what description more minute, of the universality and glory of this dominion? In like manner, we read in the prophetic record the testimony of Daniel: "I saw in the night visions, and behold, one like the Son of Man came with the clouds of heaven, and came to the Ancient of Days, and they brought him near before him; and there was given him dominion and glory, and a kingdom, that all people, nations, and languages should serve him. His dominion is an everlasting dominion, which shall not pass away, and his kingdom that which shall not be destroyed" (Dan. 7:13–14). The evangelical Isaiah, too, lifts up the voice of the ancient church: "For unto us a child is born, unto us a son is given, and the government shall be upon his shoulders; and his name shall be called Wonderful, Counselor, the Mighty God, the Everlasting Father, the Prince of Peace. Of the increase of his government and peace there shall be no end, upon the throne of David and upon his kingdom to order it, and to establish it with judgment and with justice, from henceforth even forever" (Isa. 9:6–7). Our Lord himself asserts his claim of universal empire and founds upon it the Great Commission of the church: "All power is given unto me in heaven and upon earth—go, therefore, and teach all nations" (Matt. 28:18–19). Finally, the lonely seer on Patmos turns his telescopic gaze into the heavens, and reveals the Grand Assembly in their solemn worship around the throne, "and the number of them was ten thousand times ten thousand, and thousands of thousands, and every creature which is in heaven and on the earth, and under the earth, and such as are in the sea, and all that are in them, heard I saying, blessing and honor, glory and power, be unto him that sits upon the throne, and unto the Lamb forever and ever" (Rev. 5:11–13). Such is the testimony of prophecy, both as it begins and as it closes the sacred canon.

Observe, however, of whom all this is affirmed. It is not alone of the Eternal Word which dwelt in Christ—but of the Christ in whom these two natures meet and are indissolubly united. So that we are compelled to look upon both the terms of his complex person before we can apprehend the nature and the greatness of his supremacy. We shall discover reasons in both for the sublime agency assigned to him as "the whole creation's head."

I. A. Looking, then, upon the divine side, it is obvious:

1. That all the perfections of God are indispensable to the fulfillment of this amazing trust. Recurring to the passages already quoted, this headship clearly includes universal conservation and rule. The whole administration of Providence and law over matter and over mind is delegated to this head, who cannot, therefore, be a mere creature, lacking the first attributes necessary to the execution of his task. Suppose the universe of matter to be created, yet is it throughout, from the atom to the mass, senseless and inert. The mechanical forces pent up within its gigantic frame slumber in a repose deep as that of death, until evoked and put in play by the operative will of the Great Designer; and the constant pressure of the same external will is the secret power by which the wheels and pistons of the blind machine are driven.

Proudly as science may descant upon the laws of nature which it is her province to explore, they are at last but the formulas into which our knowledge, drawn from extended observation, is generalized. It would be sad if reason should be deceived by the pompous phraseology which often serves but as the cover for that ignorance it is too proud to confess. These physical laws are but records of facts inductively classified, not producing causes to which these facts owe existence. They are only statements of the modes through which nature is seen to work, and not the secret power to which that working is due. Providence stands over against creation thus as its correlate, precisely the same energy being required in *the continuing* which was first put forth in *the producing*. The agent, then, to whom this administration of Providence is assigned must possess the attributes of God. His influential presence must pervade all nature, upholding its separate parts, balancing its discordant forces, adjusting in exact proportions its constituent elements, reconstructing it amid constant change—its omnipotent and supporting head.

The same is true in the domain of mind. Myriads of beings, for example, have pressed this globe, each of whom has a history of his own, and each history a separate thread in the great web of Providence. The slenderest of them may not be drawn without a rent in the general tissue. The tiniest babe that wakes but for a moment to an infant's joy and then closes its eyes in sleep forever was born for a purpose, though born but to die. But see these countless units as they are massed together in society, compacted into states, and living under government and law. What complications are here to be mastered by him who is placed as head over all! Alas, the best statesmanship of earth breaks down in the management even of its subdivided trusts. Contingencies it had not the wisdom to foresee, and too stubborn for control, bring its counsels to naught; and the web so patiently woven by day is unraveled in the night. What creature, then, may aspire to the premiership of the universe? As the thought ranges upward from the earth through the grand hierarchy of the skies, who among the creatures can take the scale of such an empire, grasp the law which angels and seraphim obey, weave the destinies of all into one historic conclusion, and draw it up finished and entire before the judgment throne? Just here, then, in the attributes of his Godhead, we discern the competency of Christ to be the head over all things—equal to the statesmanship of the universe, in the perfect administration of a perfect law.

Thus far we have pressed up to the divinity of Christ, but not to his personal distinction in the Godhead as the only begotten of the Father. I remark, then:

2. That this agency is suitably assigned to him as the middle person of the adorable Trinity, by whose immediate efficiency all things were created. We may not too curiously pry into the mystery of this plural subsistence in the Godhead, revealed to us as the object of faith rather than as the subject of speculation. Unquestionably, God is infinitely blessed and glorious in the ineffable fellowship of these persons as well as in the unity of his being. But as these personal distinctions have their ground in that singleness of nature, they must equally concur in all the external operations of the Deity; and so the Scriptures variously ascribe the works of creation, providence, and grace to each respectively. In this there is no contradiction, since they are assigned comprehensively to all in their unity, and distributively to each in their separateness. However unable we may be to trace the grounds of that distribution, they must be found in the reciprocal relations of those persons in the mystery of the Godhead. Cer-

tainly the Scriptures, however they may generally refer the work of creation to God absolutely, as clearly assert the special intervention of the second person as its immediate author. Paul, speaking of the Son whom God "has appointed heir of all things," adds, "by whom he also made the worlds" (Heb. 1:2). John in the opening of his gospel declares with emphasis of the Word that "all things were made by him, and without him was not anything made" (John 1:3). And in Colossians, "by him were all things created that are in heaven, and that are in earth, visible and invisible, whether they are thrones or dominions or principalities or powers; all things were created by him and for him—and he is before all things, and by him all things consist" (Col. 1:16–17). If then in the outworking of this mighty plan the control and government of all created things should be delegated to an agent who must possess the attributes of the Almighty, which of the sacred three may occupy this trust more suitably than he who in the economy of the Godhead executively and directly brought all things into being? Who shall more perfectly grasp the design of creation than he who articulately wrought it out in all its parts? Who shall better gather up all things into himself as the center and the head, and administer that Providence which is but the continuation of the creative energy which he first put forth?

Unsearchable as the mystery of God's being doubtless is, three facts are certainly revealed to us: the unity of the divine essence, a threefold distinction of persons in the same, and a certain order between them by which the second is *from* the first—not posterior in time, but second in the sequence of thought. It would seem to be a consequence of this personal characteristic of the Son as being *from* the Father that the total revelation of God, whether by word or work, should be through him. Thus a ground may exist in the eternal relationship of these persons for referring the works of creation, providence, and grace, distributively to the first in the way of final authority, and to the second in the way of executive production. The Father, who is before all, shall hold in his august keeping the eternal thought which drafts the mighty plan. The Son, by virtue of his personal distinction as *from* the Father, shall produce the thought, lifting it up from the abyss of the infinite mind and revealing it to the creatures. Thus the Son is also the Word, the one title being descriptive of his personal relation in the Godhead and the other of his office as the revealer flowing from the same. Hence Christ says: "No man has seen the Father, save he which is of God; he has seen the Father" (John 6:46). And again the evangelist John affirms, "No man has seen God at any time; the only begotten Son which is in the bosom of the Father, he has declared him" (John 1:18). In like manner, as the Son is from the Father, so in turn the Holy Spirit is from them both; and he who holds the middle place in this sacred triplet looks upon the first for those archetypal thoughts which he shall render into concrete facts, and then upon the third whose concurrent agency shall breathe life and order and beauty into the works of his hands. As therefore in Christ's divinity we discover the resources, so again in his personal distinction as the Son we trace the ultimate reason of this universal headship.

B. But let us turn from thoughts too high for us to contemplate the *human* aspect of his person. For if the power to wield this empire vests in him as God, no less does the form of that jurisdiction depend upon a true participation in the nature of those to whom he is the head. I may open this topic in three particulars:

1. *By his incarnation he has virtually embraced all the grades of being lying between the extremes of the scale.* The peculiar distinction of man is through his mixed composition to be the middle link of the whole creation. As to his body, he is of the earth, earthy; as to his soul, celestial and Godlike. How wonderful his bodily organization, of so many parts, and so wisely adjusted, the most singular feature of all being that the presence of an indwelling, actuating soul is the indispensable condition of its physical life. The two are distinct, yet their cooperation necessary. The anatomist can trace the impressions upon the skin with its fine tissues, and the transmission of these along the nerves to the brain, the sea of all sensation. But science will never perfect her methods so as to step from that brain to the mind which uses it as an organ, and thus explain to us the birth of a single thought. By means of the body, the soul comes forth and takes possession of a world which is foreign to itself; and man connects them both by their mysterious union in himself. So far as our knowledge extends, he is the only being who unites these contradictions; thus fitted by his very organization, he was placed by his Maker in paradise the head of the lower creation. In token of this supremacy, the beasts receive from him their baptismal names and express their allegiance to God's vice-regent upon the earth. As the

high priest of nature, he must give articulate voice to her silent praise and gather up in his censer the incense of a universal worship. Such was the glory of man's primeval state: himself a microcosm, summing together in the perfection of his animal frame all the properties of the material creation, and by the union of spirit bridging the awful gulf of separation between the two. Christ now according to Scriptures sinks through the entire scale of intelligent beings till he comes to man: "for verily, he took not on him the nature of angels, but he took on him the seed of Abraham" (Heb. 2:16). The two poles of being are thus brought together in him: of being, as it is in God, self-existent and eternal; and of being, as it is in man, dependent and derived. In the sweep of his descent he gathers up all the intervening grades, and finds in man at the bottom of the scale a nature which links all the forms of creaturely existence within itself. Thus in the incarnation he lays a broad foundation for his headship, establishing through it a relation to the creatures by which they may be recapitulated in him as their center and their rest.

2. *The human title of Christ to this headship is grounded upon that perfect obedience by which he magnified the law.* If we are overwhelmed by the condescension of the Son in stooping to become man, not less amazing is the counterpart to this in the exaltation of man to this universal headship. The incarnation lays, so to speak, a *physical* basis for this delegated rule by allying him in nature with the creature; but there must exist some *moral* ground for this apparent inversion, which transfers man from the bottom to the top of the scale.

All the terms which define a created moral being imply his subjection under law. The faculties of understanding, conscience, and will with which he is endowed must find their scope in relations which are determined and regulated through a law. What the air is to the lungs, the law is to will; it creates the moral atmosphere through which all the powers of the soul find their activity and play. Even Christ, in the assumption of our nature, was not exempt from this inexorable condition, for "God sent forth his son made of a woman, made under the law" (Gal. 4:4); "being found in fashion as a man, he became obedient unto death" (Phil. 2:8). How then shall his humanity lift itself above the law, executively to administer it, dispensing on either hand its blessing and its curse? The explanation is immediately furnished in the passage last cited. "Therefore, God also has highly exalted him"; because of this "obedience unto death, even the death of the cross," "a name is given him which is above every name, at which every knee shall bow, of things in heaven and things in earth, and things under the earth" (Phil. 2:9–10). In no way conceivable shall the man Jesus be lifted to this supremacy but by rendering a service to the law commensurate with its dignity, and to which this exaltation shall be an equal reward. The mere assumption of humanity by the Logos doubtless invests it with a sublime worth and imparts to the acts done by it an infinite value. But the natural basis thus laid for headship is quite another thing from the moral reason for appointing it. If, however, the work done in that nature shall be a work of support to the law itself, more conspicuously revealing its majesty and sustaining it against all possible impeachment; if it shall heal the dreadful breach which sin has made, and discover the love of God in the very assertion of his justice; if, in the language of the prophet, it shall "magnify the law and make it honorable," and be a lesson of holiness which the angels themselves shall study—we may then conceive that, to bring out these grand results in more open view, God may place the administration of this law in the hands of that being who has preeminently honored it, and install over the whole creation one who is fitted by his double nature to be its head. Yet the hypothesis I have suggested is only a faint outline of the work actually achieved by our incarnate Lord. Who can hope to condense into a paragraph the glories of that obedience by which he has forever magnified the law? An obedience glorious in being distinctly offered to the precept and the penalty, thus covering the whole area of law and exhausting its contents—a characteristic difference between the obedience of Christ and of all other beings throughout the universe. An obedience glorious as shut up within a limit, bounded within a period—so that Christ could testify in the hearing of heaven and earth, "It is finished"—not like the obedience of mere creatures, ever continuing but finished and entire; nothing to be added to it, nothing to be taken from it, and borne into the chancery of heaven as the plea for the sinner's discharge. An obedience glorious through the hypostatic union, which brings the splendors of his deity to illumine the acts of his humanity. If Moses breaks the tables of stone at the foot of the mount, behold one greater than Moses descending after him to gather up the broken fragments, cementing them with his blood, and pouring the rays of his divine glory upon the restored tablet, until every letter beams with light above the brightness of the sun. Well may the cherubim bend their gaze between their extended wings upon this repaired law reposing forever within the ark of the covenant. The transcendent worth of this obedience, as sustaining the majesty of God's law and upholding the integrity of the divine government, is signalized by placing him who wrought it over the whole creation; and it becomes the title by which this supremacy is held as his mediatorial reward.

3. *In this headship are blended the two methods of law and grace by which God reveals his moral perfections.* Beyond a doubt, the law was the original medium through which God's nature was disclosed to the creature, and it would not be difficult to show that his glory is stamped upon every feature of it. Indeed, springing out from the bosom of his nature, it not only asserts the claims of God and determines the duties of the creature, but it so transcribes and discovers the excellence of the Divine Being that the creature's obedience rises at once into the solemnity of worship. For the same reason, the law is generically *one* throughout the universe. Having its foundation in the nature of one God, it is essentially one over angels and men, modified only in its details to suit the different relations in which these different classes are placed. It is noticeable, moreover, that this law finds its majesty vindicated in both its grand divisions through the separate destiny assigned to two separate orders of beings: the holy angels, through their constant obedience, historically illustrating the glory of law as found in its precepts; and apostate angels, through constant endurance of its penalty. Such ample provisions has God made for securing a revenue of praise through the wisdom of his law. Last of all, in compensation of the stupendous service by which its majesty has been upheld, the administration thereof has been committed to the Mediator, and is brought to a conclusion at the day of judgment, when he shall sit upon the throne of his glory. Thus, by a method of pure law, the sunlight of Jehovah's excellence shines throughout the universe, gathering into focal splendor upon the person of our exalted Savior, the organ by whom it shall be dispensed to the redeemed forever; for it is written of the New Jerusalem that it had "no need of the sun nor of the moon to shine in it, for the glory of God did lighten it, and the Lamb is the light thereof" (Rev. 21:23).

There is reserved, however, a more interior display of divine perfections through a *method of grace*. The law discovers God to us in the attributes of wisdom, power, holiness, justice, and truth. But how shall Jehovah open to us his infinite heart—disclosing the depths of its tenderness, his boundless compassion, his inconceivable mercy and love? To do this, he must look upon the suffering and lost, and find a surety who shall bear their guilt and die their death under the curse. But where shall this substitute be found? In vain the challenge went forth from the august throne in tones which only the offended law could use: "Whom shall I send, and who will go for us?" Silence reigned throughout all the courts of heaven; for none of the sons of the morning might adventure the dreadful perils of such a trust—till a voice sounded forth from the midst of the throne, "Lo! I come; I delight to do your will, O my God! Yea, your law is within my heart" (Ps. 40:7–8). Bursting from the secret pavilion, the eternal Word leaps forth to execute the stern demand. He unclothes himself of light, lays aside the garments of praise, and takes upon himself the form of a servant, that he may sound the depths of human woe and pay the costly ransom for a guilty soul. By an obedience grander in its proportions than the aggregate obedience of all the creatures, Christ vindicates the law's injured majesty, while through his grace he brings out the tenderest affections of the Father as a God of love. Sublime is that utterance of Scripture which tells us that God is life; equally sublime the testimony which tells us he is light; but grander still, in the comprehension of them both, is the revelation which tells us God is *love*. To enthrone this grace by the side of law as the Queen Majesty, the author of grace is made the administrator of law. As the covering cloud tempered the brightness of God's presence upon the mercy seat, so forever must the law shine out from the mercy in which it is embosomed, that obedience may be sweetened—not only as a debt which conscience pays to duty, but an homage which the heart pays to love. Thus, the two lines of law and grace by which the divine glory streams forth upon the universe converge upon the person of Jesus Christ in the administration of his delegated trust as "the head over all things to the church."

II. I must now turn your thoughts from Christ to his church, here set forth as his body and fullness, only regretting that I must shut up in simple sentences what deserves expansion through paragraphs.

The church, in accordance with a very familiar distinction, may be viewed by us in two aspects. There is the *ideal church*, conformed to the pattern drafted in the divine purpose, composed of the elect in all ages, who have been washed, justified, and sanctified; and there is the *actual, visible church*, composed of those who profess faith in the Redeemer, whether they are his or not. These two interpenetrate each other and are largely identified in the statements of Scripture, and of both, in important though different senses, it may be affirmed they are the fullness of Christ.

A. 1. *The church of the elect is the object upon which the fullness of his grace expends itself.* The two, you perceive, are reciprocal, the fullness and the distribution. Thus the evangelist says: "The Word was made flesh and dwelt among us, and we beheld his glory as the glory of the only begotten of the Father, full of grace and truth"; and "of his fullness we have all received, and grace for grace" (John 1:14, 16). The same is stated with equal distinctness in Colossians 2:9–10: "For in him dwells all the fullness of the Godhead bodily—and you are complete in him, which is the head of all principality and power." The glory of Christ is not simply in being the architect of grace, by whom it was historically wrought out and engrafted upon law, but in being also the depository of grace—its dispenser no less than its procurer. The two cannot be viewed apart: Christ, the head of all principality and power, and the church complete in that gracious fullness which he imparts. Hence, true believers in every age have been drawn from all grades of society, under every degree of culture, have been placed under every variety of discipline, subjected to every form of temptation, recovered from every species of sin, and conducted through all the stages of spiritual growth, that through all might be displayed the exceeding riches of divine grace—grace for all, and according to the varying exigencies of each.

2. *The church of the elect is the body; that is to say, it is the complement of the mystical Christ.* In the covenant of redemption, the Father gave to the Son a seed to be redeemed, and constituted him their representative and surety. In all federal transactions the two ideas are conjoined. As in the covenant of works the first Adam cannot be considered in his separate personality, but also as the representative of his natural seed, so in the covenant of grace the second Adam is incomplete except as associated with his spiritual seed. The two terms are united in the very notion of a covenant. In this sense, the church is preeminently the body and fullness of Christ, and through all time Christ is reproducing himself in his members. While in his immediate person he is exalted at the right hand of the majesty in the heavens, and will never again appear but with his own glory and with the glory of the Father, yet in the church which is his body he is still "the man of sor-

rows and acquainted with grief." In all the persecutions, afflictions, temptations, and distress of his people, he renews his own humiliation and the agony of his own conflict with the powers of darkness. This is the ground of our confidence and hope, as we pass beneath the rod and stagger under our cross: that as "it behooved the great Captain of our salvation to be made perfect through suffering," so must all the members of his body drink of his cup and be baptized with the baptism with which he was baptized.

3. *This church of the elect is the fullness of Christ, as constituting the reward of his mediatorial work.* Having redeemed them with his own priceless blood, and sanctified them by his indwelling Spirit, he must, according to the stipulations of the covenant, present them to the Father, "holy and without blame before him in love." To this end, he must appear as the Resurrection and the Life, that they may "receive the adoption, that is, the redemption of their bodies." Amid the terrors of a burning world, he must sit upon the throne of judgment and pronounce the Father's authoritative benediction: "Come, you blessed of my Father, inherit the kingdom prepared for you from the foundation of the world." "Then comes the end, when he shall deliver up the kingdom to God, even the Father," that God, in the supremacy of his law, "may be all in all." Having wound up his mediatorial work in this final act of mediatorial authority, and fulfilled all the promises on which the faith of his people ever leaned, he presents them to the Father, according to his eternal pledge, "a glorious church, not having spot or wrinkle or any such thing, but holy and without blemish," "fit for the inheritance of the saints in light." This church is then given back into his hands, to be his reward and his rejoicing forevermore. They swell his train as he ascends a second time through the clouds into the heavens, shouting, as they rise, the triumphant challenge, "Lift up your heads, O you gates, and be lifted up, you everlasting doors, and the King of Glory shall come in" (Ps. 24:7). Gathered at length into "the General Assembly and church of the firstborn, which are written in heaven," they form the nearest circle around the throne and give the keynote of that song with which the arches of the great temple shall forever ring. Glorious in that righteousness of God which they have received by faith, the saints, like so many crystal pillars, shall surround the Lamb in the midst of the throne, till all heaven becomes bright with the reflected splendors of that wrought righteousness which answers to the holiness of God, expressed through the law. As the great an-

them of praise rolls up from the company of the redeemed, the High Priest of this transfigured church gathers all into his golden censer and waves it before the throne. Thus, in a sublimer sense, the God of Holiness is seen to be "all in all," and the Lamb again is seen to be the light of the New Jerusalem. In this final and exhaustive sense, this glorified church becomes the body of the great head, "the fullness of him that fills all in all."

B. It must not, however, escape us that this spiritual church has its manifestation here in the church actual and visible: the incarnation through which it becomes to us a thing tangible and known. In this view, also, Christ is still her head, and she his fullness, because:

1. *In this embodied form Christ is her only King,* enacting by his sole legislation laws for her government, appointing by his executive authority officers for her administration, instituting in his priestly jurisdiction the ordinances of her worship, and granting in the supremacy of his headship the charter by which her immunities and rights are held. In this pure theocracy, the Mediator is King, and all power under him is simply ministerial. By whatever names we choose to designate her earthly guides, their function is simply to expound a written constitution and to enforce, by spiritual censures, obedience to a spiritual and unseen Ruler.

2. *Through this visible church Christ acquires his wider mediatorial authority over the universe.* As Mediator, his prime relation is to those whom he comes to reconcile. The plan of grace, though last in development, is first in the divine thought, the most stupendous of all God's works, and the earth was built as the stage on which the sublime drama of redemption might be enacted. The whole scheme of nature is therefore subordinated to it, and the administration of Providence is committed to Christ for the prosecution of that grace which he came to inaugurate. Hence Paul testifies that he is given to be the head over all things to the church, "which is his body"; through her as his fullness he himself "fills all in all."

3. *Christ, in his precious headship, heals the breach which sin has made between the creatures; and the visible church, finally embracing all nations within her pale, embodies this grand result.* The first transgression not only separated man from God, but seemed forever to have dissolved the brotherhood between the creatures also. From that day till now, the beasts of the field have been in revolt against the dominion of man, and the elements of nature

are reclaimed under his control only through the discoveries of science. The one speech of the infant race has been broken into a thousand jarring tongues, and the earth has been covered with violence and blood. But the Reconciler came. Planting his cross as the great magnet of earth, he draws to himself his purchased seed, incorporates them into a society of love, and sends them forth to throw its bands around a shattered world. Prophecy, through her roll, shows in the dim perspective this church embracing all lands and tongues and tribes within her arms, and "the kingdoms of this world becoming the kingdoms of our Lord and of his Christ." The reconciliation ends not here. When this militant church shall be transfigured in the skies, to her visible worship and fellowship will be added the "innumerable company of angels" whom sin has never soiled. The sad breach is forever healed, and cherubim and a flaming sword shall no longer guard the way of the tree of life against guilty man. He who has "made reconciliation for iniquity and brought in everlasting righteousness" has also "made an end of sins." Sin, death, and hell are cast into the lake of fire, and the redeemed universe is brought into one under him who is head over all. Saints and angels blend in harmony of praise around his throne, and the schism of sin is canceled forever in the church fellowship of heaven.

Fathers and brethren, I must not shut down the gate upon the flood of this discourse without pointing to the consolation for us in this day of darkness and trial, wrapped up in the headship of the adorable Redeemer. *What tenderness it gives to the whole doctrine of Providence!* Once we trembled in our guilt and shame and could not look upon the angry throne; to us

A seat of dreadful wrath,
Which shot devouring flame.

But healing peace flowed into our wounded hearts as we looked upon "God in Christ, reconciling the world unto himself." In like manner the dispensations of Providence seem relentless and stern as they frown upon us from "the unknown God," but the dark clouds are drenched in soft and mellow light as they are moved by the hands of our "Immanuel, God with us." All judgment is committed to the Son of Man; can we not trust him, our elder brother, clothed with all our sympathies, who has borne our griefs and carried our sorrows, and is able to succor in that he himself has suffered? The name of this precious Jesus broke for us the spell of despair when in the hour of legal conviction conscience hung up the ghastly catalogue of our sins against the judgment throne. The name of Jesus will be the last upon our lips, softly whispered by the departing spirit as the last breath wafts it upward to the skies. It will be first upon our lips when the grave shall yield up its dead to meet the Lord in the air. Shall it not be always upon our lips, taking away the bitterness of our private and our public lot, when all these dispensations are read through an exposition of grace and are seen throughout to be a discipline of love?

What safety also to the universe in this headship of Jesus! He, who grasped the idea of creation as it lay a silent thought in the mind of God, can surely work out the eternal purpose in which it was framed. For this very end, he is given to be the head over all things—that as he is "before all things," so "by him shall all things consist." The overturnings upon earth make no fissure in the one solemn purpose of the Infinite Creator, and no sudden disclosures startle him into surprise. The shuttle of history moves swiftly and blindly from age to age, but the great web is woven according to the pattern originally designed in the council of the Godhead.

But he is head over all things to the church! While, therefore, a purpose of grace remains to be fulfilled in that church which he has graven on the palms of his hands and wears as a seal upon his heart, so long the world is safe in the keeping of him whose love is stronger than death. The Christian church is to a Christian nation the ark of Jehovah's covenant, and we are here today in sublime faith to bear that ark upon our shoulders in the presence of this infant nation as she passes under her baptism of blood. Let us gather with reverence around it and sing with Luther the 46th Psalm: "God is our refuge and strength, a very present help in time of trouble. Therefore, we will not fear, though the earth be removed and though the mountains be carried into the midst of the sea, though the waters thereof roar and be troubled, though the mountains shake with the swelling thereof, though the kingdoms be moved and the earth melted—yet the Lord of Hosts is with us; the God of Jacob is our refuge."

What glory too surrounds the church, an outer halo, a second rainbow to that which, like an emerald, John saw round the throne! She is the body of Christ, the bride, the Lamb's wife, whose "beauty" the "King hath greatly desired." She is glorious in her "raiment of needlework," "her clothing of wrought gold," "the fine linen clean and white, which is the righteousness of saints." The church of the living God!—therefore, herself living by a secret life flowing from him who is life, and bestowed by the indwelling Spirit who is the quickener. The immortal church of Christ, which survives all change and never knows decay! Alas, the paths of earth are strewn with the wrecks of broken empires, constructed by human wisdom and shattered through human folly and sin. But this church of the Redeemer moves through them all upon the grand highway of history, and "flourishes in immortal youth." She rode upon the billows of a universal deluge, beneath whose gloomy depths lay a doomed and buried world. Patriarchs gathered beneath her shade in the aged and hoary past. Moses pitched her tabernacle upon the sands of the wilderness and beneath the frowning brows of Sinai. Prophets pointed out her pathway through the uprolling mists of the distant future. Through the unfolding ages she has moved securely on, while disastrous change has ground to powder and scattered to the winds the proudest dynasties of earth. Kings have bound her with fetters of brass, but the fair captive has taken again her heart from the willows, and God has made her walls salvation and her gates praise. Amid the fires of martyrdom, she has risen younger from the ashes of her own funeral pile. Wooing the nations with her accents of love, she lengthens her cords to gather them into her broad pavilion. And when the whole frame of nature shall be dissolved, she will stand serene above the burning earth to welcome her descending Lord. Caught up by him into the heavens, she will gather into her communion there all the elder sons of God—still the immortal church of the Redeemer, outliving all time and henceforth counting her years upon the dial of eternity!

Do we understand, fathers and brethren, the mission of the church given us here to execute? It is to lift up throughout the world our testimony for this headship of Christ. The convocation of this Assembly is in part that testimony. But a little while since, it was attempted in the most august court of our church to place the crown of our Lord upon the head of Caesar—to bind that body, which is Christ's fullness, to the chariot in which that Caesar rides. The intervening months have sufficiently discovered the character of that state, under whose yoke this church was summoned to bow her neck in meek obedience. But in advance of these disclosures, the voice went up throughout our land of indignant remonstrance against the usurpation, of solemn protest against the sacrilege. And now this Parliament of the Lord's freemen solemnly declares that, by the terms of her great charter, none but Jesus may be the King in Zion. Once more in this distant age and in these ends of the earth, the church must declare for the supremacy of her head and fling out the consecrated ensign with the old inscription: "For Christ and his crown."

Let this testimony be borne upon the winds over the whole earth: that he who is "head over all things to the church" "rules in the kingdom of men, and gives it to whomever he will," until all nations are brought to "praise and extol and honor the King of heaven, all of whose works are truth and his ways judgment." Let us take this young nation now struggling into birth to the altar of God, and seal its loyalty to Christ, in the faith of that benediction which says: "Blessed is that nation whose God is the Lord." The footsteps of our King are to be seen in all the grand march of history, which begins and ends in a true theocracy. Our voice is to be the voice of one crying in the wilderness, "Prepare the way of the Lord, make straight in the desert a highway for our God." For he "will overturn, overturn, overturn, until he comes whose right it is," and "the kingdoms of this world shall become the kingdoms of our Lord and of his Christ."

Above all, it is ours to bear aloft the Redeemer's cross, and with the finger ever pointing to say, with the Baptist on the banks of the Jordan, "Behold the Lamb of God, which takes away the sin of the world!" May he who wears the crown make us to feel the power of that cross! Brethren, we have today been gazing into heaven after our ascending Lord, ascending to his headship and his crown. From his gracious throne he unfolds the sacred parchment on which our charter and commission are engrossed: "Go into all the world and disciple all nations." With pathetic gesture, he also points over mountains, continents, and seas to the "other sheep which are not of this fold," wandering upon the bleak heather, under the dark star of some idol god. May the rushing mighty wind of the Pentecostal day fill this house where we are sitting, and may the tongue of fire rest upon each of this Assembly! Emblem of the power with which the story of suffering love shall subdue an apostate world! Sinking personal ambition, and forgetful of sectional aggrandizement, let us strive to equip the church with the necessary agencies for the prosecution of her solemn work. Let us build her towers and establish her bulwarks just where the most effective assaults may be made upon the kingdoms of Satan, that "her righteousness may go forth as brightness, and her salvation as a lamp that burns," and Zion become "a crown of glory," "a royal diadem in the hand of our God."

12

Christ's Pastoral Presence with His Dying People

Psalm 23:4

JOHN L. GIRARDEAU

John Lafayette Girardeau (1825–98) has been classed as one of the four greatest pulpit orators of the Southern Presbyterian Church, along with Benjamin Morgan Palmer of New Orleans, Moses D. Hoge of Richmond, and Stuart Robinson of Louisville.[1] The remarkable thing about Girardeau's preaching ministry is that much of it was delivered to black slaves, and later freedmen, of the South Carolina seaboard and the city of Charleston.

Born on November 14, 1825 on James Island, South Carolina, of French Huguenot ancestry, Girardeau professed faith at age 14, joining the Third Presbyterian Church of Charleston on October 18, 1840. He graduated from Charleston College in 1844 and from Columbia Seminary in 1848. From his boyhood he had a concern for the welfare of the African American, and his early years of ministry involved preaching the gospel to small white congregations, but also to blacks—sometimes on the plantations

---

1. Ernest Trice Thompson, *Presbyterians in the South*, 3 vols. (Richmond, Va.: John Knox Press, 1963, 1973), vol. 2: *1861–1890*, 378.

along the seaboard, but sometimes in the churches immediately after the whites vacated services.

In 1854 he was called to be pastor of the Anson Street Church, an offspring of the Second Presbyterian Church of Charleston, built for the sake of slaves and led by John B. Adger, formerly a missionary to Armenia and subsequently a professor at Columbia Seminary. Missionary efforts to the slaves, such as those by Charles Colcock Jones (1804–63), the "Apostle to the Blacks," were supported by the Southern Presbyterian Church, but the idea of a separate building where blacks could worship, with a white pastor and white Sunday-school teachers, was novel.[2]

Normally at that time blacks worshiped from the galleries of the white churches. Adger had to resign from the work for health reasons, and when Girardeau came as pastor there were 45 members in 1855. This grew to 145 by 1857.[3]

In 1858 there came a remarkable revival in Girardeau's church. It was preceded by special prayer meetings without any preaching, until one evening he sensed the presence of the Holy Spirit. He announced, "The Holy Spirit has come; we will begin preaching tomorrow evening."

> He closed the service with a hymn, dismissed the congregation, and came down from the pulpit; but no one left the house. The whole congregation had quietly resumed its seat. Instantly he realized the situation. The Holy Spirit had not only come to him—He had also taken possession of the hearts of the people. Immediately he began exhorting them to accept the Gospel. They began to sob, softly, like the falling of rain, then, with deeper emotion, to weep bitterly, or to rejoice loudly, according to their circumstances. It was midnight before he could dismiss his congregation.[4]

---

2. Thompson, *Presbyterians in the South*, 1:441.

3. George A. Blackburn, ed., *The Life Work of John L. Girardeau* (Columbia, S.C.: The State Co., 1916), 36.

4. Benjamin Rice Lacy Jr., *Revivals in the Midst of the Years* (Hopewell, Va.: Royal Publishers, 1968), 113–14. See also Blackburn, *Life Work of Girardeau*, 79–80; Iain Murray, *Revival & Revivalism: The Making and Marring of American Evangelicalism, 1750–1858* (Edinburgh and Carlisle, Pa.: Banner of Truth Trust, 1994), 379–80, 420–21.

The revival continued for eight weeks, night after night. There were many conversions. By 1860 Zion (formerly Anson Street) Presbyterian Church had a membership of 524, of whom 462 were blacks. Typically Girardeau would preach to a congregation of up to 1,500 people. The building, built by contributions of the people of Charleston, was the largest church in the city, seating more than 1,000 blacks on the main floor and approximately 250 whites in the balcony (thus reversing the customary pattern).[5] What happened in Girardeau's church was part of the nationwide awakening that began with the Laymen's Prayer Revival in New York City. "Dr. Girardeau frequently referred to this as the Lord's mercy in gathering His elect for the great war that was soon to sweep so many of them into eternity."[6]

During the Civil War Girardeau served as a chaplain in the Confederate armies, ending up as a prisoner on Johnson Island, where he preached effectively to the prisoners of war. Upon his return to Charleston, he found his church led by a missionary of the Northern Presbyterian Church under the auspices of the Freedman's Bureau. Not until January 1867 was he able to resume his ministry with Zion Church, which consisted of 116 members. Within three months the membership had risen to 150 with another 50 prospects, and he was preaching to a congregation of 500 while also serving as pastor of the white Glebe Street Church. He continued to minister to the black congregation until 1874. While opposing segregation of blacks and whites, he would not countenance the idea of blacks' being officers in white churches. He advocated a "Separate System" of black churches with white supervision.[7] He served as moderator of the General Assembly in 1874, then was professor of didactic and polemic theology at Columbia Seminary from 1876 to 1895. In Columbia he served as pastor of Second (later known as Arsenal Hill) Presbyterian Church in 1886 and then in association with his son-in-law, George A. Blackburn, until his health failed with partial paralysis in 1895. He died on June 23, 1898.[8]

---

5. Lacy, *Revivals*, 112; Thompson, *Presbyterians in the South*, 1:442.

6. Blackburn, *Life Work of Girardeau*, 100.

7. Thompson, *Presbyterians in the South*, 2:206, 315, 209–10.

8. Blackburn, *Life Work of Girardeau*, 376–77; Morton H. Smith, *Studies in Southern Presbyterian Theology* (Jackson, Miss.: Presbyterian Reformation Society and Amsterdam: Jacob Van Campen, 1962), 234.

Girardeau's eloquence made a strong impression on all sorts of hearers. Visitors in Charleston, when inquiring where to attend church, would frequently be directed to "Dr. Girardeau's mission." One example was that of Alfred Robb of Tennessee, later a colonel in the Confederate army, and Benjamin Butler of Massachusetts, later a general in the Union army, when they were attending the Democratic national convention in 1860. In the hotel Butler asked Robb where he was going to church:

> Colonel Robb replied, "To hear a great white preacher whose life is consecrated to the salvation of negroes." General Butler exclaimed, "Well, as I have never heard of any such thing as that, I will go with you." On entering the church they found the negroes occupying the main floor, while the whites were seated in the gallery.
>
> Colonel Robb described the scene thus: "The prayer of the preacher was earnest, simple and humble as of a man pleading with God. The singing was general, heartfelt and grand. The sermon was tender and spiritual, and though profound, was plain, delivered with fire and unction. After the preacher took his seat, deeply impressed, I was with closed eyes meditating on the wonderful sermon, when I heard someone sobbing. Looking around I saw General Butler's face bathed in tears.

Butler commented, "Well, I have never heard such a man and have never heard such a sermon."[9]

People sometimes wondered how Girardeau could communicate so effectively to both whites and blacks:

> Sometimes when both races were present he would preach a profound sermon, and there would be witnessed a strange anomaly. The minds of the cultured whites would be strained to keep up with the train of thought, while the negroes seemed to clearly understand and fully appreciate the whole sermon.

Girardeau's own explanation was that he emphasized certain key words in tone and manner.[10] A more likely explanation is that he employed vivid word pictures and preached the simple gospel. An example is furnished by his associate, Joseph B. Mack:

---

9. Blackburn, *Life Work of Girardeau*, 57–58.
10. Ibid., p. 71.

Once in Zion (Calhoun Street) Church of Charleston he was preaching to a large congregation of negroes. As in plaintive tones he pictured Jesus Christ going forth to death and bending beneath the burden of the cross, every eye was opened wide and riveted upon the speaker, while each breast seemed to rise and fall, as step after step was taken up the rugged steep of Calvary. When the place of execution was reached everybody fell back and many hands were raised in horror. When the nails were driven a deep sigh swept through the house like the sad moan of the sea as it rolls in upon the shore, and when the Saviour's head was drooped in death a deep shudder convulsed the weeping throng as hundreds piteously cried, "O, my God! O, my God!"[11]

Girardeau's sermon on Psalm 23:4 was chosen for publication by the Presbyterian Committee of Publication in 1896 in the volume *Southern Presbyterian Pulpit* along with samples of thirty-two other preachers. It is not stated whether it was preached to a white or black congregation, but it would have been effective to any audience. Focusing on death as the third great epoch of a believer's life, after one's birth and the second birth, he introduces Christ as shepherd in each of his three offices of Prophet, Priest, and King. A guilty conscience is what makes death formidable, but the substitutionary atonement is the answer to that. Christ is able to sympathize compassionately, having suffered himself in our human frame. A beautiful word picture is given of the shepherd protecting and supporting the crippled ewe or the straying lamb. He concludes, "Fellow travelers to the dark valley, let us believe in Jesus as our Savior."

Girardeau once confessed that he had to accommodate his intellect to his black audience's capabilities.[12] His perception, and that of other Southern Presbyterians of his time such as theologian Robert Lewis Dabney, of the blacks as inherently inferior was no doubt influenced by their firsthand observation of many who manifested the effects of slavery on family life and education; the abilities and achievements of former slaves such as Frederick Douglass and Booker T. Washington demonstrated how mistaken they were.[13] They might be amazed today to see African Americans excelling in so many commercial, cultural, and intellectual pursuits in our contemporary society. Along with access to opportunities for education and to the

---

11. Blackburn, *Life Work of Girardeau*, 53.

12. Ibid., 34.

13. For Dabney's views, see Thompson, *Presbyterians in the South*, 2:217–19.

other blessings of American civilization, much of that success no doubt comes from the fact that the gospel was communicated compassionately, if not with full equality. One story, told for its humor, related how one of Girardeau's black members asked another black to go to church with him. "The latter, refusing on the ground that the church had a white preacher, received the prompt reply from Dr. Girardeau's friend, 'Yas, he face is white, but he heart is black.'"[14]

CHRIST'S PASTORAL PRESENCE WITH HIS DYING PEOPLE

JOHN L. GIRARDEAU

Yea, though I walk through the valley of the shadow of death, I will fear no evil, for you are with me; your rod and your staff, they comfort me. (Ps. 23:4)

In this exquisite, sacred pastoral, the psalmist of Israel celebrates, in touching strains, the constant and tender care which God exercises towards his covenant people. Under the beautiful imagery of a shepherd, leading his flock to green pastures and beside still waters, he is represented as conducting them to the rich provisions and the refreshing rest of the gospel. When, like wandering sheep, they deviate from his ways, he seeks them in love, collects them again with the pastoral crook, and guides them once more in the paths of righteousness and peace. When, in their waywardness and folly, they backslide from him, he still remembers his

---

14. Blackburn, *Life Work of Girardeau*, 104.

covenant, is faithful to his promises, and saves them for the sake of his own great name; and when they come to pass through the valley of the death-shade, his cheering presence dispels their fears, and his powerful grace proves their solace and support.

Though it is true that Jehovah, the triune God, is the Shepherd of his people, there is a peculiar and emphatic sense in which Christ is represented in the gospel as sustaining the pastoral relation and discharging its functions. The evangelist John reports him as declaring, "I am the good shepherd; the good shepherd gives his life for the sheep." The apostle Paul speaks of the God of peace as having brought again from the dead our Lord Jesus, that Great Shepherd of the sheep, through the blood of the ever-lasting covenant. The apostle Peter reminds believers that whereas they were in their natural condition as sheep going astray, they are now returned unto Christ as the Shepherd and Bishop of their souls. And the same apos-tle exhorts presbyters to feed the flock of God in view of the reward which the Great Pastor would eventually confer upon them: "And when the Chief Shepherd shall appear, you shall receive a crown of glory that fades not away." These passages make it sufficiently evident that the Lord Jesus is pe-culiarly the Shepherd of his people.

The pastoral relation is a comprehensive one, including the three of-fices which Christ, as Mediator, sustains: those of a Prophet, a Priest, and a King. As it is the province of a shepherd to feed his flock, to rule and pro-tect them from their enemies, and, if necessary, to lay down his life in their defense, the prophetical function, by which Jesus feeds his people, the kingly, by which he rules and protects them, and the sacerdotal, by which he re-deems them through his death, are all embraced in his pastoral office. It touches the interests, the experience, and the hopes of believers at every point, both in life and in death. It involves the application of a Savior's power, love, and mercy to their every emergency and their every need. With infinite tenderness, compassion, and vigilance, the great Pastor follows his sheep through every devious path of life, and extends to them his succor when they faint under burning suns, in the horrid wilderness, and amid the glooms and terrors of the shadow of death.

I. In the first place, it may be remarked in attempting to expand the com-forting truths suggested by the text that the pastoral presence of Jesus is a protection to the dying believer from the fears of evil which would otherwise distress him. "Though I walk through the valley of the shadow of death, I will fear no evil, for you are with me." I have no objection to render to the view which makes these words applicable to those critical passages in the life of God's people, which may not inappropriately be described as the valley of the death-shade. This was evidently the interpretation of that masterly delineator of Christian experience, John Bunyan, in his immortal allegory. He represents his pilgrim as struggling with the dangers and conflicts of the valley of the shadow of death before he comes to the crossing of the last river. And it cannot be disputed that there are seasons in the experience of the believer when, pressed by his besetting temptations, pursued by the malice of the devil, and fascinated by the enchantments or persecuted by the fury of the world, he encounters terrors which are akin to those of death itself. In these fearful exigencies, these periods of conflict, depression, and anguish, he appears to be passing down into the darkness and gloom of the valley of death; and it is the pastoral presence of Christ in the hour of despair which dissipates the fear of evil and lights up the soul with returning joy and peace. But although this is true, I see no reason for disturbing the ordinary interpretation placed upon the words of the text— an interpretation which makes them specially applicable to the passage of the believer through death, and one which has proved a charm to dispel the apprehensions of ill from the bosoms of thousands of Christ's people amid the doubts, the strifes, the agonies of the dying hour.

There are three great and notable epochs in the earthly history of the believer in Jesus. The first is that in which, at the creative fiat of the Almighty Maker, he springs from nonentity into being, and is confronted with the duties, the responsibilities, and the bliss or woe of an immortal career. The next is that in which, by virtue of a second creation and through the wondrous process of the new birth and conversion, he passes from the kingdom of Satan and of darkness into the kingdom of grace and of light. From being a bondsman of the devil, a slave of sin, and an heir of hell, he becomes, by a marvelous transformation, a subject of God, a citizen of heaven, and an inheritor of everlasting possessions and an amaranthine crown. It is a transitional process which awakens the pulse of a new life, engenders the habits of holiness, adorns the soul with the rich graces of the divine Spirit, and inspires the joyful hope of eternal felicity beyond the grave. The third, and it is the most solemn and terrible crisis of his being, is that of death, in which the believer passes through nature's closing conflict and the awful change of dissolution to the experience of an untried existence. The transition is suited to alarm. It is nothing less than one from time to eternity, and it is accomplished in the twinkling of an eye. At one moment he is surrounded by the familiar objects of earth, and looks upon the faces of his weeping friends who cluster around the bed of death, and in the next he opens his eyes upon eternal realities and the blaze of God's immediate presence. Nature, constructed originally for an immortal life, instinctively recoils from so violent and revolting a change as that which death involves. It shrinks back in terror from the vision of the coffin and the shroud, of the corruption and the worms of the grave. The circumstances attending the dying process are such as are suited to appall a conscious sinner, and fill him with consternation and dismay—the cruel rupture of earthly relations, the sudden withdrawal of accustomed scenes, the forced abandonment of wonted pursuits, the absolute loneliness of the passage, the dread neighborhood of the flaming bar, and the rigor of the last account. My brethren, how shall we, without apprehension, encounter so tremendous a change? The text furnishes us an answer which illumines the gloom of the dying chamber and lights up the darkness of the grave. The pastoral presence of the Lord Jesus is an antidote to the fears, and a preventive of the evils, of death. There are two modes by which this blessed result is accomplished:

1. In the first place the Great Shepherd accompanies the believer in his last passage as the Conqueror of Death. That which chiefly renders death an object of terror is the consciousness of guilt. The groans, the pains, the dissolution of our bodily organisms are confessedly dreadful and repulsive; but the great poet was right when he intimated that it is conscience, a guilty conscience forecasting the retributions of the future, which makes cowards of us all. It is this which leads us to shrink from the dying bed as an arena of battle, and from the last struggle as a hopeless conflict with an evil which the startled imagination personates as a monarch and invests with power to destroy. Death becomes the king of terrors. Were there no sin, the change which might have been necessary to remove us from the present state and to adapt us to another would have been an easy and delightful translation, a euthanasia, disquieted by no apprehensions of the soul and disturbed by no pains of the body. But sin has clothed death with its tyrannical prerog-

ative as a universal and remorseless despot, converted the world into a melancholy theater of his triumphs, and transformed the earth into a vast graveyard, whitened with the monuments of his sway. The removal from the present state becomes a passage through a valley of tears peopled with shapes of terror and encompassed with the darkness of the death-shade.

Christ has subdued this dreadful monster. He conquered death by conquering sin, and he overcomes sin by his dying obedience to law. This is the statement of the apostle in his argument touching the resurrection of the body: "The sting of death is sin." The power of death to inflict torture, to poison our happiness and blast our hopes, lies in the fact that we are guilty and are therefore completely subjected to his tyranny. "The strength of sin is the law." The punishment of our guilt is penal. Our dying sufferings are the penalty of a broken law; and sin, in inflicting them upon us, throws itself back for the enforcement of its authority upon the irreversible sanctions of that majestic and eternal rule which we have outraged and insulted. Christ has stripped sin of this strength. He has unnerved the cruel monarch and rendered him powerless to destroy his people. The glorious Redeemer, moved by compassion for our wretched estate, came down to our relief and stood forth as the champion of his church in her conflict with death. He assumed our guilt, took the sting of death in his own soul, underwent our penal sufferings and, in accordance with the law of substitution, relieved us from the obligation to suffer the same punishment, and has enlisted the divine justice on the side of our deliverance. Christ has died penally for his people. God accepts the vicarious sacrifice, and the believer cannot die in the same way. Justice cannot demand a double payment of the same debt. Death is divested of its penal feature and is transformed from a curse into a blessing, from a passage to execution into a translation to bliss. In the tragedy enacted upon the cross, Jesus, the representative of his people, engaged in a mighty wrestle with death. He fell, but his fall crushed out the life of his dread antagonist. He died, but death died with him. He was buried, but he dragged death down with him into the grave; and there, despoiling the tyrant of his diadem, he unfurled over his crownless head the ensign of his people's salvation and, in their name, took undisputed possession of his whole domain. It is true that the believer must still pass through the dying change, but the curse of it is forever gone. It is no more death in its true and awful sense as the penalty of law. "I," says the divine Redeemer, "I am the resurrection and the life; he that believes in me, though he were dead, yet shall he live; and he that lives and believes in me shall never die." "He that keeps my sayings shall never see death." It is true that the believer must die; but in dying he is privileged to suffer with his Master, that he may rise and reign with him. It is true that the believer must die; but death now constitutes part of a wholesome discipline which prepares him for glory; it is a process by which he is purged from dross, casts off the slough of corruption, and is purified for his admission into the holy presence of God and the sanctified communion of saints. It is true that he must walk through the dark valley; but the Conqueror of death descends into it by his side, illuminates its darkness by the radiance of his presence, protects him from the assaults of a now powerless foe, and, bearing in his hands the keys of death and the invisible world, peacefully dismisses the departing saint from sin to holiness, and from the stormy trials of earth to the joy and peace of an everlasting rest.

2. It may be observed further that the pastoral presence of Jesus with his dying people is manifested by the tender ministration of his sympathy. There were two great ends which the Savior contemplated in his sufferings and death—the one, that he might redeem his people from sin and everlasting punishment; the other, that he might be qualified by experience to sympathize with them while themselves passing through the afflictions of life and the pains of the dying hour. To achieve these results, he became incarnate, partook of our nature, and was made bone of our bone and flesh of our flesh. Not merely a legal substitute, but possessed of the sublime and tender spirit of a priest, he consented to be compassed with sinless infirmity, that he might be capable of compassion for the weak, the wandering, and the dying. An infirm human being, struggling under the burden of assumed guilt and confronted by the terrors of divine wrath—is it any marvel that he looked forward to death not without fear? One of the most affecting and pathetic passages in the Scriptures is that in which the apostle, discoursing on the priestly sufferings of Jesus, tells us that in the days of his flesh he offered up prayers and supplications with strong crying and tears unto him that was able to save him from death, and was heard in that he feared. For it must be remembered that the form of death which Christ encountered, while it included the experience of our sufferings, embraced incomparably more. In his own person perfectly innocent, and in his char-

acter stainlessly holy, he merited intrinsically the admiration of his fellow men and the approval of his God. So far from deserving to die, he was entitled, on the naked score of retributive justice, to the highest and most blissful life. And yet condescending, in boundless mercy, to be treated as putatively guilty for the sake of dying men, he underwent a form of death, the least element of which was the pains of dissolution—a death which involved the experience of infinite wrath and the intolerable pains of hell. The cup which was placed in the hands of Jesus in Gethsemane was one which was never offered to any other human being on earth. The trembling and consternation of his human nature as he took that chalice of woe, his thrice-repeated prayer to be relieved, if possible, from the necessity of drinking it, and the bloody sweat that swathed his body like a robe attested an anguish of soul which none but he was ever called upon to bear. The Sufferer who, for us, expired on the cross of Calvary endured a species of death which was as singular as it was comprehensive and exhaustive. In body, he suffered the keen and protracted tortures of crucifixion; and in spirit, reviled by foes, deserted by friends, and abandoned of God, he descended alone into the valley of the death-shade, which was not only veiled in impenetrable gloom but swept by the tempests of avenging wrath. Furnished with such an experience, the Good Shepherd ministers with exquisite sympathy at the couch of the dying believer. He knows his doubts, his apprehensions, his fears; and moved by a compassion which naught but a common suffering could produce, he makes all the bed under the expiring saint, smooths his last pillow, and "wipes his latest tear away."

II. In the second place, the psalmist beautifully portrays the consoling influence of Christ's presence upon the dying believer when he represents the pastoral staff as affording him protection and comfort. "Your rod and your staff, they comfort me." The staff, the appropriate emblem of the pastoral office, may be regarded in two aspects. As a rod, it is a powerful weapon of defense; and as a staff, it is an instrument of support. It is at once, therefore, the symbol of protecting power and of supporting grace. When at eventide the oriental shepherd had folded his flock and missed from the number some crippled ewe or tender lamb, he failed not, albeit through night and storm, to go in quest of the wanderer as it strayed amid the jagged rocks of the mountainside or the terrors of the howling wilderness. And when he had found it, he gathered it compassionately in his arms, laid it upon his shoulders, and took his way homeward rejoicing. But often he was compelled to pass through some deep and gloomy gorge, infested by wild beasts and rendered dangerous by the swollen torrent dashing fiercely through it and making the passage hazardous and the foothold insecure. Then, when from some neighboring thicket the young lion sprang forth and roared upon his prey, wielding his shepherd's staff as a weapon of defense, he protected the precious burden he carried and beat back the assailant to his lair; or, as he stepped from one slippery rock to another through the rapid current, he used his staff as a supporting prop and stayed both himself and the feeble wanderer which he conducted to the folded flock. Thus it is, my brethren, with the Great Shepherd and Bishop of souls, when in the night of death he leads the feeble and dying members of his flock through the valley of the death-shade to the heavenly fold. There are two difficulties which the believer has not unfrequently to encounter when he comes to die:

In the first place, he is liable to the last and desperate assaults of the adversary of souls. Baffled by the power of the everlasting covenant in his attempts to compass the destruction of the believer, he meets him at the bed of death and, taking advantage of his helplessness, endeavors, if he cannot destroy him, to mar the peace and becloud the prospect of his latest moments on earth. He showers his fiery darts upon him, injects doubts as to his acceptance with God, conjures up from the past the apparition of his sins, and calls up before his appalled imagination the vision of an angry Judge, a fiery bar, and a night of eternal despair. But another and a greater than Satan is there. The Chief Shepherd is also in that chamber of death. Standing at the dying bedside, and lifting his pastoral staff as a rod of defense, he wards off from his agonized servant the incursions of the powers of darkness and beats back the assaults of his satanic foes.

Another difficulty which is apt to disturb the peace of the departing believer is derived from his vivid remembrance of his sins and his consequent fear that he is not prepared to meet his God. In the solemn and honest hour of death, his soul, conscious of its dread proximity to the judgment seat, takes a minute and impartial survey of the past. His memory, quickened into an energy which only death can impart, with lightning rapidity sweeps, as at a glance, the whole field of his earthly history. There is no glossing process then by which the hideous features of his sins can be painted or concealed, no apology for his crimes which will stand the scrutiny of the deathbed or abide the breaking light of the eternal world. All his acts of youthful folly, all his broken vows, all his unredeemed promises to his God, all his fearful backslidings, all his sinful thoughts, words, and deeds now crowd into his dying chamber, throng around his dying bed, and threaten to go with him as swift witnesses against him before the final bar. The billows of a fiercer death than that of the body dash over his head, and, struggling in the torrent which threatens to sweep him through the last valley downward to a bottomless abyss, he cries in his extremity to the Redeemer of his soul. Never deaf to the appeals of his dying people, the Great Shepherd hastens to his relief with the succors of his supporting grace. He whispers to the sinking believer that he died to save him, that his blood has cleansed him of all his sins, and that his perfect righteousness, his atoning merit, is a ground of acceptance, a foundation that will not fail him when the wicked and unbelieving shall be driven from the divine presence like the chaff before the storm. It is enough. The dying believer, with the hand of faith, grasps the pastoral staff that Jesus thus extends to him and, leaning upon it, passes in safety through the glooms and dangers of the death-shade, emerges into the light of heaven, and is satisfied with the beatific vision of God.

Fellow travelers to the dark valley, let us believe in Jesus as our Savior. Let us put our trust in him as the Shepherd and Bishop of our souls. So when we are called to die, no guilty conscience will break our peace, no condemning law will thunder upon us, no frowns of an angry Judge will deepen the awful shadow of death; but we will fear no evil, for Christ will be with us, his rod will protect us in our last conflict, his staff will support us in our latest pang.

13

"Rabboni!"

John 20:16

GEERHARDUS VOS

In 1890 Geerhardus Vos (1862–1949) accepted an appointment to the new professorship of biblical theology at Princeton Seminary. The faculty seems to have sensed a need to include this discipline in the curriculum, but it was left to Vos to work out the implications and methods of this approach as distinct from systematic theology. His studies in Germany had exposed him to the "critical" approach to biblical theology, but he reacted against the "purely naturalistic and secular" tendency of such thought. As Richard Gaffin says: "The apparent conclusion is that Vos's work in biblical theology is largely without direct antecedents and indicates the originality with which he wrestled with the matter of biblical interpretation in the Reformed tradition."[1]

In his inaugural address in May 1894, "The Idea of Biblical Theology as a Science and as a Theological Discipline," Vos laid out his already clear conception: "It is certainly not without significance that God has embodied the contents of revelation, not in a dogmatic system, but in a book of

---

1. Richard B. Gaffin Jr., ed., *Redemptive History and Biblical Interpretation: The Shorter Writings of Geerhardus Vos* (Phillipsburg, N.J.: P&R, 1980, 2001), xii.

history, the parallel to which in dramatic interest and simple eloquence is nowhere to be found."[2] Valuable as systematic theology may be in laying out the doctrinal propositions that one may properly draw out from Scripture, Vos emphasized the importance of seeing the historical context for God's revelation of redemption through Christ. Gaffin sees this as an important fulfillment of the Protestant heritage: "It is difficult to resist the conclusion that the biblical-theological method or, better, the redemptive-historical orientation exemplified by Vos is, to date, the most fruitful and pointedly biblical realization of the Reformation insistence that Scripture interprets Scripture."[3]

Geerhardus Vos was born on March 15, 1862 in Heerenveen in the province of Friesland, the Netherlands. His parents were descendants of French Huguenots who had fled from persecution to Germany and then had moved to the Netherlands. His father was a pastor in the Christian Reformed Church who accepted a call to a church in Grand Rapids, Michigan in 1881. Vos studied theology at his denomination's school at Grand Rapids, and then at Princeton Seminary, where he won a prize for his thesis, "The Mosaic Origin of the Pentateuchal Codes," which was published in London in 1886. He studied for one year at Berlin and two years at Strassburg, where he received his doctorate in Arabic studies from the philosophical faculty in 1888. Declining an appointment to the faculty of the Free University of Amsterdam, he returned to teach for the next five years at the Theological School of the Christian Reformed Church in Grand Rapids. In 1893 he joined the faculty of Princeton Seminary, where he remained for the next thirty-nine years. In 1932, at age 70, he retired to southern California and then, after the death in 1937 of his wife, Catherine, author of the *Child's Story Bible*, to Grand Rapids, where he died on August 13, 1949.[4]

Vos was apparently not the most popular of professors, as Gaffin explains:

Gentle and naturally retiring, he did not acquire a large following among the students. By many, perhaps the majority, he was probably more respected than

---

2. Quoted in David B. Calhoun, *Princeton Seminary*, 2 vols. (Edinburgh and Carlisle, Pa.: Banner of Truth Trust, 1994, 1996), vol. 2: *The Majestic Testimony, 1869–1929*, 140.

3. Gaffin, *Redemptive History*, xviii.

4. Calhoun, *Princeton Seminary*, 2:138–39; Gaffin, *Redemptive History*, ix–xiii.

understood. No doubt his lectures were like his writings, intrinsically difficult because of the wealth of insight packed into virtually every sentence.[5]

J. Gresham Machen, in his senior year as a student at Princeton Seminary, 1904–05, wrote to his mother about a chapel message by Vos:

We heard this morning one of the finest expository sermons I ever heard. It was preached by Dr. Vos, professor of Biblical Theology in the Seminary, and brother of the Hopkins Dr. Vos, and rather surprised me. He is usually rather too severely theological for Sunday morning. Today he was nothing less than inspiring. His subject was Christ's appearance to Mary after the resurrection. Dr. Vos differs from some theological professors in having a better-developed bump of reverence.[6]

That sermon, "'Rabboni!,'" was published in a volume of his Princeton chapel messages, entitled *Grace and Glory*. In his Introduction to the expanded version of this volume, Sinclair B. Ferguson comments about these sermons:

They combine such constantly penetrating depths of biblical and theological understanding with such soaring heights of eloquence that it is difficult to imagine their like being heard in any pulpit in the world today. They are at one and the same time intensely demanding on the reader and glorious in their exposition of Scripture. These pages contain a thesaurus of theological riches, a gold mine whose every vein is packed with gleaming insight.

Ferguson continues: "He wishes to speak to his hearers about God. He wants to instill in them precisely the sense that God is gracious *and* God is glorious."[7]

The sermon entitled "'Rabboni!'" that so impressed Machen as a student declares its purpose near the beginning: to try to enter into the thoughts

---

5. Gaffin, *Redemptive History*, xiii.

6. Ned B. Stonehouse, *J. Gresham Machen, A Biographical Memoir*, 3rd ed. (Edinburgh and Carlisle, Pa.: Banner of Truth Trust, 1987), 72.

7. Sinclair B. Ferguson, "Introduction to Geerhardus Vos," *Grace and Glory: Sermons Preached in the Chapel of Princeton Theological Seminary* (Edinburgh and Carlisle, Pa.: Banner of Truth Trust, 1994), x.

and feelings of the disciples on the morning of Jesus' resurrection in order "that something of the same fresh marvel and gladness that subsequently came to them may fill our hearts also." It is to achieve "a deeper faith than that of mere acquaintance with and consent to external statements of truth." Vos's sense of redemptive history, his biblical theological emphasis, comes through in various ways. The two angels that Mary sees at the tomb remind him of the cherubim on the mercy seat of the Ark of the Covenant in the Tabernacle of Moses and the Temple of Solomon. The resurrection of Jesus is compared with the moment of creation: "The time was as solemn and majestic as that of the first creation when light burst out of chaos and darkness. Heaven and earth were concerned in this event; it was the turning point of the ages." Jesus' admonition to Mary, "Touch me not," is explained in this fashion:

> The great event of which the resurrection is the first step has not yet fulfilled itself; it requires for its completion the ascent to the Father. But when this is accomplished then all restrictions will fall away, and the desire to touch that made Mary stretch forth her hand shall be fully gratified.

This is through the gift of the Spirit dependent on Jesus' entrance into heaven.

Vos's comprehensive knowledge of the Scriptures' redemptive message is combined with a depth of psychological—or, better, spiritual—insight, into Mary, ourselves, the angels, and even Jesus in connection with this incident on the first Easter morning. Mary's lingering at the empty tomb after Peter and John have departed elicits this comment: "How striking an illustration of the Savior's word that much forgiveness creates abounding love!" Vos applies Mary's grief to ourselves: "Do we not all remember occasions when we stood outside the grave of our hopes weeping, and did not perceive the hand stretched out to prepare us by the very thing we interpreted as sorrow for a higher joy?" He enters into the angels' viewpoint:

> To the mind of the angels the resurrection was so real, so self-evident, that they could scarcely understand how to her it could be otherwise. They felt the discord between the songs of joy with which their own world was jubilant and the sound of weeping coming out of a world of darkness and despair.

He enters even into the self-consciousness of Jesus:

> Jesus felt himself the central figure in this newborn universe; he tasted the exquisite joy of one who had just entered upon an endless life in the possession of new powers and faculties such as human nature had never known before.

Finally comes the dramatic conclusion:

> "Jesus said unto her, 'Mary.' She turned and said unto him, 'Rabboni!'" It happened all in a moment, and by a simple word, and yet in this one moment Mary's world was changed for her. She had in that instant made the transition from hopelessness because Jesus was absent to fullness of joy because Christ was there. We may well despair of conveying by any process of exposition the meaning of these two words.

Exponents of biblical theology have sometimes puzzled over how to preach the results of this approach. Geerhardus Vos's sermon provides a worthy example that shows the command of Scripture and deep sensitivity both to God's redemptive plan and also to human nature that are required.

"RABBONI!"

GEERHARDUS VOS

Jesus said unto her, "Mary." She turned herself and said unto him, "Rabboni"— which is to say, "Master." (John 20:16)

ur text takes us to the tomb of the risen Lord, on the first Sabbath-morning of the New Covenant. It is impossible for us to imagine a spot more radiant with light and joy than was this place immediately after the resurrection. Even when thinking ourselves back into the preceding moments, while as yet to the external eye there was nothing but the darkness of death, our anticipation of what we know to be about to happen floods the scene with a twilight of supernatural splendor. The sepulchre itself has become to us prophetic of victory; we seem to hear in the expectant air the wingbeat of the descending angels, come to roll away the stone and announce to us: "The Lord is risen indeed!" Besides this, we have learned to read the story of our Lord's life and death so as to consider the resurrection its only possible outcome, and this has to some extent dulled our sense for the startling character of what took place. We interpret the resurrection in terms of the atoning cross, and easily forget how little the disciples were as yet prepared for doing the same. And so it requires an effort on our part to understand sympathetically the state of mind they brought to the morning of this day. Nevertheless, we must try to enter into their thoughts and feelings, if for no other reason, for this: that something of the same fresh marvel and gladness that subsequently came to them may fill our hearts also. Whether we may be able to explain it or not, the gospel tells us that, notwithstanding the emphatic prediction by the Savior of his death and resurrection, they had but little remembrance of these words, and drew from them no practical support or comfort in the sorrow that overwhelmed them. In part this may have been due to the fact of our Lord's having only predicted and not fully explained these tremendous events.

At any rate, the circumstance shows that there is need of a deeper faith than that of mere acquaintance with and consent to external statements of truth when the dread realities of life and death assail us. Dare we say that we ourselves should have proved stronger in such a trial if, over against all that mocked our hope, we had been able to see no more than a dimly remembered promise? Let us thank God that, when we ourselves enter into the valley of the shadow of death, we have infinitely more than a promise to stay our hearts upon, that ours is the fulfillment of the promise, the fact of the resurrection, the risen Lord himself present with rod and staff beside us.

Supplementing the account of John with the statements of the other evangelists, we gain the following conception of the course of events previous to what the text relates. A small company of women went out at early dawn towards the garden, carrying the spices prepared as a last offering to honor Jesus. From among these Mary Magdalene, in the eagerness of her desire to reach the place, ran forward and discovered before the others that the stone had been rolled away. Without awaiting the arrival of her companions, she hastens back to tell Peter and John what she supposed to be true: "They have taken away the Lord out of the tomb." Roused from the lethargy of their grief by this startling announcement, the apostles immediately went to the place and by their own observation verified Mary's report. John came first, but merely looked into the tomb. Peter, who followed, entered in and saw the linen cloths lying and the napkin that was upon the Savior's head rolled up and put by itself. Then John also entered, saw, and believed. As yet they did not know the Scripture that he must rise again from the dead. Their eyes were so holden that the true explanation never occurred to them. Perplexed, but not moved from a despairing state of mind, they returned to their abode.

Mary must have followed the apostles at a distance when these came in haste to see for themselves. We find her standing outside the tomb weeping. Is it not remarkable that, while both John and Peter departed, Mary remained? Although the same hopeless conclusion had forced itself upon her, yet it could not induce her to leave. In her mind it only intensified a thousand times the purpose with which she had come. How striking an illustration of the Savior's word that much forgiveness creates abounding love!

But may we not believe that still something else reveals itself in this? Mary's attitude towards Jesus, more perhaps than any other disciple's, seems to have been characterized by that simple dependence which is the consciousness of an ever-present need. It was a matter of faith, as much as of love, that made her differ at this time from the others. Unmixed with further motives, the recognition of Jesus as the only refuge from sin and death filled her heart. In a measure, of course, he had been this to the others also. But while to them he stood for many other things in addition, the circumstances under which she had become attached to him made Mary's soul the mirror of saving faith pure and simple. And because she was animated by this fundamental spiritual impulse, drawing her to the Savior more irresistibly than affection or sorrow could have done, therefore she could not but continue seeking him, even though unable for the moment to do anything else than weep near his empty tomb.

In vain does Calvary proclaim that the Lord is dead, in vain does the tomb declare that he has been buried, in vain does the absent stone suggest that they have taken him away—this threefold witness will not convince Mary that he has gone out of her life forever. And why? Because in the depth of her being there was an even more emphatic witness which would not be silenced but continued to protest that she must receive him back, since he is her Savior. Contact, communion with Christ had become to her the vital breath of her spiritual life; to admit that the conditions rendering this possible had ceased to exist would have meant for her to deny salvation itself. There is, it is true, a pathetic incongruousness between the absoluteness of this desire and the futile form in which for the moment she thought it could be satisfied. In the last analysis what was she doing but seeking a lifeless body, in order that by caring for it and feeling near it she might still the longing of a living faith? Suppose she had received what she sought; would not in the next moment the other deeper desire have reasserted itself for that in him which it was absolutely beyond the power of a dead Jesus to give her? Still, however incongruous the form of expression, it was an instinct to which an outward reality could not fail to correspond. It arose out of a primary need, for which provision must exist somewhere, if redemption exists at all. Though unaware of the resurrection as a fact, she had laid hold upon the supreme principle from which its necessity flows. Once given the intimate bond of faith between a sinner and his Savior, there can be no death to such a relationship.

Mary, in her simple dependence on Jesus, had risen to the point where she sought in him life and sought it ever more abundantly. To her faith he was Conqueror over death long before he issued from the grave. She was in rapport with that spiritual aspect, that quickening quality of his Person, of which the resurrection is the sure consequence. Here lies the decisive issue for everyone as regards the attitude to be assumed towards this great fact. Ultimately, stripped of all accidentals, the question resolves itself into this: What does Christ mean for us? For what do we need him? If we have learned to know ourselves guilty sinners, destitute of all hope and life in ourselves, and if we have experienced that from him came to us pardon, peace, and strength, will it not sound like mockery in our ears if somebody tells us that it does not matter whether Jesus rose from the dead on the third day? It is of the very essence of saving faith that it clamors for facts, facts to show that the heavens have opened, that the tide of sinful nature has been reversed, the guilt of sin expiated, the reign of death destroyed and life and immortality brought to light. And because this is the insuppressible cry of faith, what else should faith do, when it sees doubt and unbelief emptying the gospel of the living Christ—what else should it do but stand outside weeping and repeating the cry: "They have taken away my Lord, and I know not where they have laid him"?

But although these things were in principle present in Mary's heart, she did not at that moment perceive the pledge of hope contained in them. Her grief was too profound to leave room for introspection. It even hid from her vision the objective evidence of the resurrection that lay around her. Worse than this, she turned what was intended to help her into an additional reason for unbelief. But who of us shall blame her? Have not we ourselves under as favorable circumstances made the mistake of nourishing our unbelief on what was meant to be food for our faith? Do we not all remember occasions when we stood outside the grave of our hopes weeping, and did not perceive the hand stretched out to prepare us by the very thing we interpreted as sorrow for a higher joy?

From Mary's experience let us learn to do better. What the Lord expects from us at such seasons is not to abandon ourselves to unreasoning sorrow, but trustingly to look sorrow in the face, to scan its features, to search for the help and hope which, as surely as God is our Father, must be there. In such trials there can be no comfort for us so long as we stand outside weeping. If only we will take the courage to fix our gaze deliberately upon the stern countenance of grief, and enter unafraid into the darkest recesses of our trouble, we shall find the terror gone, because the Lord has been there before us and, coming out again, has left the place transfigured, making out of it by the grace of his resurrection a house of life, the very gate of heaven.

This was just what happened to Mary. She could not stand forever weeping, forgetful of what went on around her. "As she wept she looked into the tomb, and she beheld two angels in white, sitting one at the head and one at the feet, where the body of Jesus had lain." It was a step in the right direction that she roused herself from her inaction. Still, what strikes us as most characteristic in this statement is its implying that even the vision of angels did not sufficiently impress her to raise the question to what the appearance of these celestial messengers might be due. Probably this was the first time she had come in direct contact with the supernatural in that particular form. The place was doubtless charged with the atmosphere of mystery and wonder angels bring with themselves when entering into our world of sense. And yet no tremor seems to have run through her, no feeling of awe to have made her draw back. A greater blindness to fact is here than that which made her miss the sign of the empty grave. What more convincing evidence of the truth of the resurrection could have been offered than the presence of these two angels, silently, reverently, majestically sitting where the body of Jesus had lain? Placed like the cherubim on the mercy seat, they covered between themselves the spot where the Lord had reposed, and flooded it with celestial glory. It needed no voice of theirs to proclaim that here death had been swallowed up in victory. Ever since the angels descended into this tomb, the symbolism of burial has been radically changed. From this moment onward, every last resting place where the bodies of believers are laid is a furrow in that great harvest field of Christ whence heaven draws upward into light each seed sunk into it, whence Christ himself was raised, the firstfruits of those that sleep.

Let us not overlook, however, that Mary's disregard of the angels revealed in a most striking form something good also: her intense preoccupation with the one thought of finding the Lord. For him she had been looking into the tomb. He not being there, it was empty to her view, though filled with angelic glory. She would have turned aside without speaking had not the angels of their own accord spoken to her: "Woman, why do you weep?" These words were meant as an expression of sympathy quite natural in beings wont to rejoice over repenting sinners. But in this question there is at the same time a note of wonder at the fact that she should be weeping at all. To the mind of the angels the resurrection was so real, so self-evident, that they could scarcely understand how to her it could be otherwise. They felt the discord between the songs of joy with which their own world was jubilant and this sound of weeping coming out of a world of darkness and despair. "Woman, why do you weep?" Tears would be called for, indeed, had you found him in the tomb, but not at a time like this, when heaven and earth unite in announcing: he is risen in glory, the King of life!

Mary's answer to the angels shows that neither their sympathy nor their wonder had succeeded in piercing her sorrow. "She said unto them, 'Because they have taken away my Lord, and I know not where they have laid him.'" These are almost the identical words in which she had informed Peter and John of her discovery of the empty tomb. Still a slight change appears. To the apostles she had said "the Lord" and "we know not." To the angels it is "my Lord" and "I know not." In this is revealed once more her intense sense of proprietorship in Jesus. In that sense the angels could not have appropriated him for themselves. They might hail him as their matchless King, but to Mary he was even more than this—her Lord, her Savior, the One who had sought, saved, and owned her in her sins.

Having given this answer to the angels, she turned herself backward and beheld Jesus standing, and knew not that it was Jesus. No explanation is added of the cause of this movement. It matters little. Our interest at this stage of the narrative belongs not to what Mary but to what Jesus did. On his part the encounter was surely not accidental but intended. He had witnessed her coming once and again, her weeping, her bending over the tomb, her answer to the angels, and had witnessed not only these outward acts, but also the inward conflict by which her soul was torn. And he appears precisely at the point where his presence is required, because all other voices for conveying to her the gladsome tidings have failed. He had been holding himself in readiness to become in his own Person the preacher of the gospel of life and hope to Mary.

There is great comfort for us in this thought that, however dim our conscious faith and the sense of our salvation, on the Lord's side the fountain of grace is never closed, its connection with our souls never interrupted; provided there is the irrepressible demand for his presence, he cannot, he will not deny himself to us. The first person to whom he showed himself alive after the resurrection was a weeping woman, who had no greater claim upon him than any simple penitent sinner has. No eye except that of the angels had as yet rested upon his form. The time was as solemn and majestic as that of the first creation when light burst out of chaos and darkness. Heaven and earth were concerned in this event; it was the turning point of the ages. Nor was this merely objectively so: Jesus felt himself the central figure in this newborn universe; he tasted the exquisite joy of one who had just entered upon an endless life in the possession of new powers and faculties such as human nature had never known before. Would it have been unnatural had he sought some quiet place to spend the opening hour of this new unexplored state in communion with the Father? Can there be any room in his mind for the humble ministry of consolation required by Mary? He answers these questions himself. Among all the voices that hailed his triumph, no voice appealed to him like this voice of weeping in the garden.

The first appearance of the risen Lord was given to Mary for no other reason than that she needed him first and needed him most. And what more appropriate beginning could have been set for his ministry of glory than this very act? Nothing could better convince us that in his exalted state he retains for us the same tender sympathy, the same individual affection as he showed during the days of his flesh. It is well for us to know this, because otherwise the dread impression of his majesty might tend to hinder our approach to him. Who of us has not at some time of communion with the Savior felt the overwhelming awe that seized the seer on Patmos, so that we could not utter our prayer until he laid his hand upon us and said: "Fear not"?

We should be thankful, then, for the grace of Christ which has so arranged it that between his rising from the dead and his departure for heaven a season of forty days was interposed, a transition period, helping, as it were, the feebleness of our faith in the act of apprehending his glory. Perhaps the Lord for the same reason also intentionally placed his meeting with Mary at the threshold of his resurrection life. Like other acts recorded in the fourth gospel, this act rises above the momentary situation and acquires a symbolic significance, enlarging before our eyes until it reveals him in his priestly ministration conducted from the throne of glory.

However, not the fact only of his showing himself to Mary, but likewise the manner of it claims our attention. When first beholding him she did not know the Lord, and even after his speech she still supposed him to be the gardener. The chief cause for this may have lain in the change which had taken place in him when the mortal put on immortality. Now behold with what exquisite tact the Lord helps her to restore the broken bond between the image her memory retained of him and that new image in which henceforth he would walk through her life and hold converse with her spirit. Even these first words—"Woman, why do you weep? Whom do you seek?"—though scarcely differing in form from the question of the angels, go far beyond the latter in their power to reach Mary's heart. In the word "woman" with which he addresses her speaks all the majesty of one who felt himself the Son of God in power by resurrection from the dead. It is a prelude to the still more majestic "Touch me not" spoken soon afterwards. And yet in the words "Why do you weep? Whom do you seek?" he extends to her that heart-searching sympathy which at a single glance can read and understand the whole secret of her sorrow. He knew that such weeping results only there where one who is more than father or mother has been taken away. And how instantaneous the effect these words produced! Though she still supposes him the gardener, she takes for granted that he at least could not have taken the body with evil intent, that he will not refuse to restore it: "Sir, if you have borne him hence, tell me where you have laid him, and I will take him away." A certain response to his sympathy is also shown in this: that three times she refers to Jesus as "him," deeming it unnecessary to mention his name. Thus in the way she met the gardener there was already the beginning resumption of the bond of confidence between her and the Lord. And thus Jesus found the way prepared for making himself known to her in a most intimate manner. "Jesus said unto her, 'Mary.' She turned and said unto him, 'Rabboni.'" It happened all in a moment, and by a simple word, and yet in this one moment Mary's world was changed for her. She had in that instant made the transition from hopelessness because Jesus was absent to fullness of joy because Christ was there. We may well despair of conveying by any process of exposition the meaning of these two words. This is speech the force of which can only be felt. And it will be felt by us in proportion as we clearly remember some occasion when the Lord spoke a similar word to us and drew from us a similar cry of recognition. Doubtless much of the astounding effect of Jesus' word was due to the tone in which he spoke it. It was a tone calling to her remembrance the former days of closest fellowship. This was the voice that he alone could use, the same voice that had once commanded the demons to depart from her, and to which ever since she had been wont to listen for guidance and comfort. By using it he meant to assure her that, whatever transformation had taken place, there could be and would be no change in the intimate, personal character of their relationship. And Mary was quick to apprehend this. The evangelist takes pains to preserve for us the word she uttered in its original Aramaic form, because he would have us understand that it meant more at this moment than could be conveyed by the ordinary rendering of "Teacher" or "Master." "Rabboni" has a special untranslatable significance. It was the personal response to the personal

"Mary," to all intents a proper name no less than the other. By speaking it Mary consciously reentered upon the possession of all that as "Rabboni" he had meant to her. Only one thing she had yet to learn, for teaching her which the Lord did not deem even this unique moment too joyful or sacred. In the sudden revulsion from her grief Mary would have given some external expression to the tumult within by grasping and holding him. But he restrained her, saying: "Touch me not, for I am not yet ascended unto my Father; but go unto my brethren and say to them, I ascend unto my Father and your Father, and my God and your God." At first sight these words may seem a contrast to those immediately preceding. And yet no mistake could be greater than to suppose that the Lord's sole or chief purpose was to remind her of the restrictions which henceforth were to govern the intercourse between himself and her. His intention was much rather to show that the desire for a real communion of life would soon be met in a new and far higher way than was possible under the conditions of local earthly nearness. "Touch me not" does not mean that touch is too close a contact to be henceforth permissible; it means that the provision for the highest, the ideal kind of touch has not been completed yet: "I am not yet ascended to my Father." His words are a denial of the privilege she craved only as to the form and moment in which she craved it; in their larger sense they are a pledge, a giving, not a withholding of himself from her. The great event of which the resurrection is the first step has not yet fulfilled itself; it requires for its completion the ascent to the Father. But when this is accomplished then all restrictions will fall away, and the desire to touch that made Mary stretch forth her hand shall be fully gratified. The thought is not different from that expressed in the earlier saying to the disciples: "You shall see me, because I go to the Father." There is a seeing, a hearing, a touching first made possible by Jesus' entrance into heaven and by the gift of the Spirit dependent on that entrance. And what he said to Mary he commissioned her to repeat to his brethren, that they also might view the event in its proper perspective.

May we not suitably close our study by reminding ourselves that we too are included among the brethren to whom he desired these tidings be brought? Before this he had never called the disciples by this name, as he had never until now so suggestively identified himself with them by speaking of "your Father and my Father" and "your God and my God." We are once more assured that the new life of glory, instead of taking him from us, has made us in a profounder sense his brethren and his Father our Father. Though, unlike Mary and the disciples, we have not been privileged to behold him in the body, yet together with the believers of all ages we have an equal share in what is far sweeter and more precious, the touch through faith of his heavenly Person for which the appearances after the resurrection were but a preparation. Let us then not linger at the tomb, but turn our faces and stretch our hands upwards into heaven, where our life is hidden with him in God, and from where he shall also come again to show himself to us as he did to Mary, to make us speak the last great "Rabboni," which will spring to the lips of all the redeemed when they meet their Savior in the early dawn of that eternal Sabbath that awaits the people of God.

14

Shall Unbelief Win?
An Answer to Dr. Fosdick

CLARENCE EDWARD MACARTNEY

On May 21, 1922 Harry Emerson Fosdick preached at the First Presbyterian Church of New York City a sermon entitled "Shall the Fundamentalists Win?" Although a Baptist, Fosdick had been the regular pulpit supply at First Presbyterian since 1918 while he also served as a professor of practical theology at Union Theological Seminary in New York. As Fosdick said in his autobiography, *The Living of These Days*, published in 1956, his sermon "was a plea for tolerance, for a church inclusive enough to take in both liberals and conservatives without either trying to drive the other out." He continued:

> If ever a sermon failed to achieve its object, mine did. It was a plea for good will, but what came of it was an explosion of ill will, for over two years making headline news of a controversy that went the limit of truculence. The trouble was, of course, that in stating the liberal and fundamentalist positions, I had stood in a Presbyterian pulpit and said frankly what the modernist position on some points was—the virgin birth no longer accepted as historic fact, the literal inerrancy of the Scriptures incredible, the second coming of Christ from the skies an outmoded phrasing of hope.[1]

1. Harry Emerson Fosdick, *The Living of These Days: An Autobiography* (New York, Evanston, and London: Harper & Row, 1956), 145–46.

Fosdick's sermon was reproduced in pamphlet form and then published and distributed widely under the title "The New Knowledge and the Christian Faith."

A response was offered by the pastor of Arch Street Presbyterian Church in Philadelphia, Clarence E. Macartney (1879–1957), who was gaining a reputation as "Philadelphia's foremost preacher."[2]

Macartney had previously crossed swords with Fosdick. The latter in a January 1919 *Atlantic Monthly* article had claimed that soldiers returning from World War I would never accept the traditional beliefs and teachings of yesterday's Christianity, and therefore the church would need to accommodate its views and practices to the spirit of the age. In the March 6, 1919 issue of *The Presbyterian*, Macartney had responded:

> If men like Dr. Fosdick have ceased to feel the grip of Christian truth, we shall be sorry because of that fact; we regret their falling out of the ranks. But when they call upon the church to reform herself by abandoning all that is distinctively Christian in her teaching, and put this demand of their own into the mouth of lads returning from the battlefields of Europe, it is the privilege and the duty of those who love the church and would be loyal to their Master to let men know what they think and feel.[3]

It was also in *The Presbyterian*, for July 13 and July 20, 1922, that Macartney's sermon was published as "Shall Unbelief Win? An Answer to Dr. Fosdick."

Macartney followed this up by preparing an overture that the Philadelphia Presbytery sent to the General Assembly to require the Presbytery of New York to ensure that the preaching in the First Church of New York conform with the doctrines of the Presbyterian church as set forth in the Westminster Confession of Faith.[4] The 1923 General Assembly approved this overture by only a 55 percent majority, 439–359, and also reaffirmed five doctrines—the inerrancy of Scripture, the virgin birth of Christ, the

---

2. Bradley J. Longfield, *The Presbyterian Controversy: Fundamentalists, Modernists, and Moderates* (New York and Oxford: Oxford University Press, 1991), 113.

3. Ibid., 113–14.

4. Clarence E. Macartney, *The Making of a Minister: The Autobiography of Clarence E. Macartney*, ed. J. Clyde Henry (Great Neck, N.Y.: Channel Press, 1961), 184–85.

substitutionary atonement, the bodily resurrection of Christ, and his supernatural miracles—as essential to the faith. In response to this action, 150 Presbyterian ministers on December 26, 1923 issued the "Auburn Affirmation," which claimed that the five doctrines could not constitutionally be elevated to requirements for ordination and that they were not essential to the Presbyterian system of doctrine but were merely possible interpretations of the faith.

At the 1924 General Assembly in Grand Rapids, Michigan, Macartney was nominated for moderator by William Jennings Bryan with these flamboyant words:

> It was his vigilance that detected the insidious attack made upon the historic doctrines of the Presbyterian Church; it was his courage that raised the standard of the protest about which the church rallied; it was his leadership that won a decisive victory for evangelical Christianity and historical Presbyterianism. He was the man of the hour and linked himself with the fundamental tenets of the creed of our church.[5]

Macartney won the election by only a 51 percent margin, 464–446, over the moderate candidate, Charles R. Erdman. Although as moderator Macartney could and did appoint conservative figures to crucial positions, discipline of the signers of the Auburn Affirmation was not pursued, and by the 1925 General Assembly the tide had turned in the liberal, or at least broadly tolerant, direction. Fosdick, though urged by his congregation to submit to Presbyterian jurisdiction, could not in good conscience do so and resigned from the pulpit of First Presbyterian Church in New York in 1925. He then became pastor of Park Avenue Baptist Church, which in 1930 erected Riverside Church in New York as an interdenominational ministry, from which Fosdick retired in 1946 before his death in 1969 at age 91. His autobiography records his summary of the "Fundamentalist–Modernist Controversy":

> We . . . thought that the controversy, despite the noise it made, was an ephemeral affair, with the matters in dispute, such as the five points the General Assembly raised, insufficient in importance to disrupt the historic

---

5. Quoted in C. Allyn Russell, *Voices of American Fundamentalism: Seven Biographical Studies* (Philadelphia: Westminster Press, 1976), 208.

churches. I often confided to my friends my sense of shame that I was unwittingly made the front and center of a controversy over such belated issues. The questions in dispute were not the great matters that confronted modern Christianity; they were trivial in comparison with the real issues of the day; and the whole uproar was not the noise of the main battle but the flare-up of a rear-guard action. The idea of splitting the great churches over such obscurantism as William Jennings Bryan stood for seemed to us absurd; the slow but inevitable processes of education were bound in time to put an end to such outdated thinking; and meanwhile our place was inside the evangelical churches, patiently standing our ground, claiming our liberty, and biding our time. The outcome, I am sure, has validated our stand.[6]

Clarence Macartney's perspective was quite different. Born on September 18, 1879 in Northwood, Ohio to parents of Scottish Covenanter background, Macartney grew up in Beaver Falls, Pennsylvania, where his father taught at Geneva College. He graduated from the University of Wisconsin in 1901 and then attended Princeton Seminary, where he was a classmate of J. Gresham Machen. From 1905 to 1914 he served as pastor of the First Presbyterian Church in downtown Paterson, New Jersey, where the membership grew from 258 in 1906 to 506 in 1913. Then he was at Arch Street Presbyterian Church in Philadelphia from 1914 to 1927, where the membership grew from 481 to 708 and the evening service attendance jumped from around 100 to more than 1,000. From 1927 to 1953 he was pastor of First Presbyterian Church in Pittsburgh, where the membership stayed at a level of almost 2,500 despite the movement of population from downtown to the suburbs. Sunday morning attendance was 1,200 to 1,600, and the Sunday evening service averaged about 900. Macartney typically preached four sermons a week, including a Wednesday evening service and the Tuesday Noon Club for Businessmen, which he founded in 1930 with a core of twelve men and which grew to an average attendance of more than 800 and a membership of more than 2,000 representing thirty-one denominations and 656 churches.[7] His preaching style has been described as that of "a talented craftsman":

---

6. Fosdick, *The Living of These Days*, 164–65.

7. Russell, *Voices of American Fundamentalism*, 197; Longfield, *Presbyterian Controversy*, 217.

He brought to his discourses careful organization, excellent diction, vivid imagination, superb illustrative ability, a thorough knowledge of the scriptures, depth of conviction, and supremely important for holding the attention of his "subjects," a freedom from all notes and manuscripts.[8]

Macartney was elected to the board of directors of Princeton Seminary in 1922, but when Westminster Seminary was established in 1929 by his former classmates, J. Gresham Machen and Oswald T. Allis, he resigned to become a member of its board. He gave the address at Westminster's first commencement in 1930:

> A deleted Bible has resulted in a diluted Gospel. Protestantism, as it loses its faith in the Bible, is losing its religion. . . . Men who desire such dilutions can drink de-caffeined coffee and smoke de-nicotined tobacco; and now we have on every hand, without money and without price, de-christianized Christianity.[9]

When Machen and the Westminster faculty supported the Independent Board for Presbyterian Foreign Missions and the formation of a new, orthodox Presbyterian denomination, Macartney and twelve other trustees resigned from the board in January 1936. He believed that his role was to remain in the Presbyterian Church, USA, providing a witness for biblical truth through his preaching. This he did until his retirement from First Church in Pittsburgh in September 1953. A lifelong bachelor, he returned to his parents' former home, Fern Cliffe, on the campus of Geneva College in Beaver Falls, Pennsylvania, where he stayed until his death on February 19, 1957.

In his sermon "Shall Unbelief Win?" Macartney stresses the need to contend for the faith. The spirit of the time is that the church "is *not* to defend the faith, it is *not* to point out the errors and inconsistencies of those who stand as the interpreters of Christianity." He believes that "in this day one of the greatest contributions that a man can make to the success of the gospel is to contend earnestly and intelligently and in a Christian spirit, but nevertheless *contend*, for the faith." Fosdick himself indicated that

---

8. Russell, *Voices of American Fundamentalism*, 195–96.
9. Quoted in Russell, *Voices of American Fundamentalism*, 199.

Macartney was "personally fair-minded and courteous" and engaged him in "frank and not unfriendly correspondence."[10] Macartney appreciated Fosdick's candor about his liberal views and in his sermon urges that people read Fosdick's "Shall the Fundamentalists Win?"

> Those who above all others ought to read this sermon are not the conservatives and not the rationalists, but the middle-of-the-road people, who are fondly hoping that these schools are divided only by a difference in word and names and that the two positions can and will be reconciled. Dr. Fosdick's sermon shows the impossibility and the non-desirability of such reconciliation.

Macartney then deals with the main points that Fosdick had discussed: the virgin birth, the inspiration of the Bible, the second advent, and the atonement. It is this last doctrine that is most important:

> Our chief complaint against the rationalist and modernist is not their writings and sayings about the deity of our Lord, the Bible, the second advent, but their rejection of the one great truth of Christianity, that through his death we have remission of our sins and are justified with God.

The very gospel of Jesus Christ is at stake. In a moving passage Macartney pictures ministers appearing before Christ when he comes again: "No minister should preach or write a sermon which he would not be willing to place in the hands of Jesus, should he appear in person." He concludes his message with a disavowal of a desire to excommunicate false teachers by means of ecclesiastical trial. He regards the liberals as a vocal minority in the church that is really outside the church, and he prays that they may be brought back in, but then he ends with a prescient prophecy about Modernism:

> The movement is slowly secularizing the church and, if permitted to go unchecked and unchallenged, will ere long produce in our churches a new kind of Christianity, a Christianity of opinions and principles and good purposes, but a Christianity without worship, without God, and without Jesus Christ.

---

10. Fosdick, *The Living of These Days*, 146–47.

Shall Unbelief Win?
An Answer to Dr. Fosdick

Clarence Edward Macartney

There appeared recently in a number of the religious papers the copy of a sermon entitled, "Shall the Fundamentalists Win?" preached by Dr. Harry Emerson Fosdick, in the pulpit of the First Presbyterian Church of New York City. The sermon has all the lucidity of thought and outline and charm of word grouping which have won for Dr. Fosdick a well-deserved popularity. It is also free from the intolerance and the bigotry and arrogance which so often mars the writings of the so-called "liberal" schools of theologians, and whose own illiberality and childishness of spirit speaks much more loudly than anything else that they say.

The sermon by Dr. Fosdick will be read with varying emotions. Those who agree with the position held by Dr. Fosdick will hail it with delight as a sort of declaration of principles and an eloquent setting forth of the Fourteen Points of modernistic theology, a manual by which all on that side can march and drill and fight. Persons who are a-theological in their thinking, but who always applaud the revolt against what has been held, taught, and believed in the church, will also rejoice in it. But there are not a few others who do not think of themselves as either "Fundamentalists" or "Moderns," but as Christians, and are striving amid the dust and confused clamor of this life to hold to the Christian faith and follow the Lord Jesus Christ, who will read this sermon with sorrow and pain. The Presbyterians who read it will deeply regret that such an utterance, so hopelessly irreconcilable with the standard of belief required by the Reformed churches, could be made by the stated occupant of a Presbyterian pulpit, and apparently without any protest or wonder on the part of the session of the church or the presbytery to which the church belongs. I have just read a letter from a minister in the West in which the writer expresses the earnest hope that Dr. Fosdick will awaken to the inconsistency of his position and the non-Christianity of his views, and return, like many another wanderer, to the cross of Christ. In this pious wish I am sure that all right-minded ministers who differ with Dr. Fosdick will join. One of his own school of thought, in conversation with me, declared that Dr. Fosdick must be retained to the church because of his splendid emphasis on the social side of Christianity. None would deny that emphasis. But why not keep him for a greater service, for an emphasis on the redemptive side of Christianity, the truth that takes in all else? We may feel that there are few instances of men who have gone as far from historic Christianity as he has gone ever returning to the fold. But what about Romanes? What about Reginald Campbell and his "New" Theology, now long since recanted? The citation of these names gives one hope that Dr. Fosdick, too, may yet speak in accents which will rejoice the hearts of believers, instead of causing them anxiety and sorrow.

But a sincere desire for the return of Dr. Fosdick to evangelical faith, and the sense of pain and anxiety which his sermon occasions, must not be permitted to stand in the way of an emphatic and earnest rejoinder on the part of those who hold the opposite views and who believe that the views held by Dr. Fosdick are subversive to the Christian faith. The greatest need of the church today is a few men of ability and faith who are not afraid of being called and thought "bigots," "narrow," "medieval" in their religious thought. I do not mean to infer that Dr. Fosdick ever so thinks of those who repudiate his views, for he goes out of his way to rebuke those of his side who indulge in this childish pastime. But more and more there is a tendency to brand as illiberal, medieval, and narrow any man who differs from the current of popular religious thought and declares it to be non-Christian in its tendencies. There is great discussion in the pulpit and out of it as to what the church is to do or not to do. The state of opinion on this subject is singularly chaotic at present. But with all the divergence of opinion as to the work of the church, there seems to be a pretty general agreement as to the one thing which the church is *not* to do. Whatever the church is to do or not to do, it is not to defend the faith, it is not to point out the errors and inconsistencies of those who stand as the interpreters of Christianity. This amazing agreement would have struck the Christian believers of almost any age in church history, save our own, as a very extraordinary one. The writer of this article dissents entirely from this popular view that when a Christian man hears or reads an utterance of Christian teachers and leaders which he believes to be irreconcilable with the gospel, the thing to do is to do *nothing*. Certainly this is not the course followed by those who are blasting at the Rock of Ages and consciously or unconsciously adulterating distinctive and New Testament Christianity with the conclusions and vagaries of this world's life and thought. I do not believe in letting them hold the field all to themselves. I believe that in this day one of the greatest contributions that a man can make to the success of the gospel is to contend earnestly and intelligently and in a Christian spirit, but nevertheless *contend*, for the faith.

Whatever one's theological position may be, one cannot but feel glad that Dr. Fosdick has spoken so frankly as he has. He, at least, cannot be charged with the offense of subtly corrupting Christian doctrines by pretending to honor them while all the time evacuating them of their meaning. The recent book by Dr. Sterrit on "What Is Modernism?" is a good example of the fog and bog of much of the rationalistic movement in the church. One is puzzled to know just what the man does believe. As an elder in one of our Presbyterian churches said of his own minister, "I really do not know what our minister believes!" He knew it was something strange, something perhaps out of harmony with historic Christianity, but just why or how, he could not tell. But none can charge Dr. Fosdick with such obscurity. Both rationalists and evangelicals, therefore, will rejoice that Dr. Fosdick in this sermon leaves no reader or hearer in the least doubt as to what he believes or disbelieves about the cardinal doctrines of the Christian religion.

It is unfortunate that Dr. Fosdick uses the name "Fundamentalist." It is a grand name, and the man who claims it certainly puts the burden of proof on those who differ from him. But in recent years the name has come to be applied to a group, especially in the Baptist churches, who indeed hold to conservative views, but whose chief emphasis is on the premillennial reign of Christ on this earth. In this sense we are not interested in the controversy, for we do not believe that an opinion or a conviction or an expectation as to the time of the second epiphany of Christ is a fundamental of the Christian faith. Historic Christianity has been wisely guided here, for no great body of the Christian church has ever made an opinion about the *time* of Christ's advent an article of its creed. In any recent controversy between rationalists and evangelicals there has been a tendency on the part of the former to use chiliasm as a sort of smoke screen and raise the cry of "premillenarian," whereas they know that the strongest and most influential currents of thought in conservative Protestantism run in an altogether different direction. The Princeton "school" of theology, for example, as summed up in Charles Hodge's famous eight reasons against premillennialism, has never had any chiliastic leanings whatever. But as we shall see, Dr. Fosdick not only, and with some cause, protests against premillenarian propaganda, but goes far beyond that and reduces the great New Testament teaching of the second advent of Jesus Christ to a "glittering generality."

Let us now take up, one by one, the different Christian doctrines mentioned in the sermon, and see how Dr. Fosdick views them. His claim is that a group of "fundamentalists" are drawing a "dead line" in theory across which no man may step and live. In stating the views of the so-called "fundamentalists," which is of little consequence, Dr. Fosdick states his own views and those of his school of thought, and this is of the greatest consequence, for it clears the atmosphere and lets us see the state of religious chaos which reigns in rationalist circles. Those who above all others ought to read this sermon are not the conservatives and not the rationalists, but the middle-of-the-road people, who are fondly hoping that these schools are divided only by a difference in word and names and that the two positions can and will be reconciled. Dr. Fosdick's sermon shows the impossibility and the non-desirability of such reconciliation. If Dr. Fosdick is right, his views ought to prevail, and the creed of the Presbyterian church and of every other church in Christendom (save the smaller humanitarian bodies, like the Unitarians, and which are really creedless, either as to a formal or written creed) ought to be revised. If this is truth, then let it prevail, no matter how many churches sink into oblivion. But whether he is right or whether the evangelical position is right, one thing all must now admit: both positions cannot be right; one *must* be wrong.

1. *The Virgin Birth:* Dr. Fosdick does not accept the virgin birth as a historic fact. He rejects what he calls "a special biological miracle" as the explanation for the way in which Christ came into the world. The virgin birth

to him is merely an effort on the part of religious devotion and faith to account for the manifest superiority of the character and person of Jesus. But lest I should do him any injustice in my summary of this paragraph of his sermon, let me quote his own words:

> To believe in virgin birth as an explanation of great personality is one of the familiar ways in which the ancient world was accustomed to account for unusual superiority. Many people do suppose that only once in history do we run across a record of supernatural birth. Upon the contrary, stories of miraculous generation are among the commonest traditions of antiquity. Especially is this true about the founders of great religions. According to the records of their faith, Buddha and Zoroaster and Lao-Tsze and Mahavira were all supernaturally born. Moses, Confucius, and Mohammed are the only great founders of religions in history to whom miraculous birth is not attributed. That is to say, when a personality arose so high that men adored him, the ancient world attributed his superiority to some special divine influence in his generation, and they commonly phrased their faith in terms of miraculous birth. So Phythagoras was called virgin born, and Plato, and Augustus Caesar and many more. Knowing this, there are within the evangelical churches large groups of people whose opinion about our Lord's coming would run as follows: those first disciples adored Jesus—as we do; when they thought about his coming, they were sure that he came specially from God—as we are; this adoration and conviction they associated with God's special influence and intention in his birth—as we do; but they phrased it in terms of a biological miracle that our modern minds cannot use. So far from thinking that they have given up anything vital in the New Testament's attitude toward Jesus, these Christians remember that the two men who contributed most to the church's thought of the divine meaning of the Christ were Paul and John, who never even distantly allude to the virgin birth.

This speaks for itself. There was no virgin birth. The opening chapters of St. Matthew and St. Luke are pure myth, and the alleged facts and acts of those pages are merely a pious, devout, and natural effort of believing men to account for the personality of Jesus, in much the same way that the followers of Buddha, Zoroaster, Lao-Tsze, and Mahavira tried to account for them. Not only does he repudiate the virgin birth, but he states that opinions on the subject are of little importance, in no way affecting vital Christianity. In this connection he makes the stock remark of the rationalist about the two great teachers of Christianity, St. John and St. Paul, never even distantly alluding to the virgin birth. I have often been asked if Dr. Fosdick believes in the divinity or, better, the deity of our Lord. I hope that he does, for even if in our New Testament we did not have the accounts of Matthew and Luke, the deity of Jesus Christ would everywhere confront us. We must grant, too, that God becoming flesh is a mystery which the virgin birth only partially explains. Nevertheless, that is the explanation given in the gospels, and the *only* explanation given. Moreover, if we are to take that part of the gospels as mere pious musings and guessing, will it not weaken our regard for the other parts? If, for example, the stories of the nativity of Jesus are mere human effort to account for a personality who defied human classification, then who can find fault with the man who says that the accounts of the crucifixion of Jesus are merely imaginations on the part of his followers who wished to have him die a glorious and sacrificial death? Or that the accounts of the resurrection are merely the tributes of devotion and admiration, not the records of fact, but stories arising out of the conviction that Christ was too great and holy a man to be held of death, and thus in keeping with other tales of the reappearance and reincarnation of great men? And so with the ascension and the second epiphany. The moment we take this view of the account of the virgin birth, do we not prepare the way for the repudiation of any other part of the gospel story by any man who wills to do so?

No intelligent Christian is disturbed by the reference that neither John nor Paul "even distantly allude" to the virgin birth of Jesus. It is partly amusing and partly irritating, the way the rationalists make use of Paul and John. When they are talking on the virgin birth of Jesus, they cite Paul and John as the great authorities of the church, and yet men who are silent on this subject. But when they are on a subject such as the atonement or the fate of the unbelievers in the next world, there John and Paul appear in an altogether different light. Now no one knows whether John wrote the gospel that bears his name—probably not; and as for Paul, he took the simple teachings of the Galilean peasant and grafted upon them a mass of doctrines about sin and atonement and justification by faith which are entirely foreign to true Christianity. For this reason, it is amusing to hear them cite John and Paul as on either side when it comes to the virgin birth. The fact is that both St. John and St. Paul, above all other writers of the New Testament, teach the incarnation of God in Jesus and the supernatural manner of the entrance of the Son of God into this world. The fact that Paul, for example, while he says that Christ was born of a woman, does not say that he was born of a virgin in no way invalidates the authority of Matthew or Luke, or implies that he had never heard of the birth of "that holy thing" in the womb of the virgin Mary.

Dr. Fosdick is not a Presbyterian, but he stands in a Presbyterian pulpit and gets his bread from a Presbyterian congregation. In view of this fact, how can his holding the purely naturalistic account of the stories of the birth of Jesus be in harmony with his preaching in the pulpit of a church whose creed, never revoked, declares in the Confession of Faith, Chapter VIII, article II: "The Son of God, . . . when the fullness of time was come, did take upon him man's nature, . . . being conceived by the power of the Holy Ghost, in the womb of the Virgin Mary, of her substance"? This article of the creed may be impossible for the "modern" mind to hold; it may be myth and rubbish. But myth or fact, truth or rubbish, it is a solemn declaration of the church from which Dr. Fosdick takes his bread.

2. *The Inspiration of the Bible:* Dr. Fosdick describes two ideas of the inspiration of the Bible, neither of which, however, are held by a great number of intelligent and devout Christians. On the one side, there is what he calls the "static [note the word, for it is *the* word of the rationalists, and should it go out of currency, we know not what they would do] and mechanical theory of inspiration." According to this theory, "all parts of the Bible, from the Dukes of Edom to the thirteenth chapter of 1 Corinthians, were inerrantly dictated by God to men a good deal as a man might dictate to a stenographer." We pass by the irreverence of this statement, with its offense not so much against orthodoxy as against good taste, and remark that those who hold the New Testament idea of inspiration, that holy men of old "spoke as they were moved by the Holy Ghost," have never thought of the Holy Ghost dictating to Moses, Isaiah, or St. Paul as Dr. Fosdick, for instance, to use his own illustration, might dictate one of his sermons to a stenographer. Nor have multitudes of Christians ever felt that for Paul to remind Timothy to fetch the cloak which he left at Troas in the house of Carpas required the inspiration of the Holy Ghost, or any kind of inspiration save that of the gloom and damp of the Mamertime dungeon. But there

are places in the writings of St. Paul where he makes the most careful and solemn claim to divine inspiration and that what he declares, that is, his magnificent interpretation of the gospel of Christ, has been revealed to him by the Holy Spirit. Every intelligent Christian knows that it is not correct to say that Christianity depends upon the Scriptures in the political sense, for Christianity had established itself in the world as a conquering and re-generating power before there was any New Testament. The New Testament was the expression of that Christian life and faith and the record of its establishment. Therefore, every intelligent Christian knows, too, that while Christianity came before the New Testament, if the New Testament is false, Christianity also must be false. The great question at issue is not any peculiar theory of inspiration, but the credibility and authority of the Bible. Personally, I have never been troubled by the controversies which have raged over the question of inspiration, ranging all the way from harsh, petrified, and illogical theories which would have made a genealogical cat-alogue with its graveyard of names of equal authority with St. Paul's state-ment of the redeeming and reconciling love of God in Christ—all the way from that to Dr. Fosdick's rationalistic theory, namely, that God revealed himself, or rather mis-revealed himself, in crude and false ways in times past, sanctioning and approving much that was false, but gradually drew away from that misrepresentation and gave a clearer knowledge of himself in the New Testament, but which representation will undoubtedly be much improved on in the future, since there is no reason to believe that this "pro-gressive" revelation came to a sudden stop with St. John or St. Paul. For me, the great question is this: Can we rely upon the Bible as giving us the great facts about what God requires of man and that plan of redemption which God has revealed through Jesus Christ? Does it contain the way of life eternal? If so, it is inspired of God. Theories of inspiration are of little consequence, for the inspiration of the Holy Spirit is like the wind—you hear the sound thereof, but cannot tell from where it comes or where it goes. But although there is such a thing as accepting the inspiration of the Bible and not being sure as to how it was inspired, that is an altogether dif-ferent thing from a theory of inspiration which breaks down the whole au-thority of the Bible. Whenever we hear men speak as Dr. Fosdick does about the Bible, the question of a mode of inspiration sinks out of sight and the greater question emerges: Do these men believe that the Bible has any special authority? Do they believe that God spoke in times past by the prophets to the fathers in any clearer note than he did to Socrates, Confucius, or Buddha? Do they really believe that the prophets, to quote the words of Dr. Gore in his recent and notable book, "Belief in God," "were in touch—as other men were not—with reality, with the real God; and that in a long and continuous process, more or less gradual, he was really communicating to them the truth by which man could live, both about the divine nature and purpose and about human nature"? The Confession of Faith of the Presbyterian Church commences with a declaration about the Scriptures, which says: "Although the light of nature and the works of creation and providence do so far manifest the goodness, wisdom, and power of God as to leave men inexcusable, yet they are not sufficient to give that knowledge of God, and of his will, which is necessary unto salvation; therefore it pleased God to reveal himself and declare his will unto his church." One lays by a sermon of Dr. Fosdick and all his school with the impression that the light of nature was sufficient for the salvation of men, and that the Bible is but a reflection of that light of nature, coming from man only, and not from God.

I am sure that even the most emancipated modernists will regret Dr. Fosdick's unhappy comparison of the Bible with the Koran, and all believers in the Bible who not only talk about it but read it will indignantly repudiate his assertion that most of the repulsive ideas which are taught in the Koran are taught somewhere in the Bible. I deny that the Bible teaches that "God is an Oriental monarch, fatal submission to his will men's chief duty, the use of force on unbelievers, polygamy and slavery." When we come to appalling statements such as this, the best plan is not to argue, but to deny.

3. *The Second Advent:* I have already intimated that I do not adhere to the premillennial school of the New Testament interpretation. I do believe that the church has been inexcusably silent and negligent in its teaching as to the future chapters in the drama of divine redemption, and that this wide neglect has prepared the way for much of the extravagance and petrified literalism of the popular premillenarian. Thoughtful conservatives are not a little perplexed over the attitude of the aggressive premillenarians and sometimes feel that their defense of historic Christianity is not altogether a helpful one; and when we hear our premillenarian brethren dwell

with more emphasis and zeal upon the mechanism of the temporal kingdom that is to be set up here upon this earth than they do upon the redeeming love of Christ and the conquest of human nature through the mild reign of the Holy Spirit, we are tempted to become impatient with them and to cry out as the princes of the Philistines did when, about to campaign against Israel, they saw David and his men in their ranks, and said to Achish, "What do these Hebrews here?" But there is one thing about the premilleniarian concerning which there is no doubt, and that is his loyalty to the Person and the claims of Jesus Christ. However much he may be tempted to write history before it has been made, his absolute loyalty to the deity of Jesus, his atonement, and his reign of righteousness and judgment is never questioned. This is far more than we can say about the rationalists and the modernists. We feel that it is but a poor Christ that they have left us, only a shadow of the tremendous personality of the New Testament.

If perchance the premillenarian has been a little too sure in his exegesis and in casting the horoscope of the church and the race, the rationalist has gone to the other extreme and has reduced the great doctrine of the second advent of Christ to a mere figure of speech. So Dr. Fosdick regards it, for he says, "They" (that is, the rationalists and modernists), "too, say 'Christ is coming!' They say it with all their hearts, but they are not thinking of an external arrival on the clouds. They have assimilated as part of the divine revelation the exhilarating insight which these recent generations have given us, that development is God's way of working out his will. Man's music has been developed from the rhythmic noise of beaten sticks; man's painting from the crude outlines of the caveman; man's architecture from the rude huts of primitive man. And these Christians, when they say that Christ is coming, mean that slowly it may be, but surely, his will and principles will be worked out by God's grace in human life and institutions, until he shall see of the travail of his soul and be satisfied!" The best possible comment on this idea of the second advent of Christ and the final jurisprudence of our species is to set it alongside of the mysterious yet tremendous utterances of Jesus in the last part of Matthew's gospel or the equally mysterious and tremendous utterances of St. Paul and of St. Peter. Whatever Christ or Paul or Peter mean or do not mean, we can be sure of this: that they imply a process of progress and arrival at perfection which is something far different from Dr. Fosdick's mild working out of the tangles of life.

The Bible teaches progress and development, and a final arrival at a state of universal peace and righteousness, but it also teaches that crisis and cataclysm play their part in bringing the great goal which seers, prophets, and poets have saluted afar off and contemplated through their tears.

The first advent of Christ was not accounted for by any long-drawn-out natural development, although it did come in the "fullness of time," and it is quite possible that the second advent will be just as much of an intervention and interruption as the first advent was. The rationalists do not do justice to this plain portion of eschatological teaching of the Bible. And even were their absurd dream to come true, even should the world by the slow working out of the powers and principalities now lodged in humanity arrive at moral perfection, still the goal would not have been reached, for there would yet remain a fearful contrast between this perfect creature and his environment. So Father Tyrrell, a much more thoughtful modernist than those who today are so vocal, asks: "Shall progress ever wipe away the tears from all eyes? Prolong life as it will, can progress ever conquer death, with its terrors for the dying, its tears for the surviving? Can it ever control the earthquake, the tempest, the lightning, the cruelties of a nature indifferent to the lot of man?"

What Father Tyrrell meant by these questions was that not only man, but man's environment, the platform of his civilization and life, must be changed and reconstructed. Have Dr. Fosdick and his fellow rationalists any prescriptions for the securing of that great end? They have not, and they know that they have not. Thus, even if it had not been revealed in Scripture, common sense and common experience would demand some such intervention and summing up of human affairs as is involved in the doctrine of the second advent. Then we shall not only have a messianic race of redeemed men, but a messianic world, in which there shall be complete and blessed peace, not only between man and God, but between man and man, between man and beast, and between man and the earth. This was the age saluted by rapt Isaiah when he sang, "And the wolf shall also dwell with the lamb, and the leopard shall lie down with the kid; and the calf and the young lion and the fatling together; and a little child shall lead them. And the cow and the bear shall feed; their young ones shall lie down together, and the lion shall eat straw like the ox, and the sucking child shall play on the hole of the asp, and the weaned child shall put his hand on the cockatrice's den. They shall not hurt or destroy in all my holy mountain; for the earth shall be full of the knowledge of the Lord, as the waters cover the sea."

The great error of the rationalists in their sketch of the future and in their dealing with the New Testament teaching of the coming of Christ is that they confine themselves to laws and principles, and forget that there is something beyond this. "And these Christians," writes Dr. Fosdick, meaning himself and other rationalists, "when they say that Christ is coming, mean that slowly it may be, but surely, his will and principles will be worked out by God's grace in human life and institutions until he shall see of the travail of his soul and be satisfied." Evangelical, New Testament Christians believe that, too. But they believe that the coming of Christ means more than just the establishment of justice in the earth. To them it means also the beatific vision; it means the presence and the companionship of him whom, not having seen, we yet love, on whom, though now we see him not, yet believing, we rejoice with joy unspeakable. This and scores of passages like it in the New Testament can have only one meaning, namely, that though rich and precious the present relationship of the believer with Jesus Christ is, there is something yet greater in store. When according to the old legend Jesus appeared to Thomas Aquinas and said to him, "Thomas, you have written well of me; what would you have?" the great schoolman replied, "Yourself, Lord!" "Yourself, Lord"—that is the consummation of the Christian life and experience. Here we have it in faith and anticipation, but when Christ comes the second time, we shall have it in glorious reality. Righteousness is to come, and the church is to be vindicated, and sinners are to be judged and crooked ways made straight and the rough places plain. It ought not to be necessary, but apparently is, to remind the rationalists that Christ is more than a principle of righteousness and justice, and that the coming of him upon whose breast John leaned at the Supper, who said to the fishermen of Galilee, "Follow me"; to Peter, "Do you love me?"; to Paul, "Why do you persecute me?"—the coming of this Christ must mean nothing less than a personal and blessed and glorious manifestation of himself to those who have believed on him and who, amid the shadows and trials of this world, have followed him as Lord and Master. To the rationalists this blessed consummation of the Christian experience seems to mean nothing. They talk about Christ as if he were only a name for a principle, and seem not to know that Jesus to whom Thomas cried out, "My Lord and my God!" And when Christ comes, how shall they greet him who in this life, and even as his ministers, have spoken of him in such a way as to lead men to believe that he was not conceived by the Holy Ghost and born of the virgin Mary; that he did not take our place and bear our sins on the cursed tree; that he did not rise again from the dead; and that he will not come again in glory? How shall they greet him, and what shall they say to him? To talk acceptably to skeptical university boys or persons inclined to unbelief and write for rationalistic papers is one thing; it is another thing to stand before the judgment seat of Christ. Now those great swelling words about "progressive" revelation, "dynamic Christianity," "the modern mind," etc., etc., sink and shrivel and disappear. No minister should preach or write a sermon which he would not be willing to place in the hands of Jesus, should he appear in person. Could the authors of these rationalistic sermons which tend to destroy men's faith in the Eternal Son of God as their only Redeemer meet Christ with confidence, and would they feel like placing in his hands the sermon which has denied him before men?

4. *The Atonement:* Dr. Fosdick does not dwell at length on this central doctrine of Christianity, but in the very sentence in which he caricatures the traditional evangelical belief in the atonement he reveals his complete and profound aversion to the New Testament teaching on that great and mysterious subject. He thus describes the theory of the atonement as held by the evangelical school: "That the blood of our Lord, shed in a substitutionary death, placates an alienated deity and makes possible welcome for the returning sinner."

Every Christian knows that there is a difference between the *fact* of the atonement and any *theory* of it. But it is inconceivable that any man should receive the fact of the atonement, the death of Christ for sin, and not be interested in the explanation of that fact. The rationalists now write of the theology of St. Paul as an intelligent man's honest effort to give some rational explanation of how he is saved, and how it is that the death of Christ makes possible the forgiveness of sin. Why, may we ask, are the rationalists not interested in giving some explanation of the atonement? If the great primary fact of Christianity, the death of Christ for the remission of sins, is the rock upon which their feet stand, their refuge and their hope, why are they not more interested in the meaning of that fact? Why is it that the only time they talk about the atonement is when they are assailing the traditional views of historic Christianity? Why is it that the only interest they betray in the atonement is to deny the explanations of other believers? St. Paul, whom Dr. Fosdick quotes as one of the two great Christian teachers, made the death of Christ, and the substitutionary and vicarious explanation of that death, the one grand theme of his preaching. To the Corinthians he said: "I delivered unto you, *first of all*, how that Christ died for our sins according to the Scriptures." Is there in the whole world today a rationalist or a modernist who can say that to any city or church where he has preached?

In the close of his sermon, Dr. Fosdick says: "It is almost unforgivable that men should tithe mint and anise and cumin, and quarrel over them, when the world is perishing for lack of the weightier matters of the law, justice, mercy, and faith." He thus likens the question of the virgin birth of our Lord, the inspiration of the Bible, the second advent of Christ, and the atonement to mint, anise, and cumin. To me, this seems an almost unpardonable flippancy on the part of one who speaks as a teacher of Christianity. Especially astounding it is to hear a man so speak of the death of the Lord Jesus Christ. Francis Turretin, whom Dale calls the greatest of Calvinistic theologians, evidently thought differently about the atonement, for he wrote of it as "the chief part of our salvation, the anchor of Faith, the refuge of Hope, the rule of Charity, the true foundation of the Christian religion, and the richest treasure of the Christian church. So long as this doctrine is maintained in its integrity, Christianity itself and the peace and blessedness of all who believe in Jesus Christ are beyond the reach of danger; but if it is rejected, or in any way impaired, the whole structure of the Christian faith must sink into decay and ruin."

Our chief complaint against the rationalist and modernist is not their writings and sayings about the deity of our Lord, the Bible, the second advent, but their rejection of the one great truth of Christianity, that through his death we have remission of our sins and are justified with God.

Dr. Fosdick contends against a conspiracy on the part of those whom he calls "Fundamentalists," and who perhaps so name themselves, to put out of the church all those who do not agree with them in every particular. I have not heard of such a conspiracy and have never been asked to join it. At the same time, I believe that so long as the Presbyterian church has not abandoned and repudiated its Confession of Faith, any man in any of its pulpits holding and declaring the views of Dr. Fosdick occupies an anomalous and inconsistent position. As for putting them out, that could be easily done, for they are very small in the church, although at present the *vocal* minority. But I am coming to think less and less of excision and excommunication as a means of preserving the church from false teaching, not because of any base and ignoble fear on the part of those who might so proceed of being called "heresy hunters," "medieval," etc., but because I am convinced that the far more useful course to pursue is to declare the whole counsel of God so clearly and fearlessly that the whole world may know that there is a difference between what is Christianity and what is not Christianity. Dr. Fosdick and his companions need not worry about processes of excision and ecclesiastical trial, and so being put out of the church. The sad thing is that in the minds of thousands upon thousands of Christians, they are already *out* of the church, and no act of an ecclesiastical court could make the fact more real. Our duty is to pray that they may be brought back into the church and help to build up and adorn where formerly they have only wounded his mystical Body, which is the church.

In his celebrated autobiography, John Stuart Mill, in describing the attitude of his father towards Christianity, says that he looked with indignation upon the identification of the worship of the Christian God with Christianity. The son confesses the same aversion, and thinks the day will come when we shall have a Christianity with God left out. For me, this sums up better than anything I have ever read the menace of the rationalistic and modernist movement in Protestant Christianity. The movement is slowly secularizing the church and, if permitted to go unchecked and unchallenged, will ere long produce in our churches a new kind of Christianity, a Christianity of opinions and principles and good purposes, but a Christianity without worship, without God, and without Jesus Christ.

15

Constraining Love

2 Corinthians 5:14–15

J. GRESHAM MACHEN

J. Gresham Machen (1881–1937) was recognized as the intellectual leader of the opposition to Liberalism in the American church of the 1920s and '30s. Pundit Walter Lippmann in his 1929 book *A Preface to Morals* wrote concerning Machen's *Christianity and Liberalism*, published in 1923:

> It is an admirable book. For its acumen, for its saliency, and for its wit, this cool and stringent defense of orthodox Protestantism is, I think, the best popular argument produced by either side in the controversy. We shall do well to listen to Dr. Machen. The Liberals have yet to answer him.[1]

Machen was a professor of New Testament at Princeton Seminary at the time he published *Christianity and Liberalism*, which makes the claim that Liberalism is not merely another form of Christian thinking, but really a distinct religion from biblical Christianity. His major scholarly books included *The Origin of Paul's Religion* (1921) and *The Virgin Birth of Christ*

---

1. Quoted in Ned B. Stonehouse, *J. Gresham Machen: A Biographical Memoir*, 3rd ed. (Edinburgh and Carlisle, Pa.: Banner of Truth Trust, 1987), 348.

(1930). Other books published during his lifetime included *What Is Faith?* (1925) and *The Christian Faith in the Modern World* (1936), with *The Christian View of Man* published in the year of his death, 1937. Posthumously there appeared *God Transcendent* (1949) and *What Is Christianity? and Other Addresses* (1951), both edited by Ned B. Stonehouse.

Besides his books, Machen's legacy was in several institutions he helped to found in order to stem the tide of Liberalism and to advance the kingdom of Jesus Christ. In 1929 it was Westminster Theological Seminary, in 1933 the Independent Board for Presbyterian Foreign Missions, and in 1936 the Orthodox Presbyterian Church as a new denomination. Westminster Seminary was established by Machen and a few others who left the faculty of Princeton Seminary when it was reorganized in a way that tipped the balance of control away from those who stood for orthodox Reformed doctrine. The Independent Board was formed when conservative Presbyterians could no longer support in good conscience the denominational board of the Presbyterian Church, USA. These two institutions reflected the twin concerns of Machen: the sound theological training of faithful ministers of the gospel and the spread of the one true means of salvation around the world.

The third institution, the Orthodox Presbyterian Church (originally named the Presbyterian Church of America), reflects, however, the deepest longing of Machen's heart. As early as 1921 Machen had seen a separation of true believers from the church as the only real hope. In a letter to his mother after the death of Princeton professor Benjamin B. Warfield on February 16 he described his final conversation with Warfield some weeks earlier:

> In the course of the conversation I expressed my hope that to end the present intolerable condition there might be a great split in the Church, in order to separate the Christians from the anti-Christian propagandists. "No," he said, "you can't split rotten wood." His expectation seemed to be that the organized Church, dominated by naturalism, would become so cold and dead, that people would come to see that spiritual life could be found only outside of it, and that thus there might be a new beginning.[2]

---

2. Stonehouse, *J. Gresham Machen*, 310.

In his chapter on "The Church" in *Christianity and Liberalism* Machen said, "A separation between the two parties in the Church is the crying need of the hour."[3] After a dozen years of contending for the faith within the Northern Presbyterian Church, Machen was offered help as counsel from Clarence Macartney in his trial before the Judicial Commission of the General Assembly in 1936. Macartney later wrote:

> He replied with a kind letter, but declined my offer, saying that if I defended him, he might be acquitted, and that was not what he wanted. He had already made up his mind to secede, and promptly did so, establishing the Orthodox Presbyterian Church.[4]

When the First General Assembly of the Orthodox Presbyterian Church was held on June 11, 1936, Machen declared that with the establishment of the new denomination "we became members, at last, of a true Presbyterian Church."[5] Under the title "A True Presbyterian Church at Last," his column in the *Presbyterian Guardian* exulted: "With what lively hope does our gaze turn now to the future! At last true evangelism can go forward without the shackle of compromising associations. The fields are white to the harvest. The evangelists are ready to be sent."[6] Machen's ultimate concern was for a sound, biblical church, true to the Reformed faith, that could effectively carry out the Great Commission.

J. Gresham Machen was born July 28, 1881 in Baltimore to parents from Southern ancestry, his father from Washington, D.C. and his mother from Macon, Georgia. He graduated from Johns Hopkins University in 1901 with a major in classics. He then went to Princeton, where he earned an M.A. in philosophy from the University while gaining a B.D. from the Seminary in 1905. He then spent a year in Germany, where his faith was par-

---

3. J. Gresham Machen, *Christianity and Liberalism* (Grand Rapids: Eerdmans, 1923, 1968), 160.

4. Clarence E. Macartney, *The Making of a Minister: The Autobiography of Clarence E. Macartney*, ed. J. Clyde Henry (Great Neck, N.Y.: Channel Press, 1961), 189.

5. D. G. Hart, *Defending the Faith: J. Gresham Machen and the Crisis of Conservative Protestantism in Modern America* (Baltimore and London: Johns Hopkins University Press, 1994), 158.

6. Stonehouse, *J. Gresham Machen*, 502.

ticularly challenged by the learning and piety of Professor Wilhelm Herrmann at Marburg. Upon returning to Princeton, he accepted in 1906 an appointment as instructor in Greek and New Testament, which did not require that he subscribe to a statement of faith. By 1913 Machen's doubts and sense of calling were resolved, and he received ordination from the New Brunswick Presbytery in June 1914 and was promoted to assistant professor of New Testament at Princeton Seminary.[7]

By the time of Warfield's death and the publication of *The Origins of Paul's Religion* in 1921, Machen was becoming recognized as a leader for the cause of orthodoxy and was becoming exceedingly busy in speaking engagements as well as his teaching and writing. The 1922–23 academic year found him traveling to speak on almost every weekend in churches and on college campuses.[8] From October 1923 to the summer of 1924 he was the regular pulpit supply for the First Presbyterian Church of Princeton. Eight of his sermons from that time were later printed in *God Transcendent*. On one occasion Princeton University's professor of English literature Henry Van Dyke walked out after Machen's sermon, wrote a protest to the church's session, and released the letter to the press. This publicity called greater attention to Machen's book *Christianity and Liberalism*, whose sales jumped from about 1,000 copies in 1923 to more than 4,000 in 1924, and may have contributed to an increase in Princeton Seminary's enrollment from 156 in 1919–20 to 224 in 1923–24 and 255 in 1928–29.[9]

Tensions within the faculty and administration at Princeton Seminary led to President J. Ross Stevenson's opposition to Machen's transfer to the chair of apologetics and to the General Assembly's investigation of the Seminary. This resulted in the reorganization of 1929 and Machen's departure to establish Westminster Seminary in Philadelphia. The formation of the Independent Board for Presbyterian Foreign Missions in 1933 led to Machen's trial in the New Brunswick Presbytery for what was deemed schismatic undermining of the denomination's board. He was suspended from the ministry by his presbytery on March 29, 1935. This was appealed to the

---

7. Bradley J. Longfield, *The Presbyterian Controversy: Fundamentalists, Modernists, and Moderates* (New York and Oxford: Oxford University Press, 1991), 43, 48.

8. David B. Calhoun, *Princeton Seminary*, 2 vols. (Edinburgh and Carlisle, Pa.: Banner of Truth Trust, 1994, 1996), vol. 2: *The Majestic Testimony, 1869–1929*, 336–37.

9. Calhoun, *Princeton Seminary*, 2:348–49, 508 n.18, 510 n.4.

Synod and General Assembly, but the Assembly of 1936 in Syracuse rejected the appeal.

Anticipating this action, Machen and his supporters were prepared to constitute themselves as the Presbyterian Church of America (renamed the Orthodox Presbyterian Church in 1939) in Philadelphia on June 11, 1936. Machen was elected moderator. Most of the work of this First Assembly was involved in electing committees to prepare for the Second General Assembly, to be held November 12–15 of the same year.[10] It was at the opening session of this Second Assembly that Machen preached the moderator's address on "Constraining Love" before the communion service. Little did the Assembly or he realize that this would be his valedictory to the church. Although he would deliver four radio addresses in December, this address as retiring moderator would be his final public preaching appearance. During the holiday break from Westminster Seminary he journeyed to North Dakota to discuss the current issues with churches there, but in the frigid twenty-below-zero weather he contracted pneumonia and died on January 1, 1937.

Machen's sermon as retiring moderator exemplifies his clear and logical style of presentation. His command of the Greek text of 2 Corinthians 5:14–15 is manifested in his concise exposition. He makes effective use of the words of popular hymns, "When I Survey the Wondrous Cross" and "There Is a Green Hill Far Away," and he employs a dialogue between the law of God and a sinner. In regard to doctrine he rejoices in the particularity of the atonement in Calvinism over against the generality of Arminianism's universal atonement, expressing thankfulness for the "warm and tender individualism of our Reformed faith." He points out that Christ's love that constrains us is not merely a restraint that keeps one from those things that displease Christ, but much more a new freedom to do the things that are good, including things in the arts and sciences as well as evangelism. In all that one does, one remembers the One who died and rose again. Machen concludes:

> This morning we, a little branch of his church universal, are gathered for the first time together around his table. We shall go forth from this service into the deliberations of this Assembly and then into the varied work of the church.

---

10. Edwin H. Rian, *The Presbyterian Conflict* (Grand Rapids: Eerdmans, 1940), 227–28.

He makes a threefold application of the constraint of Christ's love: the new church must not weaken the stand taken for the sake of Christ, there must not be a seeking of personal advantage or preferment, and there must not be a stifling of discussion for the sake of peace. If these things are achieved, then Machen foresees a marvelous opportunity in the privilege of proclaiming the full system of truth revealed in God's Word and summarized in the Westminster Standards in the pulpit, in the Christian home and school, in foreign lands.

Machen was not to live to see this vision fulfilled, but it would be carried out not only in the separation of the Orthodox Presbyterian Church out of the Northern Presbyterian Church but also a generation later in the separation out of the Southern Presbyterian Church that produced the new Presbyterian Church in America in 1973.

CONSTRAINING LOVE

J. GRESHAM MACHEN

For the love of Christ constrains us; because we thus judge, that if one died for all, then were all dead, and that he died for all, that they which live should not henceforth live unto themselves, but unto him which died for them, and rose again. (2 Cor. 5:14–15)

In these great verses Paul speaks of love as a constraining force. Love, he says, hems us in. There are certain things which love prevents us from doing.

Earlier in the passage he has spoken of another restraining force—namely, fear. "Knowing therefore the terror of the Lord," he says, "we persuade men." Since we must all appear before the judgment seat of Christ, it behooves us to stand in fear of him; and there are many things which, because we shall stand before his judgment seat, we are afraid to do.

That motive of fear is used in many places in the Bible. It is used in the Old Testament. It is used in the New Testament. It is used with particular insistence in the teaching of Jesus. I think it is one of the strangest of modern aberrations when men say it is a degrading and sub-Christian thing to tell man to stand in fear of God. Many passages in the Bible might be summarized by the words: "The fear of God constrains us."

In our text, however, it is something other than fear that is the thing that is said to constrain us or hem us in. It is love. "The love of Christ," Paul says, "constrains us."

What then is here meant by the love of Christ? Our first impulse, perhaps, might be to say that it is our love of Christ, the love which we bear to Christ, the love in our hearts for Christ our Savior. The comparison with verse 11 might perhaps suggest that view. As there the fear which is in our hearts when we think of our standing before the judgment seat of Christ constrains us from doing things that we might otherwise do, so here the love which is in our hearts when we think of what Christ has done for us might seem to be the second constraining force of which Paul speaks.

Now if that is the right interpretation, the verse tells us something that is certainly true. It is certainly true, and eminently in accordance with Paul's teaching elsewhere, that the love of Christ which we have in our hearts restrains us from doing things which otherwise we might do. We refrain from doing those things not only because we are afraid to do them, but also because we love Christ too much to do them. Ah, how powerful a restraining force in the Christian's life is the love he bears to Christ, his Savior! That love in the Christian's heart is a restraining force even more powerful than any fear.

As a matter of fact, however, that is not Paul's meaning here. The love of Christ which he here says constrains us is not our love for Christ, but it is Christ's love for us. We are restrained from doing evil things, Paul says, by that unspeakable love which Christ manifested when he died for us on the cross.

Well, then, if it is Christ's love for us which constrains us according to this verse, how does Christ's love for us produce that constraining effect in our lives?

The following words give the answer. "The love of Christ constrains us," Paul says, "because we thus judge, that if one died for all, then were all dead." I do not think that the translation "because we thus judge," though it appears in both the Authorized and in the Revised Version, is strictly accurate. It ought rather to be "because we have thus judged." The great conviction that Christ died for all and that therefore all died is not formed again and again in Paul's mind as though it were a new conviction, but it has already been formed. It is one of the basic convictions underlying all Paul's Christian life. "The love of Christ constrains us," Paul says, "because we formed the conviction long ago that Christ died for all and that therefore all died." Those who have that conviction, as Paul had, already formed in their minds are restrained ever after from doing certain things which otherwise they might do. Since they are convinced that Christ died for them, they cannot thereafter do the things that are displeasing to him—to him who by his death for them showed that he loved them with such a wonderful love. Once they are convinced that Christ's death was a death for them, their gratitude to the one who died hems them in, restrains them from evil, more effectively than they could have been restrained by prison bars.

That much, I think, is certain in this passage. We have here a true scriptural basis for the great hymn of Isaac Watts:

When I survey the wondrous cross
On which the Prince of Glory died,
My richest gain I count but loss,
And pour contempt on all my pride.

The overpowering love of Christ for us, manifested when he died for us on the cross, calls forth our all in response. Nothing can be so precious to us that we should not give it up to him who gave himself there for us on the tree.

But although that is no doubt taught or implied in the passage, a great deal more is taught. There are great depths of additional meaning in the passage, and we must try to explore those depths just a little further before we sit at the table of the Lord.

"The love of Christ constrains us," Paul says, "because we have thus judged, that one died for all, *therefore all died*." Those are rather strange words, when you come to think of it—"One died for all, therefore all died." How does the second of these two propositions follow from the former?

Why should we draw from the fact that one died for all the inference that therefore all died? A very different inference might conceivably be drawn. It might be said with more apparent show of reason: "One died for all, therefore all did *not* die; one died for all, therefore all lived." When one man dies for others, the usual purpose of his dying is that those others may not have to die; he dies that those others may live.

Yet here we have it said that one died for all and then all died. Apparently the death of Christ did no good to those for whom he died. Apparently he did not succeed in rescuing them from death. Apparently they had to die after all.

It might look at least as though Paul ought to have recognized the contradiction. It might look as though he ought to have said: "One died for all, *nevertheless* all died." But he does not recognize the contradiction at all. He puts the death of Christ not as something that might conceivably prevent the death of others, but as something that actually brought with it the death of others. He says not: "One died for all, nevertheless all died," but: "One died for all, *therefore* all died."

The thing might seem strange to the unbeliever; it might seem strange to the man who should come to this passage without having read the rest of the Bible and in particular the rest of the epistles of Paul. But it does not seem at all strange to the Christian; it does not seem at all strange to the man who reads it in connection with the great central teaching of the Word of God regarding the cross of Christ.

Christ died for all, therefore all died—of course, that is so because Christ was the representative of all when he died. The death that he died on the cross was in itself the death of all. Since Christ was the representative of all, therefore all may have been said to have died there on the cross outside the walls of Jerusalem when Christ died.

We may imagine a dialogue between the law of God and a sinful man.

"Man," says the law of God, "have you obeyed my commands?"

"No," says the sinner, "I have transgressed them in thought, word, and deed."

"Well, then, sinner," says the law, "have you paid the penalty which I have pronounced upon those who have disobeyed? Have you died in the sense that I meant when I said, 'The soul that sins, it shall die'?"

"Yes," says the sinner, "I have died. That penalty that you pronounced upon my sin has been paid."

"What do you mean," says the law, "by saying that you have died? You do not look as though you had died. You look as though you were very much alive."

"Yes," says the sinner, "I have died. I died there on the cross outside the walls of Jerusalem; for Jesus died there as my representative and my substitute. I died there so far as the penalty of the law was concerned."

"You say Christ is your representative and substitute," says the law. "Then I have indeed no further claim of penalty against you. The curse which I pronounced against your sin has indeed been fulfilled. My threatenings are very terrible, but I have nothing to say against those for whom Christ died."

That, my friends, is what Paul means by the tremendous "therefore," when he says: "One died for all, *therefore* all died." On that "therefore" hangs all our hope for time and for eternity.

But what does he mean by "all"? "One died for *all*," he says, "therefore all died." He seems to lay considerable emphasis upon that word "all." What does he mean by it?

Well, I suppose our Christian brethren in other churches, our Christian brethren who are opposed to the Reformed faith, might be tempted to make that word "all" mean, in this passage, "all men"; they might be tempted to make it refer to the whole human race. They might be tempted to interpret the words, "Christ died for all men everywhere, whether Christians or not."

But if they are tempted to make it mean that, they ought to resist the temptation, since this passage is really a very dangerous passage for them to lay stress on in support of their view.

In the first place, the context is dead against it. It is rather strongly against the view that "Christ died for all" means here "Christ died for all men." All through this passage Paul is speaking not of the relation of Christ to all men, but of the relation of Christ to the church.

In the second place, the view that "Christ died for all" means "Christ died for all men" proves too much. The things that Paul says in this passage about those for whom Christ died do not fit those who merely have the gospel offered to them; they fit only those who accept the gospel for the salvation of their souls. Can it be said of all men, including those who reject the gospel or have never heard it, that they died when Christ died on the cross; can it be said of them that they no longer live unto themselves but unto the Christ who died for them? Surely these things cannot be said of all men, and therefore the word "all" does not mean all men.

Perhaps, indeed, it will be said that Paul is speaking only of the purpose of Christ in dying for all men, without implying that that purpose was accomplished. Perhaps, it will be said, he means only that Christ died for all men with the purpose that all men might live to him who died for them, without at all implying how many of those for whom Christ died actually accomplished that purpose by living in that way.

Well—quite aside from the difficulty of supposing that God's purposes ever fail—I can only say that if that meaning is attributed to the passage, the force of the passage is, to say the least, seriously impaired. Did Christ upon the cross die merely to make possible my salvation? Did he die merely for the great mass of humanity and then leave it to the decision of individuals in that mass whether they would make any use of what Christ purchased for them at such cost? Was I, in the thought of the Son of God when he died there on Calvary, merely one in the great mass of persons who might possibly at some future time accept the benefits of his death?

I tell you, my friends, if I thought that—if, in other words, I became a consistent Arminian instead of a Calvinist—I should feel almost as though the light had forever gone out of my soul. No, indeed, my friends, Christ did not die there on Calvary merely to make possible our salvation. He died to save us. He died not merely to provide a general benefit for the human race from which we might at some future time draw, as from some general fund, what is needed for the salvation of our souls. No, thank God, he died there on the cross for us individually. He called us, when he died for us, by our names. He loved us not as infinitesimal particles in the mass of the human race, but he loved us every one.

Do you ask how that could be? Do you ask how Christ when he died could have in his mind and heart every one of the millions of those who had been saved under the old dispensation and who were to be saved in the long centuries that were to come? I will tell you how it could be. It could be because Christ is God. Being God, he knows us every one, with an intimacy that is far greater than the intimacy of the tenderest mother's love.

People say that Calvinism is a dour, hard creed. How broad and comforting, they say, is the doctrine of a universal atonement, the doctrine that

Christ died equally for all men there upon the cross! How narrow and harsh, they say, is this Calvinistic doctrine—one of the "five points" of Calvinism—this doctrine of the "limited atonement," this doctrine that Christ died for the elect of God in a sense in which he did not die for the unsaved!

But do you know, my friends, it is surprising that men say that. It is surprising that they regard the doctrine of a universal atonement as being a comforting doctrine. In reality it is a very gloomy doctrine indeed. Ah, if it were only a doctrine of a universal salvation, instead of a doctrine of a universal atonement, then it would no doubt be a very comforting doctrine; then no doubt it would conform wonderfully well to what we in our puny wisdom might have thought the course of the world should have been. But a universal atonement without a universal salvation is a cold, gloomy doctrine indeed. To say that Christ died for all men alike and that then not all men are saved, to say that Christ died for humanity simply in the mass, and that the choice of those who out of that mass are saved depends upon the greater receptivity of some as compared with others—that is a doctrine that takes from the gospel much of its sweetness and much of its joy. From the cold universalism of that Arminian creed we turn ever again with a new thankfulness to the warm and tender individualism of our Reformed faith, which we believe to be in accord with God's holy Word. Thank God we can say every one, as we contemplate Christ upon the cross, not just: "He died for the mass of humanity, and how glad I am that I am amid that mass," but: "He loved me and gave himself for me; my name was written from all eternity upon his heart, and when he hung and suffered there on the cross he thought of me, even me, as one for whom in his grace he was willing to die."

That is what Paul means when he says, "One died for all, therefore all died." But is that all that Paul says? No, he says something more; and we must consider briefly that something more before we turn away from this marvelous passage.

"All of us died," Paul says, "since it was as our representative that Christ died." But what then? What becomes afterwards of those who have thus died to the curse of the law? Are they free thereafter to live as they please because the penalty of their sins has been paid?

Paul gives the answer in no uncertain terms. "One died for all," he says, "therefore all died, that they which live should not henceforth live unto themselves but unto him which died for them, and rose again."

Some people upon this earth, he says, have passed through a wonderful thing! They have died. That is, Christ died for them as their representative. They have died so far as concerns the death which the law of God pronounces as the penalty of sin. They died there on Calvary in the Person of Christ their Savior. But what of them now? Look at them, and you might think if you were a very superficial observer that they are living very much as before. They are subject to all the petty limitations of human life. They are walking the streets of Corinth or of Philadelphia. They are going about their daily tasks. They might seem to be very much the same. Ah, but, says Paul, they are not really the same; a great change has taken place in them. They are living upon this earth. Yes, that is granted. They are living in the flesh. Very true. But their lives—their humdrum, working lives upon this earth—have now an entirely new direction. Formerly they were living unto themselves; now they are living unto Christ. What greater change could there possibly be than that?

Christ had that change definitely in view, Paul says, when he died for them on the cross. He did not die for them on the cross in order that they might live with impunity in sin. He did not die for them on the cross in order that they might continue to live for themselves. He died that they might live for him.

"One died for all, therefore all died; and he died for all that they which live should not henceforth live unto themselves"—let us stop just there for a moment to notice that at that point the grand circle is complete. Paul has got back to the assertion with which he began; only now he has shown gloriously how it is that that assertion is true. He began by saying, "The love of Christ constrains us," and now he has shown how that constraint has been brought about. "The love of Christ constrains us; because we have thus judged, that one died for all, therefore all died; and that he died for all, that they which live should not henceforth live for themselves." "Should not henceforth live unto themselves"—that is the constraint of which Paul started out to speak. A man who may not live unto himself is indeed under constraint. All the impulses of fallen man lead him to live unto himself. A hundred selfish passions and appetites crave free course. Yet here are fallen men who check the free course of those selfish passions and appetites. What has caused them to do so? The answer is "Christ's love." He loved them. Loving them, he died for them on the cross. Dying for them on the cross, he wiped out the curse of the law against them, that in the new life that they then began by his Spirit to live they might by thinking on his death be led to live no longer unto themselves. What a wonderful restraining force was exerted by Christ's dying love! How many things freely done by the men of the world the Christian is restrained by Christ's love from doing!

Yes, it is indeed true that if we are real Christians "the love of Christ constrains us." Paul is not afraid to use a very drastic word in this connection. He is not afraid to say: "The love of Christ hems us in, surrounds us on every side as with a barrier or wall."

The reason why he is not afraid to say that is that he is going to wipe the paradox out in this very same verse; he is going to show his readers at once that the restraint of which he speaks is the most glorious freedom; he is going to make abundantly plain right in this very passage that the Christian life is not a cabined and confined life at all but a life that is marvelously rich and free. The Christian is restrained from doing certain things. True! But he is restrained from doing those things not in order that he may do nothing at all, but in order that he may do other things that are infinitely more worthwhile. He is restrained from doing evil things that he may do the things that are good; he is restrained from doing things that bring death in order that he may do things that belong to eternal life.

What are those good things in the doing of which Christian freedom is shown? Ah, how wonderfully does Paul sum them up in this glorious verse! Listen to the grand climax with which the sentence ends. "The love of Christ constrains us," he says, "because we have thus judged, that one died for all, therefore all died; and that he died for all, that they which live should not henceforth live unto themselves, *but unto him which died for them.*" "But unto him which died for them"—ah, there is the refutation forever of the charge brought by carnal men that the Christian life is a narrow and restricted life, life hemmed in by "Thou shalt nots" but without high aspirations or a worthy goal. No, it is not a narrow and restricted life at all. What sweet and lovely thing in human living may not be included in that one great business of living unto Christ? Art, you say? Is that excluded? No, indeed! Christ made the beauty of the world, and he made men that they might enjoy that beauty and celebrate it unto his praise. Science? All the wonders of the universe are his. He made all, and the true man of science has the privilege of looking just a little way into his glorious works. Every high and worthy human pursuit may be ennobled and enlarged by being consecrated unto Christ. But highest of all is the privilege of bringing other souls to him. That privilege belongs not only to the wise and learned. It belongs to the humblest Christians. To be the instrument in saving a soul from death—what more wonderful adventure can there be than that? No, the Christian life is not a narrow and restricted life. It is a life most wonderfully free. What rich harvest fields it offers, what broad prospects, what glittering mountain heights!

In all that life of high endeavor the Christian thinks always of the One to whom he owes it all, the One who died. Ever does he remember that one died for all and that therefore all died. What depth of love in the Christian's heart is called forth by that story of the dying love of Christ! What a barrier it is against selfishness and sin, what an incentive to brave and loving deeds! He died for all, and in the true Christian's life the purpose of his dying is indeed fulfilled, that they which live should not henceforth live unto themselves but unto him which died for them.

We have almost finished. We have read the passage almost to the end. But there is one word that we have so far not touched. It is the very last word. Sadly incomplete would our exposition be if we did not now notice that tremendous word.

> For the love of Christ constrains us; because we have thus judged, that one died for all, therefore all died; and that he died for all, that they which live should not henceforth live unto themselves, but unto him which died for them, and *rose again*.

"And *rose again*"—that is the word (one word it is in the Greek) that we must notice at last before we sit down together at the table of our Lord.

How does our thought of the death of Christ restrain us from evil and inspire us to good? Is it merely like the thought of some dear one who has gone? Is it merely the thought of that last smile on a mother's face; is it merely like our thought of the last touch of her vanished hand; is it merely like the memory of those last loving words when she bade us to be true and good?

Well, we do think of the death of our Lord in some way as that. We commemorate that death today in the broken bread and the poured-out cup. We think of that simple story in the gospels which tells how he broke the bread with his disciples, endured mocking of wicked men, was taken outside the walls, and died for the love that he bore to us sinners. And as we think on that story, our hearts melt within us and we are ashamed to offend against such love. We say to ourselves, in the words of the sweet Christian hymn:

O, dearly, dearly has he loved!
And we must love him too,
And trust in his redeeming blood,
And try his works to do.

But is that all? No, it is not all, my friends. It is not all, because that One who there died for us is now alive. He is not dead but is with us in blessed presence today. He died for all that they which live should not live unto themselves, but unto him which died for them and *rose again*. We do more than commemorate his death when we sit around the table this morning. We rejoice also in his presence. And as we go forth from this place we must live as those who are ever in his sight. Are we in temptation? Let us remember that he who died for us, and who by his dying love constrains us that we fall not into sin, is with us today, and is grieved if we dishonor him in our lives. It is not to a memory merely that we Christians have dedicated ourselves. It is to the service of a living Savior. Let us remember always that "he died for all, that they which live should not henceforth live unto themselves, but unto him which died for them and *rose again*."

This morning we, a little branch of his church universal, are gathered for the first time together around his table. We shall go forth from this service into the deliberations of this Assembly and then into the varied work of the church.

If we remember what this service commemorates, there are certain things which we shall be constrained by Christ's love not to do.

We shall be constrained, for example, not to weaken in the stand which we have taken for the sake of Christ. How many movements have begun bravely like this one, and then have been deceived by Satan—have been deceived by Satan into belittling controversy, condoning sin and error, seeking favor from the world or from a worldly church, substituting a worldly urbanity for Christian love. May Christ's love indeed constrain us that we may not thus fall!

We shall be constrained, in the second place, from seeking unworthily our own advantage or preferment, and from being jealous of the advantage or preferment of our brethren. May Christ's love indeed constrain us that we fall not into faults such as these!

We shall be constrained, in the third place, from stifling discussion for the sake of peace and from (as has been said) "shelving important issues in moments of silent prayer." May Christ's love constrain us from such a misuse of the sacred and blessed privilege of prayer! May Christ's love prevent us from doing anything to hinder our brethren from giving legitimate expression to the convictions of their minds and hearts!

We shall be constrained, in short, from succumbing to the many dangers which always beset a movement such as this. Christ's love alone will save us from such dangers.

But Christ's love will do more than restrain us from evil. It will lead us also into good. It will do more than prevent us from living unto ourselves. It will also lead us to live unto him.

What a wonderful open door God has placed before the church of today. A pagan world, weary and sick, often distrusting its own modern gods. A saving gospel strangely entrusted to us unworthy messengers. A divine book with unused resources of glory and power. Ah, what a marvelous opportunity, my brethren! What a privilege to proclaim not some partial system of truth but the full, glorious system which God has revealed in his Word, and which is summarized in the wonderful Standards of our faith! What a privilege to get those hallowed instruments, in which that truth is summarized, down from the shelf and write them in patient instruction, by the blessing of the Holy Spirit, upon the tablets of the children's hearts! What a privilege to present our historic Standards in all their fullness in the pulpit and at the teacher's desk and in the Christian home! What a privilege to do that for the one reason that those Standards present, not a "man-made creed," but what God has told us in his holy Word! What a privilege to proclaim that same system of divine truth to the unsaved! What a privilege to carry the message of the cross, unshackled by compromising associations, to all the world! What a privilege to send it to foreign lands! What a privilege to proclaim it to the souls of people who sit in nominally Christian churches and starve for lack of the bread of life! Oh, yes, what a privilege and what a joy, my brethren! Shall we lose that joy for any selfishness or jealousy; shall we lose it for any of the sins into which every one of us without exception is prone to fall?

Only one thing can prevent us from losing it, my brethren. Only one thing can bestow it upon us in all its fullness. That one thing is the love of Jesus Christ our Savior—the love that we celebrate as we sit this morning around the table of our Lord. That love alone can restrain us from the sins that will if unchecked destroy this church's life—the sins of the preacher of this morning, the sins of those to whom he preaches. That alone can send us forth rejoicing to live for him who died. As we sit now at his table, and commemorate his dying love, may the blessed words that we have read together this morning sink deep into our minds and hearts and bear fruit in our lives. May it now indeed be true of us that "the love of Christ con-strains us; because we thus judge, that if one died for all, then were all dead, and that he died for all, that they which live should not henceforth live unto themselves, but unto him which died for them, and rose again."

16

No Little People, No Little Places

Exodus 4:1−2; Mark 10:42−45

FRANCIS A. SCHAEFFER

Looking back from 1986, a seminary professor described an experience when he was an undergraduate at Harvard University:

> In the spring of 1960 I walked down a Swiss mountainside to laugh at the psychological ploys of a fundamentalist preacher. With considerable cynicism, I watched a small man with a high voice stand in front of his living room fireplace to lead a congregation of about fifteen in singing Bach chorales. The cynicism changed as he began to preach. Although I was not prepared to believe what he was saying, I recognized immediately that Francis Schaeffer's preaching was not a psychological game, but a reflection of his passionate commitment to a God whom he knew. His presentation was forceful and his message clear. To this day, whenever I preach on the serpent in the wilderness, I make use of points that Schaeffer made on that Sunday.[1]

The experience of Jim Hurley was not unlike that of hundreds who came from all over the world, but particularly from North America, to visit the

---

1. James B. Hurley, "Schaeffer on Evangelicalism," in *Reflections on Francis Schaeffer*, ed. Ronald W. Ruegsegger (Grand Rapids: Zondervan, 1986), 269.

Swiss chalet ministry of Francis (1912–84) and Edith Schaeffer known as L'Abri. Beginning this unique ministry of study center and Christian community in Huemoz, Switzerland in 1955, Schaeffer by the late 1960s had gained a reputation as a leading evangelical thinker who had a gift for giving "honest answers to honest questions" from the inquiring and challenging younger generation. Tapes of his L'Abri lectures spread abroad, so that sometimes he was recognized by total strangers just from his distinctive high-pitched voice. As he gained invitations to speak on college and university campuses, his lectures became books, especially his trilogy of *Escape from Reason* (1968), *The God Who Is There* (1968), and *He Is There and He Is Not Silent* (1972), which gave him a reputation as a philosopher. These and other books led to his producing two film series with his son, Franky Schaeffer, *How Should We Then Live?* (1977) and *Whatever Happened to the Human Race* (1979).[2]

Schaeffer always disavowed being a scholar and viewed himself more as an evangelist and defender of the faith to the intellectual. And yet the testimony of many who went to L'Abri to seek honest answers to their honest questions about the Christian faith was that even more important than the intellectual help was the compassion shown to them by the Schaeffers in their home and community:

> Edith Schaeffer has said of her husband that he was "really . . . a very emotional person." That part of his character became evident to many who went to L'Abri over the years; he took immense care with each one. As his son-in-law Ranald [Macaulay] put it, Schaeffer had compassion for the "little people."[3]

Francis Schaeffer himself could be viewed as one of the "little people" whom God used in a mighty way. Not only small of stature, he came from a background that was not promising either educationally or spiritually. He was born on January 30, 1912 in Germantown, Pennsylvania to working-

---

2. Chronologies of the life of Schaeffer are to be found in Louis Gifford Parkhurst Jr., *Francis Schaeffer: The Man and His Message* (Wheaton, Ill.: Tyndale House, 1985), 213–15, and in Lane T. Dennis, ed., *Francis A. Schaeffer: Portraits of the Man and His Work* (Westchester, Ill.: Crossway, 1986), 207–11.

3. Christopher Catherwood, *Five Evangelical Leaders* (Wheaton, Ill.: Harold Shaw, 1985), 122.

class parents who had only a nominal commitment to the Lutheran church. He gained exposure to various walks of life by working with his father on carpentry and also working on a fish wagon in Philadelphia at age 17. He became a committed Christian at that age, largely from merely reading the Bible, which answered the questions of his agnosticism. Excelling in school, he entered Drexel Institute in Philadelphia in 1930 to study engineering; however, he soon sensed God's call to ministry. In 1931 he entered Hampden-Sydney College in Virginia and graduated second in his class in 1935. That summer he married Edith Seville, the daughter of missionaries to China, and in the fall entered Westminster Seminary, which was led by J. Gresham Machen. Following the death of Machen in 1937, Schaeffer switched to the newly founded Faith Seminary in Wilmington, Delaware. Upon his graduation from Faith in 1938, he became the first ordinand of the Bible Presbyterian Church, which had split off from Machen's Orthodox Presbyterian Church. Schaeffer served as pastor of Covenant Presbyterian Church in Grove City, Pennsylvania (1938–41) and then the associate pastor of the Bible Presbyterian Church of Chester, Pennsylvania (1941–43) before accepting a call to the Bible Presbyterian Church (now Covenant Presbyterian Church) in St. Louis, Missouri. It was in St. Louis that he started a ministry called "Children for Christ" that led in 1947 to his touring post–World War II Europe to survey how best to meet the spiritual needs of the rising younger generation. In February of 1948 he and his family moved to Switzerland under the auspices of the Independent Board for Presbyterian Foreign Missions.

It was in 1951 that Schaeffer experienced a major spiritual crisis in which he questioned the authenticity of his own faith and of the lives of Christians he observed. "I had to go back and rethink my whole position. . . . I told Edith that for the sake of honesty I had to go all the way back to my agnosticism and think through the whole matter."[4] The result was an experiential as well as intellectual commitment to the reality of God and the resolve to live in a way that would demonstrate that reality. Out of this resolve came the establishment of L'Abri through much prayer and many remarkable providential circumstances in 1954–55. His 1971 book *True Spirituality* expresses this crucial turning point in his ministry, which was

---

4. Catherwood, *Five Evangelical Leaders*, 120.

FRANCIS A. SCHAEFFER

reflected in his speaking across the United States during a missionary furlough of 1953–54.

Schaeffer's influence spread in the 1960s and '70s through his lectures, books, and film series. His 1971 book *The Church Before the Watching World* had a profound effect on conservatives within the Southern Presbyterian Church. He was invited to speak at a crucial gathering in Atlanta on February 15–16, 1973 to those who would lead in the founding of the Presbyterian Church in America that December; and at the Second General Assembly of the PCA in 1974, he commended it for standing for the truth in a loving way that avoided some of the harsh bitterness of the separation from the Northern Presbyterian Church in 1936. In 1982 he expressed his approval when his own denomination, by then named the Reformed Presbyterian Church, Evangelical Synod, joined the PCA.[5]

The year 1974 marked another turning point in Schaeffer's ministry as he spent less time at Swiss L'Abri and more time in lecturing abroad. He addressed the Lausanne International Congress on World Evangelization that year and also began his work on the film series. In the films he wore his characteristic Swiss mountain garb of knickers and turtleneck sweater, which made him appear to many as some kind of guru. In a November 1982 review of his book *A Christian Manifesto*, a *Newsweek* article actually labeled him the "Guru of Fundamentalism."[6] But to the end of his life Schaeffer sought to compassionately communicate his commitment to truth and also to love. He was discovered to have lymph cancer in October 1978. He battled it through prayer and chemotherapy treatments and continued his active ministry almost up to his death on May 15, 1984.

Preaching was an essential part of Schaeffer's reaching of those who came to L'Abri:

> First were the sermons, which were usually kept as simple as possible, so that even children could understand. He would take his text and go through it logically in an expository way, building up the total picture so that the essential truth in each passage would be revealed.

---

5. Kennedy Smartt, *I Am Reminded: An Autobiographical, Anecdotal History of the Presbyterian Church in America* (Chestnut Mountain, Ga.: n.p., 1994), 35, 56, 65–66, 82–83, 113, 155–56.

6. Catherwood, *Five Evangelical Leaders*, 149, 155.

Then, second, there would be the lectures, either on tape or in person. And finally there would be one-on-one conversations, around the table or on a hike in the mountains. Schaeffer's sermons were both full of content to make one think and also full of passion, expressing the urgency of the subject:

> Schaeffer's Sunday preaching was . . . about ideas, "flaming ideas, brought to men as God has revealed them to us in Scripture. It is not a contentless experience internally received, but it is contentful ideas internally acted upon that make the difference."[7]

His sermon "No Little People, No Little Places" is the lead sermon of sixteen preached in the chapel of L'Abri and published under that title in 1974.[8] It was probably given fairly early in L'Abri's existence and most likely was repeated in his travels. His very personal style is apparent from the start, as he frequently makes reference to his own experiences. It is clear that the lessons that he is applying to his listeners are ones that he has applied also to himself. Referring to the rod of Moses, he views himself as like a stick of wood in the hands of God. Commenting on Jesus' words in Mark 10:42–45, he says:

> Every Christian, without exception, is called into the place where Jesus stood. To the extent that we are called to leadership, we are called to ministry, even costly ministry. The greater the leadership, the greater is to be the ministry. The word *minister* is not a title of power but a designation of servanthood. There is to be no Christian guru.

The basic relation of Christians is not as elder and people, or pastor and people, but as brothers and sisters in Christ. He addresses the temptation to take a larger place in order to have a greater influence for Christ. One should not take the larger place unless God "extrudes" him into that greater role. Choosing the lesser place of service allows one to be quiet before God, an essential quality if one is to serve the Lord. But this does not mean that Christians are to be passive. Christianity is active, not monastic. But the

---

7. Catherwood, *Five Evangelical Leaders*, 131, 125.

8. From Francis A. Schaeffer, *No Little People: Sixteen Sermons for the Twentieth Century* (Downers Grove, Ill.: InterVarsity, 1974), 13–25.

only good fighter for Jesus Christ is the person who does not like to fight. Schaeffer concludes:

> Only one thing is important: to be consecrated persons in God's place for us, at each moment. Those who think of themselves as little people in little places, if committed to Christ and living under his Lordship in the whole of life, may, by God's grace, change the flow of our generation.

No Little People, No Little Places

Francis A. Schaeffer

As a Christian considers the possibility of being *the Christian glorified* (a topic I have discussed in *True Spirituality*), often his reaction is, "I am so limited. Surely it does not matter much whether I am walking as a creature glorified or not." Or, to put it in another way, "It is wonderful to be a Christian, but I am such a small person, so limited in talents—or energy or psychological strength or knowledge—that what I do is not really important."

The Bible, however, has quite a different emphasis: With God there are no little people.

Moses' Rod

One thing that has encouraged me, as I have wrestled with such questions in my own life, is the way God used Moses' rod, a stick of wood. Many years ago, when I was a young pastor just out of seminary, this study of the use of Moses' rod, which I called "God so used a stick of wood," was a crucial factor in giving me the courage to press on.

The story of Moses' rod began when God spoke to Moses from the burning bush, telling him to go and challenge Egypt, the greatest power of his day. Moses reacted, "Who am I, that I should go unto Pharaoh, and that I should bring forth the children of Israel out of Egypt?" (Ex. 3:11), and he raised several specific objections: "They will not believe me, nor hearken unto my voice: for they will say, The LORD hath not appeared unto thee. And the LORD said unto him, What is that in thine hand? And he said, A rod" (Ex. 4:1–2). God directed Moses' attention to the simplest thing imaginable—the staff in his own hand, a shepherd's rod, a stick of wood somewhere between three and six feet long.

Shepherds are notorious for hanging onto their staves as long as they can, just as some of us enjoy keeping walking sticks. Moses probably had carried this same staff for years. Since he had been a shepherd in the wilderness for forty years, it is entirely possible that this wood had been dead that long. Just a stick of wood—but when Moses obeyed God's command to toss it on the ground, it became a serpent, and Moses himself fled from it. God next ordered him to take it by the tail, and when he did so, it became a rod again. Then God told him to go and confront the power of Egypt and meet Pharaoh face to face with this rod in his hand.

Exodus 4:20 tells us the secret of all that followed: *The rod of Moses had become the rod of God.*

Standing in front of Pharaoh, Aaron cast down this rod and it became a serpent. As God spoke to Moses and Aaron was the spokesman of Moses (Ex. 4:16), so it would seem that Aaron used the rod of Moses which had become the rod of God. The wizards of Egypt, performing real magic through the power of the devil, not just a stage trick through sleight of hand, matched this. Here was demonic power. But the rod of God swallowed up the other rods. This was not merely a victory of Moses over Pharaoh but of Moses' God over Pharaoh's god and the power of the devil behind that god.

This rod appeared frequently in the ensuing events:

> Get thee unto Pharaoh in the morning; lo, he goeth out unto the water; and thou shalt stand by the river's brink against he come; and the rod which was turned to a serpent shalt thou take in thine hand. And thou shalt say unto him, The LORD God of the Hebrews hath sent me unto thee, saying, Let my

people go, that they may serve me in the wilderness: and, behold, hitherto thou wouldst not hear. Thus saith the LORD, In this thou shalt know that I am the LORD: behold, I will smite with the rod that is in mine hand upon the waters which are in the river, and they shall be turned to blood. (Ex. 7:15–17)

The rod of God indeed was in Aaron's hand (Ex. 7:17, 19–20) and the water was putrefied, an amazing use for a mere stick of wood. In the days that followed, Moses "stretched forth his rod" and successive plagues came upon the land; after the waters no longer were blood, after seven days, there came frogs, then lice, then thunder and hail and great balls of ball lightning running along the ground, and then locusts (Ex. 8:1–10:15). Watch the destruction of judgment, which came from a dead stick of wood that had become the rod of God.

Pharaoh's grip on the Hebrews was shaken loose, and he let the people go. But then he changed his mind and ordered his armies to pursue them. When the armies came upon them, the Hebrews were caught in a narrow place with mountains on one side of them and the sea on the other. And God said to Moses, "Lift thou up thy rod" (Ex. 14:16). What good is it to lift up a rod when one is caught in a cul-de-sac between mountains and a great body of water with the mightiest army in the world at his heels? Much good, if the rod is the rod of God. The waters divided and the people passed through. Up to this point, the rod had been used for judgment and destruction, but now it was a rod of healing for the Jews, as it was the rod of judgment for the Egyptians. That which is in the hand of God can be used in either way.

Later, the rod of judgment also became a rod of supply. In Rephidim the people desperately needed water.

And the LORD said unto Moses, Go on before the people, and take with thee of the elders of Israel; and thy rod, wherewith thou smotest the river, take in thine hand, and go. Behold, I will stand before thee there upon the rock in Horeb; and thou shalt smite the rock, and there shall come water out of it, that the people may drink. And Moses did so in the sight of the elders of Israel. (Ex. 17:5–6)

It must have been an amazing sight to stand before a great rock (not a small pebble but a face of rock such as we see here in Switzerland in the mountains) and to see a rod struck against it, and then to watch torrents of life-giving water flow out to satisfy thousands upon thousands of people and their livestock. The giver of judgment became the giver of life. It was not magic. There was nothing in the rod itself. The rod of Moses had simply become the rod of God. We too are not only to speak a word of judgment to our lost world, but are also to be a source of life.

The rod also brought military victory as it was held up. It was more powerful than the swords of either the Jews or their enemy (Ex. 17:9). In a much later incident the people revolted against Moses, and a test was established to see whom God had indeed chosen. The rod was placed before God and it budded (Num. 17:8). Incidentally, we find out what kind of tree it had come from so long ago because it now brought forth almond blossoms.

The final use of the rod occurred when the wilderness wandering was almost over. Moses' sister Miriam had already died. Forty years had passed since the people had left Egypt, so now the rod may have been almost eighty years old. The people again needed water, and though they were now in a different place, the desert of Zin, they were still murmuring against God. So God told Moses:

> Take the rod, and gather thou the assembly together, thou, and Aaron thy brother, and speak ye unto the rock before their eyes; and it shall give forth his water, and thou shalt bring forth to them water out of the rock: so thou shalt give the congregation and their beasts drink. And Moses took the rod from before the LORD, as he commanded him. (Num. 20:8–9)

Moses took the rod (which verse 9 with 17:10 shows was the same one which had been kept with the ark since it had budded) and he struck the rock twice. He should have done what God had told him and only spoken with the rod in his hand, but that is another study. In spite of this, however, "water came out abundantly" (Num. 20:11).

Consider the mighty ways in which God used a dead stick of wood. "God so used a stick of wood" can be a banner cry for each of us. Though we are limited and weak in talent, physical energy, and psychological strength, we are not less than a stick of wood. But as the rod of Moses had to become the rod of God, so that which is *me* must become the *me* of God. Then I can become useful in God's hands. The Scripture emphasizes that much can come from little if the little is truly consecrated to God. There are no little people and no big people in the true spiritual sense, but only consecrated and unconsecrated people. The problem for each of us is applying this truth to ourselves: Is Francis Schaeffer the Francis Schaeffer of God?

No Little Places

But if a Christian is consecrated, does this mean he will be in a big place instead of a little place? The answer, the next step, is very important: As there are no little people in God's sight, so there are no little places. To be wholly committed to God in the place where God wants him—this is the creature glorified. In my writing and lecturing I put much emphasis on God's being the infinite reference point which integrates the intellectual problems of life. He is to be this, but he must be the reference point not only in our thinking but in our living. This means being what he wants me to be, where he wants me to be.

Nowhere more than in America are Christians caught in the twentieth-century syndrome of size. Size will show success. If I am consecrated, there will necessarily be large quantities of people, dollars, etc. This is not so. Not only does God not say that size and spiritual power go together, but he even reverses this (especially in the teaching of Jesus) and tells us to be deliberately careful not to choose a place too big for us. We all tend to emphasize big works and big places, but all such emphasis is of the flesh. To think in such terms is simply to hearken back to the old, unconverted, egoist, self-centered Me. This attitude, taken from the world, is more dangerous to the Christian than fleshly amusement or practice. It is the flesh.

People in the world naturally want to boss others. Imagine a boy beginning work with a firm. He has a lowly place and is ordered around by everyone: Do this! Do that! Every dirty job is his. He is the last man on the totem pole, merely one of Rabbit's friends-and-relations, in Christopher Robin's terms. So one day when the boss is out, he enters the boss's office, looks around carefully to see that no one is there, and then sits down in the boss's big chair. "Someday," he says, "I'll say 'run' and they'll run." This is man. And let us say with tears that a person does not automatically abandon this mentality when he becomes a Christian. In every one of us there remains a seed of wanting to be boss, of wanting to be in control and have the word of power over our fellows.

But the Word of God teaches us that we are to have a very different mentality:

> But Jesus called them [his disciples] to him, and saith unto them, Ye know that they which are accounted to rule over the Gentiles exercise lordship over them; and their great ones exercise authority upon them. But so shall it not be among you: but whosoever will be great among you, shall be your minister: And whosoever of you will be the chiefest, shall be servant of all. For even the Son of man came not to be ministered unto, but to minister, and to give his life a ransom for many. (Mark 10:42–45)

Every Christian, without exception, is called into the place where Jesus stood. To the extent that we are called to leadership, we are called to ministry, even costly ministry. The greater the leadership, the greater is to be the ministry. The word *minister* is not a title of power but a designation of servanthood. There is to be no Christian guru. We must reject this constantly and carefully. A minister, a man who is a leader in the church of God (and never more needed than in a day like ours when the battle is so great), *must* make plain to the men, women, boys, and girls who come to places of leadership that instead of lording their authority over others and allowing it to become an ego trip, they are to serve in humility.

Again, Jesus said, "But be not ye called Rabbi: for one is your Master, even Christ; and all ye are brethren" (Matt. 23:8). This does not mean there is to be no order in the church. It does mean that the *basic* relationship between Christians is not that of elder and people, or pastor and people, but that of brothers and sisters in Christ. This denotes that there is one Father in the family and that his offspring are equal. There are different jobs to be done, different offices to be filled, but we as Christians are equal before one Master. We are not to seek a great title; we are to have the places together as brethren.

When Jesus said, "He that is greatest among you shall be your servant" (Matt. 23:11), he was not speaking in hyperbole or uttering a romantic idiom. Jesus Christ is the realist of all realists, and when he says this to us, he is telling us something specific we are to do.

Our attitude toward all men should be that of equality because we are common creatures. We are of one blood and kind. As I look across all the world, I must see every man as a fellow creature and I must be careful to have a sense of our equality on the basis of this common status. We must be careful in our thinking not to try to stand in the place of God to other men. We are fellow creatures. And when I step from the creature-to-creature relationship into the brothers-and-sisters-in-Christ relationship within the church, how much more important to be a brother or sister to all who have the same Father. Orthodoxy, to be a Bible-believing Christian, always has two faces. It has a creedal face and a practicing face, and Christ emphasizes that that is to be the case here. Dead orthodoxy is always a contradiction in terms, and clearly that is so here; to be a Bible-believing Christian demands humility regarding others in the body of Christ.

Jesus gave us a tremendous example:

> Jesus knowing that the Father had given all things into his hands, and that he was come from God, and went to God; he riseth from supper, and laid aside his garments; and took a towel, and girded himself. After that he poureth water into a bason, and began to wash the disciples' feet, and to wipe them with the towel wherewith he was girded. . . . Ye call me Master and Lord: and ye say well; for so I am. If I then, your Lord and Master, have washed your feet; ye also ought to wash one another's feet. For I have given you an example, that ye should do as I have done to you. Verily, verily, I say unto you, The servant is not greater than his lord; neither he that is sent greater than he that sent him. If ye know these things, happy are ye if ye do them. (John 13:3–5, 13–17)

Note that Jesus says that if we do these things there will be happiness. It is not just knowing these things that brings happiness, it is doing them. Throughout Jesus' teaching these two words *know* and *do* occur constantly, and always in that order. We cannot do until we know, but we can know without doing. The house built on the rock is the house of the man who knows and does. The house built on the sand is the house of the man who knows but does not do.

Christ washed the disciples' feet and dried them with the towel with which he was girded, that is, with his own clothing. He intended this to be a practical example of the mentality and action that should be seen in the midst of the people of God.

Taking the Lowest Place

Yet another statement of Jesus bears on our discussion:

> And he put forth a parable to those which were bidden, when he marked how they chose out the chief rooms; saying unto them, When thou art bidden of any man to a wedding, sit not down in the highest room; lest a more honourable man than thou be bidden of him; and he that bade thee and him come and say to thee, Give this man place; and thou begin with shame to take the lowest room. But when thou art bidden, go and sit down in the lowest room; that when he that bade thee cometh, he may say unto thee, Friend, go up higher: then shalt thou have worship in the presence of them that sit at meat with thee. For whosoever exalteth himself shall be abased; and he that humbleth himself shall be exalted. (Luke 14:7–11)

Jesus commands Christians to seek consciously the lowest room. All of us—pastors, teachers, professional religious workers, and non-professional included—are tempted to say, "I will take the larger place because it will give me more influence for Jesus Christ." Both individual Christians and Christian organizations fall prey to the temptation of rationalizing this way as we build bigger and bigger empires. But according to the Scripture this is backwards: We should consciously take the lowest place unless the Lord himself extrudes us into a greater one.

The word *extrude* is important here. To be extruded is to be forced out under pressure into a desired shape. Picture a huge press jamming soft metal at high pressure through a die so that the metal comes out in a certain shape. This is the way of the Christian: He should choose the lesser place until God extrudes him into a position of more responsibility and authority.

Let me suggest two reasons why we ought not grasp the larger place. First, we should seek the lowest place because there it is easier to be quiet before the face of the Lord. I did not say easy; in no place, no matter how small or humble, is it easy to be quiet before God. But it is certainly easier in some places than in others. And the little places, where I can more easily be close to God, should be my preference. I am not saying that it is impossible to be quiet before God in a greater place, but God must be allowed to choose when a Christian is ready to be extruded into such a place, for only he knows when a person will be able to have some quietness before him in the midst of increased pressure and responsibility.

Quietness and peace before God are more important than any influence a position may seem to give, for we must stay in step with God to have the power of the Holy Spirit. If by taking a bigger place our quietness with God is lost, then to that extent our fellowship with him is broken and we are living in the flesh, and the final result will not be as great, no matter how important the larger place may look in the eyes of other men or in our own eyes. Always there will be a battle, always we will be less than perfect, but if a place is too big and too active for our present spiritual condition, then it is too big.

We see this happen over and over again, and perhaps it has happened at some time to us: Someone whom God has been using marvelously in a certain place takes it upon himself to move into a larger place and loses his quietness with God. Ten years later he may have a huge organization, but the power has gone, and he is no longer a real part of the battle in his generation. The final result of not being quiet before God is that less will be done, not more—no matter how much Christendom may be beating its drums or playing its trumpets for a particular activity.

So we must not go out beyond our depth. Take the smaller place so you have quietness before God. I am not talking about laziness; let me make that clear. That is something else, something too which God hates. I am not talking about copping out or dropping out. God's people are to be active, not seeking, on account of some false mystical concept, to sit constantly in the shade of a rock. There is no monasticism in Christianity. We will not be lazy in our relationship with God, because when the Holy Spirit burns, a man is consumed. We can expect to become physically tired in the midst of battle for our King and Lord; we should not expect all of life to be a vacation. We are talking about quietness before God as we are in his place for us. The size of the place is not important, but the consecration in that place is.

It must be noted that all these things which are true for an individual are true also for a group. A group can become activistic and take on responsibilities God has not laid upon it. For both the individual and the group the first reason we are not to grasp (and the emphasis is on *grasp*) the larger place is that we must not lose our quietness with God.

The second reason why we should not seek the larger place is that if we deliberately and egotistically lay hold on leadership, wanting the drums to beat and the trumpets to blow, then we are not qualified for Christian leadership. Why? Because we have forgotten that we are brothers and sisters in Christ with other Christians. I have said on occasion that there is only one good kind of fighter for Jesus Christ—the man who does not like to fight. The belligerent man is never the one to be belligerent for Jesus. And it is exactly the same with leadership. The Christian leader should be a quiet man of God who is extruded by God's grace into some place of leadership.

We all have egoistic pressures inside us. We may have substantial victories over them and we may grow, but we never completely escape them in this life. The pressure is always there deep in my heart and soul, needing to be faced with honesty. These pressures are evident in the smallest of things as well as the greatest. I have seen fights over who was going to be the president of a Sunday school class composed of three members. The temptation has nothing to do with size. It comes from a spirit, a mentality, inside us. The person in leadership for leadership's sake is returning to the way of the world, like the boy dusting off the boss's chair and saying, "Someday I'll sit in it, and I'll make people jump."

One of the loveliest incidents in the early church occurred when Barnabas concluded that Paul was the man of the hour and then had to seek him out because Paul had gone back to Tarsus, his own little place. Paul was not up there nominating himself; he was back in Tarsus, even out of communication as far as we can tell. When Paul called himself the chief of sinners, "not meet to be called an apostle" (1 Tim. 1:15; 1 Cor. 15:9), he was not speaking just for outward form's sake. From what he said elsewhere and from his actions, we can see that this was Paul's mentality. Paul, the man of leadership for the whole Gentile world, was perfectly willing to be in Tarsus until God said to him, "This is the moment."

Being a Rod of God

The people who receive praise from the Lord Jesus will not in every case be the people who held leadership in this life. There will be many persons

FRANCIS A. SCHAEFFER

who were sticks of wood that stayed close to God and were quiet before him, and were used in power by him in a place which looks small to men.

Each Christian is to be a rod of God in the place of God for him. We must remember throughout our lives that in God's sight there are no little people and no little places. Only one thing is important: to be consecrated persons in God's place for us, at each moment. Those who think of themselves as little people in little places, if committed to Christ and living under his Lordship in the whole of life, may, by God's grace, change the flow of our generation. And as we get on a bit in our lives, knowing how weak we are, if we look back and see we have been somewhat used of God, then we should be the rod "surprised by joy."

17

Christ the Calvinist

John 10:27–29

JAMES MONTGOMERY BOICE

Historic Tenth Presbyterian Church in Philadelphia, founded in 1829 and located at the corner of Seventeenth and Spruce Streets since 1856, has represented through its long life an evangelical outreach and a commitment to the Reformed faith. Its strong characteristics of expository preaching and extensive missionary support were maintained in the mid–twentieth century by Senior Pastors Donald Grey Barnhouse (1927–60) and Mariano Di Gangi (1961–67). In 1968 James Montgomery Boice (1938–2000) became senior pastor, and during his tenure until his death in 2000 he further developed the contributions of Tenth Church to the evangelical cause while also firmly deepening its commitment to Reformed, or Calvinistic, theology. An example of the former was his service as chairman of the International Council on Biblical Inerrancy (ICBI) from 1977 to 1987, which brought together a broad network of evangelicals from many denominations to reaffirm belief in the full authority, proper interpretation, and due application of the Scriptures' teaching. An example of the latter was his establishment in 1974 of the Philadelphia Conference on Reformed (now "Reformation") Theology (PCRT), which took leading Reformed thinkers not only to Philadelphia but to various other cities

378

of North America in order to reassert the distinctives of Reformed doctrine. But the most regular manifestations of these twin commitments were the support of missions at Tenth Church and especially the faithful preaching of books of the Bible from the pulpit. These sermons typically became radio broadcast messages on "The Bible Study Hour," with tapes distributed widely around the world, and then became published commentaries. Boice's sermons, which he characteristically referred to as "studies," sometimes covered a single significant book of the Bible over a period of years and then would be published in multiple-volume commentaries, such as his *The Gospel of John: An Expositional Commentary* in five volumes (1975–79, reprinted in 1999), *Genesis: An Expositional Commentary* in three volumes (1982–87), *Romans* in four volumes (1992–94), *Psalms* in three volumes (1994–99), and *Matthew* in two volumes (2001).

James Boice was born on July 7, 1938 in Pittsburgh. His parents moved to Philadelphia for further training in orthopedic surgery for his father, and in the early 1940s the family was influenced by the ministry of Donald G. Barnhouse at Tenth Presbyterian Church. After their return to the Pittsburgh area in 1945 they continued contact with Barnhouse, who put them in touch with Frank Gaebelein, headmaster of Stony Brook School on Long Island, to gain Jim admission to the school in 1951. From there Boice went in 1956 to Harvard, where he majored in English and attended Boston's Park Street Congregational Church, pastored by Harold John Ockenga. Graduating with high honors in 1960, he next went to Princeton Seminary, where he focused on New Testament studies under Professor Bruce Metzger. He married Linda McNamara on June 9, 1962 in Montclair, New Jersey, and they moved that summer to Washington, D.C. to begin working with Carl F. H. Henry at *Christianity Today*. After graduation from Princeton Seminary in 1963, the Boices moved to Switzerland, where he pursued his doctor of theology degree at the University of Basel with studies under Professors Bo Reicke and Oscar Cullmann. During their three years in Switzerland he started, with the encouragement of a couple from the Philippines, the Basel Community Church, leading worship and Bible study for an English-speaking fellowship. By December 1966 he was back in Washington as assistant editor at *Christianity Today*, but when Carl Henry announced his plan to leave his editor's position late in 1967, Boice made clear his intention to pastor a church. It was Frank Gaebelein who made the connection with Philadelphia's Tenth Presbyterian Church, whose pulpit had been vacant since the resignation of Mariano Di Gangi in June 1967. James Boice received the call and began his ministry as senior pastor of Tenth on Easter Sunday, April 14, 1968.[1]

At that time a congregation of the Northern Presbyterian Church (known then as the United Presbyterian Church in the U.S.A.), Tenth Presbyterian Church had gone through a difficult transition since the death of Barnhouse in 1960. As senior pastor, Di Gangi had opened the doors of the church to African Americans, but the racial and other controversies of the 1960s, including the denomination's adoption of the new "Confession of 1967," had produced some turmoil at Tenth. Membership had declined from a peak of 824 in 1948 to 535 in 1968.[2] Attendance at the beginning of Boice's ministry was 386 on Sunday morning and 270 at the evening service. The budgets for 1969 were $60,000 for the general budget and $40,000 for missions. By the final year of his pastorate, 2000, attendance averaged 1,200 per Sunday, and the annual budget was $2.1 million ($1.3 general, $600,000 missions, and $200,000 building).[3]

Barnhouse had developed a significant radio ministry with the Bible Study Hour in 1949. Within months of his arrival at Tenth, Boice took up the radio preaching, and by 1977 the broadcasts were carried on seventy-seven stations with 100 airtimes. In 1978 these messages began to be carried in Asia, and in 1980 his sermons on John were translated into Mandarin and broadcast into China. By 2000 the weekly program was heard on 248 stations in the U.S.[4] Although located in center-city Philadelphia, Tenth Church had more the character of a metropolitan church than an urban ministry, with a strong pulpit ministry attracting regular attenders not only from the Pennsylvania suburbs, but also from New Jersey and Delaware. Under Boice's leadership the church continued this character and also developed ministries suited to its urban setting. Concern for their

---

1. *The Life of Dr. James Montgomery Boice, 1938–2000*, ed. Philip G. Ryken (Philadelphia: Gerald Stevens, Inc., 2001), 4–9, by Linda M. Boice.

2. James M. Boice, ed., *Making God's Word Plain: One Hundred and Fifty Years in the History of Tenth Presbyterian Church of Philadelphia* (Philadelphia: Tenth Presbyterian Church, 1979), 99.

3. *Life of Boice*, 12.

4. *Life of Boice*, 20–23, by C. Everett Koop; *Philadelphia Inquirer* obituary, June 17, 2000, E10.

two younger daughters' high-school education led Linda and Jim Boice in 1983 to found City Center Academy, which provides a college-preparatory curriculum for an ethnically mixed enrollment of more than eighty students.[5] As members of the congregation became burdened for various needs in the community, Boice and the session would encourage the development of a ministry, which might eventually spin off to have its own board and means of support. These included a crisis pregnancy counseling service, an outreach to homosexuals, and a ministry to those with HIV disease and their families. Tenth also sought to plant daughter churches in the region. Its outstanding outreach, however, was in foreign missions, with a congregational commission established to maintain communication and support for scores of international missionaries, including the sending of tapes of Boice's weekly sermons.[6]

In 1974 Boice began the Philadelphia Conference on Reformed Theology (PCRT), which continues to meet every April in Philadelphia and two or three other cities. Speakers included such Reformed leaders as Roger Nicole, John Gerstner, and R. C. Sproul from America and J. I. Packer, Eric Alexander, and Sinclair Ferguson from Great Britain as well as Boice himself. Attracting thousands of listeners and learners, PCRT also gave rise to similar conferences on Reformed theology in other regions of the U.S. In 1976 a group including Gerstner, Packer, and Sproul meeting in California conceived of the International Council on Biblical Inerrancy as a means to undergird a flagging evangelical conviction concerning the authority of Scripture. Seeking a leader with proper academic and spiritual credentials, they tapped Jim Boice to be chairman. The organization held two "Summits" and two "Congresses on the Bible" in various parts of the country from 1977 to 1987, when it concluded its meeting and publishing efforts, having agreed in advance to terminate after ten years in order not to create another self-perpetuating ecclesiastical bureaucracy.[7]

Two other organizations that displayed Boice's ability to combine his Reformed doctrinal commitment with broad evangelical cooperation were the Bible Study Fellowship International (BSF) and the Alliance for Confessing Evangelicals (ACE). From 1981 to 1999 Boice was one of the sum-

---

5. *Life of Boice*, 30–33, by D. Marion Clark.

6. *Life of Boice*, 16–19, by Eugene Betts.

7. *Life of Boice*, 28–29, by Karen C. Hoyt.

mer teachers of the numerous Bible teachers for the widespread, mostly women's groups of BSF. In 1994 he launched ACE with Michael Horton and others for the sake of reviving knowledge and understanding of Protestantism's Reformation heritage. Horton commented on Boice's ability to achieve unity out of the rich diversity of evangelical Baptists, Anglicans, Lutherans, and Presbyterians:

> He taught us that truth is the source of, not the obstacle to, the power that we lack in our churches today, and the fountain of the evangelistic zeal, intellectual rigor, and action in the world that our various "relevance" operations these days cannot match.[8]

Commitment to biblical truth not only brought unity out of diversity, but also led to necessary separation. In 1980 Boice and the session led Tenth to leave the Northern Presbyterian Church, which was tolerating denial of the deity of Christ while at the same time enforcing the ordination of women as elders and ministers, and in the next year to join the Reformed Presbyterian Church, Evangelical Synod (RPC,ES). In 1982 the RPC,ES was received into the Presbyterian Church in America, which had formed in 1973 for the sake of biblical orthodoxy.

Returning exhausted from the travels of the 2000 PCRT, Boice was diagnosed on Good Friday to have an aggressive form of liver cancer. His last sermon at Tenth was preached on Easter Sunday, April 23. On May 7 he appeared in the pulpit to explain his rapidly deteriorating physical condition before giving the call to worship. His last time to be in the sanctuary of Tenth Church was on May 14 when he slipped into the choir loft to hear the children's choir sing a hymn he had written for them. During the last year of his life he wrote with organist Paul Jones twelve hymns that well expressed his Reformed beliefs. The third stanza of "Give Praise to God" is as follows:

> Nothing exists that God might need
> For all things good from him proceed.
> We praise him as our Lord, and yet
> We never place God in our debt.

---

8. Michael S. Horton, in *Life of Boice*, 37–38.

Come, lift your voice to heaven's high throne,
And glory give to God alone!⁹

Jim Boice's deep and mellow voice would characteristically respond, "Amen and amen!" He died on June 15, 2000.

Boice's sermon "Christ the Calvinist," based on John 10:27–29, expresses these same Reformed convictions. He claims that the distinctive points of Calvinistic theology are at the core of Christian proclamation in all the great ages of the church. They are not to be held back as possibly offensive, for Jesus spoke these truths plainly to his enemies. The human condition is one of being lost in sin. The initiative in salvation lies with God. This includes Christ's death for the sins of his people. Those who are Christ's hear him (including in the Sunday service) and follow him. Finally, God perseveres with his saints. In straightforward exposition of three verses of John's gospel, Boice has illuminated the distinctive points of Calvinist theology. He concludes with illustration and application from the conversion experience, at age 15, of Charles Haddon Spurgeon. Boice was sometimes criticized for his lack of illustration and application; however, as one elder of Tenth Church put it:

> Dr. Boice's expositional style with few illustrations transcended cultural differences. This direct preaching of God's Word allowed the Holy Spirit freedom to speak to listeners, whatever their nationality. As a result, the tapes of his sermons sent to Tenth's missionaries were frequently circulated among English-speaking nationals.¹⁰

As another elder described Boice's preaching style:

> Carrying on the legacy of the Barnhouse era, Dr. Boice tackled a biblical text like a tenacious bulldog by analyzing and searching for its meaning and application. His easy-to-understand yet profound teaching captivated young and old alike. In many lives this ministry of the Word became profitable for "correction, reproof, and instruction in righteousness" (2 Timothy 3:16).¹¹

---

9. *Life of Boice*, 40–45.
10. Eugene K. Betts, in *Life of Boice*, 19.
11. George K. McFarland, in *Life of Boice*, 12.

CHRIST THE CALVINIST

JAMES MONTGOMERY BOICE

*My sheep hear my voice, and I know them, and they follow me.
And I give unto them eternal life; and they shall never perish,
neither shall any man pluck them out of my hand. My Father,
which gave them me, is greater than all; and no man is able to
pluck them out of my Father's hand. (John 10:27–29)*

One week, after I had preached a sermon from John touching
on some of the main points of the Reformed faith, I found
a bulletin from the service upon which someone had scrib-
bled his opinion of the message. It said, "I'm sick of Calvinism in every
sermon."

The message did not particularly bother me. Notes like that seldom do.
But I found it surprising that the person who wrote the note somehow regarded Calvinism as a system of thought that could well be dispensed with
while nevertheless, as he assumed, still preserving Christianity. In other
words, this person, like many others, somehow regarded the doctrines that
go by the name of Calvinism as at best an addition to the pure gospel and
at the worst a system which is opposed to it. Is this true? Are the doctrines
of grace wrong? One proof that they are not is seen in the verses to which
we come in this chapter.

HISTORIC CALVINISM

The verses I have in mind are those in which the Lord Jesus Christ spoke
plainly to his enemies, saying that those who do not believe on him do not
believe because they are not his sheep, that those who are his sheep be-

lieve and follow, that this is true because they are given to him by the Father, that these who are given to him by the Father inevitably come to him, and finally, that these who come will never be lost. This is a message of man's complete ruin in sin and God's perfect remedy in Christ, and it can be expressed in the distinctive points of Calvinistic theology. Before we look at these points in detail, however, we should see that far from being an aberration or addition to the gospel, these truths have always belonged to the core of the Christian proclamation and have been characteristic of the church at its greatest periods.

To begin with, the doctrines of grace known as Calvinism were most certainly not invented by Calvin, nor were they characteristic of his thought alone during the Reformation period. As we shall see, these are the truths taught by Jesus and confirmed for us in Scripture by the apostle Paul. Augustine argued for the same truths over against the denials of Pelagius and those who followed him. Luther was a Calvinist. So was Zwingli. That is, they believed what Calvin believed and what he later systematized in his influential *Institutes of the Christian Religion*. The Puritans were also Calvinists; it was through them and their teaching that both England and Scotland experienced the greatest and most pervasive national revivals the world has ever seen. In that number were the heirs of John Knox: Thomas Cartwright, Richard Sibbes, Richard Baxter, Matthew Henry, John Owen, and others. In America thousands were influenced by Jonathan Edwards, Cotton Mather, and George Whitefield, all of whom were Calvinists.

In more recent times the modern missionary movement received nearly all its direction and initial impetus from those in the Calvinistic and Puritan tradition. The list includes such men as William Carey, John Ryland, Henry Martyn, Robert Moffat, David Livingstone, John G. Paton, John R. Mott, and many others. For all these the doctrines of grace were not an appendage to Christian thought but were rather that which was central and which most fired and gave form to their preaching and missionary efforts.[12]

This, of course, is precisely why I am reviewing this history—to show that the doctrines known as Calvinism are not something that emerged late in church history but rather are that which takes its origins in the teachings of Jesus, which has been found throughout the church in many peri-

---

12. For a similar review of this history, see Volume 2 ("Those Who Shall Come," John 6:36–37), 166–67.

ods, and which has always been characteristic of the church at its greatest periods of faith and expansion. It follows from this that the church of Jesus Christ will again see great days when these truths are widely proclaimed, and proclaimed fearlessly.

Jesus is our example. We sometimes think of these doctrines as household doctrines; that is, as truths to be proclaimed only to those who already believe. But this was not Jesus' procedure. He taught them also to his enemies. In this case, they had come to him with the implication that he was responsible for their failure to believe; they had said, "If thou be the Christ, tell us plainly." He answered this, not so much with a statement concerning his identity as the Messiah (although he did say that his words and works authenticated him), but much more importantly by a full statement of man's utter inability to choose God and of the necessity for divine grace in each step of salvation. Did they want it told plainly? Well, this is the truth told plainly: "Ye believe not, because ye are not of my sheep. . . . My sheep hear my voice, and I know them, and they follow me. And I give unto them eternal life; and they shall never perish, neither shall any man pluck them out of my hand. My Father, which gave them me, is greater than all; and no man is able to pluck them out of my Father's hand" (vv. 26–29).

STATE OF THE LOST

First of all, Christ's words reflect the desperate state of the lost; that is, the state of all men as they are apart from Christ. The teachings on this point are not so much direct as indirect. Still they underlie the positive points made in this passage.

In reference to man's desperate state apart from Christ, these verses show that he has lost spiritual life; otherwise, it would not be necessary for Christ to speak of it as a gift. Originally, man had life. When the first man and woman were created by God, they were created with that life that shows itself in communion with him. Consequently, we learn that they communed with God in the garden in the cool of the day. When they sinned, this life was lost, a fact evidenced by their hiding from God. This has been the state of men ever since. Consequently, when the gospel is preached, those who hear it turn away unless God intervenes to do a supernatural work of regeneration in their hearts.

Moreover, the desperate state of men apart from Christ is suggested by the fact that no one can recover this life except as a free gift from God. Jesus calls it a gift, for it is undeserved and unearned. If it were earned, it would be wages; if it were merited, it would be a reward. But eternal life is neither of these. It is a gift, which means that it originates solely in God's goodwill toward men.

As a last thought on this subject, it is also true, is it not, that men and women will perish except for this gift. Jesus says of those to whom he gives life that "they shall never perish." But if he makes this promise, it must be because there is a danger for us of perishing without his intervention. We are sinners. Sin makes us heirs of God's wrath. If God does not intervene, we stand under divine judgment, without hope, facing the punishment due us for our own sins. According to these verses, we cannot even come to Christ, for we are not of his sheep and so lack the ability to hear his voice and turn to him.

GRACE

This brings us to the next thought. For while it is true that in ourselves we cannot come to Christ and so lie under God's just condemnation, the main point of these verses is that God has nevertheless acted in grace toward some. Earlier this was expressed by saying that Christ died for the sheep; in other words, by the doctrine of a particular redemption (v. 11). In this section we are told that Jesus has given eternal life to the same people (v. 28), and that these are those whom God has given him (v. 29).

You cannot trace the origins of our salvation further back than that. In this, as in all things, the origins are to be found in God. Some say, "But surely God called them because he foresaw that some would believe." But it does not say that. Others say, "He chose them because he knew in advance that they would merit salvation." It does not say that either. What it does say is that the initiative in salvation lies with God and that this is found, on the one hand, in God's electing grace whereby he chooses some for salvation entirely apart from any merit on their own part (which, of course, they do not have) and, on the other hand, in Christ's very particular atonement by which he bore the penalty for the sins of his people.

I need to say also, however, that there are aspects of the death of Christ which apply to the world at large. I am not denying that. The death of the

Lord Jesus Christ is a revelation of the nature of God. It is a revelation of his hatred of sin in that Christ died for it. It is most certainly a revelation of God's love, for love lay behind it. It is an example to the race. These things are true. But in addition to these, there is also a sense in which the Lord Jesus Christ died particularly and exclusively for his own, so that he literally bore the penalty for their particular sins, that they might be forgiven.

These truths do not make us proud, as some charge. Rather, they increase our love for God, who out of pure grace saves some when none deserve it.

AN EFFECTIVE CALL

The third of the Reformed doctrines presented by Jesus is the effective call: that is, that God's call of his people is accompanied by such power that those whom he calls necessarily come to him, believing on Christ and embracing Christ for salvation. Jesus expresses this by saying: "My sheep hear my voice, and I know them, and they follow me" (v. 27). It is a mark of the sheep that they both hear and follow their shepherd.

In the Puritan era it was the habit of many preachers to play on these two characteristics, calling them the marks of Christ's sheep. In days when there were many flocks of sheep, it was necessary to mark the sheep to distinguish them. In our day, at least on cattle, this is done by branding. On sheep it was often done by cutting a small mark into the ear. "Well," said the Puritans, "each of Christ's sheep has a double mark—on his ear and on his foot. The mark on his ear is that he hears Christ. The mark on his foot is that he follows him."

This is true, of course. It leads us to ask, "Do we hear? Do we follow?"

How many of those who come to church on a typical Sunday morning really hear the voice of Christ or have ever heard it? They hear the voice of the preacher; they hear the voices of the members of the choir. But do they hear Christ? If they do, why are they so critical of what they hear? Why are their comments afterward so much more about the Lord's servant than the Lord? Those who are Christ's hear *Christ*. And they follow him. But how many who come to church are really following? Most seem to make good leaders—in their own cause—but they are poor followers. They make good critics—of the Bible and of Christ's people—but they are poor disciples. They make respectable wolves, for they ravage the flock, but they do not have the traits of the sheep and would even be contemptuous of them if they had an understanding of what those traits are.

Do not presume on your relationship to Christ. You are not his unless you hear his voice and follow him. Jesus said, "If ye love me, keep my commandments" (John 14:15). He said, "He that hath an ear, let him hear what the Spirit saith unto the churches" (Rev. 2:7 et al.).

NEVER LOST

Finally, notice that these verses also speak at length of God's perseverance with his saints. That is, they teach us that none whom God has called to faith in Christ will be lost. Indeed, how can they be, if God is responsible for their salvation? Jesus says, "I give unto them eternal life; and they shall never perish, neither shall any man pluck them out of my hand" (v. 28).

"But," says someone, "suppose they jump out of their own accord?"

"They shall never perish," says the Lord.

"Never?"

"No, never," says Jesus. "They shall never perish, neither shall any man pluck them out of my hand."

This does not mean that there will not be dangers, of course. In fact, it implies them; for if Jesus promises that no one will succeed in plucking us from his hands, it must be because he knows that there are some who will try. The Christian will always face dangers—dangers without, from enemies, and dangers within. Still, the promise is that those who have believed in Jesus will never be lost. We may add that the Christian may well be deprived of things. He may lose his job, his friends, his good reputation. Still, he will not be lost. The promise, you see, is not that the ship will not go to the bottom, but that the passengers will all reach shore. It is not that the house will not burn down, but that the people will escape safely.

Do you believe this promise, that you are safe in Jesus' hands, that you will never be lost? Are you able to trust God for this as you have for other truths? I suppose there is a way of explaining away almost everything, but I must say that I do not see how the opponents of eternal security can explain away this text. Am I Christ's? Then it is he who has promised that neither I nor any who belong to him shall perish. If I do perish, then Jesus has not kept his word, he is not sinless, the atonement was not adequate, and no one in any place can enter into salvation.

I wish that all God's children might come to know and love these truths. I wish that many might be saved by them.

We live in a day that is so weak in its proclamation of Christian doctrine that even many Christians cannot see why such truths should be preached or how they can be used of the Lord to save sinners. But this was not always so, and it was not always the case that these truths were unused by God in saving sinners.

Did you know that it was these doctrines, particularly the doctrine of God's perseverance with his people, that God used to save Charles Haddon Spurgeon, one of the greatest preachers who ever lived? Spurgeon was saved when he was only fifteen years old, but before that time he had already noticed how friends of his, who had begun life well, made shipwreck of their lives by falling into gross vice. Spurgeon was appalled by such things. He feared that he himself might fall into them. He reasoned like this: "Whatever good resolutions I might make, the probabilities are that they will be good for nothing when temptation [assails] me. I [will] be like those of whom it has been said, 'They see the devil's hook and yet cannot help nibbling at his bait.' I [will] disgrace myself." It was then that he heard of the truth that Christ will keep his saints from falling. It had a particular charm for him, and he found himself saying, "If I go to Jesus and get from him a new heart and a right spirit, I shall be secured against these temptations into which others have fallen. I shall be preserved by Him."[13] It was this truth along with others that brought Spurgeon to the Savior.

I wish it might be the same with you! I do not preach a gospel that has a shaky foundation. I do not proclaim a religion of percentages and probabilities. I proclaim the message of Christ, Paul, Augustine, Luther, Calvin, and all others who have found God to be their pure hope and salvation. It is the message of man's complete ruin in sin and of God's perfect remedy in Christ, expressed in his election of a people to himself and his final preservation of them. God grant that you might believe it wholeheartedly.

---

13. Charles Haddon Spurgeon, "Perseverance Without Presumption," in *Metropolitan Tabernacle Pulpit*, vol. 18 (Pasadena, Tex.: Pilgrim Publications, 1971), 347, 348.

18

Truth, Tears, Anger, and Grace

John 11:20–53

TIMOTHY KELLER

On Tuesday morning, September 11, 2001, four U.S. commercial airliners were hijacked by nineteen radical Islamist terrorists. Two were purposely crashed into the twin towers of the World Trade Center in New York City, and a third was crashed into the Pentagon in Washington, D.C. The fourth crashed in a field in western Pennsylvania, evidently brought down short of another Washington target by alerted passengers who sought to overwhelm the terrorists. All passengers and crews on the flights were killed, and thousands of lives were lost, especially among those in offices and others seeking to rescue them in Lower Manhattan. As a result of the events of September 11, President George W. Bush declared a war on such terrorist organizations as have a global reach and also warned those governments that harbor such organizations. The attack on the United States having been linked with the al-Qaida organization, with a worldwide network of cells but with a base in Afghanistan, where the Taliban government gave it support, the first battles were waged in that Central Asian country, where the Taliban regime was toppled by December 2001.

On Sunday, September 16, with New York City still reeling from the shock of the collapse of the two over-100-story towers of the World Trade Center, the destruction of the surrounding sixteen acres of business district, and the loss of hundreds of firefighters and policemen as well as approximately 3,000 in the World Trade Center, Tim Keller (1950–), pastor of Redeemer Presbyterian Church in mid-Manhattan, preached his sermon "Truth, Tears, Anger, and Grace," based on the account of Jesus' raising of Lazarus from the dead in John 11:20–53.

Redeemer Presbyterian Church was a relatively recent plant under the auspices of Mission to North America of the Presbyterian Church in America (PCA), having been started in 1989 with Tim Keller as organizing pastor with a nucleus of fewer than 100. By 1992 there were close to 1,000 in attendance, and new churches were being started among Hispanics and Portuguese-speaking Brazilians with the help of Redeemer as a flagship church. Subsequently, Redeemer led in the formation of a new Metropolitan New York Presbytery of the PCA, with churches established in Greenwich Village, in Rye, and in Harlem among African Americans. By September 11, 2001, Redeemer Church had an average attendance of 3,000. On the Sunday after the attacks, there were 5,100 in attendance. In the months following, the attendance leveled off to approximately 4,000.

Timothy J. Keller was born on September 23, 1950 in Allentown, Pennsylvania. Graduating from Bucknell University in Lewisburg, Pennsylvania in 1972, he received his M.Div. degree from Gordon-Conwell Seminary in South Hamilton, Massachusetts in 1975. He married Kathy Louise Kristy in Monroeville, Pennsylvania on January 4, 1975 and was ordained in August of that year by the Mid-Atlantic Presbytery of the PCA upon his call to be pastor of the West Hopewell Presbyterian Church in Hopewell, Virginia. This was a daughter church of West End Presbyterian Church in Hopewell, where such leaders in the establishment of the PCA in 1973 as William E. "Bill" Hill, Donald B. Patterson, and Kennedy Smartt had served. In 1962, whereas the percentage of Presbyterians in Virginia was from 3 to 4 percent, in Hopewell it was about 14 percent. The West End Church had planted four daughter churches and had established a strong ministry of evangelism and social outreach, including to the black community.[1]

---

1. Kennedy Smartt, *I Am Reminded: An Autobiographical, Anecdotal History of the Presbyterian Church in America* (Chestnut Mountain, Ga.: n.p, 1994), 22–23, 28–29, 30, 32, 41.

Keller served as pastor of the West Hopewell Presbyterian Church from 1975 to 1984.

In 1981 he gained his D.Min. degree from Westminster Theological Seminary in Philadelphia, and in 1984 he joined the faculty of that institution as a professor of practical theology. He also served part-time as Director of Mercy Ministries for the PCA's Mission to North America 1984–89 and was author of *Resources for Deacons* (1985) and *Ministries of Mercy* (1989). It was in 1989 that he was called by MNA to be organizing pastor of the new mission in Manhattan that became Redeemer Presbyterian Church.

Keller's sermon of September 16, 2001 is of significance for its biblical response to the historic events of the terrorist attacks of September 11, but it is also characteristic of his preaching. The congregation is constantly engaged because there is immediate application throughout the sermon. Frequently he suggests two improper extreme reactions before presenting the appropriate biblical answer, as in his call to worship when he says it was right to grieve but not to grieve as those without hope. Drawing the analogy with the devastation of Lazarus' death, which his sisters Martha and Mary knew Jesus could have prevented, Keller says that Jesus moves through the ruins of this tragedy with truth, tears, anger, and grace. Dealing first with Mary's tears and Jesus', he says that Jesus does not just fix the problem, but enters into the grief. Dealing next with Jesus' anger, he points out that those on both the left and the right were employing a story line to explain the attacks as a judgment on America. Another story line demonizes the enemy. But Jesus' anger was at death, and the gospel story line is the resurrection. Then Keller talks about the truth that Jesus discussed with Martha. Jesus offers not a consolation but a resurrection if one will believe. This leads, after references to Dostoyevsky's *Brothers Karamazov* and Tolkien's *Lord of the Rings*, to a brief presentation of the gospel of Jesus' paying the penalty so we could participate in all that resurrection means. Those who do not really believe are invited to keep coming and explore the claims of Christ. Finally, Keller develops the point of grace. Jesus knew that the only way to get Lazarus out of death was for himself to be killed. Christianity alone of all the religions tells us that God lost his Son in an unjust attack. Jesus is the perfect counselor, who knows who needs what and when: tears, truth, anger, but most of all his grace. Tim Keller tells his congregation that they need to stay to be neighbors and friends in the great but devastated city of New York, and he concludes that the grace of Jesus "is what you need most, and that is what he came to give. That is what we are going to keep giving here." Redeemer Presbyterian Church's proclamation and demonstration of the hope and love from Jesus' resurrection shows the relevance of the Reformed faith in the midst of the most shocking event of recent history.

Truth, Tears, Anger, and Grace

Timothy Keller

P eace I leave with you; my peace I give you. I do not give to you as the world gives. Do not let your hearts be troubled and do not be afraid" (John 14:27). Let me call you to worship today in a quiet way, a way that's appropriate today, this week.

In 1 Thessalonians 4, Paul says to Christians, "Grieve, but don't grieve as those without hope." Paul is saying that there are two opposite mistakes you can make in the face of tragedy, death, and suffering. On the one hand, you can try to avoid grief. You can try to avoid weeping. You can try to put it out of your mind and get past it right away. That will either make you hard and inhuman or else it will erupt later on and devastate you.

The other mistake is to grieve without hope. The Bible indicates that the love and hope of God, and the love and hope that come from one another, have to be rubbed into our grief the way you rub salt into meat to keep it from spoiling. Your grief will make you bleaker and weaker or it will make you far more wise and good and tender, depending on what you rub into it. That is why we are here today. We are here not just to weep but to rub hope and love into our tears.

When John the Baptist was cut down in the middle of his life in an unjust attack, that is what his disciples did in Matthew 14:12. First, they came, took up his body, and buried it. That is the grieving. But then they went and told Jesus.

All week we have been bearing up under an incredible load. Now it is time to tell Jesus. It is time to lay it at his feet. If you go and tell Jesus about your trouble and sorrows and all that is on your heart, he will speak to you. He will say something like, "That soul that on Jesus has leaned for repose I will not, I will not, desert to its foes. That soul though all hell should endeavor to shake, I'll never, no never, no never forsake."

Let us pray. Almighty and most merciful God, you are the consolation of the sorrowful, you are the support of the weary. Look down now in tender love and pity on us whose joy has been turned into mourning, so that while we mourn and grieve, we may not have our hearts darkened, but rather might learn wisdom and grow strong in hope; that we might resign ourselves into your hands to be taught and comforted, remembering all your mercies and promises and love in Jesus Christ, who brings life out of death and can turn all grief into deep and eternal joy.

In our midst today we have people whose hearts are broken. Father, others can work on broken buildings and broken bodies, but only you can heal the broken souls, the fears, the grief, the rage, the despondency. Some of us have come very close to death; some of us have people dear to us who have died. Many of us are shattered. Bind us up.

Father, as your people, make us what we need to be for our city. To a great degree, Father, we have been participating in the self-absorption of the great cities of our world. People come to the cities to take, to get, to build themselves up, to build up their résumés, to consume. Father, we ask that you get us out of ourselves. We ask that you humble us and purify us. Make us servants. Make us what we need to be in order to show the glory and love of Jesus to the people around us. Help us to be what the city needs us to be now, the kind of people the city needs us to be, the kind of neighbors and citizens we need to be.

Lastly, we pray for the churches of the city. Make us wise enough to know how to work together and use our resources to meet the needs. Make us generous. Teach us how to be Christian communities in a place that might be harder than ever to be a Christian community economically, socially, and physically. Father, we ask that you will protect us by your power and nurture us with newness and the sense of your presence. Fill us with your peace so that we can be like Jesus, who came not to be served but to serve and give his life for many. We ask all this in Jesus' name, Amen.

Our Scripture reading is the famous passage where Jesus is at the tomb of Lazarus in John 11.

When Martha heard that Jesus was coming, she went out to meet him, but Mary stayed at home.

"Lord," Martha said to Jesus, "if you had been here, my brother would not have died. But I know that even now God will give you whatever you ask."

Jesus said to her, "Your brother will rise again."

Martha answered, "I know he will rise again in the resurrection at the last day."

Jesus said to her, "I am the resurrection and the life. He who believes in me will live, even though he dies; and whoever lives and believes in me will never die. Do you believe this?"

"Yes, Lord," she told him, "I believe that you are the Christ, the Son of God, who was to come into the world. . . ."

When Mary reached the place where Jesus was and saw him, she fell at his feet and said, "Lord, if you had been here, my brother would not have died."

When Jesus saw her weeping and the Jews who had come along with her also weeping, he was deeply moved in spirit and troubled. "Where have you laid him?" he asked.

"Come and see, Lord," they replied.

Jesus wept. . . .

Jesus, once more deeply moved, came to the tomb. It was a cave with a stone laid across the entrance. "Take away the stone," he said.

"But, Lord," said Martha, the sister of the dead man, "by this time there is a bad odor, for he has been there four days."

Then Jesus said, "Did I not tell you that if you believed, you would see the glory of God? . . ."

When he had said this, Jesus called in a loud voice, "Lazarus, come out!" The dead man came out, his hands and feet wrapped with strips of linen, and a cloth around his face.

Jesus said to them, "Take off the grave clothes and let him go."

Therefore many of the Jews who had come to visit Mary, and had seen what Jesus did, put their faith in him. But some of them went to the Pharisees and told them what Jesus had done. . . . So from that day on they plotted to take his life.

This is God's Word.

Mary and Martha were facing the same problem we face today. They were looking at a tragedy and saying, "Where were you, Lord, in all of this? How do we make sense of this?" Jesus moves through the ruins with four things: truth, tears, anger, and, finally, grace. The truth he wields with Martha; the tears he sheds with Mary; the anger he directs at the tomb; and the grace he extends to everybody. Let's look at the way those four things fit together.

Let's begin with the tears of Jesus. What do we learn from them? When Jesus reaches Mary, she asks him a major theological question: "Lord, why weren't you here? You could have stopped this." She asked him a question, but he couldn't even speak. He just wept. All he could do is ask, "Where have you laid him?" He is troubled. He is deeply moved.

This reaction is startling because when Jesus entered this situation, he came with two things that you and I don't have. First, he comes in knowing why it happened. He knows how he is going to turn it into a manifestation of the glory of God. He knows what he is going to do, and that in ten minutes they will all be rejoicing. When you and I enter into these tragic situations, we have no idea.

The second thing he had was power. He could do something about the problem. You and I can't do a thing to undo it. Yet still he weeps. Why? Why doesn't he just come in and say, "Wait until you see"? If you knew you were about to turn everything around, would you be drawn down into grief, entering into the trauma and pain of their hearts? Why would Jesus do that? Because he is perfect. He is perfect love. He will not close his heart even for ten minutes. He will not refuse to enter in. He doesn't say, "There's not much point in entering into all this grief." He goes in.

We learn two things from that. The first is simple but needs to be said: There is nothing wrong with weeping at a time like this. Jesus Christ was the most mature person who ever lived, yet he is falling into grief. It is not a sign of immaturity or weakness. The people who are more like Jesus don't avoid grief. They find themselves pulled into the grief of those who are hurting. There is something very right about that.

Jesus' tears also suggest something about our need to "fix it." There are a lot of people who are coming to New York to fix things. We are glad for them. They will try to fix the buildings. We need that. And eventually they will leave. But when Jesus weeps, we see that he doesn't believe that the ministry of truth (telling people how they should believe and turn to God) or the ministry of fixing things is enough, does he? He also is a proponent of the ministry of tears. The ministry of truth and power without tears isn't Jesus. You have to have tears.

Do we do volunteer work? Yes. Do we help the people who have been displaced? Do we help the people who are bereaved? Yes. But consider this. Over the next months and years, New York may become a more difficult, dangerous place to live economically, politically, vocationally, or emotionally. It feels like it today, does it not? But if that happens, let's stay. Let's enter into the problems.

The city is going to need neighbors and friends and people who are willing to live here and be part of a great city. It may be more difficult and expensive just to be Redeemer for the next few months and years; I don't know. But if it does, the best thing we can do for the city is to stay here and be ourselves, even though it might cost more money or take more time. Maybe we are going to have to be a little less concerned about our own careers and more concerned about the community. So let's enter in. Let's not just "fix it." Let's weep with those who weep. This is the first lesson about suffering, learned from the tears of Jesus.

The second thing we learn about suffering we learn from the anger of Jesus. Did you notice anything in the text I read that indicated that Jesus was angry? In verse 33, when Jesus saw Mary and the others weeping, it says, "He was deeply moved in spirit and troubled." But the original Greek word means "to quake with rage." In verse 38 as Jesus came to the tomb, it says he was "deeply moved." The original Greek word there means to roar or snort with anger like a lion or a bull. So the best translation would be, "Bellowing with anger, he came to the tomb." That must at least mean that his nostrils flared with fury. It might mean that he was actually yelling in anger.

TIMOTHY KELLER

This is relevant to us because we are all going through this corporately. Our shock and grief are giving way to fear and anger. There's a lot of rage around. In this passage, Jesus is filled with rage. So are we. What does Jesus do with it?

There are two things he does *not* do. First, he does not become a "Job's friend." Do you know what a "Job's friend" is?

In the book of Job, a series of terrible things happened to Job. His children died, he lost all of his money, and he became sick. Job's friends said, "Clearly, you are not living right! God must be judging you for your sins or these bad things would not happen."

Does Jesus speak that way to Mary and Martha? Is he angry at them or at the victims today? Does he say, "If this young man, Lazarus, is cut off in the prime of life, he must be receiving judgment for his sins"? No. He is not mad at them.

He is also not mad at himself. Isn't that interesting? Here is the one who claims to be God, who could have prevented this, now filled with rage, but not at himself. He says to Martha, "I am the resurrection and the life," one of the most stupendous claims that anyone has ever made. He doesn't just say, "I am a healer." He says, "I am the resurrection and the life. I am the offer of life." He is claiming to be God! But when he gets to the tomb, he does not demonize anyone, including the victims, and including God.

I bring this up because everyone who is speaking publicly about this event must put it into a narrative structure to make sense of it. You cannot make sense of things unless you find a story line. There are two story lines that people are using today that Jesus is rejecting here.

The first story line is that this is happening because America is being judged for its sins. Interestingly enough, the left and the right are both using it. People on the left are saying that America asked for it because of our social injustice. People on the right are saying, "Look at all our immorality! God is punishing us." In both cases, the story line is "God is punishing us." Blame the victims.

Let's think biblically about this. How do you decide whether God is mad at you personally or at your nation? How do you know whether God is mad at you or pleased with you? Do you decide by looking at how life is going? No. Jesus Christ—who was a pretty good person, don't you think?—had a lousy life! Rejection! Loneliness! Everything went wrong!

In Luke 13 some people came up to Jesus and asked about two incidents. One was a political massacre in which a group of people was killed by Pilate. In the other incident, a tower fell on thirteen people. The question was, were they being judged? Were they worse sinners than the others?

Do you know what Jesus says? *No.* And then he asks, "Why don't *you* repent?"—almost as if he is irritated with the question. How do I decide whether God is mad at me or pleased with me? I read the Bible. The Bible says, "Love God, love your neighbor." If I am not doing that, he is mad at me. If I am doing that, he is pleased with me. I can't decide, "I just lost my job so he is mad at me." "I was just in a car accident. I am paralyzed. He must be mad at me." That's not how it works! Jesus did not suffer for us so that we would not suffer. He suffered so that *when* we suffer, it makes us like him. The story line that God is judging America for its sins is not a good one. Jesus is not mad at the victims.

There is another story line that seems to have more justification to it, and for that reason is somewhat dangerous.

This second story line is to demonize our enemy. *We* represent goodness. *They* are absolute evil. There is more warrant to this story line because what happened was evil. Justice has to be done. But that story line overreaches. Miroslav Volf is a Croatian Christian who has been through his share of suffering. It so happened that he was speaking at the United Nations prayer breakfast on September 11. He put it this way: "Enormous poison comes into my heart and into the culture of the world if I forget this." Enormous problems happen "when I exclude my enemy from the community of humans and when I exclude myself from the community of sinners," when I forget that my enemy is not a subhuman monster but a human being, when I forget that I am *not* the perfect good but also a flawed person. But by remembering that, my hatred doesn't kill me or absorb me, and I can actually go out and work for justice.

Jesus does not conform to the second story line. He does not say, "I am mad at God. Demonize God. Demonize Middle Easterners. Demonize anybody who is Muslim. Shoot out the windows of their mosques." What does he do with his rage? He does not direct it against the people who have done this or against God. He focuses his rage on death itself. He is angry at the tomb. And this is the story line that the best leaders are using.

Jesus says, "I am going to turn this death into a resurrection. I am going to bring out of this something even greater than was there before."

That's the gospel story line, by the way. Out of the cross comes the resurrection. Out of the weakness comes real strength. Out of repentance and admitting you are weak comes real power. Out of giving away and serving others comes real strength. Out of generosity and giving your money away comes real wealth. That's the gospel story line.

Our most effective civic leaders are not saying we are being judged, and they are not saying we are completely good and our enemies completely evil. What they are saying is that we can bring something even better out of this horrible event. Out of this death we can bring a resurrection!

Think about it. New York is filled with people who don't give a rip about New York. All they wanted to do was to get ahead. There was so much fun, so much money around.

Now do you want to be a part of it? Here is what could happen. What if New York became a community? Through this death couldn't there be a resurrection? Instead of a bunch of self-aggrandizing individuals and individualists, what if we actually became a community? What if the United States was truly humbled in realizing we are part of the rest of the world? We are not invulnerable. At the same time, we would become prouder in the best sense, in terms of the democracy project that we are. Out of this loss of goodness can come something even better. Out of this death we can see a resurrection. We can be a better city, better people, a wiser and better country. That is the right story line, and it actually incorporates what little truth there is in the others—our need to humble ourselves, to recognize the need for change and to do justice.

Here's the point. Unless you learn how to handle your anger, unless you know what story line to put it into, you can be railing and angry against America or railing and angry against God. Or railing against the demons out there who all look alike so we can beat them up when we see them on the street.

Or out of this death can come a resurrection. That is what you should do with your anger. Don't get rid of it—be angry at death! "Rage against the dying of the light." Say, "I'm going to put this light on. I am going to make it brighter."

Somebody says, "That's pretty hard to do. First you tell me to keep my heart open and weep with those who weep. Then you tell me not to use my rage in a way that short-circuits that whole process. I don't know if I can manage that!"

That is why Jesus gives us a third thing. It's the ministry of truth—not just his tears, not just his anger, but truth. He says to Martha, "I am the resurrection and the life. Do you believe this?"

The governor and mayor, whether they know it or not, are using the gospel story line. It's the best one there is. The moralistic story line is, "We are the good people. You are the bad people." That doesn't really help much in the long run. When your stance is, "We are the good people. We have been telling you that you have been sinning, and now you finally got what you deserved," it doesn't work terribly well.

The gospel story line is the one that works. To the extent that it is working in our culture right now, we can bring a better city out of the ashes. But Jesus says, "I can give you something so much more. If you want an even greater resource—the ultimate power to handle this apart from a kind of altruistic wishful thinking— you have to believe."

He looks at Martha and says, "I can give you this power, but do you believe that I am the Son of God who has come into the world, that I am the one from heaven who has come down into this planet to die and rise again? Do you believe that?" He has a reason to ask, "Do you believe?" Because unless you believe that he is the Son of God who has come into the world, you don't have access to this incredible thing I am about to tell you. Martha says, "Yes, I do."

Do you? I hope you do. What I am about to tell you is contingent on your having a personal encounter in faith with the Son of God. Here is what he offers—not a consolation but a resurrection. What do I mean by that?

Jesus does not say, "If you trust in me, someday I will take you away from all this." He does not say, "Someday if you believe in me, I will take you to a wonderful paradise where your soul will be able to forget about all this." I don't want a place like that right now. I am upset and mad about what we have lost.

But Jesus Christ does not say he will give us consolation. He says he is giving us resurrection. What is resurrection? Resurrection means "I have come not to take you out of the earth to heaven but to bring the power of heaven down to earth—to make a new heaven and new earth and make everything new. I am going to restore everything that was lost, and it will be a million times better than you can imagine. The power of my future, the power of the new heaven and new earth, the joy and the wholeness and the health and the newness that will come, the tears that will be gone, and the suffering and death and disease that will be wiped out—the power of all that will incorporate and envelop everything. Everything is going to be made better. Everything is going to be made right."

Every year or so, I have a recurring nightmare that my wife is very flattered by. The nightmare is that my wife dies. Something has happened to her, and I'm trying to make it without her. My wife is very flattered by it because it is obviously my greatest fear.

But let me tell you something really weird. I almost like having the nightmare now. Do you know why? Because the first minute after you wake up is so unbelievably great! To wake up and say, "Oh my, it was only a bad dream. Everything bad I was living through has come untrue." It is not like being awakened to have someone give me something to make it better, in the sense of "Here's another wife." No. What I like about waking up is that the dream becomes untrue! It is a wonderful feeling to say, "It is morning. It was only a bad dream!"

Do you know what Jesus Christ is saying when he says, "I am the resurrection"? He is not saying that he will give us a nicer place. He is going to make everything that happened this week be a bad dream. He is not just giving you a consolation. He is going to make it come untrue. He is going to incorporate even the worst things that have ever happened to you. They will be taken up into the glory that is to come in such a way that they make the glory better and greater for having once been broken.

No one puts this truth better than Dostoevsky. In *The Brothers Karamazov*, there is this fascinating passage: "I believe like a child that suffering will be healed and made up for, that all the humiliating absurdity of human contradictions will vanish like a pitiful mirage. In the world's finale, at the moment of eternal harmony, something so precious will come to pass that it will suffice. It will comfort all resentments. It will atone for all the crimes, for all the blood that has been shed, that it will make it not only possible to forgive but to justify everything that happens."

I feel like I am looking into a deep abyss when he says that. I know what he means. What he is trying to say is that we are not just going to get some kind of consolation that will make it possible to forget. Rather, everything bad is going to come untrue.

At the end of *Lord of the Rings*, the hobbit Sam, who thought everything was going wrong, woke up and the sun is out. He sees Gandalf, the great wizard. To me, this is the quintessence of Jesus' promise. Sam says, "Gandalf, I thought you were dead. I thought I was dead. Is everything sad going to come untrue?" The answer of Jesus is, "Yes." Someday will be the great morning, *the* morning, not m-o-u-r-n but m-o-r-n-i-n-g, the great morning that won't just console us. Jesus will take all of those horrible memories, everything bad that has ever happened, and they will actually be brought back in and become untrue. They will only enrich the new world in which everything is put right—everything.

Do you believe this? Jesus says, "Do you believe this?" You say, "I want to believe this." If Jesus is the Son of God who has come from heaven, if he is the incarnate Son of God who died on the cross so that we could be forgiven, so God could someday destroy evil and suffering without destroying us, he paid the penalty so that we could participate in this.

Do you believe the gospel? If you believe the gospel, then you have to believe that. There are a lot of people in this room who do believe the gospel, but they haven't really activated it this week. That is what I am here to help you do. You have not thought about that. Your heart hasn't leapt. You haven't wept when you thought about it. I hope today is a start!

If, on the other hand, you do not really believe that Jesus is the Son of God, I ask you to keep coming and explore it. Jesus says, "Unless you believe in me, all that is just a pipe dream." If there is a God up there who has never become human, and you are down here hoping that someday you will be good enough for him to take you to heaven, it won't work. But if you believe in a God who is willing to come to die, to resurrect the whole world, a God who would come into our lives, that is the gospel.

C. S. Lewis at one point says, "If we let him, he will make the feeblest and filthiest of us into dazzling, radiant, immortal creatures pulsating through with such energy and joy and wisdom and love as we cannot now imagine. He will make us into bright, stainless mirrors that reflect back to

God perfectly, though, of course, on a smaller scale, his own boundless power and delight in goodness. That is what we are in for, nothing less."

Do you believe that? "Do you believe this, Martha?" Then you can face anything.

Everyone is wondering what kind of power New York is going to put back. I know that God is going to put something back. In the new heavens and new earth, everything we have here—even the best things we have here—will be just a dim echo of what we are going to have there.

Finally, somebody says, "How do I know this is going to happen? I would love to believe this, but how do I know?" There is one more thing in this story you have to recognize. Jesus offered tears, truth, and anger, but did you notice the last line of the story, the last line of the text I read? It said, "From that day on they plotted to take his life."

Now that Jesus had raised Lazarus from the dead, his enemies said, "Now he's got to go. He is the most dangerous man there is. We've got to get rid of him now."

Don't you think Jesus knew that when he was raising Lazarus from the dead? Yes, he did. Jesus Christ knew and made a deliberate choice. He knew that the only way to interrupt Lazarus's funeral was to cause his own. The only way to bring Lazarus out of the grave was to bury himself. The only way he could get Lazarus out of death was for him to be killed. He knew that.

Isn't that a picture of the gospel? We have a God who is so committed to ending suffering and death that he was willing to come into the world and share in that suffering and death himself. There are an awful lot of people praying to a general God—"I am sure that God somehow is loving us." I *don't* know that. Or rather, I know that only because Christianity alone of all the religions tells us that God has specifically loved us: God lost his Son in an unjust attack. Only Christianity tells us that God has suffered.

When somebody says to me, "I don't know that God cares about our suffering," I say, "Yes, he does." They say, "How do you know?" If I were in any other religion, I wouldn't know what to say. But the proof is that he was willing to suffer himself.

I don't know why he hasn't ended suffering and evil by now, but the fact that he was willing to be involved and that he himself got involved is proof that he must have some good reason. He cares. He is not remote. He is not away from us.

Isn't it amazing that Jesus was so different with Martha and Mary? Martha and Mary, two sisters with the same situation, same circumstances, same brother. They even had the same question. Martha and Mary asked Jesus the same question word for word. But in Martha's case, Jesus' words were almost a rebuke as he laid truth on her. In Mary's case, Jesus just wept with her. Why? Because he is the perfect counselor. Not like me. I try, but I tend to be a "truther." I tend to say, "I have all this information. I don't want to waste your time, so let me try to fix things." I want to say, "You need to know this and this and this." Sometimes you just need somebody to weep with you, and I am not the guy. Then sometimes you go to a counselor, and all the counselor wants to do is weep, when you really need somebody to tell you the truth and bring you up short.

But Jesus is the perfect counselor. He will always give you what you need. If you need truth, if you need tears, he will give it to you the day you need it. He will give it to you in the dosage you need it. He will give it to you in the order you need it. He is the only perfect counselor there is. You need to go to him. You need to get his tears, you need to get his truth, you need to get his anger. You need all those things, but most of all you need to get his grace. That is what you need most, and that is what he came to give. That is what we are going to keep giving here.

Let's pray. Now, Father, we ask that you give us the possibility of growth and healing as a congregation, as a people, and as a city because we have seen that your Son is the resurrection and he died to prove it. With that hope we can face the future. Now we ask simply that you apply this teaching to our hearts in the various ways we need it applied so that we are able to be the neighbors and friends the city needs us to be. We pray this in Jesus' name. Amen.

Sources

1 **John Cotton**, "God's Promise to His Plantation." From John Cotton, *God's Promise to His Plantation* (London: Printed by William Jones for John Bellamy, 1630). Courtesy of the Cambridge University Library, Cambridge, England.

2 **John Winthrop**, "A Model of Christian Charity." From John Winthrop, *Papers of John Winthrop*, vol. 2 (Boston: Massachusetts Historical Society, 1931), pp. 282–95. Used by permission.

3 **Cotton Mather**, "The Death of Desirable Relatives, Lamented and Improved, in a Sermon Occasioned by the Death of Mrs. Abigail Mather." From Cotton Mather, *Meat out of the Eater; or, Funeral Discourses, Occasioned by the Death of Several Relatives . . .* (Boston: Printed for Benjamin Eliot, 1703). Courtesy of the Free Library of Philadelphia.

4 **Jonathan Edwards**, "The Distinguishing Marks of a Work of the Spirit of God." From Jonathan Edwards, *The Distinguishing Marks of a Work of the Spirit of God, Applied to That Uncommon Operation That Has Lately Appeared on the Minds of Many of the People of New England . . .* In Jonathan Edwards, *The Works of Jonathan Edwards*, ed. Edward Hickman, 2 vols. (Edinburgh: Banner of Truth, 1974), 2:260–77. Courtesy of the Christian Classics Etherial Library (http://www.ccel.org).

5 **Gilbert Tennent**, "The Danger of an Unconverted Ministry." From Gilbert Tennent, *The Danger of an Unconverted Ministry, Considered in a Sermon on Mark 6:34, Preached in Nottingham, in Pennsylvania, March 8, Anno 1739, 40* (Philadelphia: Printed by Benjamin

Franklin, 1740). Courtesy of Princeton Theological Seminary's Archives Division.

6 **Jonathan Mayhew**, "Discourse Concerning Unlimited Submission and Non-Resistance to Higher Powers." From Jonathan Mayhew, *A Discourse Concerning Unlimited Submission and Non-Resistance to the Higher Powers: With Some Reflections on the Resistance Made to King Charles I and on the Anniversary of His Death: In Which the Mysterious Doctrine of That Prince's Saintship and Martyrdom Is Unriddled* . . . (Boston: Printed by D. Fowle, 1749/50). Courtesy of Princeton Theological Seminary's Archives Division.

7 **Ezra Stiles**, "The United States Elevated to Glory and Honour." From Ezra Stiles, *The United States Elevated to Glory and Honour: A Sermon Preached before His Excellency Jonathan Trumbull, Esq., L.L.D., Governour and Commander in Chief, and the Honourable the General Assembly, of the State of Connecticut Convened at Hartford, at the Anniversary Election, May 8th, 1783* . . . (Worcester, Mass.: Printed by Isaiah Thomas, 1785). Courtesy of Princeton Theological Seminary's Archives Division.

8 **Archibald Alexander**, "A Sermon Delivered at the Opening of the General Assembly." From Archibald Alexander, *A Sermon Delivered at the Opening of the General Assembly of the Presbyterian Church in the United States, May 1808* (Philadelphia: Hopkins and Earle, 1808), pp. 3–38. Courtesy of the Princeton Theological Seminary's Archives Division.

9 **Asahel Nettleton**, "Professing Christians, Awake!" From Asahel Nettleton, *Sermons from the Second Great Awakening*, ed. Tom Nettles (Ames, Iowa: International Outreach, 1995), pages 1–8. Used by permission.

10 **James Waddel Alexander**, "God's Great Love to Us." From J. W. Alexander, *God Is Love* (Edinburgh: Banner of Truth, 1985), pages 31–55. Used by permission.

11 **Benjamin Morgan Palmer**, "The Headship of Christ over the Church." From *Minutes of the General Assembly of the Presbyterian*

Church in the Confederate States of America . . ., vol. 1 (Augusta, Ga.: Steam Power Press Chronicle and Sentinel, 1861), pages 61–72. Courtesy of the Princeton Theological Seminary's Archives Division and of the Presbyterian Historical Society, Philadelphia.

12 **John L. Girardeau**, "Christ's Pastoral Presence with His Dying People." From *Southern Presbyterian Pulpit: A Collection of Sermons by Ministers of the Southern Presbyterian Church* (Richmond, Va.: Presbyterian Committee of Publication, 1896), pages 74–85. Courtesy of the Presbyterian Historical Society, Montreat, and of Princeton Theological Seminary's Archives Division.

13 **Geerhardus Vos**. "Rabboni!" From Geerhardus Vos, *Grace and Glory: Sermons Preached in the Chapel of Princeton Theological Seminary* (Edinburgh: Banner of Truth, 1994). Used by permission.

14 **Clarence Edward Macartney**, "Shall Unbelief Win? An Answer to Dr. Fosdick." From *The Presbyterian*, 13 July 1922, 8–10, 26; 20 July 1922, 8–10. Courtesy of Westminster Theological Seminary.

15 **J. Gresham Machen**, "Constraining Love." From J. Gresham Machen, *God Transcendent*, ed. Ned Bernard Stonehouse (1949; reprint ed., Edinburgh: Banner of Truth, 1982), pages 141–56. Used by permission.

16 **Francis A. Schaeffer**, "No Little People, No Little Places." From Francis A. Schaeffer, *No Little People: Sixteen Sermons for the Twentieth Century* (1974), pages 21–32. Used by permission of Crossway Books, a division of Good News Publishers.

17 **James Montgomery Boice**, "Christ the Calvinist." From James Montgomery Boice, *The Gospel of John*, 5 vols. (Grand Rapids: Baker, 1999), 3:128–34. Used by permission of Baker Book House Company.

18 **Timothy Keller**, "Truth, Tears, Anger, and Grace." From "Truth, Tears, Anger, and Grace," *Journal of Biblical Counseling* 20 (Fall 2001): 2–8. Courtesy of Redeemer Presbyterian Church, New York. Used by permission of *Journal of Biblical Counseling*.

William S. Barker (B.A., Princeton University; M.A., Cornell University; B.D., Covenant Theological Seminary; Ph.D., Vanderbilt University) is professor of church history emeritus at Westminster Theological Seminary. He taught at Covenant Theological Seminary from 1972 to 1984, serving as president during his last seven years. Before joining Westminster's faculty in 1987, he served as editor of *Presbyterian Journal* for three years. He is the author of *Puritan Profiles* and coaeditor of *Theonomy*. He has contributed to *Dictionary of Christianity in America*, *Blackwell Dictionary of Evangelical Biography*, *To Glorify and Enjoy God*, and *The Practice of Confessional Subscription*. His articles have appeared in *American Presbyterians* and *Westminster Theological Journal*.

Samuel T. Logan Jr. (B.A., Princeton University; M.Div., Westminster Theological Seminary; Ph.D., Emory University) is professor of church history and president of Westminster Theological Seminary. Before joining Westminster's faculty in 1979, he taught American studies at Barrington College. He edited *The Preacher and Preaching: Reviving the Art in the Twentieth Century*. He has contributed to *Dictionary of Christianity in America*, *Pressing Toward the Mark*, *Theonomy*, and *To Glorify and Enjoy God*, and his articles have appeared in *Christian Scholar's Review* and *Westminster Theological Journal*.